156
68
171
172

ENGINEERING APPROACHES FOR LAKE MANAGEMENT
Volume 2 : Mechanistic Modeling

ENGINEERING APPROACHES FOR LAKE MANAGEMENT
Volume 2 : Mechanistic Modeling

By

STEVEN C. CHAPRA
Department of Civil Engineering
Texas A&M University

KENNETH H. RECKHOW
School of Forestry and Environmental Studies
Duke University

With a chapter on Nutrient/Food Chain Models in collaboration with Donald Scavia, Research Scientist, and Gregory A. Lang, Physical Scientist, Great Lakes Environmental Research Laboratory; and a chapter on Assimilative Capacity Models and Water Quality Management in collaboration with Heather D. Wicke, Legislative Analyst, Senate Committee on Environment and Public Works.

Cover Design by S. C. Chapra

BUTTERWORTH PUBLISHERS
Boston·London
Sydney·Wellington·Durban·Toronto

An Ann Arbor Science Book

Ann Arbor Science is an imprint of Butterworth Publishers

Library of Congress Catalog Card Number 79-56115
ISBN 0-250-40392-7

10 9 8 7 6 5 4 3 2 1

Butterworth Publishers
10 Tower Office Park
Woburn, MA 01801

Printed in the United States of America

FOREWORD

Over the last two decades or so, limnology, the science of lakes and running waters, has moved out from its primarily academic realm to become a science which more and more is called on to help solve pollution problems threatening the health and ecological state of freshwater bodies throughout the world. In part due to this increased involvement in practical application, there has been a shift in emphasis in the approach to studying limnological phenomena, from an originally more qualitative to a more quantitative orientation. Parallel to this, a shift in disciplinary orientation has also occurred, which was foreseen in principle by the founding fathers of limnology. Although limnology grew primarily from biology, masters of the stature of Forel, Theinemann, Naumann, Birge and Juday recognized the need to link and integrate freshwater biology with other disciplines; with this in mind they and their schools led the way for the development of a systems approach to limnology. The first broadly based account of this evolution is found in Hutchinson's *Treatise on Limnology*.

Of further importance for the multidisciplinary integration of limnology was the recognition that the properties and behaviors of bodies of water are closely related and are an expression of the properties of their catchment systems; in other words, bodies of water are open, not closed, systems. This change in conception met with the evolving science of systems analysis and brought about a fruitful marriage between the classically field- and experiment-oriented scientists and the more abstract-oriented mathematicians. The result of this marriage was a quantum leap in predictive capability that represented an essential bridge to practical applicability.

Though the search has progressed considerably in the desired direction, it is not finished yet. Due to the number of subsystems to be considered and the enormous complexity of their interactions, and considering also the tremendous variability in properties of natural systems, many questions regarding ways and methodologies are still open. In this regard, two basic approaches are possible: (1) pursuing a broadly based elaboration of information from as many systems as possible using statistical techniques, and (2) performing an in-depth analysis and integration of the various processes pertaining to a single system.

The two approaches — each with its own spectrum of methodologies — are not mutually exclusive, but complementary. Questions that may be addressed with one of the approaches may not be possible with the other, and vice versa. At the same time, a realm of overlapping competence can also be recognized. Steve Chapra's and Ken Reckhow's work presents these facets and integrates them as far as possible into a consistent framework.

These two volumes are not intended for the often remote though highly qualified systems analysts, but rather for students, research workers, engineers and managers of more practical orientation searching for those aspects in the vast literature on the subject that have immediate applicability. As one who has experienced and observed for many years the various transitions in approach and orientation of limnology and its application to practical problems, I take great pleasure in introducing the work of my friends and followers to the scientific community. I hope that many old and new limnologists will find it stimulating to their work, as it was stimulating to mine.

Richard A. Vollenweider
Canada Centre for Inland Waters

PREFACE

A scientist, an engineer and a lawyer were asked the question: "What
is two plus two?"
The scientist immediately answered: "Two plus two equals four."
The engineer shook his head and retorted: "Approximately two plus
approximately two equals approximately four."
Both then turned to the lawyer and demanded: "What is your
answer? What is two plus two?"
The lawyer stared back and calmly replied: "Well, what would you
like it to be?"

Aside from its commentary on the varying perspectives of the three
participants, this story illustrates how the engineer often finds himself
midway between objective reality and subjective aspirations of society.
In essence, the engineer's traditional task has been to marshal information of a scientific and economic nature to solve practical problems. For
example, the civil engineer uses relationships derived from physical laws
to construct dams and aqueducts to provide fresh water for a variety of
uses by humans. In food processing, the chemical engineer applies
knowledge of thermodynamics, chemistry, bacteriology and economics
to insure a fresh, safe and economical product for human consumption.

One of the engineer's major roles in the area of water pollution control
has been the development of mathematical models to predict the effect of
waste discharges on natural bodies of water. Dating from Streeter's and
Phelp's (1925) classic studies of stream oxygen dynamics, a well
developed theory and a wide variety of analytical techniques have been
derived to approach the problem of predicting the effect of pollutants on
natural waters. However, most of the engineering theory prior to 1970
dwelt on the water quality of streams and estuaries with little emphasis
on lakes.

The impact of pollutants on lakes also was neglected by those who
studied them for scientific reasons. Although the effect of a lake's
drainage basin on its water quality has been recognized for many years,

most limnologists prior to the late 1960s studied lakes as isolated entities, with the shoreline demarcating the area of their investigations.

In 1968, Richard Vollenweider published a report that has become a landmark in lake analysis. The report presented a body of evidence and some statistical models demonstrating the connection between a lake's trophic state and the characteristics of its drainage basin as a framework for the consideration of human impact on lake quality. Thus, although Vollenweider's contribution had a strong scientific orientation, its consideration of human impact on lake quality was similar to the problem-solving perspective of the engineers. Since the publication of his report coincided with a growing public concern about lake pollution, the succeeding decade has seen numerous attempts to elaborate on Vollenweider's approach. While many of the studies have contributed greatly to our understanding of how lakes respond to external influences, they often have been developed without familiarity with the analytical techniques that are part of the engineering repertoire. The primary purpose of this book, therefore, is to describe many of these techniques and to illustrate their application to lake analysis. In general, the book has four underlying themes that we believe are essential to an effective analysis of lake water quality, as well as indicative of what we call the engineering approach.

The first is the importance of a strong data base. As Mortimer (1975) put it, "Any model remains an intellectual plaything of limited impact... unless it can be tested and verified by experiment, or by field observation, or both. A combined two-pronged approach — modeling coupled with direct study of the system or its components — holds the greatest promise of success." In too many cases, lake models have been developed on the "feet of clay" of weak data bases and inadequate verification. Thus, the preliminary sections of the first volume of our book are devoted to a variety of techniques that can contribute to the sound observational program that is the prerequisite for an effective modeling effort.

The second theme is the importance of model uncertainty, as suggested by the "approximate" nature of the engineer's response to the question: "What is two plus two?" We believe that the explicit consideration of uncertainty is a necessity in the complete prediction of a lake's water quality. Thus, throughout the book, techniques for the estimation of uncertainty and its effect on model calculations are delineated.

The third theme of the book is the need for simplicity in lake modeling. As Einstein stated, "Everything should be as simple as possible, but no simpler." While many areas of engineering make use of elaborate computations, traditional engineering relies heavily on simple relationships (for example, nomographs) as design tools. In a sense, Vollenweider's statistical models have been of this variety. Although some of the techniques described in this book require sophisticated computers, many (particularly in Volume 1) can be implemented on a pocket calculator or with a sheet of graph paper.

Finally, the use of mathematical techniques can become a sterile exercise without a strong scientific understanding of the problem. Therefore, many of the examples in this book are devoted to eutrophication because that area has been the subject of concentrated research in recent years. However, given strong limnological understanding, most of the methods are general enough to be applied to a broad variety of lake quality problems. Without such understanding, the application of the present techniques could be futile and possibly self-defeating. If applied with a strong theoretical and observational underpinning, however, they can contribute greatly to the management of lake water quality.

NOTES AND ACKNOWLEDGMENTS FOR VOLUME 2

Practice is required to attain mastery of any craft. Although water quality modeling is based on scientific principles, there is a certain amount of judgment or art that is required for its effective implementation and that is difficult to transmit verbally. Only by building models over a period of time can such intuition be developed and honed. This volume is designed as a starting point for those wishing to gain proficiency in the art of water quality analysis. It is not intended as a complete treatise, but as an introduction to some mathematical techniques and organizing principles that constitute the "grammar" of mechanistic lake quality modeling. Together with practice and a strong scientific understanding of the system and problem, it will prove useful to those wishing to attain fluency in this area.

The introductory nature of the volume also is intended to serve people such as managers and lake scientists, who must interact with modelers and thus would like to acquaint themselves with their basic perspective and orientation. For them, we have made a conscious effort to intersperse our technical discussions with descriptions and examples that elucidate the fundamental — and easily understood — concepts that underlie most models. We believe that such understanding is essential for effective use of models in the decision-making process.

Acknowledgments. In writing the present volume, we owe much to the research of Professors Donald J. O'Connor, Robert V. Thomann and Dominic M. Di Toro of Manhattan College. These investigators have developed efficient and elegant solutions to most of the critical analytical problems connected with predicting the response of natural water bodies to pollutant inputs. Although some of their most significant contributions have been developed for lake systems, many of their techniques have been derived for streams, estuaries and the ocean. Therefore, one purpose of this volume is to demonstrate how these techniques can be applied to lake water quality analysis.

In addition, Professors Thomann and Richard A. Vollenweider provided guidance on the overall structure and content of this volume. We would like to acknowledge reviews of individual chapters by Gene Aubert, Bill Batchelor, John Bennett, John Connolly, Brian Eadie, Ray Ferrara, Dieter Imboden, Greg Lang, Kate Lartigue, James Martin, Mike McCormick, Don Scavia, Heather Wicke and Rick Winfield. Lori Bateman did a masterful job of editing the manuscript. Thanks are also extended to the Department of Civil Engineering at Texas A&M University, the NOAA Great Lakes Environmental Research Laboratory, the School of Forestry and Environmental Studies at Duke University and the Department of Resource Development at Michigan State University for secretarial and graphics support and for the time necessary to prepare this book. In particular, Gene Aubert of NOAA and Roy Hann of Texas A&M were very supportive of this endeavor. Finally, we would like to thank our families, friends, colleagues and students who have endured, with understanding, the many hours "stolen" to complete the work presented in the chapters that follow.

Steven C. Chapra
College Station, Texas

Kenneth H. Reckhow
Durham, North Carolina

REFERENCES

Mortimer, C. H. 1975. "Modelling of Lakes as Physico-Biochemical Systems — Present Limitations and Needs," in *Modeling of Marine Systems,* J. C. J. Nihoul, Ed. (New York: Elsevier), p. 217.

Streeter, H. W. and E. B. Phelps. 1925. "A Study of the Pollution and Natural Purification of the Ohio River, III, Factors Concerned in the Phenomena of Oxidation and Reaeration," Publ. Health Bull. 146, U.S. Public Health Service.

Vollenweider, R. A. 1968. "The Scientific Basis of Lake and Stream Eutrophication, with Particular Reference to Phosphorus and Nitrogen as Eutrophication Factors," Technical Report DAS/DSI/68.27, Organization for Economic Cooperation and Development, Paris, France.

Chapra   **Reckhow**

Steven C. Chapra is an Associate Professor in the Environmental Engineering Division of the Civil Engineering Department of Texas A&M University. He formerly was a Physical Scientist with the National Oceanic and Atmospheric Administration's Great Lakes Environmental Research Laboratory (1974–1982) and an Environmental Engineer with the Environmental Protection Agency (1972–1974). Dr. Chapra received his PhD in Water Resources and Environmental Engineering from the University of Michigan and an ME in Environmental Engineering and BE in Civil Engineering from Manhattan College. He is the author of numerous technical publications including 20 articles in refereed journals. He has contributed chapters to several books and is the author of a textbook on numerical methods. Dr. Chapra is active in a number of professional societies and serves on several governmental and professional committees related to water quality modeling. His work has been used in a variety of decision-making contexts including legislative testimony and the 1978 Great Lakes Water Quality Agreement.

Kenneth H. Reckhow is an Assistant Professor in the School of Forestry and Environmental Studies and in the Department of Civil and Environmental Engineering at Duke University. He received his PhD in Environmental Sciences and Engineering from Harvard University and a BS in Engineering Physics from Cornell University. Dr. Reckhow was an Assistant Professor in the Department of Resource Development at Michigan State University from 1977 to 1980. He is the author of more than 30 publications on water quality, modeling, applied statistics and decision analysis. He has served as chairman of technical sessions at several conferences and is active in a number of professional societies. Dr. Reckhow is an associate editor for *Water Resources Research* and *Water Resources Bulletin,* and he prepares the annual literature review on systems analysis for the *Journal of the Water Pollution Control Federation.*

to
Christian

CONTENTS
VOLUME 2

Section 4
Basic Concepts

Section 5
Models of Spatial Resolution

Section 7
Model Implementation

SECTION 4

BASIC CONCEPTS

CHAPTER 10

MECHANISTIC MODELING
OF LAKE WATER QUALITY

The previous volume, subtitled *Data Analysis and Empirical Modeling,* dealt primarily with the use of statistical techniques to discern patterns or relationships underlying data for large samples of lakes. Although preconceived notions usually influence such an exercise, e.g., in the choice of variables included in the analysis, the resulting models do not necessarily have a theoretical basis. In other words, they do not have to be designed with an idea of how a lake works. In the present volume, we discuss those models that attempt to explicitly account for the mechanisms underlying lake dynamics.

There are certain situations in which each type is appropriate for use. As an example, consider models of the oceanic tides. If we desire a predictive model for estimation of the high and low tides, then observation of the periodicity could lead to the development of a simple empirical model. Minimal theoretical understanding would be necessary to develop a fairly accurate empirical model. However, if, as scientists, we want to understand the tidal motion, then clearly cause-effect relationships must be studied and described. When expressed mathematically, this description is called a mechanistic model.

These theoretically descriptive models, like their empirical counterparts in Volume 1, have been employed in the study of a variety of topics related to lake water quality. It is hoped that, in the end, both approaches will converge on unified insights regarding lake behavior. Before describing details of specific mechanistic models, a number of concepts fundamental to their derivation and use will be reviewed.

10.1 CONSERVATION OF MASS

The basic organizing principle of mechanistic water quality models is the conservation of mass, i.e., within a finite volume of water, mass is neither created nor destroyed. In quantitative terms, the principle is expressed as a mass balance equation that accounts for all transfers of matter across the system's boundaries and all transformations occurring within the system. For a finite period of time, this can be expressed as

$$[accumulation] = [loadings] \pm [transport] \pm [reactions] \qquad (10.1)$$

Figure 10.1 depicts mass conservation for two hypothetical substances that flow through and react within a volume of water. The movement of matter through the volume, along with water flow, is termed *transport*. In addition to this flow, mass is gained or lost by transformations or *reactions* of the substances within the volume. Reactions either add mass by changing another constituent into the substance being modeled or remove mass by transforming the substance into another constituent, as in Figure 10.1, where "X" reacts to form "Y". Finally, the substances can be increased by external *loadings*.

By combining all the above factors in equation form, the mass balance represents a bookkeeping exercise for the particular constituent being modeled. If, for the period of the calculation, the sources are greater than the sinks, the mass of the substance within the system increases. If

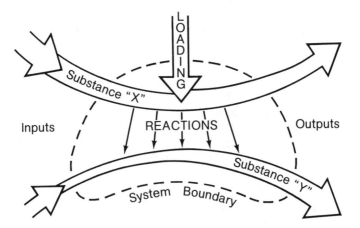

Figure 10.1 A schematic representation of the loading, transport and transformation of two substances moving through and reacting within a volume of water.

sinks are greater than sources, the mass decreases. If sources are in balance with sinks, the mass remains at a constant level and the system is said to be at a steady-state or dynamic equilibrium. The mathematical expression of mass conservation, therefore, provides a framework for calculating the response of a body of water to external influences.

Since the system in Figure 10.1 includes two substances, separate mass balances should be written for "X" and "Y". Each should include mathematical terms to account for the transport of substances into and out of the system. In addition, the balance for "X" should include a term to reflect the loss of "X" to "Y" by reaction. Likewise, the equation for "Y" should include the same term but with a positive sign to reflect the gain of mass by "Y" due to the same process. Finally, the balance for "X" should include a term for the mass gained by loading.

For situations where more than two substances interact, additional equations could be written. Similarly, an investigator might be interested in the levels of substances at various locations within the volume. The system can then be divided into subvolumes for which separate mass balance equations would be developed. Additional transport terms could be included to account for the mass transfer between the subvolumes. This mathematical division of space and matter into compartments— termed *segmentation*—is fundamental to the application of mass conservation to lake water quality problems. Before embarking on a discussion of segmentation, we will discuss the two major processes underlying the mass balance: transport and reactions. In addition, we will present the concept of *assimilative capacity,* which is the basis for integrating models into the decision-making process.

10.2 MASS TRANSPORT

Numerous types of water motion transport matter in lake systems. Mass typically enters and leaves a lake via inlet and outlet streams. Within the lake, wind energy and density differences impart motion to the water that leads to mass transport. In the present context, within-lake motion can be divided into two general categories: advection and diffusion.

Advection is due to flow that is unidirectional and does not change the identity of the substance being transported. As in Figure 10.2a, advection moves matter from one position in space to another. A simple example of transport that is primarily of this type is the flow of water through a lake's outlet. Another is transport by an imposed current system. The rate of movement of mass out of a volume of water via advection can be represented as

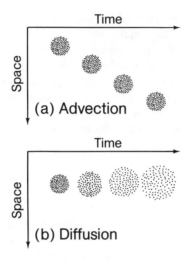

Figure 10.2 Pictorial representation of the transport of a dye patch in space and time via (a) advection and (b) diffusion.

$$[\text{transport}]_{\text{advection out}} = -Qc \qquad (10.2)$$

where   Q = the rate at which water flows through the volume $[L^3T^{-1}]$*
         c = the concentration of the substance in the volume $[ML^{-3}]$
         − = denotes a loss of mass from the system

Likewise, movement of mass into the volume by advection from an adjacent volume can be expressed as

$$[\text{transport}]_{\text{advection in}} = Q_a c_a \qquad (10.3)$$

where Q_a = the rate of flow from the adjacent volume $[L^3T^{-1}]$
         c_a = the concentration of the adjacent volume $[ML^{-3}]$

Diffusion refers to the movement of mass due to random water motion or mixing. Such transport causes the dye patch depicted in Figure 10.2b to spread out over time with negligible net movement of its center of mass. A simple example of diffusive transport would be the sloshing motion of water caused by seiches and eddys in lakes. After a long enough time period, such mixing would result in a uniform concentration of the substance throughout the lake. This tendency to minimize gradients (i.e.,

---

*The bracketed letters refer to the units of the quantity where M = mass, L = length and T = time.

differences in concentration) by moving mass from regions of high to low concentration is also indicated by a simple mathematical representation of the process

$$[\text{transport}]_{\text{diffusion}} = E'(c_a - c) \qquad (10.4)$$

where E' is a bulk diffusion coefficient $[L^3 T^{-1}]$, which is a parameter that reflects the magnitude of the mixing process between the two volumes.

Note that, according to Equation 10.4, the movement of mass is positive (i.e., from the adjacent volume into the volume for which the balance is taken) when $c_a > c$. Conversely, the movement is negative or out of the volume when $c_a < c$. In addition, the magnitude of the movement is proportional to the concentration difference or gradient between the volumes. Thus, if at $t = 0$, c_a is much larger than c, random turbulent water motion between the two volumes would initially transport large quantities of mass from the adjacent high concentration volume into the low concentration volume. With time, this rate would decrease as the concentrations in the volumes approached each other. Finally, the concentrations would become so close that random movements from one to the other would, in effect, be equivalent and the net transport would be zero. Figure 10.3 is a pictorial representation of this process.

The breakdown of the motion into the two idealized forms of advec-

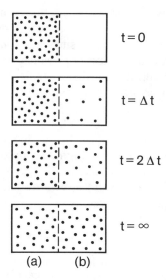

Figure 10.3 The diffusion of mass between two completely mixed volumes.

tion and diffusion is influenced by the scales of the phenomena being modeled. For example, the motion of water between an embayment and a main lake might be perceived as primarily advective on a short time scale, as a receding, or relaxing, seiche causes water to move unidirectionally out of the bay. If the modeling problem concerns the effect of bacterial pollution from a short-term storm water overflow episode, characterization of the transport as advection would be necessary. On a longer time scale, however, the seiche would move water back and forth between the water bodies in a cyclical fashion and the motion might be primarily classified as diffusive. In many cases, within-lake transport is considered a combination of the two modes, with the emphasis dependent on the scale of the problem.

Water motion within a lake is a complicated process and, as with any idealization, the above concepts are intended as a brief introduction to some of the essential features. In-depth discussions of the subtleties of mixing (Fischer et al., 1979) and lake hydrodynamics (Hutchinson 1957, Mortimer 1974, Boyce 1974) are presented elsewhere. In addition, a more detailed discussion of the mathematics and physics of transport processes is included in Chapter 12.

10.3 REACTION KINETICS

Just as mass is transported in space by water motion, it is "moved" between chemical forms by a variety of chemical and biochemical reactions. The *kinetics* or speed of such reactions can be expressed quantitatively by the *law of mass action,* which states that the rate is proportional to the concentration of the reactants. For example, a general chemical reaction can be represented as

$$aA + bB \rightleftharpoons cC + dD \qquad (10.5)$$

where the upper case letters designate concentrations and the lower case denote stoichiometric coefficients. For a volume of water, the rate of mass exchange in the forward direction (i.e., of A and B to form C and D) can be generally expressed as

$$[reaction]_{forward} = k_f V c_A{}^w c_B{}^x \qquad (10.6)$$

where

k_f = a coefficient that depends on a number of factors including temperature and the chemical characteristics of the reacting substances $[T^{-1}(ML^{-3})^{1-w-x}]$

V = the size of the volume $[L^3]$

c_A and c_B = the concentrations of A and B $[ML^{-3}]$

w and x = empirically derived exponents

In a similar fashion, the backward reaction can be expressed as

$$[reaction]_{backward} = k_b V c_C{}^y c_D{}^z \tag{10.7}$$

After a period of time, the forward movement will equal the backward movement as in

$$[reaction]_{forward} = [reaction]_{backward} \tag{10.8}$$

and the reaction is said to be at an equilibrium. At this point, Equations 10.6 and 10.7 can be substituted into 10.8 and solved for

$$K = \frac{k_f}{k_b} = \frac{c_C{}^y c_D{}^z}{c_A{}^w c_B{}^x} \tag{10.9}$$

where K is the equilibrium constant of the reaction. This relationship indicates that, at equilibrium, the reactants and products exhibit a constant proportionality. In lake modeling, some reactions can be considered to be at an equilibrium state, depending on the speed of the reaction and the time scale of the simulation. As explained in a subsequent section, this greatly simplifies the computation. In most cases, however, reactions must be modeled dynamically with a mathematical representation of their kinetics based generally on Equation 10.6 or 10.7.

Temperature Dependence of Reactions. The rates of most reactions in natural waters increase with temperature. A general rule of thumb is that the rate will approximately double for a temperature rise of 10°C. This temperature dependence is given quantitative expression by the van't Hoff-Arrhenius equation,

$$\frac{d(\ln k)}{dT_a} = - \frac{E_a}{RT_a^2} \tag{10.10}$$

where T_a = the absolute temperature (expressed as °K) at which the reaction occurs
E_a = a constant called the activation energy
R = the universal gas constant [199 cal °K^{-1} mole^{-1}]

Equation 10.10 can be integrated between limits to yield

$$\ln \frac{k_2}{k_1} = \frac{E_a(T_{a,2} - T_{a,1})}{RT_{a,2}T_{a,1}} \tag{10.11}$$

where k_2 and k_1 are the reaction rates at $T_{a,2}$ and $T_{a,1}$, respectively.

By convention, chemical and biological reaction coefficients are often reported at 20°C (293°K). Equation 10.11 can, therefore, be used to compute the reaction rate at another temperature as in

$$k_{T_a} = k_{293°K} e^{E_a(T_a - 293)/RT_a293}$$ (10.12)

where the subscripts designate the temperatures at which the rate coefficients apply. Equation 10.12 can be simplified by realizing that: (1) since temperatures in most lakes vary over a narrow range (273–303°K), the product of $T_{a,1}$ and $T_{a,2}$ is relatively constant and (2) a difference in temperature $(T_{a,2} - T_{a,1})$ is the same whether an absolute or centigrade scale is used. Therefore, the exponential in Equation 10.12 may be assumed to be essentially constant. Setting this term equal to θ yields

$$k_T \cong k_{20°C} \theta^{T - 20°C}$$ (10.13)

where T is temperature in degrees centigrade. Equation 10.13 is commonly used to estimate the change in the reaction rate associated with a change in temperature. It should be noted, however, that for some reactions θ can vary significantly within the temperature fluctuations encountered in natural waters. Care should be exercised, therefore, in using Equation 10.13 to extrapolate beyond the limits for which θ was determined empirically.

The temperature dependence of biologically mediated reactions often is expressed as the quantity, Q_{10}, which is defined as the ratio of the rate at 20°C to the rate at 10°C. Using Equation 10.13, Q_{10} and θ are related by

$$Q_{10} = \theta^{10}$$ (10.14)

Although Equation 10.13 can be used to characterize many biological reactions, it does not hold at high temperatures where the reaction rate decreases. Thus, some investigators have developed relationships that increase to an optimal temperature and then decrease at higher levels. However, for many cases, Equation 10.13 is an adequate approximation.

As with our discussion of transport processes, the foregoing has been a brief introduction to a complex subject. The key concept is that reactions can be characterized as the product of the concentration of the reactants and a temperature dependent constant. The application of this concept to lake modeling will be illustrated in subsequent chapters. For additional information on the subject, the reader is referred to Stumm and Morgan (1981) and Moore (1972).

10.4 ASSIMILATIVE CAPACITY

The previous sections indicate that if a lake is subject to inputs of material from external sources, there are processes that act to remove or "assimilate" these substances. Although these processes take a variety of mathematical forms, their magnitude is generally dependent on the within-lake concentrations of the substances as in Equations 10.2, 10.4, 10.6 and 10.7. This dependence can be reexpressed as

$$\text{assimilative processes} = \P\,[\text{within-lake levels}] \qquad (10.15)$$

where $\P$ is an *assimilation factor* representing the net effect of the transport coefficients and reaction rates that contribute to removal of the pollutant from the system $[MT^{-1}\,(ML^{-3})^{-1}]$. Note that in practice $\P$ is often not the simple proportionality constant expressed in Equation 10.15. However, for the purposes of the present discussion, it can be represented in this way.

For a system where accumulation is zero (i.e., at steady state), the external loadings and the assimilative forces would be in balance,

$$[\text{loadings}] = \P[\text{within-lake levels}] \qquad (10.16)$$

There are two ways in which Equation 10.16 can be applied to water quality analysis. First, it can be used to determine lake response to given loadings,

$$[\text{within-lake levels}] = \frac{[\text{loadings}]}{\P} \qquad (10.17)$$

Much of the remainder of the volume is devoted to techniques for solving the equation in this way.

The second application, which is more typical of the model's use in a management context, is the determination of the loading necessary to meet a desired in-lake concentration. This loading is called the *assimilative capacity*. It is truly an engineering computation since it specifies a human manipulation necessary to attain a goal. In a broader sense, the assimilative capacity is a concept reflecting the complex subjective tradeoffs among environmental quality, economics and engineering. Most of the models developed in this book can be used to determine the assimilative capacity.

§ § §

Example 10.1. Lake Ontario, in the early 1970s, had a total phosphorus loading of approximately 10,500 metric tons per year and an in-lake concentration of 21 μg/l (Chapra and Sonzogni 1979). A crude estimate of the lake's assimilation factor can be determined by assuming a linear relationship between loadings and concentration and rearranging Equation 10.16 to yield

$$\P = \frac{[\text{loadings}]}{[\text{within-lake levels}]} = \frac{10,500}{21} = 500 \ \frac{\text{metric tons/yr}}{\mu\text{g/l}}$$

In 1973, the state of New York and the province of Ontario ordered a reduction of detergent phosphate levels. This reduction resulted in a loading decrease to approximately 8000 metric tons per year.

(a) What in-lake concentration level would result from this action? Using Equation 10.17,

$$[\text{within-lake levels}] = \frac{8000}{500} = 16 \mu\text{g/l}$$

(b) If the water quality objective is to bring the in-lake levels down further to 10 μg/l, how much additional load reduction is needed? Using Equation 10.16,

$$[\text{loadings}] = 500(10) = 5000 \ \frac{\text{metric tons}}{\text{year}}$$

Therefore, 3000 additional metric tons per year must be removed.

§ § §

10.5 SEGMENTATION AND MODEL RESOLUTION

The final concepts that must be explored before developing mechanistic water quality models are segmentation and model resolution. As stated previously, segmentation is the process of dividing space and matter into increments. In space, a lake can be divided into volumes for which mass balance equations are written. Within each volume, matter, in turn, may be divided into different chemical and biological forms for which separate equations would again be written. Thus, if a lake was divided into n segments in space and matter was divided into m substances, m × n mass balance equations would be used to define the system.

Aside from space and matter, there is a temporal aspect to segmentation related to the fact that the mass balance defines changes in the water body *over a finite period of time.* Although this concept will become clearer in the subsequent development of actual models, the key point is that, just as a model describes additional spatial and material detail by using more segments, the model also has a temporal focus that can be increased by using a shorter "finite period" or *time step* for the mass balance computation. For example, as in Figure 10.4b, phytoplankton undergo seasonal cycles due to, among other things, fluctuating light and temperature levels over the course of the year. At the same time, the lake may be undergoing a significant yet gradual change due to longer-term phenomena such as increases in nutrient loads (Figure 10.4a). By

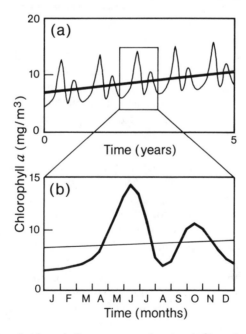

Figure 10.4   Plot of chlorophyll *a* concentration (mg/m^3) vs time. (a) depicts the long-term trend (heavy line) along with the underlying seasonal cycle (light line). (b) depicts the seasonal cycle (heavy line) along with the underlying long-term trend (light-line).

adjusting the time step of the computation, the model can be designed to resolve part or all of this variability. In a sense, this can be thought of as segmentation in time.

The degree to which space, time and matter are segmented is called *model resolution*. This concept is analogous to photography where the camera's lens is adjusted to bring different parts of the field of vision into focus. At times, the foreground is important; at others, distant details might be of interest.

In the present context, there are two basic ways in which the "focus" or resolution of a model has significance for water quality analysis. First, the fine-scale phenomenon may have a direct, causative influence on predictions made on the coarser scale. This is primarily a function of the substance's properties and the physical characteristics of the system. For example, certain pollutants (e.g., enteric bacteria) die rapidly upon entering a lake. Therefore, they typically are at high levels near a sewage outfall and then decrease rapidly so that by mid-lake they are at "background" levels. Thus, a model of nearshore bacterial pollution would require relatively fine spatial and temporal segmentation around sewage outfalls. In contrast, conservative or slowly reacting substances often can be modeled with coarser schemes that treat the whole lake as a single well-mixed segment.

The physical characteristics of the system also can dictate the required level of segmentation. For example, dendritic lakes have numerous embayments that make treatment of the system as a single segment unrealistic. In addition, problems such as eutrophication that are strongly influenced by thermal stratification may need multiple vertical segments for adequate characterization.

The second way in which model resolution has significance is the influence of the problem context on the choice of scales. For example, although phytoplankton go through growth cycles on seasonal time scales and exhibit patchiness on small space scales, a water quality planner might not have the funds to develop models to simulate such short-term variability. This would often occur when large numbers of small lakes were being evaluated. Alternatively, the issue of concern to the planner may be such that spatial and temporal aggregation results in a negligible loss of relevant planning information. In these cases, the manager might opt for a coarser scale model. In other situations, as with bacterial contamination of beaches, a finer scale approach would be necessary to handle the problem effectively.

The temporal, spatial and kinetic scales of a problem often are interrelated. As depicted in Figure 10.5, fast kinetic processes such as jet mixing of thermal effluents or bacterial die-off, tend to manifest themselves

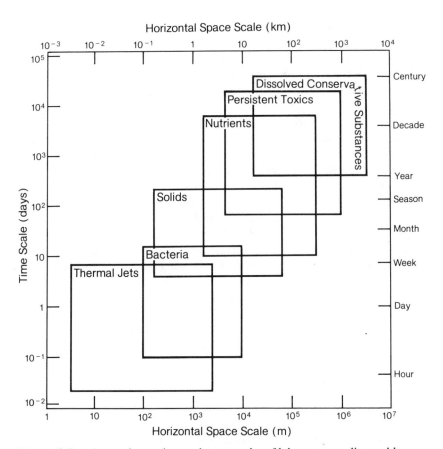

Figure 10.5 Approximate time and space scales of lake water quality problems.

on local (i.e., small) time and space scales. In contrast, problems determined by slow reactions such as the decay of persistent contaminants are more likely to be important on a whole-lake, long-term basis.

Because of the importance of segmentation and model resolution to effective lake quality simulation, the present volume is organized around these concepts. Chapter 11 is devoted to derivation and discussion of the simplest lake model—the completely mixed, input-output approach. In this way, the basic principles underlying mechanistic modeling can be elucidated without complicating factors. The remaining chapters then are designed to discuss various ways in which the basic model can be refined.

For example, Chapter 12 is devoted to a variety of analytical techniques to predict water quality in the nearshore zone, embayments, river-run lakes, and other systems with strong pollutant gradients in the horizontal dimension. Similarly, there are a variety of processes that contribute to large differences in the distribution of matter in the vertical dimension. Chapter 13 presents a number of models that have been developed to simulate the effect on water quality of two of the most important vertical processes—stratification and sediment-water exchange.

In Chapters 12 and 13, special emphasis is placed on the physical aspects that contribute to horizontal and vertical distribution of substances in lakes. Thus, while more detailed spatial resolution is used, the models are primarily designed to simulate the dynamics of a single pollutant with simple reaction kinetics.

In contrast, Chapters 14 and 15 use simple spatial segmentation schemes, but go into what might be called fine-scale kinetic segmentation, i.e., they are designed to simulate the partitioning of mass into various chemical and biological forms within a lake. Chapter 14 describes the nutrient/food chain models that have been developed to predict the cycling of matter and energy through lake ecosystems. Chapter 15 is devoted to the simulation of the accumulation and fate of toxic contaminants in lakes.

Chapter 16 deals with the subject of model confirmation. Finally, Chapter 17 provides a discussion of the use of mechanistic models for water quality management.

REFERENCES

Boyce, F. M. 1974. "Some Aspects of Great Lakes Physics of Importance to Biological and Chemical Processes," *J. Fish. Res. Bd. Can.* 31:689-730.

Chapra, S. C., and W. C. Sonzogni. 1979. "Great Lakes Total Phosphorus Budget for the mid 1970's," *J. Water Poll. Control Fed.* 51:2524-2533.

Fischer, H. B., E. J. List, R. C. Y. Koh, J. Imberger and N. H. Brooks. 1979. *Mixing in Inland and Coastal Waters* (New York: Academic Press), 483 pp.

Hutchinson, G. E. 1957. *A Treatise on Limnology, Volume 1, Geography, Physics and Chemistry* (New York, NY: John Wiley and Sons, Inc.), 1015 pp.

Moore, W. J. 1972. *Physical Chemistry* (Englewood Cliffs, NJ: Prentice-Hall, Inc.), 977 pp.

Mortimer, C. H. 1974. "Lake Hydrodynamics," *Mitt. Internat. Verein. Limnol.* 20:124-197.

Stumm, W. and J. J. Morgan. 1981. *Aquatic Chemistry.* (New York: Wiley-Interscience), 780 pp.

CHAPTER 11

INPUT-OUTPUT MODELS

As the name implies, input-output models are designed to predict the state of a lake by determining the flows of matter across its boundaries. Thus, the internal structure or resolution of the system is only important if it influences inputs and outputs. As a rule, input-output models describe a lake as being internally homogeneous or well mixed and a single mass balance equation is used to characterize its dynamics. Because of their simplicity, such models provide easily calculated estimates of lake quality that often are quite useful in broad planning and management contexts. In addition, their lack of complexity makes them an ideal starting point for the derivation of mechanistic lake quality models. Finally, as we saw in Volume 1, input-output models are simple enough to easily accommodate an error analysis for the estimation of prediction uncertainty.

In the following sections, a mass balance equation for a single, completely mixed lake is derived and solutions for two general categories are presented. The first is for those cases where exact or closed form solutions are possible. These solutions are algebraic equations that can be computed on a pocket calculator and are possible where the input to the lake can be represented as an idealized function of time, e.g., as a straight line, a sinusoid, etc. The second category is for more realistic cases, where the input and other model parameters vary nonuniformly in time. In these cases, approximate, numerical solution techniques are used. In addition, methods for the error analysis of such models are presented.

11.1 MASS BALANCE FOR A COMPLETELY MIXED LAKE

A completely mixed model, as schematized in Figure 11.1, is appropriate for a system in which the contents are well mixed and uniformly distributed. Such a model is a good first approximation for many lakes in which wind-induced turbulence causes substances to be dispersed fairly homogeneously in the horizontal plane. Although there are a variety of ways in which this idealization might be violated for a particular lake (e.g., gradients due to vertical thermal stratification, heightened concentrations in the vicinity of sewage outfalls and river mouths, etc.), the model has found broad application because of its simplicity and success in providing order of magnitude estimates of lake water quality. It is thus a good context for demonstrating how the conservation of mass can be expressed in mathematical terms.

For the completely mixed model, the volume of water around which the mass balance is taken is the entire lake. For a finite period of time, the balance can be expressed as

$$[\text{accumulation}] = [\text{inputs}] - [\text{outputs}] \pm [\text{reactions}] \qquad (11.1)$$

In this case, the inputs, or loadings, may consist of mass carried by tributary streams, in precipitation, from sediment feedback or from

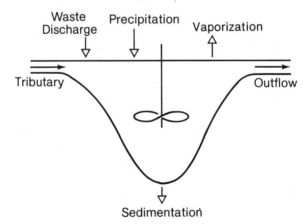

Figure 11.1   Schematic of a mass balance around a completely mixed lake showing some typical inputs and outputs of matter. Aside from these sources and sinks, mass may also be transformed by reactions within the lake.

municipal sewer systems. Output could be via sedimentation, vaporization or flow through the lake's outlet. In addition, the substance being modeled can be transformed into another compound by reaction. The mathematical forms of the terms in Equation 11.1 will now be elaborated.

Accumulation

For a lake of constant volume, the rate of change of the mass of a substance (i.e., accumulation) is represented as

$$\frac{dm}{dt} = V \frac{dc}{dt} \tag{11.2}$$

where m = the mass of the substance [M]
          d/dt = the change with respect to time [T^{-1}]
          V = the lake's volume [L^3]
          c = the concentration of the substance [$M\ L^{-3}$]

Thus, mass accumulates as concentration increases with time (positive dc/dt) and diminishes as concentration decreases with time (negative dc/dt). For the steady-state case, mass remains constant ($dc/dt = 0$). The units of accumulation (as with all other terms in the balance) are mass per time [$M\ T^{-1}$].

Loadings

Mass enters a lake from a variety of sources and in a number of different ways. For example, mass carried by tributary streams enters a lake at its periphery and is dependent on the magnitude of stream flow, as well as on drainage basin characteristics, such as soil types, land use and population density. Similarly, sources from the direct discharge of human waste also enter at the periphery and are dependent on such factors as waste treatment and population. In contrast, atmospheric sources, such as precipitation and dry fallout, enter across the air-water interface and are, in part, dependent on the size of the lake's surface area and the amount of rainfall. Feedback of matter from the bottom sediments also enters the lake on an areal basis. While the position and manner of entry of loadings will have fundamental importance to the simulation of horizontal gradients in lakes (Chapter 12), they are less important for completely mixed models since by definition all inputs are instantaneously distributed throughout the volume. Therefore, in the present section, the emphasis is on the fact that inputs generally can be characterized by their temporal characteristics, i.e., by their changes with time. This is expressed mathematically as

$$\left(V \frac{dc}{dt} \right)_{inputs} = W(t) \tag{11.3}$$

where $W(t)$ is the rate of mass loading $[M \ T^{-1}]$ and (t) designates it as a function of time. For example, human sources in many drainage basins have been increasing exponentially in recent years due to population growth. Sources related to the hydrologic cycle, such as mass carried by runoff or precipitation, often can be characterized by periodic functions. This is because the general pattern of high spring runoff, with relatively low and constant flow for other seasons, is repeated in a fairly predictable manner from year to year. On a longer time scale, cycles of wet and dry periods often can be represented by sinusoidal functions. Specific examples of the idealized loading functions for which solutions will be given are presented in Table 11.1. A useful feature of the models developed here is that they are linear and the solutions will be additive. Thus, if a lake is being subjected to an exponentially increasing human waste load, a constant precipitation load and a periodic runoff load, the model can be solved for each case separately and the results added for a total solution.

Outputs

Just as the formulation of inputs was reduced in complexity because of complete mixing, there are a number of ways in which the losses of mass are simplified. Since only movement of matter across the boundaries is important, the complex internal transport regimes that exist in most lakes are disregarded. Further, since the lake is assumed to be well mixed, the outputs, which are dependent on in-lake levels, can be formulated as a function of a single concentration. This is in contrast to systems, such as river-run lakes, in which strong spatial gradients can have a pronounced effect on how matter leaves the lake. With this in mind, the outputs can be divided into two general categories according to the manner and location of mass transport across the boundary. The primary distinction is between flow-related transport through the lake's outlet and areal losses (such as sedimentation and vaporization) through the lake's surface or bottom.

One way for mass to leave a lake is to be borne along with water flowing through its outlet. Since this flow is advective, it can be formulated in a manner similar to Equation 10.2 as in

Table 11.1   Idealized Forms of W(t), the Rate of Mass Loading of a Substance to a Lake

Type of Input	Mathematical Form	Graphical Representation
Impulse	$W(t) = 0 \quad t \neq 0$ $W(t) = m\delta \quad t = 0$	
Step	$W(t) = 0 \;@\; t < 0$ $W(t) = \overline{W} \;@\; t > 0$	
Linear	$W(t) = \overline{W} \pm \beta_l t$	
Exponential	$W(t) = W_e e^{\pm \beta_e t}$	
Periodic	$W(t) = \overline{W} + W_o \sin(\omega t - \theta)$ $(\omega = 2\pi / T_p)$	

$$\left(V \frac{dc}{dt} \right)_{\text{outflow}} = -Qc \qquad (11.4)$$

In contrast to outflow losses, mass can exit the system across the air-water and the sediment-water interfaces. In these cases, the loss can be formulated in proportion to the lake's concentration and surface area* as in

$$\left(V \frac{dc}{dt} \right)_{\text{areal loss}} = -vA_s c \qquad (11.5)$$

where v = the mass transfer velocity across the interface $[L\ T^{-1}]$
        A_s = the lake's surface area $[L^2]$, which is assumed equivalent to the sediment surface area

This linear expression is based on the assumption of identical and independent (e.g., no coagulation) behavior of the individual pollutant particles. As will be shown in the next section, Equation 11.5 is of the same mathematical form as a first-order decay reaction. In fact, although the process is one of mass transport, it usually is treated as a reaction.

Reactions

Since the present model development is concerned with the dynamics of a single substance, Equation 10.6 can be reexpressed as

$$\left(V \frac{dc}{dt} \right)_{\text{reaction}} = -kVc^n \qquad (11.6)$$

where k = the reaction's coefficient $[T^{-1}\ (M\ L^{-3})^{1-n}]$
        n = the order of the reaction

The negative sign indicates that in this reaction the mass of the reactant is lost or transformed to another substance. By far the most common formulation used to characterize reactions in natural waters is the first-order (i.e., $n=1$) reaction,

$$\left(V \frac{dc}{dt} \right)_{\text{first-order reaction}} = -kVc \qquad (11.7)$$

where k has units of $[T^{-1}]$. This formulation has been used to charac-

---

*Other formulations for this sink term are proposed and empirically fitted in Chapter 8.

terize a number of different transformations in natural waters, including radioactive decay, bacterial die-off and biochemical oxidation of organic matter. In these cases, the transformation takes place in one phase (phases being solid, liquid or gas) and is termed a *homogeneous* reaction. This is in contrast (see Figure 11.2) to a *heterogeneous* reaction, which involves more than one phase. An example of a heterogeneous reaction in water quality analysis is the movement of mass from the water (liquid) to the lake bottom (solid) via sedimentation. Another is the adsorption of a dissolved constituent onto the surface of a suspended particle.

Note that for a lake of constant depth, Equations 11.5 and 11.7 are of equivalent mathematical form. This can be seen by realizing that

$$V = A_s z \qquad (11.8)$$

where z is the mean depth of the lake [L]. Equation 11.5 can be rewritten, therefore, as

$$\left(V \frac{dc}{dt} \right)_{sedimentation} = - \left(\frac{v}{z} \right) Vc \qquad (11.9)$$

Thus, since v and z are constants, both Equations 11.7 and 11.9 represent mass loss as a product of concentration, volume and a constant.

Besides first-order reactions, there are numerous other ways to characterize transformations of matter in lakes. Solutions for some of the more common types will be derived in Section 11.2.2. Before proceeding to solutions for the first-order reactions, we will combine the preceding formulations into the complete mass balance equation.

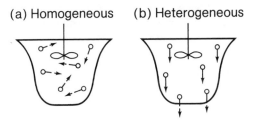

(a) Homogeneous   (b) Heterogeneous

Figure 11.2   Schematic representation of (a) homogeneous and (b) heterogeneous reactions in completely mixed lakes.

Total Balance

The foregoing terms can now be combined to yield the following mass balance for a completely mixed lake

$$V \frac{dc}{dt} = W(t) - Qc \pm \left(V \frac{dc}{dt} \right)_{reaction} \tag{11.10}$$

Note that areal losses are not included and the form of the reaction is not specified. The former was done because areal outputs often can be treated as first-order reactions. The latter was done because the following sections will provide solutions for various types of reactions. Before proceeding to these solutions we should note some nomenclature. In Equation 11.10, c and t can be thought of as the *dependent* and the *independent variables,* respectively, since essentially the model is designed to predict concentration over time. The loading term W(t) is often referred to as the *forcing function.* Finally, the quantities Q, V and k are called *coefficients* or *parameters.*

11.2 EXACT SOLUTIONS

For the general n^{th} order reaction, Equation 11.10 can be reexpressed as

$$\frac{dc}{dt} = \frac{W(t)}{V} - \frac{Q}{V} c - kc^n \tag{11.11}$$

This equation is an ordinary differential equation that defines changes in the lake's concentration (dc) with respect to changes in time (dt). If the concentration at a particular time is known and if values for the terms on the right-hand side of Equation 11.11 are available, the relationship provides a way to estimate the state of the lake at a future time as in

$$c(t + \Delta t) = c(t) + \frac{dc}{dt} \Delta t \tag{11.12}$$

where Δt represents the increment of time into the future for which the estimate is made. This operation could then be repeated any number of times to predict the lake's trajectory through time under changing conditions. As described in subsequent sections of this volume, most mathematical models of lake water quality use such incremental approaches to obtain their solutions. However, because actual changes in the lake are occurring continuously, some error is associated with the predictions. They are, therefore, referred to as *approximate* approaches.

In contrast, for certain forms of Equation 11.11 (constant coefficients and certain forcing functions), *exact* solutions are possible. These solutions consist of two parts.

$$c = c_g + c_p \qquad (11.13)$$

where c_g = the general solution when W(t) is zero
        c_p = the particular solution for specific forms of W(t)

In the following sections these solutions are derived for various types of reactions.

11.2.1 First-Order Reactions

For the case of a first-order reaction (n = 1), Equation 11.11 can be reformulated as

$$\frac{dc}{dt} + \alpha c = \frac{W(t)}{V} \qquad (11.14)$$

where*

$$\alpha = \frac{Q}{V} + k \qquad (11.15)$$

Before deriving time variable solutions, the steady-state case will be examined.

The Steady-State Solution

If a system is subject to a constant load, $\overline{W}$, for a long enough time, it will attain a dynamic equilibrium condition called the *steady state*. In mathematical terms, this means that accumulation is zero. Equation 11.14 can be solved for the lake's steady-state concentration, $\bar{c}$, since accumulation (dc/dt) equals zero. Therefore,

$$\bar{c} = \frac{\overline{W}}{\alpha V} = \frac{\overline{W}}{Q + kV} \qquad (11.16)$$

---

*Note that if a pollutant settles and decays, the sedimentation rate could be included as a first-order loss (Equation 11.5) and $\alpha = Q/V + k + v/z$.

§ § §

Example 11.1. Green Lake has the following characteristics:

$Q = 20 \times 10^6 \, m^3/yr$ $\qquad\qquad$ $A_s = 10 \times 10^6 \, m^2$

$z = 10 \, m$ $\qquad\qquad$ $V(Eq. \ 11.8) = 100 \times 10^6 \, m^3$

For the past 50 years, the only source of "Pollutant X" has been the town of Chilton, which has discharged its wastewater directly into the lake. The town has had a fairly stable population of 200 people over the same time period. If human beings generate approximately 0.115×10^6 g of "Pollutant X" per year, what is the lake's steady-state concentration if the substance decays at a rate of $1.05/yr$?

The loading of "Pollutant X" can be calculated as a product of Chilton's population and the human generation rate as in

$$\overline{W} = 200 \times (0.115 \times 10^6) = 23 \times 10^6 \, g/yr$$

From Equation 11.15

$$\alpha = \frac{20 \times 10^6}{100 \times 10^6} + 1.05 = 1.25/yr$$

From Equation 11.16

$$\bar{c} = \frac{23 \times 10^6}{(1.25)(100 \times 10^6)} = 0.184 \, g/m^3$$

§ § §

Time Variable Solutions

As shown in Equation 11.13, the time variable solution consists of two parts: a general and a particular solution. The general solution to Equation 11.13 relates to how the lake would respond in the absence of inputs, i.e., with W(t) equal to zero as in

$$\frac{dc}{dt} + \alpha c = 0 \qquad\qquad (11.17)$$

With an initial condition of $c = c_o$, Equation 11.17 can be integrated as in

$$\int_{c_0}^{c} \frac{dc}{c} = - \int_{0}^{t} \alpha \, dt \qquad (11.18)$$

This can be solved for

$$\ln c - \ln c_0 = -\alpha t \qquad (11.19)$$

which can be reexpressed as

$$c_g = c_0 e^{-\alpha t} \qquad (11.20)$$

Equation 11.20 indicates that, in the absence of loadings, the initial concentration in the lake decreases with time as in Figure 11.3. The rate of decrease is a function of α which reflects the lake's flushing and reaction rates.

§ § §

Example 11.2. For the same lake used in Example 11.1, determine the response if all loadings were terminated at $t = 0$.

Since the concentration in Green Lake is 0.184 g/m³, Equation 11.20 becomes

$$c_g = 0.184 e^{-1.25t}$$

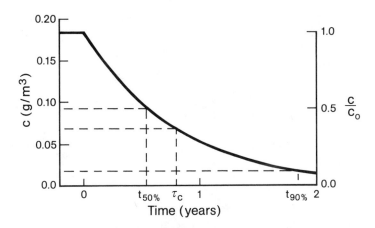

Figure 11.3 Graphical depiction of the general solution (i.e., the response if loadings are discontinued at $t = 0$). Values of the pollutant residence time, τ_c, and the 50% (half-life) and 90% response times are also shown.

which can be solved for the following values of time:

t (yr)	$c_g(g/m^3)$
0	0.184
0.5	0.098
1.0	0.053
1.5	0.028
2.0	0.015

The calculation can be continued with the results as in Figure 11.3.

§ § §

In addition to the initial condition, the lake's response to its input or forcing function, W(t), is needed for a complete solution of Equation 11.14. In the following paragraphs, some particular solutions for ideal forms of W(t) are presented (Table 11.1). Most of this material originated in the work of O'Connor and Mueller (1970).

The equation for a time-variable loading to a well-mixed lake is

$$\frac{dc}{dt} + \alpha c = \frac{W(t)}{V} \tag{11.21}$$

This equation can be solved by multiplying it by the integrating factor, $e^{\alpha t}$,

$$e^{\alpha t} \frac{dc}{dt} + e^{\alpha t} \alpha c = e^{\alpha t} \frac{W(t)}{V} \tag{11.22}$$

Now, realizing that

$$\frac{d}{dt} (e^{\alpha t} c) = e^{\alpha t} \frac{dc}{dt} + e^{\alpha t} \alpha c \tag{11.23}$$

Equation 11.22 becomes

$$\frac{d}{dt} (e^{\alpha t} c) = e^{\alpha t} \frac{W(t)}{V} \tag{11.24}$$

Integrating this equation for the interval 0 to t yields

$$e^{\alpha t} c \Big|_o^t = \frac{1}{V} \int e^{\alpha t} W(t) dt \tag{11.25}$$

or

$$ce^{\alpha t} - c_o = \frac{1}{V} \int e^{\alpha t} W(t)dt \qquad (11.26)$$

Dividing by $e^{\alpha t}$ and rearranging gives

$$c(t) = c_o e^{-\alpha t} + \frac{1}{V} \int_o^t e^{-\alpha(t-\tau)} W(\tau)d\tau \qquad (11.27)$$

where τ is a dummy variable. Thus, the first term on the right-hand side of the equal sign is the general solution (as in Equation 11.20) and the second term is the particular solution

$$c_p = \frac{1}{V} \int_o^t e^{-\alpha(t-\tau)} W(\tau)d\tau \qquad (11.28)$$

Note that the integrand is composed of two parts. The fixed portion, $e^{-\alpha(t-\tau)}$, is called the *kernel* and will not vary when we use Equation 11.28 to evaluate various particular solutions. The second term, $W(\tau)$, represents a general, time-variable, waste loading function. The following pages present solutions for Equation 11.28 for a number of ideal forms of $W(\tau)$.

§ § §

Example 11.3. If the waste loading is of an exponentially increasing form

$$W(\tau) = W_e e^{\beta_e t} \qquad (i)$$

use Equation 11.28 to evaluate the particular solution.
Substituting Equation (i) into 11.28 yields

$$c_p = \frac{1}{V} \int_o^t e^{-\alpha(t-\tau)} W_e e^{\beta_e \tau} d\tau$$

or

$$c_p = \frac{W_e e^{-\alpha t}}{V} \int_o^t e^{(\alpha + \beta_e)\tau} d\tau$$

which can be integrated to yield

$$c_p = \frac{W_e e^{-\alpha t}}{V} \left[\frac{e^{(\alpha + \beta_e)\tau}}{\alpha + \beta_e} \right]_o^t$$

or

$$c_p = \frac{W_e e^{-\alpha t}}{V} \left[\frac{e^{(\alpha + \beta_e)t} - 1}{\alpha + \beta_e} \right]$$

or

$$c_p = \frac{W_e}{V(\alpha + \beta_e)} (e^{\beta_e t} - e^{-\alpha t})$$

§ § §

Impulse Function. The most fundamental time variable loading is the impulse, or delta, function representing the discharge of waste over a relatively short time period. The accidental spill of a contaminant to a lake would be of this type. Mathematically, the *Dirac delta function,* $\delta(t - t_o)$, has been developed to represent such phenomena. The δ function can be visualized as an infinitely thin spike centered at $t = t_o$ and having unit area (Table 11.1 and Figure 11.4). It has the following properties

$$\delta(t - t_o) = 0 \quad \text{at } t \neq t_o \tag{11.29}$$

and

$$\int_{-\infty}^{\infty} \delta(t - t_o)dt = 1 \tag{11.30}$$

These lead to the important result

$$\int_{-\infty}^{\infty} \delta(t - t_o)f(t)dt = f(t_o) \tag{11.31}$$

The impulse load of mass to a lake can be represented in terms of the delta function as

$$W(t) = m\delta(t - t_o) \tag{11.32}$$

where m is the quantity of pollutant mass discharged during a spill [M] and the delta function has units of $[T^{-1}]$. Physically, Equation 11.32 indicates that the discharge of mass, m, occurs only at t_o and is zero elsewhere. Equation 11.32 can be substituted into Equation 11.28 giving

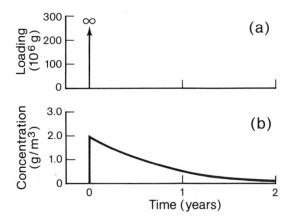

Figure 11.4   Plot of (a) loading and (b) response for an impulse loading.

$$c_p = \frac{1}{V} \int_0^t e^{-\alpha(t-\tau)} m\delta(\tau - \tau_0) d\tau \qquad (11.33)$$

If the spill occurs at time zero [i.e., t_0 (or τ_0) = 0], Equation 11.33 can be solved for

$$c_p = \frac{m}{V} e^{-\alpha t} \qquad (11.34)$$

This solution indicates that the spill is instantaneously distributed throughout the lake's volume resulting in an initial concentration of m/V. Thereafter, the pollutant is purged from the system by assimilative factors represented collectively by the parameter α.

§ § §

Example 11.4. At $t = 0$, 200×10^6 g of "pollutant X" is accidentally input to Green Lake over a 3-hour period. Compute the response of the lake to this spill. Using Equation 11.34 and data from Example 11.1

$$c_p = \frac{200 \times 10^6}{100 \times 10^6} e^{-1.25t}$$

which can be solved for the following values of time:

t (yr)	c_p (g/m^3)
0	2.000
0.5	1.071
1.0	0.573
1.5	0.307
2.0	0.164

The computation is displayed in Figure 11.4b.

§ § §

Step Input. If at $t = 0$ the lake's loading is changed to a new constant level, the forcing function is called a step input and is represented as (Figure 11.5a).

$$W (t < 0) = 0$$

$$W (t > 0) = \overline{W} \qquad (11.35)$$

where $\overline{W}$ is the new constant level of loading [M T^{-1}]. For this case, the particular solution is

$$c_p = \frac{\overline{W}}{\alpha V} (1 - e^{-\alpha t}) \qquad (11.36)$$

Note that this solution starts at zero and then converges on a new steady-state concentration, as in Figure 11.5a. At $t = \infty$, Equation 11.36 becomes equivalent to Equation 11.16 since the exponential term becomes very small as time progresses. The time variable model discussed previously in Chapter 8 results simply from the combination of this particular solution (Equation 11.36) with the general solution (Equation 11.20).

§ § §

Example 11.5. At $t = 0$, a new industry begins discharging 50×10^6 g/yr of "Pollutant X" into Green Lake. Calculate the lake's response to this step input.
Equation 11.36 becomes

$$c_p = \frac{50 \times 10^6}{1.25(100 \times 10^6)} [1 - e^{-1.25t}]$$

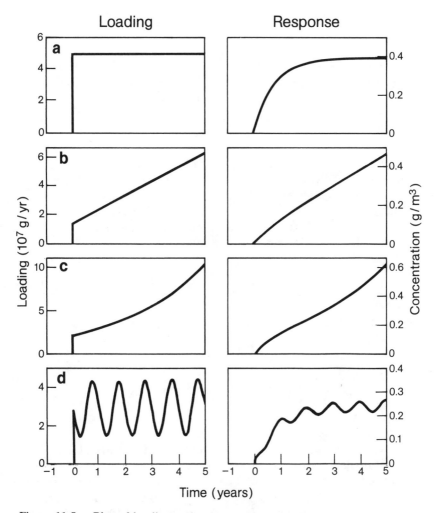

Figure 11.5   Plot of loading and response for (a) step input, (b) linear input, (c) exponential input and (d) sinusoidal input.

which can be solved for the following values of t:

t (yr)	$c_p(g/m^3)$
0	0.000
0.5	0.186
1.0	0.285
1.5	0.339
2.0	0.367
∞	0.400

The results of the computation are plotted in Figure 11.5a.

§ § §

Linear Input. The simplest representation of a trend is a straight line. Waste inputs can often be represented in this way as in

$$W(t) = \overline{W} \pm \beta_\ell t \tag{11.37}$$

where β_ℓ is the rate of change or slope of the trend $[M \ T^{-2}]$. Notice that Equation 11.37 is composed of a constant part (which is equivalent to the step loading as described in the previous section) and a part that changes linearly with time. Since the model itself (Equation 11.14) is linear, it can be solved separately for each of these parts. In the latter case, O'Connor and Mueller (1970) have derived the following solution

$$c_p = \mp \frac{\beta_\ell}{\alpha^2 V} (1 - e^{-\alpha t} - \alpha t) \tag{11.38}$$

which can be combined with Equation 11.36 to yield the total particular solution

$$c_p = \frac{\overline{W}}{\alpha V} (1 - e^{-\alpha t}) \mp \frac{\beta_\ell}{\alpha^2 V} (1 - e^{-\alpha t} - \alpha t) \tag{11.39}$$

§ § §

Example 11.6. At $t = 0$, a cattle feedlot is built on Green Lake with an initial population of 150 animals. For the next decade, the facility will be expanded to accommodate 100 additional animals per year. Assuming that all wastes are discharged directly to the lake, calculate the effect of the feedlot on Green Lake if cattle generate 0.1×10^6 g of "Pollutant X" per year.

The feedlot's waste discharge can be estimated as a product of the animal population and the pollutant generation rate as in

$$W(t) = (0.1 \times 10^6)(150 + 100t) = 15 \times 10^6 + (10 \times 10^6)t$$

Thus, $\overline{W} = 15 \times 10^6$ and $\beta_\ell = 10 \times 10^6$. Equation 11.39 can then be used to calculate the future concentrations as in

$$c = \frac{15 \times 10^6}{1.25(100 \times 10^6)} (1 - e^{-1.25t}) - \frac{10 \times 10^6}{(1.25)^2(100 \times 10^6)} (1 - e^{-1.25t} - 1.25t)$$

which can be solved for the following values of t:

t (yr)	$c_p(g/m^3)$
0	0
0.5	0.066
1.0	0.120
1.5	0.167
2.0	0.211

The results of the computation are displayed in Figure 11.5b.

§ § §

Exponential Input. Another standard way to characterize loading trends is as an exponential function as in

$$W(t) = W_e e^{\pm\beta_e t} \qquad (11.40)$$

where W_e [M T^{-1}] and β_e [T^{-1}] are coefficients. Such a function characterizes waste sources that grow (or decay) in proportion to their own magnitude. For example, O'Connor and Mueller (1970) used an exponential equation to characterize waste sources due to population growth in the Great Lakes.

The particular solution for this case is (recall Example 11.3)

$$c_p = \frac{W_e}{V(\alpha \pm \beta_e)}(e^{\pm\beta_e t} - e^{-\alpha t}) \qquad (11.41)$$

§ § §

Example 11.7. Because of the increased development in its watershed, it is anticipated that the stable population of Chilton will grow. It is estimated that this growth will proceed exponentially at a rate of 0.3/yr. Determine the effect of this growth on Green Lake. The population of Green Lake after t = 0, can be represented as

$$P = 200e^{0.3t}$$

With the same per capita pollutant generation rate as in Example 11.1, the waste loading due to the town can be represented as

$$W(t) = (200e^{0.3t})(0.115 \times 10^6) = 23 \times 10^6 e^{0.3t}$$

Thus, $W_e = 23 \times 10^6$ and $\beta_e = 0.3$. For this case, Equation 11.41 can be used to calculate the lake's response as in

$$c_p = \frac{23 \times 10^6}{(100 \times 10^6)(1.25 + 0.3)} (e^{0.3t} - e^{-1.25t})$$

which can be solved for the following values of t:

t(yr)	$c_p(g/m^3)$
0	0.000
0.5	0.093
1.0	0.158
1.5	0.210
2.0	0.258

The results of this computation are displayed in Figure 11.5c.

§ § §

Sinusoidal Inputs. A simple periodic input is the sinusoidal function (see Table 11.1 and Figure 11.5d) that can be represented mathematically as

$$W(t) = \overline{W} + W_o \sin(\omega t - \theta) \tag{11.42}$$

where $\overline{W}$ is the constant part of the loading [M T^{-1}], W_o is the amplitude (i.e., the distance between the constant part and the extremes) of the sine wave [M T^{-1}], θ is the phase shift [radians or degrees], defined as

$$\theta = \left(t_m - \frac{T_p}{4}\right)\omega \tag{11.43}$$

where t_m is the time of occurrence of the peak or maximum loading [T], ω is the frequency of the oscillation [radians (or degrees)/T] which can be calculated from

$$\omega = \frac{2\pi}{T_p} \quad \text{or} \quad \frac{360°}{T_p} \tag{11.44}$$

where T_p is the period of time over which a complete oscillation occurs [T]. The particular solution for this case is

$$c = \frac{\overline{W}}{\alpha V}(1 - e^{-\alpha t}) + \frac{W_o}{V\sqrt{\alpha^2 + \omega^2}} \sin\left(\omega t - \theta - \arctan\frac{\omega}{\alpha}\right)$$

$$-\frac{W_o}{V\sqrt{\alpha^2 + \omega^2}}\sin\left(-\theta - \arctan\frac{\omega}{\alpha}\right)e^{-\alpha t} \qquad (11.45)$$

§ § §

Example 11.8. At $t=0$ a canning plant begins operation and discharges "Pollutant X" into Green Lake. Because of the seasonal nature of the product being canned, peak waste discharges occur in fall (October 1) and minimum levels in spring (April 1). The discharge has a mean level of 30×10^6 g/yr, with a difference between the mean and the extremes of 15×10^6 g/yr. Compute the response of Green Lake to this discharge with a sinusoidal input to approximate the loading.

Since the loading pattern repeats itself every year, $T_p = 1$ yr and ω (Equation 11.44) $= 2\pi$ yr^{-1}. The peak loading occurs at $t_m = 3/4$ yr; thus from Equation 11.43,

$$\theta = (\tfrac{3}{4} - \tfrac{1}{4})2\pi = \pi$$

Therefore, the loading function in this case is

$$W(t) = 30 \times 10^6 + 15 \times 10^6 \sin(2\pi t - \pi)$$

Using Equation 11.45, the solution is

$$c = \frac{30 \times 10^6}{1.25(100 \times 10^6)}(1 - e^{-1.25t})$$

$$+ \frac{15 \times 10^6}{(100 \times 10^6)\sqrt{1.25^2 + (2\pi)^2}}\sin\left(2\pi t - \pi - \arctan\frac{2\pi}{1.25}\right)$$

$$- \frac{15 \times 10^6}{(100 \times 10^6)\sqrt{1.25^2 + (2\pi)^2}}\sin\left(-\pi - \arctan\frac{2\pi}{1.25}\right)e^{-1.25t}$$

which can be solved for the following values of t:

t(yr)	c_p(g/m^3)
0	0.000
0.25	0.043
0.50	0.076
0.75	0.142
1.00	0.188
1.25	0.180
1.50	0.177
1.75	0.215
2.00	0.241

The result is shown in Figure 11.5d.

§ § §

Total Solution

The preceding particular solutions represented a lake's response to individual types of waste loadings. In each case, if that type of loading were the sole input, the total solution would be obtained by combining the particular solution with the general solution (Equation 11.20). For example, if Green Lake were only affected by the exponential growth of the town of Chilton, the total solution would be attained by combining Equations 11.20 and 11.41. If other sources (such as the feedlot or the factories) also affected the lake, their effect would merely be added to the other equations.

§ § §

Example 11.9. Determine the total response of Green Lake to the developments described in Examples 11.1, 2, 5, 6, 7 and 8.

The total solution is obtained by combining the general and particular solutions as in

$$c = c_g (\text{Eq. } 11.20) + c_p (\text{Eq. } 11.36 + \text{Eq. } 11.39 + \text{Eq. } 11.41 + \text{Eq. } 11.45)$$

Information from the previous examples can be used to calculate the response for a number of values of t as in:

t	General	Step	Linear	Exp.	Sine	Total
0	0.184	0.000	0.000	0.000	0.000	0.184
0.5	0.098	0.186	0.066	0.093	0.076	0.520
1.0	0.053	0.285	0.120	0.158	0.188	0.803
1.5	0.028	0.339	0.167	0.210	0.177	0.921
2.0	0.015	0.367	0.211	0.258	0.241	1.093

The above, along with other values, are plotted Figure 11.6.

§ § §

Assimilative Capacity, Loading Plots, Residence and Response Time

Assimilative Capacity. As described in Section 10.4, *assimilative capacity* is the amount of loading that a lake can bear and still attain a

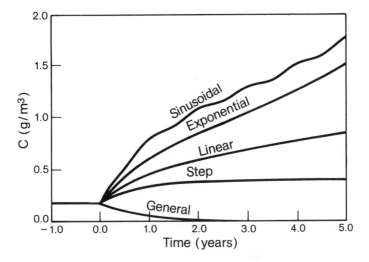

Figure 11.6 Plot of total lake response to a combination of loadings.

water quality objective. For the simple model described above, the ability to assimilate pollutant inputs is a function of a combination of factors, including lake size, flow rate and reaction characteristics as defined for a steady-state lake as (note: $\P = Q + kV$)

$$\bar{c} = \frac{\overline{W}}{Q + kV} = \frac{\overline{W}}{\P} \qquad (11.46)$$

If a concentration level is set as a water quality goal, Equation 11.46 can be rearranged* to estimate the loading level that would be required to reach the goal as in (recall Equation 10.16)

$$\overline{W} = \bar{c}(Q + kV) = \bar{c}\P \qquad (11.47)$$

Loading Plots. Although Equation 11.47 provides a direct estimate of assimilative capacity, it can also be expressed graphically to facilitate its application by lake managers. For example, both Vollenweider (1975) and Dillon (1975) have used completely mixed mass balance models to derive loading plots for eutrophication management. These loading plots are presented in Chapter 8 along with additional graphical methods for reexpression of the assimilative capacity in a probabilistic form.

---

*Depending on the approach used to estimate k, this may also require reestimation of the parameter. As we note in Chapter 6, the least squares regression of y on x is generally not equivalent to the least squares regression of x on y.

The basic idea behind loading plots is to map the equation onto two-dimensional space with loading as the dependent variable. For Equation 11.47 this can be done by dividing by V and taking the logarithm to yield

$$\log_{10}(\overline{W}/V) = \log_{10}(\bar{c}) + \log_{10}(\alpha) \tag{11.48}$$

where α represents the assimilative forces of the lake. Equation 11.48 can be plotted in two ways. In Figure 11.7a, $\log_{10}(\overline{W}/V)$ is mapped on $\log_{10}(\alpha)$, with $\log_{10}(\bar{c})$ treated as a parameter. This format is similar to that used by Vollenweider (1975) and Dillon (1975) in the sense that the abscissa is a measure of the assimilative forces and the contours represent the water quality objective, or standard. The plot indicates that, for a given in-lake concentration, a low flushing/slow decaying system can assimilate less loading (where loading is defined as $\overline{W}/V$; see Chapter 1) than a fast decaying substance in a fast flushing lake.

An alternative expression is shown in Figure 11.7b, where loading is mapped on the water quality standard. In this case, α is allowed to vary. This plot indicates that for a given assimilative capacity, the standard varies directly with the lake loading.

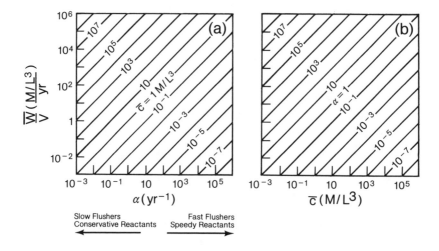

Figure 11.7   Two loading plots based on the completely mixed model with first-order decay reaction. (a) Volumetric loading versus the assimilation rate, with contours indicating various in-lake water quality standards. (b) Volumetric loading versus the water quality standard for various levels of assimilation.

Residence Time. The residence time (or equivalently, the detention time), τ_E [T], of a substance E is defined for a steady-state, constant volume system as (Stumm and Morgan 1970)

$$\tau_E = \frac{E}{|dE/dt|_{\pm}} \qquad (11.49)$$

where

E = the quantity of the element which can be expressed as either mass [M] or concentration [M L^{-3}]

$|dE/dt|_{\pm}$ = the absolute value of either the sources or the sinks of the element in units of [M T^{-1}] or [M L^{-3} T^{-1}]

The residence time represents the mean amount of time that a particle of E would stay or "reside" within the system.

One of the simpler applications of Equation 11.49 is the determination of the residence time of water in a lake. Since the density of water is by definition approximately 1.0 g/cm^3, the quantity of water in a lake is equivalent to the lake's volume. In a similar sense, the "sink" of water from a lake is measured by the magnitude of its outflow (assuming that evaporation = precipitation*). Substituting these values into Equation 11.49 yields the water residence time,

$$\tau_w = \frac{V}{Q} \qquad (11.50)$$

This relationship is useful for understanding the general notion of residence time since it has a straightforward physical interpretation—it is the amount of time that would be required for the outflow to replace the quantity of water in the lake. Thus, it is a measure of the lake's flushing rate. If the volume is large and the flow is small, the lake has a long residence time, i.e., it is a slow flusher. If such a lake were subjected to a pollutant load, the lake would have a relatively poor ability to cleanse itself by flushing. For this reason, lake quality is often empirically related to flushing rate and some attempts to develop lake assimilative capacity models have used water residence time as a primary independent variable.

While water residence time does provide an estimate of a lake's ability to flush pollutants, as we have seen in the previous sections, other mechanisms can contribute to assimilative capacity. A more direct estimate of a lake's resistance to pollution would therefore be provided by a relationship that accounted for the other cleansing mechanisms. This is done by combining Equation 11.49 with the simple first-order mass balance (Equation 11.14) to develop a "pollutant residence time."

---

*Note that even without this assumption the relationship holds if Q is generalized to *all* inputs or outputs.

The pollutant sinks for Equation 11.14 expressed on a concentration per time basis are

$$\left.\frac{dc}{dt}\right|_{-} = \frac{Qc}{V} + \frac{kVc}{V} \tag{11.51}$$

Substituting this into Equation 11.49 and simplifying yields

$$\tau_c = \frac{V}{Q + kV} = \frac{1}{\alpha} \tag{11.52}$$

Note that Equations 11.50 and 11.52 are similar in form, with the exception that magnitude of the pollutant residence time is affected by the rate of reaction in addition to the outflow. Thus, if a "pollutant" has a very high reaction rate, cleansing by reaction would remove the pollutant from the water column at a high enough rate so that an individual particle would reside in the water for a short time period. Thus, it might be assumed that the pollutant would have less of an impact than a substance with a lower reaction rate (other things being equal). However, one problem with the direct use of Equation 11.52 as a measure of "assimilative capacity" is that it includes the effect of volume in its numerator. Thus, it does not necessarily indicate how much waste the lake is capable of assimilating (see Example 11.10).

Response Time. Whereas the residence time of a lake is useful in comparing the relative assimilative capacity of lakes, another measure of interest is the time required for a lake to respond to loading changes. To derive such a quantity, assume that a lake is in a steady-state condition with a concentration of $\bar{c}_i$. At $t = 0$, the lake's loading is changed to a level that will, in time, bring the lake to a new steady-state concentration of $\bar{c}_f$. From Equations 11.20 and 11.36, the response of the lake can be calculated as in

$$c = \bar{c}_i e^{-\alpha t} + \bar{c}_f (1 - e^{-\alpha t}) \tag{11.53}$$

Algebraically, this equation can be rearranged to yield

$$\frac{c - \bar{c}_f}{\bar{c}_i - \bar{c}_f} = e^{-\alpha t} \tag{11.54}$$

Inverting Equation 11.54, taking its natural logarithm and dividing by α gives

$$t = \frac{\ln (\bar{c}_i - \bar{c}_f)/(c - \bar{c}_f)}{\alpha} \qquad (11.55)$$

Now, we define a new quantity, ϕ, which is the percentage of the new steady state that has been attained as in

$$\phi = \frac{c - \bar{c}_i}{\bar{c}_f - \bar{c}_i} \times 100\% \qquad (11.56)$$

which can be solved for c as in

$$c = \frac{\phi (\bar{c}_f - \bar{c}_i) + 100\% \, \bar{c}_i}{100\%} \qquad (11.57)$$

Equation 11.57 may then be substituted into Equation 11.55 and simplified to

$$t_\phi = \frac{\ln 100/(100 - \phi)}{\alpha} \qquad (11.58)$$

where t_ϕ is the $\phi\%$ response time that is equal to the time required to reach $\phi\%$ of a new steady state following a step change in loading.

With the arbitrary setting of a value of ϕ, Equation 11.58 represents an estimate of a lake's response characteristics. For example, if we are interested in knowing how long it takes to reach 90% of a new steady state, Equation 11.58 becomes*

$$t_{90} = \frac{\ln 100/(100 - 90)}{\alpha} = \frac{2.3}{\alpha} \qquad (11.59)$$

One interesting result of this exercise is that for $\phi = 63.2\%$

$$t_{63.2} = \frac{1}{\alpha} = \frac{V}{Q + kV} \equiv \tau_c \qquad (11.60)$$

Note that this is equivalent to Equation 11.52. Therefore, aside from representing the mean time that a pollutant particle resides in a lake, this pollutant residence time, identified as τ_c, also is equivalent to the time

---

*Similarly, the half-life (t_{50}) could be calculated as $0.693/\alpha$.

required to reach 63.2% of a new steady state following a step change in its loading. Figure 11.3 depicts several typical values of t_ϕ.

§ § §

Example 11.10. The Twin Lakes have the following characteristics

	Twin Lake I	Twin Lake II
Mean depth (m)	10	20
Surface area (10^6 m^2)	10	10
Outflow (10^6 m^3/yr)	10	20
Volume (10^6 m^3)	100	200

Both lakes receive equal loadings (50×10^6 g/yr) of a pollutant that settles at a rate of 5 m/yr and decays at a rate of 0.2/yr. Calculate the following quantities for both lakes: (a) steady state concentration, (b) water residence time and (c) pollutant residence time.

Equation	Twin Lake I	Twin Lake II
a) α (Eq. 11.15)*	0.80/yr	0.55/yr
$\bar{c}$ (Eq. 11.16)	0.625 g/m^3	0.455 g/m^3
b) τ_w (Eq. 11.50)	10 yr	10 yr
c) τ_c (Eq. 11.52)	1.25 yr	1.82 yr

Note that both lakes have the same residence time, yet have different concentrations even though they have the same loading. In addition, although Twin Lake II has a higher pollutant residence time (indicating that a particle stays in its volume longer), its concentration is lower. To make this clearer, determine d) the loading that is necessary to attain a water quality goal of $\bar{c} = 0.250$ g/m^3 in each lake and e) determine the 50%, 75%, 90% and 95% response times required to reach this goal.

Equation	Twin Lake I	Twin Lake II
d) $\overline{W}$ (Eq. 11.47)	20×10^6 g/yr	27.5×10^6 g/yr

Thus, Twin Lake II has a higher assimilative capacity although it also has a higher pollutant residence time.

Equation	Twin Lake I	Twin Lake II
e) t_{50} (Eq. 11.58)	0.87 yr	1.26 yr
t_{75}	1.73 yr	2.52 yr

---

*Remember that α includes the effect of decay *and* sedimentation as well as flushing, as noted in the footnote for Equation 11.15.

t_{90}	2.88 yr	4.18 yr
t_{95}	3.75 yr	5.45 yr

§ § §

11.2.2 Other Single Species Reactions

Zero-Order Reactions. Aside from the first-order reaction, there are as many forms of Equation 11.6 as there are values of n. However, very few of them are applicable to transformations in natural waters. An exception is the *zero-order reaction* where Equation 11.6 becomes

$$\left(V\,\frac{dc}{dt} \right)_{\text{zero-order reaction}} = -kVc^0 = -\psi \qquad (11.61)$$

ψ is a constant $[M\,T^{-1}]$ since a quantity raised to zero is equal to unity. Consequently, for a zero-order reaction, the transformation is independent of the reactant's concentration. Equation 11.61 can be substituted into Equation 11.10 to yield

$$\frac{dc}{dt} + \alpha'c = \frac{W'(t)}{V} \qquad (11.62)$$

where

$$W'(t) = W(t) - \psi \qquad (11.63)$$

and

$$\alpha' = \frac{Q}{V} = \frac{1}{\tau_w} \qquad (11.64)$$

Thus, the model is identical in form to the mass balance for the first-order model with $k = 0$, and all the previously derived solutions apply (with the proper substitutions as indicated above). For example, the steady-state solution for the zero-order reaction is

$$\bar{c} = \frac{\overline{W'}}{Q} \qquad (11.65)$$

and the general solution is

$$c_g = c_0 e^{-t/\tau_w} \qquad (11.66)$$

Note that, since the reaction is independent of concentration, the pollutant's response characteristics are defined solely by the water residence time, i.e., the lake is cleansed by flushing alone.

There are a few reactions in natural waters that can be described by the above relationships. The most common are conservative substances, such as chloride, that do not react. For this particular case $\psi = 0$.

Another use of zero-order reactions is to characterize removal mechanisms that occur so quickly that they can be treated as a constant fraction of the incoming load. For example, a portion of a lake's phosphorus loading might be associated with suspended particulate matter that settles rapidly upon entering a lake. For the steady-state case, this portion could be defined as (Piontelli and Tonolli 1964)

$$\psi = f_s \overline{W} \tag{11.67}$$

where f_s is that fraction of the loading that settles rapidly. The steady-state solution for this case is

$$c = \frac{(1 - f_s)\overline{W}}{Q} \tag{11.68}$$

This approach, as applied to phosphorus modeling, was explored in greater depth in Chapter 8.

11.2.3 Coupled Reactions and Equilibria

All the foregoing derivations have been for a single reactant. As will be discussed later (Chapters 14 and 15), there are a variety of lake problems that require the modeling of more than a single substance for adequate characterization. The simplest system of this type consists of two constituents linked by first-order reactions as in Figure 11.8. Mass balances for this system can be written as

$$V\frac{dc_1}{dt} = W_1(t) - Qc_1 - k_{12}Vc_1 + k_{21}Vc_2 \tag{11.69}$$

and

$$V\frac{dc_2}{dt} = W_2(t) - Qc_2 - k_{21}Vc_2 + k_{12}Vc_1 \tag{11.70}$$

or

$$\frac{dc_1}{dt} + \alpha_1 c_1 = \beta_1 c_2 + \Omega_1 \tag{11.71}$$

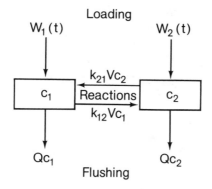

Figure 11.8 Coupled system of reactants.

and

$$\frac{dc_2}{dt} + \alpha_2 c_2 = \beta_2 c_1 + \Omega_2 \tag{11.72}$$

where

$$\alpha_1 = \frac{Q}{V} + k_{12} \tag{11.73}$$

$$\beta_1 = k_{21} \tag{11.74}$$

$$\alpha_2 = \frac{Q}{V} + k_{21} \tag{11.75}$$

$$\beta_2 = k_{12} \tag{11.76}$$

$$\Omega_1 = \frac{W_1(t)}{V} \tag{11.77}$$

$$\Omega_2 = \frac{W_2(t)}{V} \tag{11.78}$$

Steady-State Solution. At steady state, Equations 11.71 and 11.72 can be solved for (setting $dc_1/dt = dc_2/dt = 0$, and solving for two unknowns)

$$\bar{c}_1 = \frac{\overline{\Omega}_1 \alpha_2 + \overline{\Omega}_2 \beta_1}{\alpha_1 \alpha_2 - \beta_1 \beta_2} \tag{11.79}$$

$$\bar{c}_2 = \frac{\overline{\Omega}_2 \alpha_1 + \overline{\Omega}_1 \beta_2}{\alpha_1 \alpha_2 - \beta_1 \beta_2} \tag{11.80}$$

Time-Variable Solution. The general solutions (i.e., with $W = 0$) can be obtained with Laplace transforms for the case where we set the initial conditions $c_1 = c_{10}$ and $c_2 = c_{20}$ at $t = 0$.

$$c_{1g} = \frac{\lambda\gamma - \Delta}{\lambda - \mu} e^{-\lambda t} + \frac{\Delta - \mu\gamma}{\lambda - \mu} e^{-\mu t} \qquad (11.81)$$

and

$$c_{2g} = \frac{\sigma - \lambda\delta}{\mu - \lambda} e^{-\lambda t} + \frac{\delta\mu - \sigma}{\mu - \lambda} e^{-\mu t} \qquad (11.82)$$

where

$$\lambda = \frac{(\alpha_1 + \alpha_2) + \sqrt{(\alpha_1 + \alpha_2)^2 - 4(\alpha_1\alpha_2 - \beta_1\beta_2)}}{2} \qquad (11.83a)$$

$$\mu = \frac{(\alpha_1 + \alpha_2) - \sqrt{(\alpha_1 + \alpha_2)^2 - 4(\alpha_1\alpha_2 - \beta_1\beta_2)}}{2} \qquad (11.83b)$$

$$\gamma = c_{10} \qquad (11.84)$$

$$\Delta = c_{10}\alpha_2 + c_{20}\beta_1 \qquad (11.85)$$

$$\delta = c_{20} \qquad (11.86)$$

$$\sigma = c_{20}\alpha_1 + c_{10}\beta_2 \qquad (11.87)$$

A number of lake water quality contexts can be idealized as coupled systems. Examples include an embayment and main lake as described in Chapter 12. Additionally, the epilimnion and hypolimnion or a mixed sediment layer and the overlying water can sometimes be characterized in this way. However, the inclusion of only one additional reactant adds great complexity to the solutions. For this reason, most multicomponent systems are modeled with numerical solution techniques as described in Section 11.3. Before proceeding to these techniques, two situations where multicomponent analyses can be simplified will be reviewed.

Equilibria Solutions. If the first-order reactions linking the reactants in Equations 11.69 and 11.70 are much quicker than the input-output terms of the model, they will reach a dynamic equilibrium on the time frame of the calculation. For example, if the k_{12} and k_{21} were on the order of 1/hr and the residence time of the lake were a year, the reactions would always be at a *local equilibrium* on an annual or even weekly time frame. In this case, Di Toro (1976) has shown that Equations 11.69 and 11.70 can be added together to yield

$$V \frac{dc_t}{dt} = W_t(t) - Qc_t \qquad (11.88)$$

where

$$c_t = c_1 + c_2 \qquad (11.89)$$

and

$$W_t(t) = W_1(t) + W_2(t) \qquad (11.90)$$

Notice that the terms representing the kinetic interaction between c_1 and c_2 were cancelled out by the addition. They can then be calculated using the following relationships

$$c_1 = \frac{c_t}{1 + (k_{12}/k_{21})} \qquad (11.91)$$

$$c_2 = \frac{k_{12}}{k_{21}} c_1 \qquad (11.92)$$

Thus, the above manipulation effectively reduces a set of two differential equations to a single differential and two algebraic equations. Considering the difficulty of solving a set of coupled equations, this operation greatly simplifies the solution of such systems.

Di Toro's (1976) local equilibrium technique is especially useful in modeling chemical reactions that typically go to completion on short time scales. For example, inorganic carbon variations due to phytoplankton production and respiration can be modeled as an equilibrium process (see Chapter 14). Other quick transformations, such as adsorption/desorption can also be handled in this way (see Chapter 13).

11.2.4 Lakes in Series

If a number of lakes are linked by short stretches* of river, they usually must be managed collectively because modification of the upstream lakes

---

*By short stretch, we formally mean that the residence time of substances in the interconnecting rivers is short enough that pollutants undergo negligible changes during inter-lake transport. Also, the residence times of the rivers should be much shorter than in the lakes.

could have significant effects downstream. Such lake chains occur naturally as well as due to man's influence. For example, the Laurentian Great
Lakes and the Madison (Wisconsin) Lakes are noteworthy natural systems. In addition, the construction of impoundments can result in the
transformation of a free-flowing river into a series of lakes.

O'Connor and Mueller (1970) have developed a general computational
framework for modeling such systems for pollutants undergoing first-
order reactions. The approach is based on a mass balance around the nth
lake of a series (Figure 11.9),

$$\frac{dc_n}{dt} + \alpha_n c_n = \frac{W_n}{V_n} + \frac{Q_{n-1}}{V_n} c_{n-1} \tag{11.93}$$

where n is the lake in question and $n-1$ designates the upstream lake. As
was done previously for a single lake (Equations 11.22–27), Equation
11.93 can be multiplied by an integrating factor to give

$$c_n = c_{no} e^{-\alpha_n t} + \frac{1}{V_n} \int_0^t e^{-\alpha_n(t-\tau)} [W_n(\tau) + Q_{n-1} c_{n-1}] d\tau \tag{11.94}$$

Note that Equation 11.94 is identical to Equation 11.27 with the exception that the former includes a term, $Q_{n-1} c_{n-1}$, accounting for the effect
of the upstream lake. Thus, starting from the first lake in the series, we
can obtain solutions for the entire system by a recursive method.

§ § §

Example 11.11. Use Equation 11.94 to obtain the response of the
second in a series of lakes to a constant loading introduced into the first
lake. Assume that both lakes have zero concentration at time zero (i.e.,
$c_{n-1,o} = c_{n,o} = 0$). For a constant loading, the response of the first lake can
be represented using Equation 11.94 by

$$c_1 = \frac{1}{V_1} \int_0^t e^{-\alpha_1(t-\tau)} \overline{W} d\tau \tag{i}$$

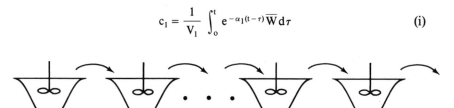

Figure 11.9   A series of n well-mixed lakes.

From our previous derivations we know that the solution is (as in Equation 11.36),

$$c_1 = \frac{\overline{W}}{\alpha_1 V_1} (1 - e^{-\alpha_1 t}) \qquad \text{(ii)}$$

This result can then be substituted into Equation 11.94 (for $n = 2$) to give

$$c_2 = \frac{1}{V_2} \int_o^t e^{-\alpha_2(t-\tau)} Q_1 \frac{\overline{W}}{\alpha_1 V_1} (1 - e^{-\alpha_1 \tau}) d\tau \qquad \text{(iii)}$$

which can be rearranged

$$c_2 = \frac{Q_1}{V_2} \frac{\overline{W}}{\alpha_1 V_1} e^{-\alpha_2 t} \int_o^t e^{\alpha_2 \tau} - e^{(\alpha_2 - \alpha_1)\tau} d\tau \qquad \text{(iv)}$$

and integrated to yield

$$c_2 = \frac{Q_1}{V_2} \frac{\overline{W}}{\alpha_1 V_1} \left[\frac{1}{\alpha_2} (1 - e^{-\alpha_2 t}) - \frac{1}{\alpha_1 - \alpha_2} (e^{-\alpha_2 t} - e^{-\alpha_1 t}) \right] \qquad \text{(v)}$$

For a third lake, Equation (v) could be multiplied by Q_2, substituted into Equation 11.94 and solved.

Notice that the solution is composed of two parts related to the form of the response of the first lake. As in Equation (ii) the solution for the first lake includes a constant part, $\overline{W}/\alpha_1 V_1$, and a negative, decaying exponential, $-\overline{W}/\alpha_1 V_1 e^{-\alpha_1 t}$. These are then multiplied by the interconnecting flow, Q_1, to become the "loading" to the second lake. Thus, the input to the second lake from the first lake is identical in form to a direct constant and a direct exponential loading. The solution, therefore, has two components reflecting these two effects. This can be seen by comparing the solution (Equation v) with Equations 11.36 and 11.41.

§ § §

The solution for the nth lake due to a waste load introduced in the ith can now be written in general form as*

$$c_{ni} = \frac{(Q_{n-1} Q_{n-2} \cdots Q_i)}{V_n V_{n-1} \cdots V_{i+1}} e^{-\alpha_n t} \int_o^t e^{\alpha_n t} e^{-\alpha_{n-1} t} \int_o^t e^{\alpha_{n-1} t}$$

$$\cdots e^{-\alpha_i t} \int_o^t W(t) e^{\alpha_i t} dt_i \cdots dt_{n-1} dt_n \qquad (11.95)$$

---

*Note that because of errata in the original publication, this differs from the comparable equation in O'Connor and Mueller (1970).

where c_{ni} designates the concentration of lake n due to a loading of W(t) to lake i.

§ § §

Example 11.12. During the late 1950s and early 1960s, nuclear weapons testing introduced large quantities of radioactive substances into the atmosphere. As in Figure 11.10 this resulted in a fallout flux of these substances to the surface of the earth. Although the fallout has continued to the present time, the pronounced peak in the early 1960s allows idealization of the resulting load as an impulse function centered in 1963. For ^{90}Sr, this function is

$$W(t) = J_{Sr} A_s \delta(t - t_o) \qquad (i)$$

where
J_{Sr} = the impulse flux of strontium-90 delivered to the lake = 70×10^{-9} Ci/m^2 (Ci designates the radioactivity unit, the Curie)
A_s = the lake's surface area [m^2]
$\delta(t - t_o)$ = the unit impulse function [yr^{-1}]
t_o = 1963

Using O'Connor and Mueller's (1970) method predict the response of the Laurentian Great Lakes to this flux.

Equation 11.95 can be used to derive the following relationships for the impulse load. For example, the effect of the impulse load to the first lake on the concentration of the first lake is

$$c_{11} = c_{10} e^{-\alpha_1 t} \qquad (ii)$$

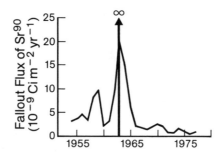

Figure 11.10 Fallout flux of ^{90}Sr to the Great Lakes (from Lerman 1972) along with the impulse load used in Example 11.12 to approximate the input.

where

$$c_{10} = \frac{J_{Sr,1} A_{s,1}}{V_1}$$ (iii)

Similarly, the concentration of subsequent lakes down the chain could be computed as

$$c_{21} = \frac{Q_1}{V_1} c_{10} \frac{e^{-\alpha_1 t} - e^{-\alpha_2 t}}{\alpha_2 - \alpha_1}$$ (iv)

$$c_{31} = \frac{Q_2 Q_1}{V_3 V_2} c_{10} \left[\frac{e^{-\alpha_1 t} - e^{-\alpha_3 t}}{(\alpha_3 - \alpha_1)(\alpha_2 - \alpha_1)} - \frac{e^{-\alpha_2 t} - e^{-\alpha_3 t}}{(\alpha_3 - \alpha_1)(\alpha_2 - \alpha_3)} \right]$$ (v)

$$c_{41} = \frac{Q_3 Q_2 Q_1}{V_4 V_3 V_2} c_{10} \left[\frac{e^{-\alpha_1 t} - e^{-\alpha_4 t}}{(\alpha_2 - \alpha_1)(\alpha_3 - \alpha_1)(\alpha_4 - \alpha_1)} \right.$$

$$- \frac{e^{-\alpha_3 t} - e^{-\alpha_4 t}}{(\alpha_2 - \alpha_1)(\alpha_3 - \alpha_1)(\alpha_4 - \alpha_3)} - \frac{e^{-\alpha_2 t} - e^{-\alpha_4 t}}{(\alpha_2 - \alpha_1)(\alpha_3 - \alpha_2)(\alpha_4 - \alpha_2)}$$

$$\left. + \frac{e^{-\alpha_3 t} - e^{-\alpha_4 t}}{(\alpha_2 - \alpha_1)(\alpha_3 - \alpha_2)(\alpha_4 - \alpha_3)} \right]$$ (vi)

The Great Lakes can be represented as a series of reactors as in Figure 11.11. Note that both Lakes Michigan and Superior are "first" upstream lakes. Their outflows feed into Lake Huron which discharges to Lake Erie. Lake Ontario is the last lake in the system. Equations ii and iv–vi

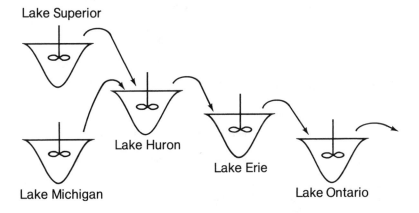

Lake Superior

Lake Huron

Lake Erie

Lake Michigan

Lake Ontario

Figure 11.11   The Laurentian Great Lakes as a series of well-mixed reactors.

can be applied to the Great Lakes and the total solution arrived at by summing the individual components as in

$$c_{st} = c_{ss} \tag{vii}$$

$$c_{mt} = c_{mm} \tag{viii}$$

$$c_{ht} = c_{hh} + c_{hs} + c_{hm} \tag{xi}$$

$$c_{et} = c_{ee} + c_{eh} + c_{es} + c_{em} \tag{x}$$

$$c_{ot} = c_{oo} + c_{oe} + c_{oh} + c_{os} + c_{om} \tag{xi}$$

where subscripts, s, m, h, e and o designate Superior, Michigan, Huron, Erie and Ontario, respectively, and t designates total concentration. Using the data in Table 11.2 and the decay rate of ^{90}Sr ($= 0.024 \ yr^{-1}$), the results can be computed and compared with data (Figure 11.12). The simulation duplicates the general trend of the measurement with the exception that the computation decreases somewhat faster than the data. This is due, in part, to our use of an impulse function to idealize the continuous loading function (Figure 11.10).

§ § §

Some interesting insights can be drawn from Example 11.12. First, note that Lake Erie's initial response to the impulse flux is generally four times higher than for the other lakes. This is due to its shallow depth since the initial concentration can be reexpressed as

$$c_{no} = J_{Sr} \frac{A_{s,n}}{V_n} = \frac{J_{Sr}}{z_n} \tag{11.96}$$

where z_n is the mean depth of lake n. Therefore, if two lakes receive an

Table 11.2.   Model Parameters for the Great Lakes

Parameter	Units	Superior	Michigan	Huron	Erie	Ontario
Mean Depth	m	146	85	59	19	86
Surface Area	$10^6 \ m^2$	82,100	57,750	59,570	25,212	18,960
Volume	$10^9 \ m^3$	12,000	4,900	3,500	468	1,634
Outflow	$10^9 \ m^3 yr^{-1}$	67	36	161	182	212

equal impulse flux of a pollutant, their response is inversely proportional to their depth.*

Figure 11.12 also indicates that for a slowly decaying contaminant such as ^{90}Sr (half life = 29 years), the upstream Great Lakes have a signif-

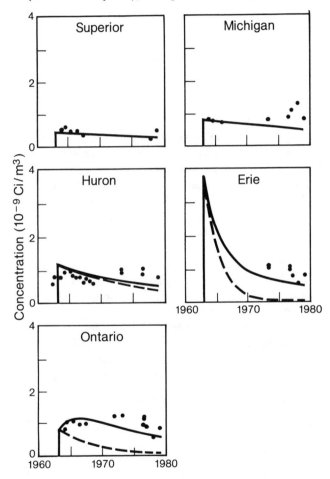

Figure 11.12 Response of Great Lakes to impulse loading of ^{90}Sr in 1963. Data (•) from Lerman (1972), Alberts and Wahlgren (1981), and International Joint Commission (1979). Dashed line represents the response of the lake to its own loading excluding the effect of upstream lakes.

---

*Note that if two lakes receive an equal impulse of mass (in contrast to equal flux) of a contaminant, their response is inversely proportional to volume.

icant effect on Lakes Erie and Ontario. The effect on the latter is so pronounced that its peak concentration does not occur in 1963 but lags 2 to 3 years due to upstream effects. Thus, contamination of the upper Great Lakes with long-lived pollutants could take decades to be purged from the system.

11.3 NUMERICAL SOLUTIONS

The exact solutions presented previously are useful for a variety of water quality analyses. This is particularly true when making predictions since idealizations are often the only way to characterize the future. In addition, even when simulating present or past conditions, an idealization may be warranted. For example, if a lake is subjected to a relatively constant loading for a long enough time, a manager might not be interested in information regarding changes in the lake's quality due to year-to-year meteorological conditions, such as high versus low flow years. In this case, he might only require an estimate of the long-term mean condition, which can be calculated exactly from a relationship such as Equation 11.16.

However, in other cases, more temporal and spatial resolution might be required. For example, particularly where there is more than one waste source, control measures could be applied at different points in time resulting in an arbitrary or nonideal form of the loading term. In other cases, particularly for short residence time systems, year-to-year (or in some cases, even shorter term) variations in flow often can have a significant impact on the calculation that should be accounted for in the analysis. For these cases, approximate or numerical solutions are required.

11.3.1 The Euler-Cauchy Method

A numerical solution, in the present context, is similar to the exact solutions described previously in the sense that we start with an initial condition and then use a differential equation, such as Equation 11.11 to calculate future values. However, in a numerical method, rather than obtaining a single function that applies to all future times, the computation proceeds step-wise to give an approximate solution. Thus, we compute a solution at $t_1 = t_0 + \Delta t$ where t_0 is the initial time and Δt is a fixed increment of time. Then the calculation is repeated at $t_2 = t_0 + 2\Delta t$ and so on into the future. At each step, the differential equation is used to extrapolate to the next time by a formula. Such formulas can be based on the Taylor series

$$c_{t+\Delta t} = c_t + \left(\frac{dc}{dt}\right)_t \Delta t + \left(\frac{d^2c}{dt^2}\right)_t \frac{(\Delta t)^2}{2} + \ldots \qquad (11.97)$$

where the subscript designates the time at which the term is evaluated. For small values of Δt, the higher order terms often can be neglected and Equation 11.97 becomes

$$c_{t+\Delta t} \cong c_t + \left(\frac{dc}{dt}\right)_t \Delta t \qquad (11.98)$$

using this formula, we can proceed by steps into the future and in this fashion obtain approximate values of the solution of c (Figure 11.13).

This simple procedure, which is called the *Euler-Cauchy method,* is a first-order method because in Equation 11.98 we take only the term with the first power of Δt. The omission of the higher order terms results in an error, called the *local truncation error,* that can be minimized by using small values of Δt. (Note that there are additional errors, owing to rounding* and to the fact that dc/dt is itself a function of the estimated value of c.) In a practical sense, an indication of the accuracy of the solu-

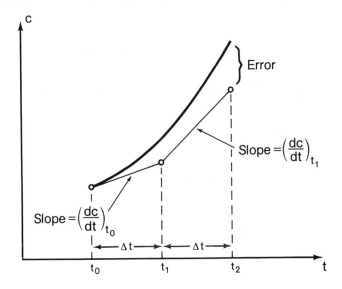

Figure 11.13 The Euler-Cauchy method.

---

*Round-off error is due to the fact that computers can retain only a finite number of significant figures. Thus, numbers with more significant figures than can be handled by the machine must be approximated by "rounded" values. These errors can become significant when using too *small* a time step.

tion can be obtained by applying the method twice with step sizes of Δt
and $\Delta t/2$, and then comparing the two results to see whether a significant
difference occurs.

§ § §

Example 11.13. A lake with the following characteristics:

$$A_s = 1 \times 10^6 m^2 \qquad Q = 5 \times 10^6 m^3/yr$$

$$\bar{z} = 10m \qquad V(Eq.\,11.8) = 10 \times 10^6 m^3$$

is subject to the following exponential loading

$$W(t) = 150 \times 10^6 e^{0.5t}$$

of a pollutant that does not react ($k = 0$), but settles at a rate of 10 m/yr.
If its initial concentration is 7.5 g/m³, calculate its concentration for the
next 2 years using (a) the exact solution of Equations 11.20 and 11.41, (b)
the approximate Euler-Cauchy solution with $\Delta t = 1.0$ yr and (c) the Euler-
Cauchy with $\Delta t = 0.5$ yr.

Since the pollutant is removed by settling, α can be calculated as

$$\alpha = \frac{Q}{V} + \frac{v}{z} = \frac{5 \times 10^6}{10 \times 10^6} + \frac{10}{10} = 1.5$$

(a) The exact solution is (Equations 11.20 and 11.41)

$$c = 7.5e^{-1.5t} + \frac{150 \times 10^6}{(10 \times 10^6)(1.5 + 0.5)} (e^{0.5t} - e^{-1.5t})$$

(b and c) the Euler-Cauchy method is (Equation 11.98)

$$c_{t+\Delta t} = c_t + \left(\frac{dc}{dt}\right)_t \Delta t$$

or using Equation 11.14 to calculate dc/dt

$$c_{t+\Delta t} = c_t + \left(\frac{W}{V} - \frac{Q}{V}c - \frac{v}{z}c\right)_t \Delta t$$

The above equations are then used to calculate c for the values of t in Table 11.3. Notice that, as the step-size of the Euler-Cauchy method is decreased, it becomes a more accurate approximation of the exact solution. Thus, we must increase the number of computations in order to attain a more accurate solution. This trade-off between accuracy and the size of a calculation (and, therefore, its cost) must be evaluated when choosing and implementing numerical solution techniques.

§ § §

Table 11.3   Results of Computations Using
the Euler-Cauchy Method

| t
 (yr) | W(t)
 (10^6 g/yr) | Euler-Cauchy Approximation | | | | Exact <br> solution
 (g/m^3) |
| | | t = 1.0 | | t = 0.5 | | |
		dc/dt (g/m^3/yr)	c (g/m^3)	dc/dt (g/m^3/yr)	c (g/m^3)	
0	150	3.750	7.500	3.750	7.500	7.500
0.5	193			5.198	9.375	9.630
1.0	247	7.856	11.250	6.770	11.974	12.365
1.5	318			8.717	15.359	15.878
2.0	408		19.106		19.717	20.387

Since the Euler-Cauchy procedure only requires information at one point in order to project forward in time, it is referred to as a *one-step method*. Other techniques make use of values at several points outside the interval from t to t + Δt in order to calculate predictions. Although these *multistep procedures* generally require fewer computations than one-step methods to attain comparable accuracy, they have several disadvantages. For example, in most problems, only one initial value is given. Since multistep methods require information at several points in time, a one-step approach must be used to generate the initial values necessary for computation. In addition, it is difficult to change the step-size once the computation has been started. This option is readily implemented with single-step methods and is particularly useful when integrating functions that go through rapid changes during the course of a calculation.* Descriptions of multistep approaches and the trade-offs between various numerical schemes are presented elsewhere (Carnahan et al. 1969).

11.3.2 Runge-Kutta Methods

Although one-step schemes of increased accuracy can be obtained by including higher order terms of Taylor's expansion, they are impractical for all but the simplest differential equations. Alternative procedures, called *Runge-Kutta methods* require only first derivatives and yield predictions equivalent in accuracy to higher order schemes. These methods have algorithms of the general form

$$c_{t+\Delta t} = c_t + \Delta t \, \phi \qquad (11.99)$$

where ϕ is called the *increment function.*
A commonly used increment function can be formulated as

$$\phi = \tfrac{1}{6}(r_1 + 2r_2 + 2r_3 + r_4) \qquad (11.100)$$

where

$$r_1 = c'(t,c_t) \qquad (11.101)$$

$$r_2 = c'(t + \tfrac{1}{2}\Delta t, c_t + \tfrac{1}{2}\Delta t\, r_1) \qquad (11.102)$$

$$r_3 = c'(t + \tfrac{1}{2}\Delta t, c_t + \tfrac{1}{2}\Delta t\, r_2) \qquad (11.103)$$

$$r_4 = c'(t + \Delta t, c_t + \Delta t\, r_3) \qquad (11.104)$$

where

$$c'(t,c) = \frac{dc}{dt}\,(\text{evaluated @ t and c}) \qquad (11.105)$$

---

*On the positive side, multistep methods have a number of advantages not the least of which is that they are less costly to run than comparable single-step algorithms. Because easy-to-use, packaged programs are available for implementing multistep methods on most computer systems, they are presently the most popular algorithms for solving ordinary differential equations. The most widely used are called the Adams methods.

§ § §

Example 11.14. Perform the same computation as in Example 11.13, but using the Runge-Kutta method and a time step of 1.0.

The mass balance for Example 11.13 yields the following differential equation

$$c'(t,c) = \frac{W(t)}{V} - \left(\frac{Q}{V} + \frac{v}{z}\right)c$$

or

$$c'(t,c) = 15e^{0.5t} - 1.5c$$

which can be used to compute (Equations 11.101-104) values of r for the interval from t = 0 to t = 1.0,

$$r_1 = 15e^{0.5(0)} - 1.5(7.5) = 3.75$$

$$r_2 = 15e^{0.5(0.5)} - 1.5(7.5 + 3.75/2) = 5.198$$

$$r_3 = 15e^{0.5(0.5)} - 1.5(7.5 + 5.198/2) = 4.112$$

$$r_4 = 15e^{0.5(1)} - 1.5(7.5 + 4.112) = 7.313$$

Substituting these values into Equations 11.99 and 11.100 yields

$$c_{1.0} = 7.5 + 1 \left\{ \frac{1}{6} [3.750 + 5.198(2) + 4.112(2) + 7.313] \right\}$$

$$c_{1.0} = 12.447$$

The computation can be repeated for the interval from 1.0 to 2.0 with the result that

$$r_1 = 6.06 \qquad r_3 = 6.680$$

$$r_2 = 8.54 \qquad r_4 = 12.084$$

which can be used to compute

$$c_{2.0} = 20.544$$

These results compare favorably with the exact solutions in Table 11.3.

§ § §

The algorithm represented by Equations 11.99–104 has a local truncation error of the order Δt^5 and the method is, therefore, a fourth-order
procedure. In general, fourth-order Runge-Kutta schemes are the most
widely used single-step methods for solving ordinary differential equations. Descriptions of these methods can be found elsewhere (Carnahan
et al. 1969). As should be obvious from the above examples, for all but
the simplest problems, numerical techniques require computers for their
implementation.

§ § §

Example 11.15. Completely mixed models have proven useful in lake
eutrophication analyses. (See Chapter 8 for a review.) One way they have
been applied is in simulation of the long-term changes of a lake's phosphorus concentration as a function of time-variable loads. Because the
loading changes are often nonuniform, numerical techniques must be
used to obtain solutions. In addition, numerical methods are also
required for cases where the model parameters vary in time.

A case in point is Lake Ontario, where a major phosphorus control
program was begun in the early 1970s. Figure 11.14a, which depicts total
phosphorus loading from 1965 through 1978 as calculated by a mathematical model (Chapra 1980), shows that loadings have dropped from a
high level of approximately 15,000 metric tons per year in the early 1970s
to present levels of approximately 10,000 metric tons per year. This
decrease is primarily due to the fact that the two governments bordering
the lake (i.e., the province of Ontario and the state of New York) passed
legislation to reduce phosphate levels in detergents in the early 1970s.
Such a strategy would be expected to be particularly effective for Lake
Ontario, where a large fraction of the phosphorus loading originates
from the major metropolitan areas (Toronto, Ont., and Buffalo and
Rochester, NY) that are situated near the lake shore. Since prelimitation
detergents accounted for about half of the phosphorus in domestic
wastewater, the reduction resulting from the detergent limitations would
be expected to yield significant results. In addition, both governments
have recently begun to upgrade facilities to remove phosphorus at sewage
treatment plants.

The response can be related to the loading changes by a completely
mixed model,

$$V_{t,w} \frac{dp}{dt} = W_p(t) - Q(t)p - v_a A_s p \qquad (i)$$

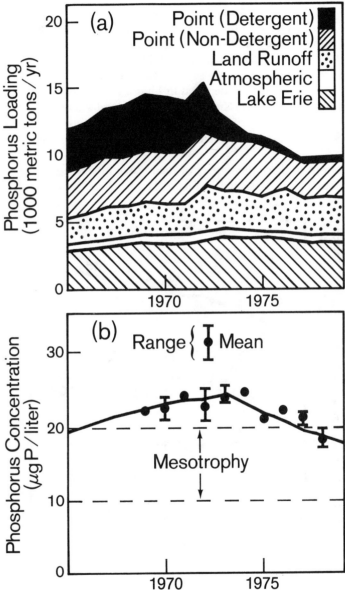

Figure 11.14 Recent trends of (a) total phosphorus loading in thousand metric tons per year, and (b) spring total phosphorus concentration in μgP/L. The curves are calculated by a mathematical model and the data in (b) are off-shore, lake-wide means for surveillance cruises of the Canada Centre for Inland Waters. Where more than one cruise occurred for a given year, the range of the cruise-means is included.

where p is total phosphorus concentration, $W_p(t)$ and $Q(t)$ are time-variable loading and outflow, respectively, and v_a is a settling velocity used to parameterize the loss of phosphorus to the lake's sediments. Chapra (1980) used Equation i, along with time-variable loadings and outflows, to simulate the response of Lake Ontario from 1965 through 1979. The model results are depicted in Figure 11.14b, along with measurements obtained by the Canada Centre for Inland Waters. The results show that a peak value of approximately 24 to 25 $\mu g/L$ occurred in spring 1973, with a gradual decline to 1978 levels of approximately 18 $\mu g/L$.

An attempt to place the impact of load reductions in a broader temporal perspective is presented in Figure 11.15, where the mathematical

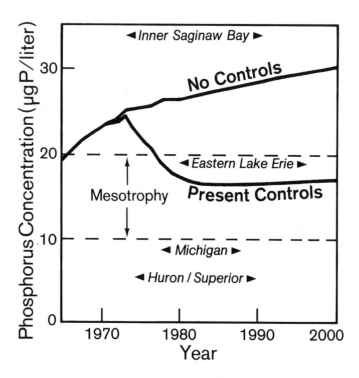

Figure 11.15   Model prediction of spring total phosphorus concentration in Lake Ontario if the present control level is maintained into the future. Projections of the effect of the absence of controls are also shown. Present spring phosphorus levels for other lakes or bays of the Great Lakes system as well as approximate bounds for mesotrophy are included to assist interpretation.

model has been used to extend the trend of spring total phosphorus concentration to the year 2000. This entailed an extrapolation of the loading information from data on the expected population growth in the basin. As can be seen, the present controls will maintain the lake at a mesotrophic level to the year 2000. More significantly, the simulation indicates that the lake would have approached a solidly eutrophic level of 30 μg/L by 2000 (which is similar to the present level of Saginaw Bay) had nothing been done after 1970 to reduce phosphorus loadings.

§ § §

11.4 ERROR ANALYSIS

The mathematically simple nature of the input-output model permits application of error analysis methodologies with little difficulty. Both first-order analysis and Monte Carlo simulation have been used to estimate the effect of error terms on the model prediction uncertainty. In Chapter 2 of Volume 1 we discuss these methods, and in Chapter 8 of Volume 1, an application of first-order analysis is presented. For purposes of continuity and completeness in Volume 2 we briefly outline these approaches below. The interested reader may consult Volume 1 for additional discussion and references.

First-order error analysis is based on the first-order terms of the Taylor series. For a single independent variable relationship, $y = f(x)$, expanded about the mean, $\bar{x}$, the first two terms of the Taylor series are

$$y = f(x) \sim f(\bar{x}) + (x - \bar{x}) \left. \frac{\partial f(x)}{\partial x} \right|_{\bar{x}} \qquad (11.106)$$

If we take the variance of each side, we find (since $\text{Var}[f(\bar{x})] = 0$)

$$\text{Var}(y) \sim \left[\left(\frac{\partial f(x)}{\partial x} \right) \Big|_{\bar{x}} \right]^2 \text{Var}(x) \qquad (11.107)$$

For a multivariable relationship this becomes

$$\text{Var}(y) \sim \sum_{i=1}^{n} \sum_{j=1}^{n} \left. \frac{\partial f}{\partial x_i} \right|_{\bar{x}_i} \left. \frac{\partial f}{\partial x_i} \right|_{\bar{x}_j} \text{Cov}(x_i, x_j) \qquad (11.108)$$

where $\text{Cov}(x_i, x_j)$ is the covariance of x_i and x_j. For two independent variables, Equation 11.107 is written

$$\text{Var}(y) \sim \frac{\partial^2 y}{\partial x_1^2} \text{Var}(x_1) + \frac{\partial^2 y}{\partial x_2^2} \text{Var}(x_2) + \partial \frac{\partial y}{\partial x_2} \frac{\partial y}{\partial x_2} \rho_{x_1 x_2}[\text{Var}(x_1)\,\text{Var}(x_2)]^{1/2}$$

$$(11.109)$$

where $\rho_{x_1 x_2}$ is the correlation between x_1 and x_2. This equation (or its univariate or multivariate analog) may be used to estimate the effect of errors, in this case the effect of errors in variables x_1 and x_2 (or parameters x_1 and x_2), on the dependent variable y.

First-order error analysis is a linearization procedure that depends on the first two moments. Thus, the acceptability of first-order analysis depends on the degree of nonlinearity in the model, the size of the error terms (and their relative importance, as measured by $\partial y/\partial x_i$), and the degree of representation of the error distribution by the first two moments. Clearly, too, the level of error acceptable to the analyst is also quite important.

Monte Carlo simulation is a conceptually simple process that was, prior to the widespread use of computers (particularly microcomputers), discouraged because of calculation tedium and cost. Under this procedure, probability density functions are identified for each uncertain characteristic (model equations, variables and parameters) in the model. The model is then run, and for each of the uncertain characteristics, a value is randomly selected from the distribution for use in the model run. This procedure is repeated a large number of times (perhaps 100 to 1000), and the result is a distribution of values for the model prediction. This prediction distribution is the prediction error, representing the combined effects of the uncertain model characteristics.

Monte Carlo simulation has advantages over first-order analysis in that complete error distributions can be employed (as opposed to the first two moments) and the model is used without modification (linearization is not required). However, first-order analysis requires fewer calculations, and for simple models first-order analysis can be easily undertaken with hand calculations alone. Therefore, the choice between these methods must be made in consideration of both the cost of analytical error and the cost of computational time. As we have unequivocally stated throughout these volumes, however, the reader should give serious consideration to the estimation of error.

REFERENCES

Alberts, J. J., and M. A. Wahlgren. 1981. "Concentrations of [239,240]Pu, ^{137}Cs, and ^{90}Sr in the Waters of the Laurentian Great Lakes. Comparison of 1973 and 1976 Values," *Environ. Sci. Tech.* 15:94–98.

Carnahan, B., H. A. Luther and J. O. Wilkes. 1969. *Applied Numerical Methods* (New York: John Wiley and Sons, Inc.).

Chapra, S. C. 1980. Simulation of Recent and Projected Total Phosphorus Trends in Lake Ontario. *J. Great Lakes Res.* 6:101-112.

Dillon, P. J. 1975. "The Phosphorus Budget of Cameron Lake, Ontario: The Importance of Flushing Rate to the Degree of Eutrophy of Lakes," *Limnol. Oceanog.* 20:28-39.

Di Toro, D. M. 1976. "Combining Chemical Equilibrium and Phytoplankton Models," in *Modeling Biochemical Processes in Aquatic Ecosystems,* R. P. Canale, Ed. (Ann Arbor, MI: Ann Arbor Science Publishers, Inc.), pp. 233-255.

International Joint Commission. 1979. "Great Lakes Water Quality 1978, Appendix D, Radioactivity Subcommittee Report," International Joint Commission, Windsor, Ontario.

Lerman, A. 1972. "Strontium 90 in the Great Lakes: Concentration-Time Model," *J. Geophys. Res.* 77:3256-3264.

O'Connor, D. J., and J. A. Mueller. 1970. "Water Quality Model of Chlorides in Great Lakes," *J. San. Eng. Div., ASCE* 96(SA4):955-975.

Piontelli, R., and V. Tonolli. 1964. "The Time of Retention of Lacustrine Waters in Relation to the Phenomena of Enrichment in Introduced Substances with Particular Reference to the Lago Maggiore," *Mem. Ist. Ital. Idrobiol.* 17:247-266.

Stumm, W., and J. J. Morgan. 1981. *Aquatic Chemistry.* (New York: Wiley-Interscience), 780 pp.

Vollenweider, R. A. 1975. "Input-Output Models with Special Reference to the Phosphorus Loading Concept in Limnology," *Schweiz. Z. Hydrol.* 37:53-84.

SECTION 5

MODELS OF SPATIAL RESOLUTION

CHAPTER 12

MODELS OF HORIZONTAL SPATIAL PROCESSES

Since most pollutants enter lakes at their periphery, gradients exist between the near- and the offshore zones of lakes. These differences are compounded and influenced by physical aspects of the system, such as irregular shorelines, embayments and current regimes, as well as by the reaction rate of the substance being modeled. An example of the latter is the fact that coliform bacteria die rapidly when introduced into natural waters. For the case of a sewage outfall on a large lake, the bacteria could die quickly enough in relation to the advective and diffusive motion of the lake currents so that minimal levels would be reached within close proximity of the injection point. Thus, a model that treated the lake as a single, homogeneous volume would miss (or average out) information on the extent of bacterial contamination that could be useful to someone interested in public health issues, such as beach closings.

In the present chapter, techniques are developed to simulate substance dynamics in lake subsystems and incompletely mixed lakes. These include river-run lakes, embayments and nearshore zones (Figure 12.1). In addition, a general numerical approach for modeling such systems is presented. However, before discussing these topics we will review some basic concepts related to within-lake transport.

12.1 MATHEMATICS OF HORIZONTAL TRANSPORT

In Chapter 10, we introduced the notion that water transport in a lake can be divided into organized (advective) and random (diffusive) motion. The present section is devoted to some basic mathematical expressions that have been developed to represent these processes.

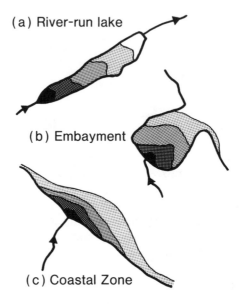

(a) River-run lake

(b) Embayment

(c) Coastal Zone

Figure 12.1   Three systems that typically exhibit strong horizontal gradients.

12.1.1 Molecular Diffusion

Molecular diffusion is defined as the net movement of matter due to the random motion of individual particles. Although it is generally unimportant in horizontal transport of pollutants, it is a useful starting point because its mathematics commonly are used to characterize turbulent transport. In addition, the fact that its theoretical basis is more developed than that for turbulent mixing can be used to gain insight into possible deviations from theory. Before presenting the mathematical formulae, it is useful to investigate the process in physical terms.

The Random Walk. Suppose that a population of particles is confined to motion along a one-dimensional line (Figure 12.2). Assume that each particle has an equal likelihood of moving a small distance Δx to either the left or right over a time interval Δt. At $t = 0$, all particles are

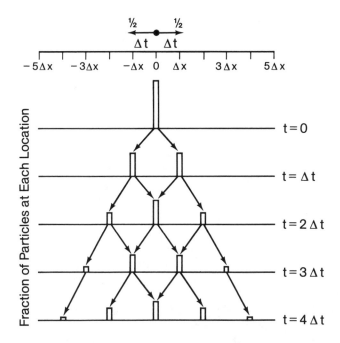

Figure 12.2   Graphic representation of a random walk. At time t = 0, all particles are grouped at the origin (x = 0). During each time step, Δt, half the particles at each location move left and half move right. The result is that over time the particles spread out in a bell-shaped pattern.

grouped at x = 0 and are allowed to take one random step in either direction. After Δt has elapsed, approximately one half of the particles would walk to the right (Δx) and the remainder would walk left (– Δx). After another time interval, i.e., after 2Δt had elapsed, approximately one fourth would be at – 2Δx, one fourth at 2Δx, and one half would have stepped back to the origin. With additional time, the particles would spread out. Note that the distribution of the population is not uniform but is greatest near the origin and diminishes at the ends. This is due to the fact that a particle would have to execute many successive moves in a single direction to reach the outskirts. For example, in Figure 12.2, after 4Δt, a particle would have had to execute four successive right steps to reach 4Δx. Since there is a 50–50 chance of moving left or right in each time interval, it is more likely that a particle would stumble around in the vicinity of the origin. The net outcome is that the random walk of the individual particles results in a spreading bell-shaped distribution of the population. In addition, note that this spreading tendency amounts to a general movement of particles from high to low concentrations.

We can begin to formulate the process mathematically by realizing that it can be represented as a binomial distribution. The binomial, or Bernoulli's distribution, results from our tendency to place observations in one or the other of two mutually exclusive categories. If p is the probability that an event will occur and $q = 1 - p$ is the probability that it will not, the probability that the event will happen exactly x times in n trials is given by

$$p(x, n) = \binom{n}{n - x} p^x q^{n - x} \qquad (12.1)$$

where the parenthetical operation represents the number of possible ways or combinations by which the event can occur x times in n trials where

$$\binom{n}{n - x} = \frac{n!}{x!(n - x)!}$$

where $n! = n(n - 1)(n - 2) \ldots$

The random walk is this sort of process since the particle is limited to two modes of motion: left or right. Thus, the binomial distribution can be used to determine the probability that, after n_t time steps, the particle will be n_x spatial intervals from the origin. To do this, the total number of steps would be divided into n_r to the right and $(n_t - n_r)$ to the left. In order to wind up at n_x, the difference between the right and left steps, $n_r - (n_t - n_r)$ would have to equal n_x. Therefore, the number of right steps would have to be $n_r = (n_t + n_x)/2$ and left steps would have to be $(n_t - n_r) = (n_t - n_x)/2$. The probability that after n_t time steps the particle would be n_x spatial intervals from the origin can be represented as (remember that there is an equal likelihood of moving left or right; i.e., $p = q = 1/2$)

$$p(n_x, n_t) = \binom{n_t}{(n_x + n_t)/2} \frac{1}{2}^{(n + r)/2} \frac{1}{2}^{(n - r)/2}$$

or

$$p(n_x, n_t) = \left(\frac{1}{2}\right)^{n_t} \frac{n_t!}{[(n_t + n_x)/2]![(n_t - n_x)/2]!} \qquad (12.2)$$

As the number of intervals become very large, the binomial distribution approaches the normal distribution. If we define continuous variables $x = n_x \Delta x$ and $t = n_t \Delta t$, the probability that the particle would be at distance x at time t can be formulated (see Pielou 1969) as a normal distribution with a mean of zero and a variance of $t(\Delta x)^2/\Delta t$ as in

$$p(x, t) = \frac{1}{2\sqrt{\pi Dt}} \, e^{-x^2/(4Dt)} \qquad (12.3)$$

where D is a diffusion coefficient defined in the limit (as Δx and Δt become small) as

$$D = \frac{\Delta x^2}{2\Delta t} \qquad (12.4)$$

If the population is grouped at the origin at time zero, the concentration at position x at a subsequent time t would be proportional to the probability of an individual particle being at x, as in

$$c(x, t) = \frac{m_p}{2\sqrt{\pi Dt}} \, e^{-x^2/(4Dt)} \qquad (12.5)$$

where m_p is the total mass of the particles per cross-sectional area of the interface $[M \, L^{-2}]$.* Thus, the distribution of a population of particles is described by a series of bell-shaped curves that spread out over time symmetrically around the origin (Figure 12.3). It should be noted that

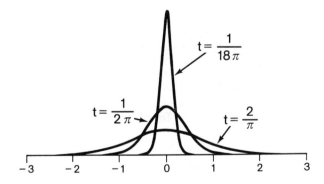

Figure 12.3   Representation of the random walk by a normal distribution.

---

*Note that m_p is formally called a "plane source" since it enters the system at a plane surface—the interface.

Equations 12.3–5 apply only if n_x and n_t are much greater than 1. In other words, the observation time (t) and the observation space (x) must be much greater than the magnitudes of the duration (Δt) and size (Δx) of the individual steps. Because the random walk is an analog of the diffusion process, these conditions will have relevance to the application of diffusion models in the real world. That is, the process holds only when the random motions, whether molecular or due to eddys, have smaller time and space scales than do the phenomena being modeled.

Fick's Laws. The physiologist, Adolph Fick, proposed that the diffusive mass flux of a solute is proportional to the gradient of its concentration. This is the same hypothesis that Fourier had proposed some time earlier to quantify heat conduction.

We can begin to formulate this process in mathematical terms by recalling the case (Figure 10.3) of the diffusion of particles between two volumes. At t = 0, all particles were in volume "a". The particles redistributed over time until they were uniformly distributed between the two volumes. This redistribution can be quantified by realizing that the rate of particle passage through the interface between the volumes is proportional to the number of particles near the interface. Thus, passage from "a" to "b" is proportional to the number of particles in "a", as defined by

$$W_{ab} = n_a m_i P = m_a P \qquad (12.6)$$

where W_{ab} = the rate of mass transfer from "a" to "b" $[M\ T^{-1}]$
        n_a = number of particles in "a"
        m_i = the mass of an individual particle [M] (note that all particles are assumed to be identical)
        P = the probability of transfer across the interface $[T^{-1}]$
        m_a = the mass of particles in "a" [M]

Likewise, the rate of mass transfer from "b" to "a" can be formulated as

$$W_{ba} = m_b P \qquad (12.7)$$

and the net transfer by

$$W_{net} = P(m_a - m_b) \qquad (12.8)$$

Now we define the *flux*, J, as the net transfer of mass per unit area of the interface per unit time $[M\ L^{-2}\ T^{-1}]$. Dividing Equation 12.8 by A_c, the cross-sectional area of the interface $[L^2]$, yields

$$J = P \frac{(m_a - m_b)}{A_c} \tag{12.9}$$

Multiplying the top and bottom of Equation 12.9 by Δx^2 and grouping terms yields

$$J = P\Delta x^2 \frac{m_a - m_b}{A_c \Delta x^2} \tag{12.10}$$

or

$$J = P\Delta x^2 \frac{c_a - c_b}{\Delta x} \tag{12.11}$$

where Δx = the length of the individual volumes [L]
c = concentration of mass in each volume $[M \ L^{-3}] = m/(A_c \Delta x)$.

Now realizing that as Δx gets small

$$\lim_{\Delta x \to 0} \frac{c_b - c_a}{\Delta x} = \frac{\partial c}{\partial x} \tag{12.12}$$

Therefore by taking the limit of Equation 12.11

$$J_x = -P\Delta x^2 \frac{\partial c}{\partial x} \tag{12.13}$$

where J_x designates the flux at the interface. Finally, since transfer across the interface should be independent of the size of the volumes, $P\Delta x^2$ should be a constant and

$$J_x = -D \frac{\partial c}{\partial x} \tag{12.14}$$

where D is the diffusion coefficient $[L^2 \ T^{-1}]$. For three dimensions using Cartesian coordinates, Equation 12.14 can be formulated as

$$J = -D \left(\frac{\partial c}{\partial x} + \frac{\partial c}{\partial y} + \frac{\partial c}{\partial z} \right) \tag{12.15}$$

Equation 12.14 is called *Fick's first law*. Among other things it indicates that (1) the flux of particles transferred by molecular diffusion is proportional to the gradient across the interface $(\partial c/\partial x)$ and (2) that net transport is always (as indicated by the negative sign) from regions of high to low concentration.

Fick's second law is merely an expression of the above relationship in terms of conservation of mass. For a one-dimensional segment (Figure 12.4) the change in mass is equal to the difference between inputs and outputs of mass.

$$\Delta m = A_c \left[J_x - \left(J_x + \frac{\partial J_x}{\partial x} \Delta x \right) \right] \Delta t \qquad (12.16)$$

or

$$\Delta m = A_c \left(- \frac{\partial J_x}{\partial x} \Delta x \right) \Delta t \qquad (12.17)$$

Dividing both sides by the volume of the segment and Δt yields

$$\frac{\Delta c}{\Delta t} = - \frac{\partial J_x}{\partial x} \qquad (12.18)$$

Then, substituting Fick's first law (Equation 12.14) and taking the limit (i.e., letting Δt and $\Delta x \rightarrow 0$) gives Fick's second law.

$$\frac{\partial c}{\partial t} = D \frac{\partial^2 c}{\partial x^2} \qquad (12.19)$$

Equation 12.19 is a *partial differential equation* (in contrast to the ordinary differential equations in Chapter 11) since it involves derivatives of more than one independent variable. It is known as the *diffusion equation* and is of the exact form as the heat conduction equation derived from Fourier's law with mass and concentration interchangeable with heat and temperature. Solutions of a great number of problems based on

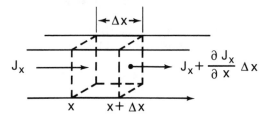

Figure 12.4 A finite volume, or slice, of thickness Δx along the longitudinal axis of a one-dimensional system. J designates fluxes (i.e., mass per unit area per unit time) crossing the surface of the volume.

the diffusion equations can be found in Carslaw and Jaeger (1959) and Crank (1975). For example, the solution for the diffusion of a substance concentrated initially at $x = 0$ is

$$c = \frac{m_p}{2\sqrt{\pi Dt}} e^{-x^2/(4Dt)} \qquad (12.20)$$

which is identical to the solution based on the random walk (Equation 12.5). Thus, the solution is a bell-shaped curve with mean at zero and variance of 2Dt.

Because the variance is a measure of spread, it would be tempting to use it as the basis of a simple engineering computation of the effect of diffusion on a pollutant discharge. For example, if a conservative contaminant were discharged in a lump sum into a water body, its tendency to spread outward from its center of mass into the environment could be represented by the standard deviation.

$$\sigma = \sqrt{2Dt} \qquad (12.21)$$

or multiples of the standard deviation as depicted in Figure 12.5.

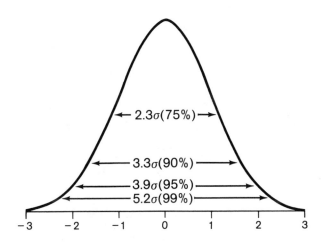

Figure 12.5 A standardized normal distribution showing the probability (expressed as percent) encompassed by various multiples of the standard deviation. For example, 2.3σ encompasses 75% of the area under the curve.

§ § §

Example 12.1. A barge releases a large quantity of a highly persistent contaminant in the center of a narrow lake. If the diffusion coefficient is approximately 10^5 m²/d, how far will the contaminant spread in one day? In two days?

Using Equation 12.21 and the relationships in Figure 12.5 that accounts for 95% of the pollutant yields

$$x_s(1\,day) = 3.9\sqrt{2Dt} = 3.9\sqrt{2(10^5)1} = 1744\,m\,(1.08\,miles)$$

and

$$x_s(2\,days) = 3.9\sqrt{2(10^5)2} = 2466\,m\,(1.53\,miles)$$

§ § §

There is a critical flaw in Example 12.1 related to the fact that it is based on a constant diffusion coefficient. Although this is appropriate for molecular diffusion, it will be shown subsequently that mass transport in lakes is primarily brought about by turbulent or eddy diffusion. A complicating feature of turbulence is that it is a function of scale. That is, the eddy diffusion coefficient is not constant but varies with the size of the phenomenon being modeled. Thus, simple Fickian diffusion models have limited utility in modeling the transient dispersal of spills in the environment. However, Fickian models provide useful engineering estimates in contexts where they are appropriate such as in lake sediments (see Example 13.14).

For two and three dimensions, the diffusion equation can be expressed as

$$\frac{\partial c}{\partial t} = D_x \frac{\partial^2 c}{\partial x^2} + D_y \frac{\partial^2 c}{\partial y^2} \tag{12.22}$$

and

$$\frac{\partial c}{\partial t} = D_x \frac{\partial^2 c}{\partial x^2} + D_y \frac{\partial^2 c}{\partial y^2} + D_z \frac{\partial^2 c}{\partial z^2} \tag{12.23}$$

with respective solutions

$$c(x, y, t) = \frac{m_\ell}{4\,\pi t\sqrt{D_x D_y}} \exp\left(-\frac{x^2}{4D_x t} - \frac{y^2}{4D_y t}\right) \tag{12.24}$$

and

$$c(x, y, z, t) = \frac{m}{(4\,\pi t)^{3/2}\sqrt{D_x D_y D_z}}\exp\left(-\frac{x^2}{4D_x t} - \frac{y^2}{4D_y t} - \frac{z^2}{4D_z t}\right) \qquad (12.25)$$

where m_ℓ is mass per unit depth $[ML^{-1}]$ called a line source and m is mass $[M]$.

For the case where diffusion is isotropic (i.e., constant in all directions), the two-dimensional equation can be expressed in radial coordinates as

$$c(r, t) = \frac{m_\ell}{4\pi Dt}\,e^{-r^2/4Dt} \qquad (12.26)$$

where r is the radius [L] defined as

$$r = \sqrt{x^2 + y^2} \qquad (12.27)$$

and Equation 12.26 is a circular normal density function with mean of zero and variance of 2 Dt. Equations similar to 12.24–26 will be used subsequently to model pollutants discharged to the coastal zone (Section 12.2.3).

12.1.2 Turbulent Diffusion

Just as mass is transported via random molecular motion, matter is mixed by larger-scale eddys or whirls in lakes. If long enough observational time and space scales are employed, this motion can be viewed as random and treated mathematically as a diffusion process. Although equations of the kind developed for molecular motion can be used to characterize turbulent mass transport, two important differences should be noted.

First, because the eddys are much larger than the "random steps" of molecules, mixing by turbulent diffusion is much greater than by molecular diffusion. As shown in Figure 12.6, turbulent diffusion coefficients are several orders of magnitude greater than those on a molecular scale. Note also that horizontal diffusion in lakes is generally much greater than vertical diffusion. Likewise, effective diffusion through porous media such as lake sediments is less than molecular diffusion in free solution due to the fact that, among other things, the solute must move around particles.

Second, in contrast to molecular diffusion where the motion of particles was assumed to be identical in scale, turbulence is comprised of a wide range of eddy sizes. Thus, it would be expected that the resulting

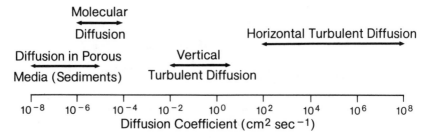

Figure 12.6 Typical ranges of the diffusion coefficient for a number of mixing processes.

diffusion would be scale dependent. It has been shown that generally the turbulent diffusion coefficient, which we will designate as E, varies with the 4/3 power of the scale of the phenomenon (Richardson 1926). This relationship is supported by observations in both the oceans and lakes (Figure 12.7).

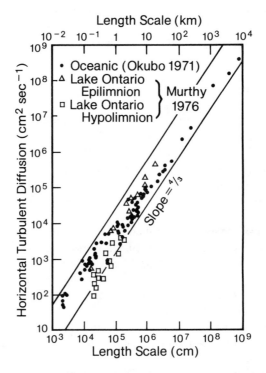

Figure 12.7 Relationship of horizontal diffusivity and length scale in the ocean and Lake Ontario. Lines define an envelope around the oceanic data with a slope of 4/3 (Okubo 1971).

The scale-dependence of eddy diffusivity has great practical consequence to modeling pollutant transport in lakes. For cases where a pollutant is discharged rapidly in a small area (i.e., a spill), the diffusion of the resulting cloud would accelerate as it grew. This is due to the fact that larger and larger eddys would play a role in its mixing as it spread. Finally, when the spill grew bigger than the largest eddy, a constant diffusion coefficient model could be used to approximate further mixing.

One way to circumvent the problem of scale-dependent diffusion is to limit the models to cases where the long-term distribution of pollutants are simulated. On a long enough time scale, we can account for the large-scale circulation of a lake as an advective term and assume that all eddys of a smaller scale can be treated as random turbulent diffusion (see Example 12.9). All models in this chapter are of this kind.*

12.1.3 Diffusion and Advection

Up to this point we have been dealing with mass transport determined solely by diffusion. In addition, matter can be transported by imposed current systems. The flux due to this advective transport can be represented in one dimension as

$$J = Uc \qquad (12.28)$$

where U is the velocity of the water [L T^{-1}]. The total flux due to both advection and diffusion would, therefore, be

$$J = Uc - D \frac{\partial c}{\partial x} \qquad (12.29)$$

Equation 12.29 can be substituted into Equation 12.18 which can be rearranged and manipulated to yield

$$\frac{\partial c}{\partial t} = D \frac{\partial^2 c}{\partial x^2} - \frac{\partial}{\partial x} Uc \qquad (12.30)$$

Equation 12.30 is called the "advection-diffusion equation." In three dimensional form it is

$$\frac{\partial c}{\partial t} = D_x \frac{\partial^2 c}{\partial x^2} + D_y \frac{\partial^2 c}{\partial y^2} + D_z \frac{\partial^2 c}{\partial z^2} - \frac{\partial}{\partial x} U_x c - \frac{\partial}{\partial y} U_y c - \frac{\partial}{\partial z} U_z c \qquad (12.31)$$

---

*Models of smaller scale phenomena are treated elsewhere (Fischer et al. 1979).

For the case of an instantaneous release of a slug of pollutant into a one-dimensional channel, the solution to Equation 12.30 (with constant advection) is

$$c(x, t) = \frac{m_p}{2\sqrt{\pi Dt}} \exp\left(-\frac{(x - Ut)^2}{4Dt}\right)$$ (12.32)

Note that in comparison with Equation 12.20, the effect of advection is to "move" the diffusion solution intact downstream at speed U (Figure 12.8).

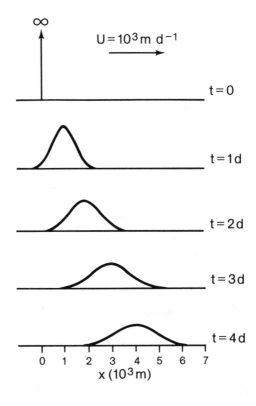

Figure 12.8   Simultaneous advection and diffusion of a conservative pollutant, discharged into a one-dimensional system as an impulse load at $x = 0$ and $t = 0$. The advective flow is from left to right and essentially moves the diffusion solution downstream at velocity U.

12.1.4 Dispersion

To this point, we have treated transport as a combination of two inde-pendent processes: organized advection and random diffusion. Although this idealization is adequate for many lake water quality simulations, the two modes are not always independent. In fact, mixing can occur as a result of advection.

This process, called *dispersion,* is the result of velocity differences within the mean advective flow regime. A simple example of dispersion is the introduction of a dye into water flowing through a pipe (Figure 12.9). In such cases, a molecule of dye near the wall of the pipe would move slower than a molecule near the center due to a velocity gradient or *shear.* The net effect of these differences in mean velocity is to spread or mix the dye along the pipe's axis. Interestingly, it can be shown (Taylor 1953, Fischer et al. 1979) that coupled with random radial movement due to diffusion, this dispersion (given enough time) can be represented as a Fickian diffusion process.

In the environment, turbulent diffusion and dispersion can, individ-ually or in consort, cause mixing of a substance. For example, in rivers and estuaries, dispersion usually predominates because of the strong shears developed by the large mean flows and constraining banks. Dis-persion can sometimes be important in highly advective river-run lakes. Additionally, for all classes of lakes, dispersion is often important on smaller time and space scales. In particular, shears can be developed near system boundaries such as the shoreline or the bottom. However, for longer-term simulations, mixing becomes more akin to a random process and can be adequately represented as turbulent diffusion. In the follow-ing models, therefore, we will limit ourselves to turbulent diffusion. The

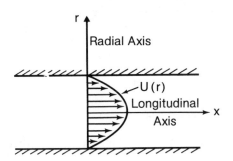

Figure 12.9   Idealized representation of flow through a pipe. Flow differences in the longitudinal direction cause dispersion, or spreading, of a substance carried by the advective flow.

reader should be cognizant of the existence of dispersion and its possible effects on pollutant transport.

The above material is a brief introduction to some basic concepts related to horizontal transport of pollutants in lakes. The reader is referred to other sources for additional information; notably, Fischer et al. (1979) and Csanady (1973) on turbulence and Boyce (1974), Hutchinson (1957) and Mortimer (1974) on lake hydrodynamics.

The remainder of this chapter is devoted to applications of advection-diffusion equations to simulate the long-term horizontal distribution of substances. This material is divided into exact (or analytical) solutions and approximate numerical methods.

12.2 EXACT SOLUTIONS

12.2.1 Completely Mixed Embayment Model

A well-mixed bay connected to a large lake is the simplest illustration of the general long-term approach to modeling horizontal subareas of lakes. It is particularly instructive since it is directly comparable with the completely mixed lake models described previously. As in Figure 12.10, the primary difference between the completely mixed lake with outlet (Figure 12.10a) and the completely mixed bay with open boundary (Figure 12.10b) is the inclusion of an additional term in the mass balance equation to characterize the turbulent or diffusive mass transport. If the main lake is assumed to be unaffected by the bay (i.e., its concentration stays at a constant level), a mass balance for the bay can be written as (Chapra 1979)

$$V_b \frac{dc_b}{dt} = W_b(t) - Q_{bm}c_b - k_b V_b c_b + E'(\bar{c}_m - c_b) \quad (12.33)$$

(accumulation) = (loading) − (advection) − (reaction) ± (diffusion)

where b = indicates that the quantity refers to the bay
Q_{bm} = the magnitude of the advective flow from the bay to the main lake $[L^3 T^{-1}]$
$\bar{c}_m$ = the constant concentration of the main lake $[M L^{-3}]$
E' = a bulk diffusion coefficient $[L^3 T^{-1}] = EA_c/\ell$

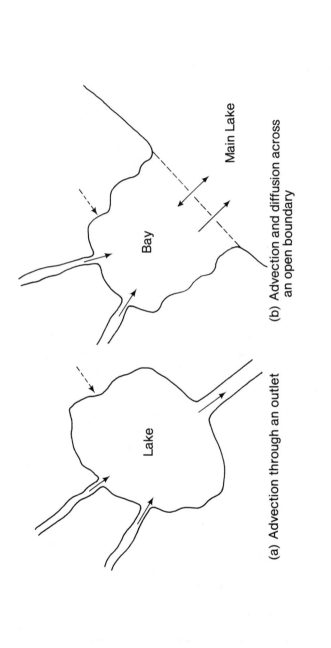

Figure 12.10 Schematic overhead views of a well-mixed (a) lake and (b) bay showing a waste input (– – –), advective mass transport (⟶) and turbulent or diffusive mass transport (⟷).

where   E = the turbulent diffusion coefficient at the interface between the
        bay and lake [$L^2 T^{-1}$]
    A_c = the cross-sectional area of the interface [L^2]
    ℓ = the mixing length of the interface [L]*

Note that diffusive transport will be positive or negative depending on the direction of the gradient.

By grouping terms, Equation 12.33 can be expressed in a form directly comparable to the basic equation for the well-mixed lake (Equation 11.14) as in

$$\frac{dc_b}{dt} + \alpha' c_b = \frac{W'(t)}{V_b} \qquad (12.34)$$

where

$$\alpha' = \frac{Q_{bm}}{V_b} + k_b + \frac{E'}{V_b} \qquad (12.35)$$

and

$$W'(t) = W_b(t) + E' \bar{c}_m \qquad (12.36)$$

Note that Equations 12.34–12.36 are similar in form to Equations 11.14–11.15, with two notable exceptions. First, the bay's loading must be increased to reflect the additional input of mass from the main lake into the bay due to diffusive transport. Second, α', which reflects the cleansing mechanisms must be modified to include the effect of diffusion. While these differences will affect the magnitude of solutions for the bay, the fact that the model is mathematically identical in form to the well-mixed model means that all the solutions derived previously hold for the bay. Thus, the steady-state solution is the same as Equation 11.16, with the exception that $\overline{W}$ and α are replaced by $\overline{W}'$ and α', as in

$$c_b = \frac{\overline{W}'}{\alpha' V_b} = \frac{\overline{W}_b + E' \bar{c}_m}{Q_{bm} + k_b V_b + E'} \qquad (12.37)$$

---

*The present model is only valid where the exchange process takes place in a zone that is short compared to the length of the embayment. This is often predicated on the existence of a constriction that reduces mixing between the two bodies of water at a fairly well-defined region along the axis of the bay. The mixing length, ℓ, is the length of this region. In other cases, where the gradient is more continuous and the boundary with the main lake is not clearly delineated, a series of completely mixed segments would be required to adequately characterize the system. A method to handle multisegment systems is described in Section 12.3.2.

where the bar indicates a constant quantity. Similarly, the residence time would be of the same form as Equation 11.50, with the exception that the magnitude of the outflow would be supplemented by diffusion, as in

$$\tau_{wb} = \frac{V_b}{Q_{bm} + E'} \tag{12.38}$$

Likewise, all the other time variable solutions (Equations 11.20–11.45) would hold if α' and W' are substituted for α and W.

The above approach can also be used to estimate the bulk diffusion coefficient for cases where there is a gradient of a conservative substance (i.e., one with $k = 0$) between the main lake and the bay. This is done by writing a mass balance for the conservative substance, as in

$$V_b \frac{ds_b}{dt} = W_s - Q_{bm} s_b + E'(s_m - s_b) \tag{12.39}$$

where s designates the concentration of the conservative substance (M L^{-3}). At steady state, Equation 12.39 can be solved for

$$E' = \frac{\overline{W}_s - Q_{bm} s_b}{s_b - \bar{s}_m} \tag{12.40}$$

§ § §

Example 12.2. Table 12.1 contains information on the Saginaw Bay-Lake Huron system. Assuming that Lake Huron is not affected by changes in the Bay, calculate (a) the bulk diffusion coefficient for turbulent exchange between the systems, (b) the phosphorus concentration in the Bay at the present loading rate if phosphorus settles at a rate of 12.4 m yr^{-1} and (c) Saginaw Bay's phosphorus concentration if its loading were reduced to 800 metric tons yr^{-1}.

(a) With the data for chloride (a conservative substance), the diffusion coefficient can be estimated from Equation 12.40.

$$E' = \frac{353 - 7(15.2)}{(15.2 - 5.4)} = 25.2 \ km^3 yr^{-1}$$

(b) Equation 12.37 can be used to calculate the total phosphorus concentration in the Bay as in

**Table 12.1   Information for
the Saginaw Bay-Lake Huron System**

	Symbol	Value
Saginaw Bay:		
Volume	V_b	8.05 km^3
Surface Area	A_{sb}	1376 km^2
Mean Depth	z_b	5.85 m
Outflow	Q_b	7.0 km^3 yr^{-1}
Chloride Concentration	s_b	15.2 mg l^{-1}
Chloride Loading	$\overline{W}_s$	353 × 10^3 metric ton yr^{-1}
Phosphorus Loading	$\overline{W}_b$	1425 metric ton yr^{-1}
Lake Huron:		
Volume	V_m	3507 km^3
Surface Area	A_{sm}	58,194 km^2
Mean Depth	z_m	60.26 m
Outflow	Q_m	186.7 km^3 yr^{-1}
Chloride Concentration	s_m	5.4 mg l^{-1}
Phosphorus Concentration	c_m	5.4 μg l^{-1}
Phosphorus Loading	$\overline{W}_m$	4047 metric ton yr^{-1}

$$\bar{c}_b = \frac{1425 + 25.2(5.4)}{7 + 25.2 + 0.0124(1376)} = 31.7\,\mu g\,l^{-1}*$$

where the term $k_b V_b$ in Equation 12.37 is replaced by $v_a A_s$ to quantify settling ($v_a = 12.4$ m yr^{-1}).

On the basis of these calculations, a total phosphorus budget for Saginaw Bay can be constructed as in Figure 12.11. Of the 1,443 t·yr^{-1} coming into the bay from direct loadings and tributaries, 38% is incorporated into the sediments, 16% leaves by advection and 46% by turbulent mixing. Thus, the inclusion of the last process accounts for nearly half the outflow of phosphorus.

(c) For a loading of 800 metric tons yr^{-1}

$$\bar{c}_b = \frac{800 + 25.2(5.4)}{7 + 25.2 + 0.0124(1376)} = 19.0\,\mu g\,l^{-1}$$

§ § §

---

*Note a metric ton per cubic kilometer equals a μg/l.

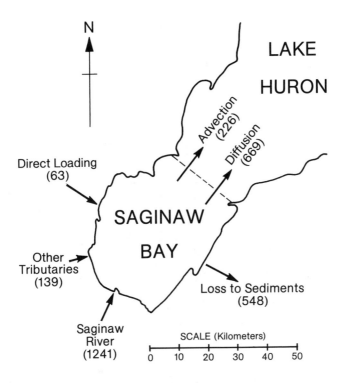

Figure 12.11 Total phosphorus budget for Saginaw Bay (all values in metric tons per year).

While the above model might be an adequate approximation for many systems, its treatment of the main lake as an "ocean" (i.e., a body of water unaffected by the state of the bay) would be untenable in many cases. For those lakes strongly affected by their embayments, an additional equation could be written for the main lake and solved simultaneously with the embayment equation. The two mass balances are

Bay:

$$V_b \frac{dc_b}{dt} = W_b(t) - Q_b c_b - k_b V_b c_b + E'(c_m - c_b) \qquad (12.41)$$

Main Lake:

$$V_m \frac{dc_m}{dt} = W_m(t) - Q_m c_m - k_m V_m c_m + E'(c_b - c_m) + Q_b c_b \qquad (12.42)$$

These equations can be reexpressed as

$$\frac{dc_b}{dt} + \alpha_b c_b = \beta_b c_m + \Omega_b \qquad (12.43)$$

$$\frac{dc_m}{dt} + \alpha_m c_m = \beta_m c_b + \Omega_m \qquad (12.44)$$

where

$$\alpha_b = \frac{Q_b}{V_b} + k_b + \frac{E'}{V_b} \qquad (12.45)$$

$$\beta_b = \frac{E'}{V_b} \qquad (12.46)$$

$$\alpha_m = \frac{Q_m}{V_m} + k_m + \frac{E'}{V_m} \qquad (12.47)$$

$$\beta_m = \frac{E'}{V_m} + \frac{Q_b}{V_m} \qquad (12.48)$$

$$\Omega_b = \frac{W_b(t)}{V_b} \qquad (12.49)$$

$$\Omega_m = \frac{W_m(t)}{V_m} \qquad (12.50)$$

Note that Equations 12.43 and 12.44 are of the same form as Equations 11.71 and 11.72. Therefore, the solutions obtained previously (Equations 11.79–11.87) can be applied to the embayment. For example, the steady-state solution (Equations 11.79 and 11.80) can be applied and simplified to yield

$$\bar{c}_b = \frac{\overline{W}_b(Q_m + k_m V_m + E') + \overline{W}_m E'}{(Q_b + k_b V_b + E')(Q_m + k_m V_m + E') - (E' + Q_b)E'} \qquad (12.51)$$

$$\bar{c}_m = \frac{\overline{W}_m(Q_b + k_b V_b + E') + \overline{W}_b(E' + Q_b)}{(Q_b + k_b V_b + E')(Q_m + k_m V_m + E') - (E' + Q_b)E'} \qquad (12.52)$$

Note how the inclusion of the additional mass balance greatly complicates the solution as compared with Equation 12.37. If the lake had two embayments, the steady-state solution would be even more unwieldy. In addition, except in the simplest cases, exact solutions for time variable forms of such equations are not possible. For these reasons, a general numerical technique for the solution of these problems is presented in Section 12.3.2.

§ § §

Example 12.3. Calculate the response of both Saginaw Bay and Lake Huron if the Saginaw Bay phosphorus loading is lowered to 800 metric tons yr^{-1}.
From Equations 12.51 and 12.52.

$$\bar{c}_b = \frac{800[186.7 + 0.0124(58194) + 25.2] + 4047(25.2)}{[7 + 0.0124(1376) + 25.2][186.7 + 0.0124(58194) + 25.2] - (25.2 + 7)25.2}$$

$$\bar{c}_b = \frac{848789}{45173} = 18.8\,\mu g\,l^{-1}$$

$$\bar{c}_m = \frac{[7 + 0.0124(1376) + 25.2]4047 + (25.2 + 7)800}{45173}$$

$$\bar{c}_m = \frac{225125}{45173} = 5.0\,\mu g\,l^{-1}$$

Thus, the inclusion of a mass balance equation for Lake Huron in the calculation has a negligible effect on the outcome for Saginaw Bay, but results in about a 10% drop in the Lake Huron concentration. For smaller lakes the effect could be even more pronounced.

§ § §

12.2.2 River-Run Lake Models

Plug Flow or River Models

The completely mixed model is appropriate for those lakes where diffusive transport is so predominant that substances are distributed uniformly throughout the system or for those situations where the modeler needs only an aggregate measure of quality. At the other end of the spectrum are bodies of water, such as streams and rivers, where advection is the primary transport mechanism. The idealization used to characterize river systems is referred to as the "plug flow model" (Figure 12.12). To derive this model, we take a mass balance around an element of thickness, Δx, as shown in Figure 12.13, over a time interval, Δt, as in

$$V_x \Delta c = Qc\Delta t - Q(c + \frac{\partial c}{\partial x}\Delta x)\Delta t - kV_x c\Delta t \qquad (12.53)$$

where V_x = the volume of the element = $\Delta x A_c$ [L^3]
   c = concentration [ML^{-3}]
   k = a first-order decay rate [T^{-1}]
   A_c = the cross-sectional area [L^2]

Dividing by Δt and V_x and simplifying and taking the limit yields

$$\frac{\partial c}{\partial t} = -U\frac{\partial c}{\partial x} - kc \qquad (12.54)$$

where U is the river's velocity [$L\,T^{-1}$] = $Q\,A_c^{-1}$.
At steady state, Equation 12.54 becomes

$$U\frac{dc}{dx} + kc = 0 \qquad (12.55)$$

With a boundary condition of $c = c_0$ at $x = o$, Equation 12.55 can be integrated to yield

$$c = c_0 e^{-kx/u} \qquad (12.56)$$

River-Run Lake Models

Between the idealizations of complete mixing and of plug flow are those lakes where both advection and diffusion are important. Such "river-run lakes," as depicted in Figure 12.14a, are typically long and narrow, with a major tributary at one end and an outlet at the other. The key feature of such systems is that the advective water movement due to the inflow and outflow is large enough to have an effect on material transport comparable to that of turbulent wind mixing. For such systems, a plug of dye introduced at one end would advect and diffuse simultaneously as it moved through the lake (Figure 12.14b).

To model such systems, we start with an idealized lake that is of constant cross-sectional area and well-mixed laterally and vertically but sub-

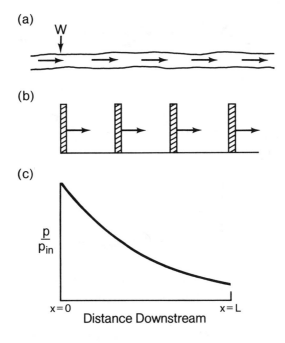

Figure 12.12   A river with waste source at $x = 0$. (a) overhead view, (b) movement of a plug of conservative dye downstream and (c) steady-state profile of concentration normalized to inflow concentration for a substance that reacts or settles at a first-order rate.

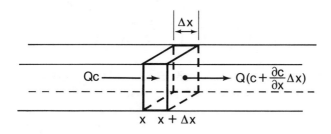

Figure 12.13   A finite slice of a river.

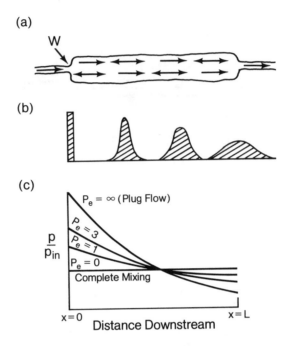

Figure 12.14 A river-run lake: (a) overhead view, (b) movement of a plug of dye through the lake and (c) steady-state concentration profiles for varying Peclet numbers.

ject to longitudinal advection and turbulent mixing. As was done in the previous section on river models, a mass balance over a time interval, Δt, can be written for the differential element, Δx, as in

$$V_x \Delta c = Qc\Delta t - EA_c \frac{\partial c}{\partial x} \Delta t - Q(c + \frac{\partial c}{\partial x} \Delta x) \Delta t$$

$$+ EA_c \left[\frac{\partial c}{\partial x} + \frac{\partial}{\partial x}\left(\frac{\partial c}{\partial x}\right)\Delta x \right] \Delta t - kV_x c\Delta t \qquad (12.57)$$

where E is a turbulent diffusion coefficient $[L^2T^{-1}]$. Dividing by Δt and V_x and simplifying and taking the limit yields

$$\frac{\partial c}{\partial t} = E\frac{\partial^2 c}{\partial x^2} - U\frac{\partial c}{\partial x} - kc \qquad (12.58)$$

At steady state, Equation 12.58 can be expressed in dimensionless form as

$$O = \frac{1}{P_e} \frac{d^2c}{d\ell^2} - \frac{dc}{d\ell} - Rc \qquad (12.59)$$

where P_e is the Peclet number ($LU E^{-1}$) which is a dimensionless group that characterizes the relative importance of advection and diffusion within the lake,* $\ell = x L^{-1}$, where L is the total length of the lake and R is a dimensionless reaction group ($kL U^{-1}$). The general solution for Equation 12.59 is

$$c = A\exp\left(\frac{P_e}{2}(1 + \gamma)x\right) + B\exp\left(\frac{P_e}{2}(1 - \gamma)x\right) \qquad (12.60)$$

where A and B are arbitrary constants and γ is defined as

$$\gamma = \sqrt{1 + 4R/P_e} \qquad (12.61)$$

Determination of the constants requires the following boundary condition

$$c_0 = c(0) - \frac{1}{P_e} \frac{dc(0)}{d\ell} \qquad (12.62)$$

which represents mass conservation at the lake's inlet, where c_0 is the concentration in the inlet river and $c(0)$ is the concentration at the head of the lake (i.e., at $\ell = 0$). The second boundary condition

$$\frac{dc(1)}{d\ell} = 0 \qquad (12.63)$$

is arrived at intuitively from the fact that no diffusion of mass is assumed to occur through the outlet; therefore, no gradients would exist [c(1) is the concentration at the end or outlet of the lake]. Application of these boundary conditions yields

$$\frac{c}{c_0} = \frac{2(1 - \gamma)}{(1 - \gamma)^2 - (1 + \gamma)^2 \exp(P_e\gamma)} \exp\left(\frac{P_e}{2}(1 + \gamma)\ell\right)$$

$$+ \left\{\frac{2}{1+\gamma} - \frac{2(1 - \gamma)^2}{(1+\gamma)[(1-\gamma)^2 - (1+\gamma)^2 \exp(P_e\gamma)]}\right\} \exp\left(\frac{P_e}{2}(1 - \gamma)\ell\right) \qquad (12.64)$$

---

*If $P_e \ll 1$, diffusion predominates. If $P_e \gg 1$, advection predominates. For intermediate levels, (e.g., $0.1 < P_e < 10$) both are important.

For large Peclet numbers (i.e., as advection becomes predominant over diffusion), the solution converges on the plug flow solution (Equation 12.56). When turbulent mixing predominates (i.e., $P_e \rightarrow 0$), the solution converges on the completely mixed solution (Equation 11.16). Figure 12.14c illustrates these solutions along with intermediate cases where both forms of transport are important.

§ § §

Example 12.4. The river run lake in Figure 12.14a has the following characteristics:

L = 1 km
Width = 0.1 km
z = 0.01 km
U = 0.05 km yr^{-1}

Assuming a pollutant that decays at a rate of 0.1 yr^{-1} enters the lake at its inlet at a concentration of c_0, calculate its distribution (i.e., $c\,c_0^{-1}$) from Equation 12.64. Perform the calculation for E = 500, 0.05, 0.01667 and 0.0 km^2 yr^{-1}.

The dimensionless reaction group R can be calculated as

$$R = \frac{(0.1/yr)(1\ km)}{0.05\ km/yr} = 2$$

The Peclet number for each case can be calculated from

$$P_e = \frac{LU}{E}$$

Equation 12.64 can then be used to calculate $c\,c_0^{-1}$ as tabulated below:

$\ell = x/L$	500 (0.0001)	0.05 (1)	0.01667 (3)	0.0 (∞)	E[km^2/yr] (P_e)
0	0.3333	0.5189	0.6870	1.0000	
0.2	0.3333	0.4333	0.5233	0.6703	
0.4	0.3333	0.3674	0.4004	0.4493	
0.6	0.3333	0.3197	0.3108	0.3012	
0.8	0.3333	0.2899	0.2517	0.2019	
1.0	0.3333	0.2794	0.2286	0.1353	

The results are shown in Figure 12.14c. Note that for high levels of turbulent mixing, the solution becomes equivalent to the completely mixed model and for zero turbulence the solution converges on the plug-flow model. This exercise leads to the general conclusion that, all other things equal, a river-run reservoir is a more efficient settling basin than a completely mixed lake. This can be seen by observing that the outlet concentration (i.e., at $x = L$) for the well-mixed system is higher than for the river-run lake. Thus, the amount of phosphorus retained by the latter would be higher. This is a necessary consequence of the direct, linear proportionality with concentration that is used to characterize sedimentation for both systems. In the well-mixed lake, sedimentation is uniform throughout the reactor since concentrations are homogeneous. In contrast, for the river-run system, settling is greater near the inlet where concentrations are high. These losses are proportionately more efficient than the reduced sediment losses near the outlet and the effect is that the net removal is higher than for the well-mixed case.

§ § §

A General Continuous Solution for River-Run Lakes. Although the above model yields general insights regarding the behavior of river-run lakes, its underlying assumptions (constant depth and cross-sectional area, no mass inputs along its length, etc.) severely limit its applicability to actual systems. For example, the model would be inappropriate for the lake in Figure 12.15 because of changes in the lake's physical and hydrologic characteristics and the presence of a major waste source down-lake from the inlet. O'Connor (1966) has presented a method for modeling such systems that is based on dividing the lake into segments with constant properties. For example, the lake in Figure 12.15 would be divided at two points to account for changes in its dimensions and water flow. In addition, a division would be made at the point where the waste input enters the lake. Thus, four segments of constant dimension would be used to define the system. A mass balance of the form of Equation 12.58 would then be written for each segment. For the steady-state case, this is

$$O = E_i \frac{d^2 c_i}{dx^2} - U_i \frac{dc_i}{dx} - k_i c_i \qquad (12.65)$$

where the subscript designates the ith segment. The general solution for this equation is

$$c_i = B_i \exp(S_i x) + C_i \exp(V_i x) \qquad (12.66)$$

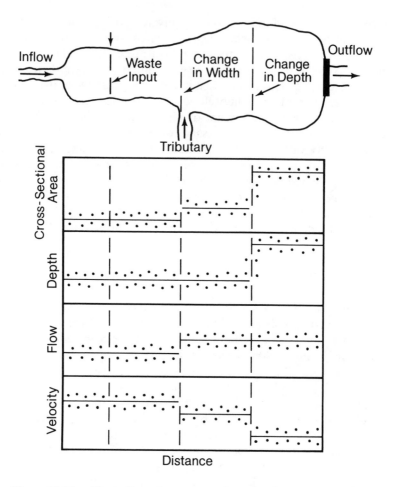

Figure 12.15   Illustration of a segmentation of a river-run reservoir.

where B_i and C_i are integration constants and

$$S_i = \frac{U_i}{2E_i}[1 + \sqrt{1 + (4E_ik_i)/U_i^2}\,]$$ (12.67a)

and

$$V_i = \frac{U_i}{2E_i}[1 - \sqrt{1 + (4E_ik_i)/U_i^2}\,]$$ (12.67b)

Therefore, for a system such as the lake in Figure 12.15, the resulting solution would consist of four equations with eight unknowns. In order to solve these equations, boundary conditions must be used to eliminate four of the unknowns. The following are some typical boundary conditions that are useful in lake analysis.

The Inlet Boundary Condition. By assuming that diffusion in the inlet river is much smaller than that in the lake, the inlet boundary condition represents a balance around a finite element at the inlet as in

$$Q_1 c_0 = Q_1 c_1 - E_1 A_{c,1} \frac{dc_1}{dx} \tag{12.68}$$

Equation 12.66 and its derivative can be substituted into Equation 12.68 to yield

$$Q_1 c_0 = Q_1 B_1 \exp(S_1 x) + Q_1 C_1 \exp(V_1 x)$$

$$- E_1 A_{c,1} B_1 S_1 \exp(S_1 x) - E_1 A_{c,1} C_1 V_1 \exp(V_1 x) \tag{12.69}$$

Since $x = 0$ at the inlet, Equation 12.69 can be simplified to yield

$$\alpha_1 B_1 + \alpha_2 C_1 = Q_1 c_0 \tag{12.70}$$

where

$$\alpha_1 = Q_1 - E_1 A_{c,1} S_1 \tag{12.71}$$

$$\alpha_2 = Q_1 - E_1 A_{c,1} V_1 \tag{12.72}$$

The Outlet Boundary Condition. As in Equation 12.63, the outlet boundary condition is

$$\frac{dc_n}{dx} (@ \, x_n = L_n) = 0 \tag{12.73}$$

where the subscript designates the last or nth segment (e.g., in Figure 12.15, n would equal 4) and L_n is the total length of the nth segment. In this case, Equation 12.66 can be differentiated and substituted into Equation 12.73 to yield

$$\alpha_3 B_n + \alpha_4 C_n = 0 \tag{12.74}$$

where

$$\alpha_3 = S_n \exp(S_n x_n) \qquad (12.75)$$

$$\alpha_4 = V_n \exp(V_n x_n) \qquad (12.76)$$

Continuity of Concentration. At the boundary between two segments the concentration must be equal. From Equation 12.66,

$$B_{j-1} \exp(S_{j-1} x_{j-1}) + C_{j-1} \exp(V_{j-1} x_{j-1}) = B_j + C_j \qquad (12.77)$$

where $j - 1$ and j designate the segments upstream and downstream from the boundary. Note that $x_j = 0$ at the boundary.

Continuity of Mass. At the boundary between two segments, mass must be conserved. A mass balance around the point of loading can be written as

$$Q_{j-1} c_{j-1} - E_{j-1} A_{c,j-1} \frac{dc_{j-1}}{dx} + W = Q_j c_j - E_j A_{c,j} \frac{dc_j}{dx} \qquad (12.78)$$

With Equation 12.66, this can be reexpressed as

$$\alpha_5 B_{j-1} + \alpha_6 C_{j-1} + \alpha_7 B_j + \alpha_8 C_j = W \qquad (12.79)$$

where

$$\alpha_5 = E_{j-1} A_{c,j-1} S_{j-1} \exp(S_{j-1} x_{j-1}) - Q_{j-1} \exp(S_{j-1} x_{j-1}) \qquad (12.80)$$

$$\alpha_6 = E_{j-1} A_{c,j-1} V_{j-1} \exp(V_{j-1} x_{j-1}) - Q_{j-1} \exp(V_{j-1} x_{j-1}) \qquad (12.81)$$

$$\alpha_7 = Q_j - E_j A_{c,j} S_j \qquad (12.82)$$

$$\alpha_8 = Q_j - E_j A_{c,j} V_j \qquad (12.83)$$

By application of the above operations, the problem can be reduced to solving a set of equations for the same number of unknowns. This is demonstrated in the following example.

§ § §

Example 12.5. From the same lake as in Example 12.4, solve for the concentration profile if the concentration of the inflow is zero and a waste source of 5×10^{-5} metric tons yr^{-1} enters the lake at a point midway along its length. Compute the profile for $E = 0.05$ km^2 yr^{-1}.

In this case, two segments are needed to model the system and the solution consists of

$$c_1 = B_1 \exp(S_1 x) + C_1 \exp(V_1 x)$$

$$c_2 = B_2 \exp(S_2 x) + C_2 \exp(V_2 x)$$

where

$$S = \frac{0.05}{2(0.05)} \left[1 + \sqrt{1 + \frac{4(0.05)(0.1)}{(0.05)^2}} \right] = 2.$$

$$V = \frac{0.05}{2(0.05)} \left[1 - \sqrt{1 + \frac{4(0.05)(0.1)}{(0.05)^2}} \right] = -1.$$

The following boundary conditions can then be applied to evaluate the unknowns:

1. Inlet boundary condition (Equation 12.70)
    $-0.00005 B_1 + 0.0001 C_1 = 0$
2. Outlet boundary condition (Equation 12.74)
    $5.4366 B_2 - 0.6065 C_2 = 0$
3. Continuity of concentration (Equation 12.77)
    $2.7183 B_1 + 0.6065 C_1 - B_2 - C_2 = 0$
4. Continuity of mass at the point of loading (Equation 12.79)
    $0.000136 B_1 - 0.000061 C_1 - 0.00005 B_2 + 0.0001 C_2 = 5 \times 10^{-5}$

These equations can be reexpressed in matrix form as

$$
\begin{bmatrix}
-0.0005 & 0.0001 & 0 & 0 \\
0 & 0 & 5.4366 & -0.6065 \\
2.7183 & 0.6065 & -1 & -1 \\
0.000136 & -0.000061 & -0.00005 & 0.0001
\end{bmatrix}
\begin{pmatrix} B_1 \\ C_1 \\ B_2 \\ C_2 \end{pmatrix}
=
\begin{pmatrix} 0 \\ 0 \\ 0 \\ 5 \times 10^{-5} \end{pmatrix}
$$

The matrix can be inverted and solved for

$B_1 = 0.138$
$B_2 = 0.042$
$C_1 = 0.069$
$C_2 = 0.374$

These values can be substituted into the solutions to yield

$$c_1 = 0.138e^{2x} + 0.069e^{-1x}$$

$$c_2 = 0.042e^{2x} + 0.374e^{-1x}$$

The results are displayed in Figure 12.16, along with the solution when the load enters the lake at the inlet.

§ § §

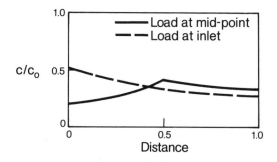

Figure 12.16　Concentration profiles along the longitudinal axis of a river-run lake for the mid-lake load (solid line) and for the same load at the inlet (dashed line).

Example 12.6. Ford Lake is a small impoundment ($\tau_w \cong 12$ days) on the Huron River in southeast Michigan. Using conductivity as a conservative tracer, it has been estimated (Beeton et al. 1980) that the diffusion coefficient for the system during mean summer flow conditions is approximately 2.6×10^5 m^2 d^{-1} (3×10^4 cm^2 sec^{-1}). Using the data in Table 12.2, compute the profiles along the lake's centerline due to total suspended solids and fecal coliform bacteria in the inflowing river. The settling rate of total suspended solids is approximately 0.5 m d^{-1} and the decay rate of the bacteria is approximately 2 d^{-1}.

To model Ford Lake we will idealize it as a one dimensional system with uniform morphometry as in Table 12.2. Using O'Connor's (1966) approach, the general solution is (Equation 12.66)

$$C_1 = B_1 \exp(S_1 x) + C_1 \exp(V_1 x) \tag{i}$$

where S_1 and V_1 can be calculated using Equation 12.67. Because a single

Table 12.2   Morphometric and Hydrologic Parameters
for Ford Lake, Michigan
During Summer Mean-Flow Conditions

Parameter	Value	Units
Depth	4.66	m
Surface Area	3.25×10^6	m^2
Volume	1.51×10^7	m^3
Cross-sectional Area	2092	m^2
Flow	1.22×10^6	$m^3 d^{-1}$
Velocity	583	$m d^{-1}$
Length	7242	m

segment is used to represent the lake, only two unknown coefficients, B_1 and C_1, must be evaluated. This can be done using the inlet (Equation 12.68) and the outlet (Equation 12.73) conditions which in the present case are

$$\alpha_1 B_1 + \alpha_2 C_1 = Q_1 c_0 \qquad \text{(ii)}$$

and

$$\alpha_3 B_1 + \alpha_4 C_1 = 0 \qquad \text{(iii)}$$

where the α's are defined in Equations 12.71, 72, 75 and 76. Equations ii and iii can then be solved simultaneously for B_1 and C_1 which can be substituted into Equation i to yield

$$\frac{c}{c_0} = \frac{Q_1}{\alpha_4 \alpha_1 - \alpha_2 \alpha_3} (\alpha_4 \exp(S_1 x) - \alpha_3 \exp(V_1 x)) \qquad \text{(iv)}$$

Using Equation iv and the data in Table 12.2, values of c/c_0 can be computed and compared with data. As in Figure 12.17, the model calculations are consistent with available measurements.

§ § §

Choice of a Diffusion Coefficient for River-Run Lakes. Mixing along the longitudinal axis of a river-run lake is a composite of turbulent diffusion and dispersion. If the lake's width is a valid approximation of the length scale (see Boyce and Hamblin 1975 and p. 114), Figure 12.7 provides a first estimate of the range of turbulent diffusion coefficients. However, because of the possible importance of dispersion, this estimate

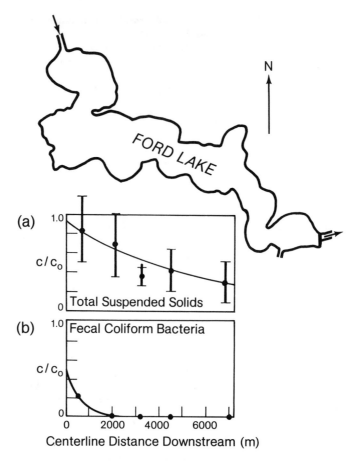

Figure 12.17   Application of continuous solution approach to Ford Lake, an impoundment on the Huron River in southeast Michigan. Profiles of dimensionless concentration (i.e., normalized to the concentration of the inflow) versus distance along the lake's centerline for (a) total suspended solids and (b) fecal coliform bacteria.

is a lower bound for the total mixing effect. Although formulae are available for computing dispersion coefficients in rivers (Fischer et al. 1979), similar schemes have not been developed for river-run lakes. For this reason, the analyst must rely on measurements (e.g., dye studies or conservative substance budgets) to estimate a total diffusion/dispersion coefficient.

Vertical and Lateral Mixing in River-Run Lakes. To this point, we have assumed that gradients occur only along the longitudinal axis of a river-run lake. Although this is a good approximation for long-term computations, significant vertical and lateral variability can be encountered on shorter spatial and temporal scales.

For example, some river-run lakes stratify during summer. Whether or not thermal stratification occurs depends on the interplay of the momentum of the through-flow and the gravitational forces due to water buoyancy. This interplay is given quantitative expression by a *densimetric Froude number,* which for a lake is approximated by (Water Resources Engineers 1969)

$$F_D = 10^{-5} \frac{L}{z\, \tau_w} \qquad (12.83a)$$

where L is the length of the lake [m], z is the mean depth [m] and τ_w is the water residence time [yr], which is equal to the volume divided by the outflow. If $F_D \gg 0.32$, the lake will be completely mixed vertically. If $F_D \ll 0.32$, it will be strongly stratified. For values in the vicinity of 0.32, weak stratification can occur.

Equation 12.83a provides a rough guideline for ascertaining when vertical stratification will occur in a river-run lake. If the substance being modeled is strongly influenced by stratification, resolution in the vertical, as well as the horizontal, dimension is called for. In Chapter 13, techniques for modeling vertical processes are discussed.

Techniques that can be used for modeling lateral pollutant gradients are developed in the remainder of this chapter. The reader is referred to Fischer et al. (1979) for additional details on modeling shorter-term mixing processes and the general topic of mixing in reservoirs and river-run lakes.

12.2.3 Near-Shore Models

Since many pollutants enter a lake at its periphery, another important water quality problem is the distribution of contaminants in the vicinity of a waste discharge or a river (Figure 12.1c). Such areas are important in a management context since human use and perception of a lake are typically intense in the coastal or nearshore zone, where beaches and other recreational areas are located.

After an initial period of mixing due to the turbulence of the discharge jet (see Fischer et al. 1979 for a discussion of modeling jets and plumes), the concentration of a nearshore input is dependent on the transport processes in the lake and the pollutant's reaction characteristics. For a vertically well-mixed, constant depth layer such as the epilimnion of a stratified lake, the distribution of a substance reacting with first-order decay is represented by

$$\frac{\partial c}{\partial t} = -U_x \frac{\partial c}{\partial x} - U_y \frac{\partial c}{\partial y} + E_x \frac{\partial^2 c}{\partial x^2} + E_y \frac{\partial^2 c}{\partial y^2} - kc \qquad (12.84)$$

where the x and y axes are defined to be parallel and perpendicular to the shoreline, respectively (Figure 12.18). The following sections present solutions to Equation 12.84.

Steady-State Case in an Infinite Fluid (*No Advection*). In situations where advective currents are negligible, the steady-state version of Equation 12.84 is (assuming that diffusion is equal in all directions)

$$E \left(\frac{\partial^2 c}{\partial x^2} + \frac{\partial^2 c}{\partial y^2} \right) - kc = 0 \qquad (12.85)$$

O'Connor (1962) transformed and solved Equation 12.85 for polar coordinates as depicted in Fig. 12.18. If r is the radial axis, Equation 12.85 becomes

$$\frac{\partial^2 c}{\partial r^2} + \frac{1}{r} \frac{\partial c}{\partial r} + \frac{1}{r^2} \frac{\partial^2 c}{\partial \theta^2} - \frac{k}{E} c = 0 \qquad (12.86)$$

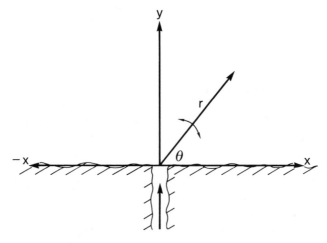

Figure 12.18   Cartesian (x,y) and radial (r) coordinates used for coastal zone models.

By assuming that c is constant for a given r, $\partial c/\partial \theta$ and $\partial^2 c/\partial \theta^2$ are zero and Equation 12.86 reduces to a Bessel equation* of order zero.

$$\frac{d^2c}{dr^2} + \frac{1}{r}\frac{dc}{dr} - \frac{k}{E}c = 0 \qquad (12.87)$$

the solution of which is

$$c = BI_0[\sqrt{kr^2/E}\,] + CK_0[\sqrt{kr^2/E}\,] \qquad (12.88)$$

where B and C are constants of integration and I_0 and K_0 are modified Bessel functions of the first and second kind, respectively.* By invoking the following boundary conditions

$$c(r_0) = c_0 \qquad (12.89)$$

and

$$c(\infty) = 0 \qquad (12.90)$$

O'Connor solved Equation 12.88 for

$$\frac{c}{c_0} = \frac{K_0[\sqrt{kr^2/E}\,]}{K_0[\sqrt{kr_0{}^2/E}\,]} \qquad (12.91)$$

O'Connor's first boundary condition (Equation 12.89) sets the concentration equal to a constant at a distance, r_0, from the origin. This distance can be thought of as the periphery of a mixing zone. Although this formulation has the disadvantage of not being directly related to the waste source at $r = 0$, it is useful in that it circumvents the problem that the solution (Equation 12.91) actually approaches infinity as r approaches zero. This can be seen from an alternative solution to Equation 12.87 that uses a boundary condition at $r = 0$,

$$c = \frac{W}{\pi zE}K_0[\sqrt{kr^2/E}\,] \qquad (12.92)$$

---

*Differential equations of a particular form (e.g., Equation 12.87) are called Bessel equations. The solutions for these equations are called Bessel functions. These functions are tabulated in numerous mathematical reference volumes and handbooks. Additionally, most computer systems carry easy-to-use library functions to compute their value.

This solution goes to infinity as r approaches zero since, mathematically, the waste source emanates from a point (or more accurately a line since the source enters over the depth of the layer) of infinitely small thickness at the shoreline. Di Toro (1972) has presented an analysis of the problem along with a tabulated solution that is finite at the origin. While the modeler should consult Di Toro's paper, Equations 12.91 and 12.92 are adequate approximations in many cases and will be used in subsequent examples.

§ § §

Example 12.7. O'Connor (1962) used Equation 12.91 to solve for bacterial distribution in the vicinity of Indiana Harbor in Lake Michigan. The radius of the mixing zone was taken to be 45.7 m which is one half of the approximate width of the harbor outlet. A diffusion coefficient of 2.6×10^6 m^2 d^{-1} (3×10^5 cm^2 sec^{-1}) was used to characterize turbulent mixing. Two decay rates, 0.5 and 3.0 per day, were used to estimate bounds for bacterial die-off under summer temperature conditions. The results in Figure 12.19 indicate general agreement between model

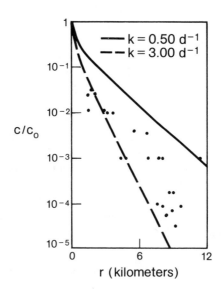

Figure 12.19   Profiles of bacterial concentration (normalized to concentration at the edge of the mixing zone) versus distance, r (kilometers) from the edge of the mixing zone in the vicinity of Indiana Harbor, Lake Michigan as originally computed by O'Connor (1962). The lines represent model calculations based on two estimates of the bacterial die-off rate. The data are three-month averages for June through August.

results and three month averages (June, July and August) of bacterial concentration.

§ § §

Steady-State Case in an Infinite Fluid (Advection Along the Shoreline). Although the preceding is appropriate where turbulent mixing is the primary transport mechanism, some lakes have persistent unidirectional currents that can advect pollutants along the shoreline. For this case, Equation 12.84 becomes, at steady state,

$$U_x \frac{\partial c}{\partial x} = E\left(\frac{\partial^2 c}{\partial x^2} + \frac{\partial^2 c}{\partial y^2}\right) - kc \tag{12.93}$$

where U_x is the current velocity along the shoreline. Boyce and Hamblin (1975) have presented the following solution

$$c = \frac{W}{\pi z E} \exp\left(\frac{U_x x}{2E}\right) K_0 \left[r \sqrt{k/E + (U_x/2E)^2}\,\right] \tag{12.94}$$

where

$$r = \sqrt{x^2 + y^2}$$

Notice that, for $U_x = 0$, Equation 12.94 reduces to Equation 12.92.

Steady-State Case in a Bounded Fluid. The preceding solutions are appropriate for situations where the reaction is rapid and/or the transport weak and/or the lake wide enough that the opposite shoreline of the lake has no effect on the solution. For example, Equations 12.92 and 12.94 would be valid for the analysis of discharge of coliform bacteria into one of the Great Lakes since the bacteria would die off within a few kilometers of shore and such lakes are on the order of a hundred kilometers wide. However, for narrow lakes or for substances that react slowly or are conservative, the effect of the opposite shoreline must be considered. In that case, Equation 12.94 is expressed directly in Cartesian coordinates as

$$c(x, y) = \frac{W}{\pi z E} \exp\left(\frac{U_x x}{2E}\right) K_0 \left[\sqrt{(x^2 + y^2)\{(k/E) + (U_x/2E)^2\}}\,\right] \tag{12.95}$$

Then, for a lake of width Y, the solution is obtained by the iterative formula (Boyce and Hamblin 1975)

$$c'(x, y) = c(x, y) + \sum_{n=1}^{\infty} [c(x, y + 2nY) + c(x, y - 2nY)] \qquad (12.96)$$

In this solution, the confining effect of the opposite shoreline is accounted for by the infinite series of additions in the second half of Equation 12.96. In practice, only a small number (i.e., ~2 or 3) are needed to characterize the effect.

§ § §

Example 12.8. A municipality discharges sewage at a rate of 4×10^4 m^3 day^{-1} at a point on a lake's shoreline. The wastewater is laden with coliform bacteria ($30 \times 10^6 / 100$ ml), which die at a rate of 1.0 day^{-1}. Calculate concentration profiles in the lake's vertically well-mixed surface layer ($z = 20$ m) for the following cases:

Case 1: Assume that the lake is infinitely long and wide and that horizontal diffusion ($E_x = E_y = 5 \times 10^6$ m^2 day^{-1}) is the sole transport mechanism.

The waste load W is calculated as the product of flow and concentration of the discharge as in

$$W = (4 \times 10^4 \text{ m}^3 \text{ day}^{-1})(30 \times 10^6 \text{ per 100 ml})$$

Equation 12.92 can then be used to determine concentrations in the lake

$$c = \frac{(4 \times 10^4)(30 \times 10^6)}{\pi(20)(5 \times 10^6)} K_0 [\sqrt{1r^2/(5 \times 10^6)} \,]$$

The results of this computation for a section of the lake are displayed in Figure 12.20a.

Case 2: Same assumptions as Case 1 but with a current of 0.5×10^4 m day^{-1} moving from east to west.

In this case, Equation 12.94 is used

$$c = \frac{(4 \times 10^4)(30 \times 10^6)}{\pi(20)(5 \times 10^6)} \exp\left(\frac{0.5 \times 10^4 x}{2(5 \times 10^6)}\right)$$

$$\times K_0 [r \sqrt{1/(5 \times 10^6) + \{[0.5 \times 10^4]/2(5 \times 10^6)\}^2} \,]$$

The results are shown in Figure 12.20b.

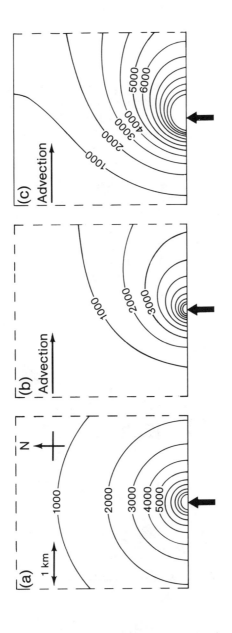

Figure 12.20 Contours of coliform bacteria (#/100 ml) as the result of a waste discharge (➤) at a point on a lake's shoreline for three cases: (a) unbounded fluid with diffusive transport, (b) unbounded fluid with diffusive and advective transport and (c) bounded fluid with diffusive and advective transport.

Case 3: Same assumptions as Case 2 but with a finite width of 4 km. In this case Equations 12.95 and 12.96 are used with $n = 2$. The results are displayed in Figure 12.20c.

§ § §

Example 12.9. Boyce and Hamblin (1974) developed Equation 12.95 and used it to simulate steady-state chloride profiles in the central basin of Lake Erie (Figure 12.21). They assumed that the controlling dimension of the lake (i.e., its narrowest width) defines the largest energy bearing eddy and specifies the point at which the acceleration of the diffusion process comes to a halt. Thus, for long-term computations, Figure 12.7 with scale length specified by the controlling width provides a first estimate of the order of magnitude of the diffusion coefficient. For example, for central Lake Erie, the minimum width is approximately 80 km (8×10^6 cm). Figure 12.7 indicates that the diffusion coefficient for this scale length ranges from approximately 5×10^5 to 8×10^6 cm^2 sec^{-1}. Figure 12.12b shows Boyce and Hamblin's (1974) simulation using Equation 12.95 and values of $E = 1.5 \times 10^6$ cm^2 sec^{-1} and $n = 2$.

§ § §

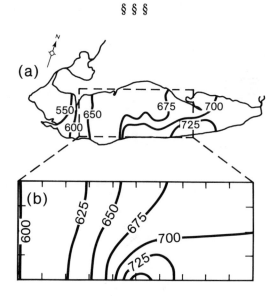

Figure 12.21   Chloride model of Lake Erie from Boyce and Hamblin (1975). (a) chloride contours in μM for Lake Erie during 1970; (b) model results using Equation 12.95.

As in Example 12.9, Figure 12.7 provides a first estimate of the expected range of the horizontal eddy diffusion coefficient for such long-term computations. However, as with any default coefficient, additional measurements, such as calibration with conservative substances, are advisable.

12.3 NUMERICAL SOLUTIONS

Although the analytical solutions provide insight into the dynamics of incompletely mixed systems, their simplicity somewhat limits their applicability. The present section describes numerical modeling techniques with which a broader class of problems can be analyzed. First, some general characteristics of finite difference schemes are discussed. Then, a specific technique that has broad applicability to engineering modeling problems is described.

12.3.1 Finite Difference Approximation of Partial Differential Equations

In Section 11.3 we described methods for solving ordinary differential equations where the dependent variable, concentration, changed in relation to one independent variable, time. These changes were approximated by dividing time into increments. In the present chapter, we have been dealing with partial differential equations where, in addition to time, concentration varies in one or more spatial dimensions. The starting point for approximating these equations is, therefore, to divide space and time into increments. Figure 12.22 shows a uniform segmentation scheme or grid that would be used for a partial differential equation that varies in time and one spatial dimension, x. For simplicity the present discussion will be limited to such one-dimensional spatial systems. Extending the analysis to multidimensional systems is straightforward. In addition, the discussion is limited to the numerical solution of the advection-diffusion equation without reactions.

$$\frac{\partial c}{\partial t} = -U \frac{\partial c}{\partial x} + E \frac{\partial^2 c}{\partial x^2} \tag{12.97}$$

Section 12.3.2 describes a more general technique that is applicable to systems with reactions as well as those with non-uniform grids.

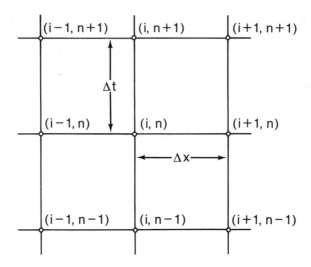

Figure 12.22 Temporal and spatial grid for a finite difference approximation of a partial differential equation.

Basic Finite Difference Forms. One way to solve Equation 12.97 numerically is to develop Taylor series expansions of its derivatives. For example, the first derivative of concentration with respect to x ($\partial c/\partial x$) can be derived by expanding forward in space as in

$$c_{i+1} = c_i + \left.\frac{\partial c}{\partial x}\right|_i \Delta x + \frac{1}{2}\left.\frac{\partial^2 c}{\partial x^2}\right|_i \Delta x^2 + \text{HOT} \qquad (12.98)$$

where HOT are higher order terms. Equation 12.98 can be solved for

$$\left.\frac{\partial c}{\partial x}\right|_i = \frac{c_{i+1} - c_i}{\Delta x} - \frac{1}{2}\left.\frac{\partial^2 c}{\partial x^2}\right|_i \Delta x + \text{HOT} \qquad (12.99)$$

or

$$\left.\frac{\partial c}{\partial x}\right|_i = \frac{c_{i+1} - c_i}{\Delta x} + 0(\Delta x) \qquad (12.100)$$

where $0(\Delta x)$ designates terms of order Δx. Therefore,

$$\left.\frac{\partial c}{\partial x}\right|_i \cong \frac{c_{i+1} - c_i}{\Delta x} \qquad (12.101)$$

is a finite difference approximation of the spatial first derivative. It is called a *forward-difference* since it is based on a projection from i "forward" to $i + 1$. Since the forward difference neglects $0(\Delta x)$, it has a truncation error of order Δx and is called "first-order accurate."

In a similar fashion, a Taylor series can be expanded backwards to $i - 1$

$$c_{i-1} = c_i - \left.\frac{\partial c}{\partial x}\right|_i \Delta x + \frac{1}{2}\left.\frac{\partial^2 c}{\partial x^2}\right|_i \Delta x^2 + HOT$$

and solved for

$$\left.\frac{\partial c}{\partial x}\right|_i \cong \frac{c_i - c_{i-1}}{\Delta x} \tag{12.102}$$

which is called a *backward-difference* which is also first-order accurate.

Finally, the forward and backward Taylor expansions can be subtracted and solved for

$$\left.\frac{\partial c}{\partial x}\right|_i \cong \frac{c_{i+1} - c_{i-1}}{2\Delta x} \tag{12.103}$$

which is called a *central or centered difference*. In contrast to the backward and forward differences, Equation 12.103 is second-order accurate. Although the central difference has this advantage it has some shortcomings related to stability as discussed subsequently. Therefore, the choice of which scheme to use is somewhat dictated by the problem context.

By analogy, approximations for the time derivative (or for first derivatives of additional space dimensions) can be developed. For example, the forward difference form of the time derivative is

$$\left.\frac{\partial c}{\partial t}\right|_i^n \cong \frac{c_i^{n+1} - c_i^n}{\Delta t} \tag{12.104}$$

where the superscript designates different points in time (as in Figure 12.22). [Note that in the spatial approximations (i.e., Equations 12.101–103) the superscript is dropped since time is constant for these cases.]

The centered-difference form of the second derivative, derived by adding forward and backwards expansions, is represented by

$$\left.\frac{\partial^2 c}{\partial x^2}\right|_i \cong \frac{c_{i+1} + c_{i-1} - 2c_i}{\Delta x^2} \tag{12.105}$$

which is second order accurate. Equation 12.105 may be expressed alternatively in a more physically tangible form as

$$\left. \frac{\partial^2 c}{\partial x^2} \right|_i = \frac{(c_{i+1} - c_i)/\Delta x \; - \; (c_i - c_{i-1})/\Delta x}{\Delta x} \tag{12.106}$$

Equations 12.103, 104 and 105 can now be substituted into Equation 12.97 to yield

$$\frac{c_i^{n+1} - c_i^n}{\Delta t} = -U \frac{c_{i+1}^n - c_{i-1}^n}{2\Delta x} + E \frac{c_{i+1}^n + c_{i-1}^n - 2c_i^n}{\Delta x^2} \tag{12.107}$$

This finite difference approximation of the advection-diffusion equation is a forward-time, centered-space difference. It is first-order accurate in time and second-order accurate in space. It can be used directly to compute concentration at time $n+1$ as a function of known values at n by rearranging Equation 12.107 to yield

$$c_i^{n+1} = c_i^n + \Delta t \left(-U \frac{c_{i+1}^n - c_{i-1}^n}{2\Delta x} + E \frac{c_{i+1}^n + c_{i-1}^n - 2c_i^n}{\Delta x^2} \right) \tag{12.108}$$

Thus, the method is simple to implement and is somewhat analogous to the Euler-Cauchy method for ordinary differential equations (Section 11.3.1). Equations are written for each spatial grid point and solved individually to predict concentration at the next time. Such methods are called *explicit* techniques and are in contrast to *implicit* methods that are more difficult to implement (simultaneous equations are solved) but have advantages related to stability.

Stability. Not all of the finite difference approximations introduced in the preceding pages yield meaningful results when substituted into the advection-diffusion equation. For example, if a centered rather than forward time difference were used in Equation 12.97, solutions would be numerically unstable—that is, chaotic predictions with no relation to the actual solution of the continuous advection-diffusion equation would result. Similarly, in the absence of diffusion, (i.e., $E = 0$), the spatially centered advection term in Equation 12.107 would result in unstable solutions.

Instability due to the choice of an inappropriate differencing scheme is termed *static instability.* As in Figure 12.23, perturbations around the solution are magnified by static instabilities and thus with time, chaos results. Additionally, if the time over which the computation is made is

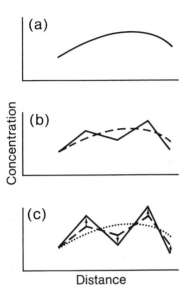

Figure 12.23   Graphical representation of static instability (redrawn from Roache 1972). (a) shows the exact solution, (b) shows the introduction of small perturbations around the true solution and (c) illustrates how these perturbations magnify with time under conditions of static instability. This magnification ultimately leads to chaos.

too long (i.e., Δt too large) a *dynamic instability* or "overshoot" can occur.

Methods are available for developing criteria for maintaining stability in numerical integration schemes. For example, it can be shown (Roache 1972) that the following two criteria guarantee stability for the forward-time, centered-space approximation of the advection-diffusion equation (12.107),

$$\frac{U\Delta x}{E} \leq 2 \qquad (12.109)$$

and

$$\frac{E\Delta t}{\Delta x^2} \leq \frac{1}{2} \qquad (12.110)$$

Given values for E and U, Equation 12.109 can be used to choose a spatial grid interval, Δx, to avoid static instability of the centered-difference advection term.* Then, Equation 12.110 is used to choose the proper time step, Δt, to avoid overshoot.

This is a very brief introduction to the complex problem of instability and is meant to acquaint the reader with the basic problem. Additional and more general criteria are presented in Section 12.3.2. The reader should also consult Roache (1972) for a straightforward exposition of the topic.

Numerical Diffusion. As stated previously, in the absence of diffusion, the spatially centered advection approximation is statically unstable. It can be shown that for cases without diffusion, the backwards difference is stable and can be used to remedy this situation. Although the use of this approximation obviates the problem it is not without its disadvantages. First, it reduces accuracy since the backwards difference is only first-order accurate. Further, the use of backwards or "upwind" differencing introduces a numerical diffusion into the computation. This diffusion is a mathematical artifact of the approximation scheme and is in addition to the actual physical diffusion occurring in the lake.

Taylor expansions can be used (Roache 1972) to show that the forward time, backward space approximation of the advection equation is equivalent to

$$\frac{\partial c}{\partial t} = -U \frac{\partial c}{\partial x} + E_n \frac{\partial^2 c}{\partial x^2} + HOT + HOD \qquad (12.111)$$

where HOD are higher order derivatives and E_n is numerical or artificial diffusion which is equal to

$$E_n = \frac{1}{2} U \Delta x \left(1 - \frac{U \Delta t}{\Delta x} \right) \qquad (12.112)$$

For the steady-state case, a different formula that is independent of the time step results,

$$E_n = \frac{1}{2} U \Delta x \qquad (12.113)$$

Thus, numerical diffusion can be minimized by reducing the grid size

---

*Note, that although by itself centered-difference advection is unstable, in the presence of diffusion it is stabilized. Equation 12.109 expresses the amount of diffusion that is needed to produce this stability.

of the computation. However, in some cases this can be quite costly and alternative, more complex methods must be used (Roache 1972).

In addition, if sufficient physical diffusion is occurring, a correction can be made by subtracting the numerical diffusion from the actual diffusion coefficient. However, for cases where real diffusion is low, this correction cannot be made and the analyst must rely on a smaller grid or more complex methods.

Numerical diffusion is not normally a problem in lake water quality modeling because large scale turbulent diffusion is usually significant. The reader should be cognizant of its existence, however, when modeling highly advective systems. One case where it is relevant is in simulating the profiles of solid-associated contaminants in compacting sediments as discussed in Section 13.2.

Implicit Methods. As noted previously, explicit finite difference forms have limitations related to stability. In addition, as depicted in Figure 12.24, they exclude information that has a bearing on the true solution of the partial differential equation. Implicit methods overcome

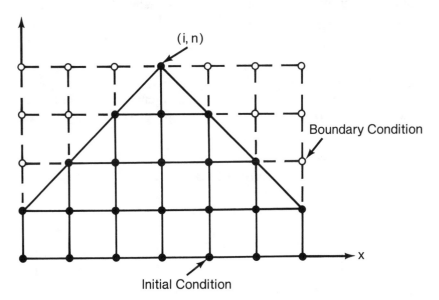

Figure 12.24 Representation of the effect of other nodes on the finite difference approximation at node (i,n) using an explicit finite difference scheme. The darkened nodes have an influence on (i,n) whereas the light nodes, which in reality do influence the approximation, are excluded (Carnahan et al. 1969).

both these difficulties at the expense of somewhat more complex algorithms.

The fundamental difference between explicit and implicit approximations is depicted in Figure 12.25. For the explicit form, we approximate the spatial derivations at time level, n (Figure 12.25a). Recall that when we substituted these approximations into the original differential equations, we obtained an approximating equation (12.108) in terms of one unknown. Thus, we can solve "explicitly" for this unknown.

In the implicit method (Figure 12.25b) we evaluate the spatial derivatives at an advanced time level, $n + 1$. For example, the finite difference approximation for the centered difference second derivative is

$$\left. \frac{\partial^2 c}{\partial x^2} \right|_i^n \cong \frac{c_{i+1}^{n+1} + c_{i-1}^{n+1} - 2c_i^{n+1}}{\Delta x^2}$$

When this equation is substituted along with the other approximations, into the original differential equation, the resulting equation contains several unknowns. Therefore, it cannot be solved by simple algebraic rearrangement as was done in going from Equation 12.107 to 12.108. Instead, the entire system of equations must be solved simultaneously. This can be done because, along with the boundary conditions, the implicit formulation results in a set of linear algebraic equations with the same number of unknowns. Thus, the problem reduces to the solution of the set of simultaneous equations at each point in time.

Although such a scheme is not as simple to implement as an explicit formulation, it has a number of important advantages. First, it includes

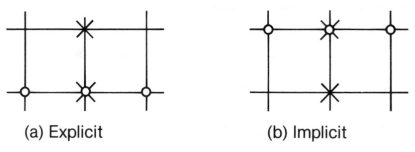

X Grid point involved in time difference
O Grid point involved in space difference

(a) Explicit   (b) Implicit

Figure 12.25 Computational molecules demonstrating the fundamental difference between (a) explicit and (b) implicit methods.

the effect of nodes that would be excluded from an explicit approach. Further, it can be shown that regardless of the value of the ratio of time and space step sizes (Equation 12.110), the method converges on the true solution as Δt and Δx approach zero. Finally, although implicit methods would seem to be more complex and costly to implement, their advantages usually outweigh these considerations. From an economic standpoint, their cost is only about 50% greater on the average than for explicit forms. This is due, in part, to the fact that the simultaneous equations can often be expressed in tridiagonal matrix form for which efficient, recursive solution techniques are available.

It should be noted that there are many varieties of implicit algorithms that are presently available. A particularly popular approach is the *Crank-Nicolson method* that has the advantage of being second order accurate in both space *and* time. Descriptions of this (and other) numerical methods, along with some computer algorithms, are found elsewhere (Carnahan et al. 1969).

12.3.2 Thomann's Control Volume Approach

Aside from Taylor series expansions, other techniques can be used for deriving finite difference approximations of partial differential equations. One of these methods, called the control volume approach, consists of treating the water body as a series of completely mixed volumes or segments. Mass balances are then written for each segment, resulting in a set of equations that can be solved simultaneously for their concentrations. The approach has a somewhat more physical basis than the previously described methods. However, if derived under similar assumptions (e.g., equally spaced segments), the two approaches yield identical finite difference representations for the original differential equations (see Roache 1972).

Thomann (1963, 1972) has developed a control volume approach that is designed for engineering computations in natural waters.* Among other things, it is particularly useful when modeling systems where variable sized segments are needed. This is often the case in real world situations where more detail might be required around river mouths or sewage outfalls. In addition, the steady-state version of the model results in the extremely useful spatial system response matrix that provides information regarding the effect of a loading to one segment on the water quality of all other segments.

---

*Thomann calls his approach a "finite section" method. We will use the terms finite section and control volume interchangeably.

This approach was first developed to model substance dynamics in estuaries, but has found widespread application to pollution analysis in a variety of water bodies including lakes. The following is a brief description of the method and examples of its use; a more detailed discussion is found in Thomann's (1972) book on water quality analysis. While the approach is applicable to multidimensional problems, it is most straightforward to derive it for a one-dimensional case and then extend it to multidimensional systems.

One-Dimensional Case. Figure 12.26 shows a one-dimensional system divided into n volumes or segments. The change in mass with respect to time in the ith segment is a combination of advection, diffusion, reactions and mass loadings as in

$$V_i \frac{dc_i}{dt} = Q_{i-1,i}c_{i-1,i} - Q_{i,i+1}c_{i,i+1} + E'_{i-1,i}(c_{i-1} - c_i)$$

$$+ E'_{i,i+1}(c_{i+1} - c_i) - kV_ic_i + W_i \qquad (12.114)$$

where E' is a bulk diffusion coefficient [$L^3 T^{-1}$] defined as

$$E' = \frac{EA_c}{\ell}$$

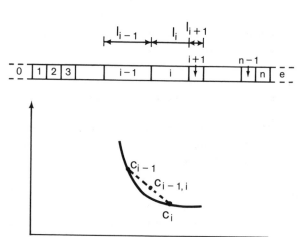

Figure 12.26 Segmentation scheme for a one-dimensional system showing how the concentration at the interface between segments $i - 1$ and i is determined by linear interpolation.

where A_c is the cross-sectional area of the interface connecting segment i with an adjacent segment, j $[L^2]$, E is the diffusion coefficient across this interface $[L^2\ T^{-1}]$ and ℓ is the average length of segments i and j $[L] = (\ell_i + \ell_j)/2$. Note that in this case, in contrast to the embayment model (Section 12.2.1), advection is represented as a product of the flow and the concentration at the interface between each segment (Figure 12.26). The concentration at the interface depends on the levels in both segments, which can be approximated by

$$c_{i-1,i} = \alpha_{i-1,i}c_{i-1} + \beta_{i-1,i}c_i \qquad (12.115)$$

and

$$c_{i,i+1} = \alpha_{i,i+1}c_i + \beta_{i,i+1}c_{i+1} \qquad (12.116)$$

where α and $\beta = 1 - \alpha$ are weighting factors. Using linear interpolation, as depicted in Figure 12.26, a first approximation to the weights is given by

$$\alpha_{ji} = \frac{\ell_i}{\ell_i + \ell_j} \quad \text{and} \quad \beta_{ji} = \frac{\ell_j}{\ell_i + \ell_j} \qquad (12.117)$$

where ℓ_i is the length of segment i and j designates an adjacent segment. An additional constraint on α and β, based on stability requirements, is that*

$$\alpha > 1 - E'/Q \qquad (12.118)$$

Equations 12.115 and 12.116 can be substituted into Equation 12.114, which then can be written for each segment in the system. The resulting set of equations can be integrated simultaneously in time. The general time step constraint for integration can be derived as (Thomann 1972)

$$1 + U\ \frac{\Delta t}{\ell}\ (\beta - \alpha) - \frac{2E\,\Delta t}{\ell^2} - k\Delta t > 0 \qquad (12.119)$$

where $U = Q/A_c$. The connection between this criterion and the time step constraint derived previously (Equation 12.110) can be demonstrated by realizing that for a central difference scheme without reaction, Equation 12.119 becomes

$$\frac{\Delta t}{\ell^2} < \frac{1}{2E} \qquad (12.120)$$

---

*Note that for a central difference ($\alpha = 1/2$), Equation 12.118 is identical with Equation 12.109.

which is identical with Equation 12.110. Thomann (1972) discusses further nuances of time-variable solutions for his approach. The present derivation will be limited to the steady-state case ($dc_i/dt = 0$), where Equation (12.114) can be rearranged by grouping terms to yield

$$[-Q_{i-1,i}\alpha_{i-1,i} - E'_{i-1,i}]c_{i-1}$$

$$+ [Q_{i,i+1}\alpha_{i,i+1} - Q_{i-1,i}\beta_{i-1,i} + E'_{i-1,i} + E'_{i,i+1} + V_i k]c_i$$

$$+ [Q_{i,i+1}\beta_{i,i+1} - E'_{i,i+1}]c_{i+1} = W_i \qquad (12.121)$$

If we define the following

$$a_{i,i-1} = -Q_{i-1,i}\alpha_{i-1,i} - E'_{i-1,i} \qquad (12.122)$$

$$a_{ii} = Q_{i,i+1}\alpha_{i,i+1} - Q_{i-1,i}\beta_{i-1,i} + E'_{i-1,i} + E'_{i,i+1} + V_i k \qquad (12.123)$$

$$a_{i,i+1} = Q_{i,i+1}\beta_{i,i+1} - E'_{i,i+1} \qquad (12.124)$$

Equation 12.121 becomes

$$a_{i,i-1}c_{i-1} + a_{ii}c_i + a_{i,i+1}c_{i+1} = W_i \qquad (12.125)$$

For the first section ($n = 1$), a similar procedure is followed, with the exception that the input from the river is prescribed, and the following equation results:

$$a_{11}c_1 + a_{12}c_2 = W_1' \qquad (12.126)$$

where

$$W_1' = W_1 + Q_0 c_0 \qquad (12.127)$$

where Q_0 and c_0 are the flow and concentration in the inflowing river and

$$a_{11} = Q_{12}\alpha_{12} + E'_{12} + V_1 k \qquad (12.128)$$

and a_{12} is as defined by Equation 12.124. In a similar fashion, the equation for the nth or outlet section becomes

$$a_{n,n-1}c_{n-1} + a_{nn}c_n = W_n \qquad (12.129)$$

where all terms are as defined previously, with the exception of

$$a_{nn} = -Q_{n-1,n}\beta_{n-1,n} + E'_{n-1,n} + V_n k \qquad (12.130)$$

The complete set of equations to be solved is given by

$$
\begin{aligned}
a_{11}c_1 + a_{12}c_2 + 0 + \cdot + \cdot + \cdot + 0 &= W_1' \\
a_{21}c_1 + a_{22}c_2 + a_{23}c_3 + 0 + \cdot + \cdot + 0 &= W_2 \\
0 + a_{32}c_2 + a_{33}c_3 + a_{34}c_4 + 0 + \cdot + 0 &= W_3 \\
&\cdot \\
&\cdot \\
&\cdot \\
0 + \cdot \quad \cdot \quad \cdot + 0 + a_{n,n-1}c_{n-1} + a_{nn}c_n &= W_n
\end{aligned}
$$

$$(12.131)$$

which can be expressed in matrix form as

$$
\begin{bmatrix}
a_{11} & a_{12} & 0 & \cdot & \cdot & \cdot & 0 \\
a_{21} & a_{22} & a_{23} & 0 & \cdot & \cdot & 0 \\
0 & a_{32} & a_{33} & a_{34} & 0 & \cdot & 0 \\
\cdot & & & & & & \cdot \\
\cdot & & & & & & \cdot \\
\cdot & & & & & & \cdot \\
0 & \cdot & \cdot & \cdot & 0 & a_{n,n-1} & a_{nn}
\end{bmatrix}
\begin{pmatrix}
c_1 \\ c_2 \\ c_3 \\ \cdot \\ \cdot \\ \cdot \\ c_n
\end{pmatrix}
=
\begin{pmatrix}
W_1 \\ W_2 \\ W_3 \\ \cdot \\ \cdot \\ \cdot \\ W_n
\end{pmatrix}
\qquad (12.132)
$$

or

$$[A](c) = (W) \qquad (12.133)$$

where [A] is an $n \times n$ matrix with units of $L^3 T^{-1}$, (c) is a $n \times 1$ vector with units of $M L^{-3}$ and (W) is an $n \times 1$ vector with units of $M T^{-1}$. The solution vector (c) is then obtained formally by inverting the [A] matrix to yield*

$$(c) = [A]^{-1}(W) \qquad (12.134)$$

---

*Recall that in Chapter 10, we presented general relationships (Equations 10.16 and 10.17) for computing assimilative capacity. These relationships are identical in form to Equations 12.133 and 12.134. Thomann's approach represents a systematic method for making assimilative capacity calculations for multiple dimensions (and reactants).

where $[A]^{-1}$ is the inverted matrix, which is termed the *spatial system response matrix* $(M L^{-3})/(M T^{-1})$. A useful property of $[A]^{-1}$ is that its elements represent the response of a segment (as represented by concentration) to a unit loading to any other segment in the system.

Multidimensional Case. An extension of the previous analysis to more than one dimension is relatively straightforward. Figure 12.27 illustrates a two-dimensional system. From the convention that flow entering a section is negative and flow out of a section is positive, an equation can be written to represent the conservation of mass for segment i

$$V_i \frac{dc_i}{dt} = \sum_k [-Q_{ik}(\alpha_{ik}c_i + \beta_{ik}c_k) + E'_{ik}(c_k - c_i)] - V_ikc_i + W_i \qquad (12.135)$$

Note, that the advection term can be generalized in this way since

$$-Q_{ik}\alpha_{ik} = Q_{ki}\beta_{ki} \qquad (12.136)$$

and

$$-Q_{ik}\beta_{ik} = Q_{ki}\alpha_{ki} \qquad (12.137)$$

At steady state, Equation 12.135 may be rewritten as

$$a_{ii}c_i + \sum_k a_{ik}c_k = W_i \qquad (12.138)$$

where

$$a_{ii} = \sum_k (Q_{ik}\alpha_{ik} + E'_{ik}) + V_ik_i \qquad (12.139)$$

and

$$a_{ik} = Q_{ik}\beta_{ik} - E'_{ik} \qquad (12.140)$$

For boundaries where advective flow enters the system at a rate Q_{oi} with a concentration c_o,*

$$W_i' = W_i + Q_{oi}c_o \qquad (12.141)$$

---

*These formulations only apply when the system's water boundaries are rivers. For open boundaries, diffusion and weighted concentrations must also be incorporated.

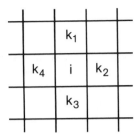

Figure 12.27   Segmentation in two dimensions.

For boundaries where advective flow leaves the section at a rate of Q_{ie},

$$a_{ii} = \sum_k [Q_{ik}\alpha_{ik} + E'_{ik}] + V_i k_i + Q_{ie} \qquad (12.142)$$

Similar to the previous analysis for one dimension, Equation 12.142, together with the appropriate boundary conditions, can be incorporated into a matrix

$$
\begin{bmatrix}
a_{11} & a_{12} & a_{13} & \cdot & \cdot & \cdot & a_{1n} \\
a_{21} & a_{22} & a_{23} & \cdot & \cdot & \cdot & a_{2n} \\
\cdot & \cdot & & & & & \cdot \\
\cdot & \cdot & & & & & \cdot \\
\cdot & \cdot & & & & & \cdot \\
a_{n1} & a_{n2} & \cdot & \cdot & \cdot & \cdot & a_{nn}
\end{bmatrix}
\begin{pmatrix}
c_1 \\ c_2 \\ \cdot \\ \cdot \\ \cdot \\ c_n
\end{pmatrix}
=
\begin{pmatrix}
W_1' \\ W_2 \\ \cdot \\ \cdot \\ \cdot \\ W_n
\end{pmatrix}
\qquad (12.143)
$$

or

$$[A](c) = (W) \qquad (12.144)$$

with a solution

$$(c) = [A]^{-1}(W). \qquad (12.145)$$

As with the previous analysis, the criterion

$$\alpha > 1 - E'/Q \qquad (12.146)$$

also applies to ensure positive results.

§ § §

Example 12.10. The lake in Figure 12.28 receives pollutant inputs that do not react ($k = 0$), but settle at a rate of 0.02 km yr^{-1}. Using the data contained in Table 12.3, calculate the system's response to the loadings. In addition, determine the improvement that would occur in segment #3 if the loading to segment #2 were reduced by 50%.

Using the convention that advection out of a segment is positive, the flows for the system are

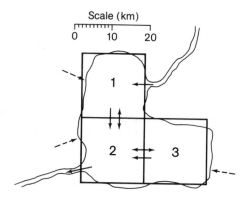

Figure 12.28 Segmentation scheme for an example of the control volume approach.

Table 12.3. Data for the Lake in Figure 12.28

Segment	A_s (km²)	z (km)	V (km³)	W (metric ton yr⁻¹)	ℓ (km)
1	280	0.0043	1.2	500	16.7
2	280	0.0043	1.2	2000	16.7
3	280	0.0043	1.2	300	16.7

Interface	Q (km³ yr⁻¹)	E (km² yr⁻¹)	A_c (km²)	Width (km)	E′ (km³ yr⁻¹)	c_o (μg ℓ⁻¹)
inlet-1	170					10
1-2	170	1500	0.072	16.7	6.5	
2-3	10	1500	0.072	16.7	6.5	
2-outlet	180					

$$Q_{10} = -170 \qquad Q_{21} = -170$$
$$Q_{12} = 170 \qquad Q_{2e} = 180$$
$$Q_{23} = -10 \qquad Q_{32} = 10$$

A first estimate of α can be determined from Equation 12.117

$$\alpha = \frac{16.7}{16.7 + 16.7} = 0.5$$

For interface 2–3, the stability criterion (Equation 12.118) is

$$\alpha > 1 - \frac{6.5}{10} = 0.35$$

Therefore, 0.5 is used since it is the larger of the two estimates. For interface 1–2, the stability criterion is

$$\alpha > 1 - \frac{6.5}{170} = 0.9618$$

Therefore, for this interface a value of 0.962 is used, resulting in the following weighting factors

$$\alpha_{12} = 0.962 \qquad \beta_{12} = 0.038$$
$$\alpha_{21} = 0.038 \qquad \beta_{21} = 0.962$$
$$\alpha_{32} = \alpha_{23} = \beta_{32} = \beta_{23} = 0.5$$

Then, Equations 12.139 through 12.142 can be used to determine the elements of the matrix as in

$$a_{11} = Q_{12}\alpha_{12} + E'_{12} + V_1 \frac{v}{z_1}$$

$$a_{22} = Q_{21}\alpha_{21} + Q_{23}\alpha_{23} + E'_{21} + E'_{23} + V_2 \frac{v}{z_2} + Q_{2e}$$

$$a_{33} = Q_{32}\alpha_{32} + E'_{32} + V_3 \frac{v}{z_3}$$

$$a_{12} = Q_{12}\beta_{12} - E'_{12}$$

$$a_{21} = Q_{21}\beta_{21} - E'_{21}$$

$$a_{23} = Q_{23}\beta_{23} - E'_{23}$$

$$a_{32} = Q_{32}\beta_{32} - E'_{32}$$

Substituting the parameter values into these equations yields the matrix:

$$\begin{bmatrix} 175.62 & -0.04 & 0 \\ -170.04 & 187.12 & -11.50 \\ 0 & -1.5 & 17.08 \end{bmatrix}$$

which can be inverted to give

$$\begin{bmatrix} 0.00570 & 0.00000 & 0.00000 \\ 0.00520 & 0.00537 & 0.00362 \\ 0.00046 & 0.00047 & 0.05887 \end{bmatrix}$$

where the elements are in $\mu g \; l^{-1}/$(metric tons yr^{-1}). The concentrations in each segment are then calculated as

$$c_1 = [500 + 170(10)]0.00570 + 2000(0.00000) + 300(0.00000) = 12.54 \; \mu g \; l^{-1}$$

$$c_2 = [500 + 170(10)]0.00520 + 2000(0.00537) + 300(0.00362) = 23.27 \; \mu g \; l^{-1}$$

$$c_3 = [500 + 170(10)]0.00046 + 2000(0.00047) + 300(0.05887) = 19.61 \; \mu g \; l^{-1}$$

The unit improvement in segment #3 due to a loading reduction in segment #2 is represented by element a_{32} of the inverted matrix $= 0.00047$. To find the total improvement due to a loading reduction of 1000 metric tons yr^{-1}, we simply multiply 0.00047 by 1000 to yield 0.47 $\mu g \; l^{-1}$.

§ § §

Example 12.11. Chapra and Sonzogni (1979) have used Thomann's approach to construct and analyze a total phosphorus budget for the Great Lakes. As depicted in Figure 12.29, the system is comprised of eleven interconnected segments. Mass balances similar to Equation 12.135 were written for each segment and solved as in Equation 12.145. The spatial system response matrix (Table 12.4) is one result of this computation.

In addition, the rates of exchange between segments were computed

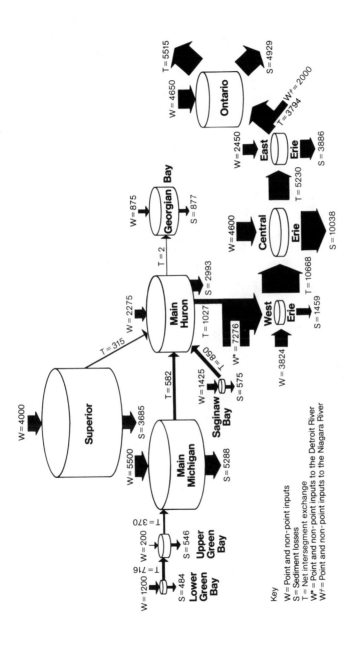

Figure 12.29 Great Lakes total phosphorus budget for the mid-1970s with major transfers shown in metric tons per year. The beakers used to represent each segment are proportional in size to the actual body of water with a 1000:1 distortion in depth; the width of the arrows is proportional to annual rate of mass transfer.

Table 12.4   Steady-State System Response Matrix for the Great Lakes Based on Mean Long-Term Flows.
[Elements are in $\mu g/1$ and correspond to the response of each segment (row) due to a loading of 1000 metric ton/yr to any other segment (column).]

Response ($\mu g/1$)	Loading										
	Superior	Lower Green Bay	Upper Green Bay	Main Michigan	Georgian Bay	Saginaw Bay	Main Huron	Western Erie	Central Erie	Eastern Erie	Ontario
Lake Superior	1.152										
Lower Green Bay	0.002	31.068	6.499	0.248	0.008	0.013	0.020				
Upper Green Bay	0.003	8.253	12.185	0.464	0.014	0.024	0.038				
Main Lake Michigan	0.008	0.427	0.631	1.293	0.040	0.066	0.107				
Georgian Bay	0.030	0.017	0.025	0.052	3.341	0.235	0.382				
Saginaw Bay	0.048	0.028	0.041	0.084	0.233	21.099	0.618				
Main Lake Huron	0.092	0.053	0.079	0.162	0.450	0.735	1.194				
Western Lake Erie	0.049	0.028	0.042	0.086	0.239	0.390	0.633	3.299	0.481	0.262	
Central Lake Erie	0.016	0.009	0.014	0.028	0.077	0.126	0.205	1.068	1.197	0.653	
Eastern Lake Erie	0.012	0.007	0.010	0.021	0.057	0.094	0.152	0.794	0.890	1.599	
Lake Ontario	0.005	0.003	0.004	0.008	0.022	0.036	0.058	0.305	0.341	0.613	2.108

and are displayed in Figure 12.29. The most striking feature of this diagram is the intense pressure on the lower Great Lakes and the impact of the Detroit River phosphorus loading. Not only does the Detroit River loading constitute the major component of the phosphorus loading to the western basin of Lake Erie, but the large water flow through the lower lakes tends to propagate its influence through the remaining basins of Lake Erie and on to Lake Ontario. This is in contrast to the upper Great Lakes (Superior, Michigan and Huron), where low flow-volume ratios tend to minimize interlake effects and, in general, a large fraction of the loading is retained by each lake.

From a management standpoint, it is useful to determine the effect of the Detroit loading on downstream segments. The spatial system response matrix (Table 12.4) provides this information. For example, the response matrix shows that a 1000 metric ton per year (mta) reduction in the annual total phosphorus load to western Lake Erie would decrease the average, whole-lake total phosphorus concentration of that basin by 3.299 μg/l. Table 12.4 also indicates that the western Erie reduction would also decrease average concentrations in central Erie, eastern Erie and Lake Ontario by 1.068, 0.794 and 0.305 μg/l, respectively. No effect would be exhibited in any of the upstream basins.

To further illustrate the use of the system response matrix, we can determine the total response of Lake Ontario and the three basins of Lake Erie to reductions of 4 thousand mta and 2.5 thousand mta in the loadings of the western and central basins of Lake Erie, respectively. The improvements can be computed using the appropriate elements of Table 12.4 as follows,

$$\Delta c_{west\ erie} = 4 \times 3.299 + 2.5 \times 0.481 = 14.4\ \mu g/l$$

$$\Delta c_{cent\ erie} = 4 \times 1.068 + 2.5 \times 1.197 = 7.3\ \mu g/l$$

$$\Delta c_{east\ erie} = 4 \times 0.794 + 2.5 \times 0.890 = 5.4\ \mu g/l$$

$$\Delta c_{ontario} = 4 \times 0.305 + 2.5 \times 0.341 = 2.1\ \mu g/l$$

Note that the load reduction in central Erie has an effect on the concentration of western Erie even though the latter segment is "upstream." This is due to the effect of diffusive transport across the open boundaries between the segments.

The value of the spatial response matrix in analyzing coupled systems is great. In particular, it provides a means for taking a global rather than a local perspective regarding pollution problems.

§ § §

12.4 GENERAL COMMENTS

The models developed in this chapter either use very simple representations of water motion or assume that the modeler has access to adequate information regarding transport. It must be stressed that this is usually not a trivial matter and the analyst may have to obtain measurements and/or use additional mathematical models to characterize water movements. In either case, substantial expense and/or expertise may be required. For additional details on the topic of hydrodynamic modeling, the reader is referred to Simons' (1980) review and critique.

Another simplification in the foregoing derivations is the use of a single variable to characterize the pollutant. This is done because the primary reason for horizontal gradients in lakes is that waste inputs enter the system in concentrated form at the periphery. Once in the lake, the diffusive and advective motion of the water transports the matter. Thus, sizeable gradients can occur even for nonreactive substances, such as chloride. Therefore, the primary features of the horizontal processes could be elucidated without introducing complicated reaction kinetics or multiple-species pollutants. It must be noted, however, that biological and chemical partitioning of matter can accentuate these gradients and is relevant to their modeling. This is particularly true for those pollutants, such as certain nutrients and toxic substances, that associate strongly with particulate matter. For these problem contexts, multicomponent models are needed for adequate characterization. Such models are described in Chapters 14 and 15 and could be used in conjunction with the computational frameworks described in the present chapter to simulate such pollutants (see, for example, Section 14.4.2).

Finally, it must be noted that error analysis is largely ignored in this chapter. This omission is representative of the state of the art in the modeling of horizontal spatial processes in lakes. Model complexity and problems with parameter estimation have clearly discouraged efforts in this area. Nonetheless, methods (e.g., Monte Carlo simulation) do exist that could be employed to estimate the effect of the errors in model terms; errors in the equations of these models pose a more difficult problem, however. In Chapter 14 we return to this topic and discuss some of the recent efforts in error analysis for aquatic ecosystem models.

REFERENCES

Beeton, A. M., J. Gannon, P. Meier and W. J. Weber, Jr. 1980. "Factors Affecting the Water Quality of the Ford Lake-Belleville Lake System," Michigan Department of Natural Resources.

Boyce, F. M. 1974. "Some Aspects of Great Lakes Physics of Importance to Biological and Chemical Processes," *J. Fish. Res. Bd. Can.* 31:689-730.

Boyce, F. M., and P. F. Hamblin. 1975. "A Simple Diffusion Model of the Mean Field Distribution of Soluble Materials in the Great Lakes," *Limnol. Oceanogr.* 20(4):511-517.

Carnahan, B., H. A. Luther and J. O. Wilkes. 1969. *Applied Numerical Methods* (New York: John Wiley and Sons, Inc.).

Carslaw, H. S., and J. C. Jaeger. 1959. *Conduction of Heat in Solids.* 2nd ed. (London: Oxford University Press).

Chapra, S. C. 1979. "Applying Phosphorus Loading Models to Embayments," *Limnol. Oceanogr.* 24(1):163-168.

Chapra, S. C. and W. C. Sonzogni. 1979. "Great Lakes Total Phosphorus Budget for the mid 1970's," *J. Water Poll. Control Fed.* 51:2524-2533.

Crank, J. 1975. *The Mathematics of Diffusion.* 2nd ed. (London: Oxford University Press).

Csanady, G. T. 1973. *Turbulent Diffusion in the Environment* (Dordrecht, Holland: D. Reidel Publishing Co.).

Di Toro, D. M. 1972. "Line Source Distribution in Two Dimensions: Applications to Water Quality," *Water Resour. Res.* 8(6):1541-1546.

Fischer, H. B., E. J. List, R. C. Y. Koh, J. Imberger and N. H. Brooks. 1979. *Mixing in Inland and Coastal Waters* (New York: Academic Press).

Hutchinson, G. E. 1957. *A Treatise on Limnology, Volume 1, Geography, Physics and Chemistry.* (New York, N.Y.: John Wiley and Sons, Inc.), 1015 pp.

Mortimer, C. H. 1974. "Lake Hydrodynamics," *Mitt. Internat. Verein. Limnol.* 20:124-197.

Murthy, C. R. 1976."Horizontal Diffusion Characteristics in Lake Ontario," *J. Phys. Oceanogr.* 6:76-84.

O'Connor, D. J. 1962. "The Bacterial Distribution in a Lake in the Vicinity of a River Discharge," in *Proceedings of the 2nd Purdue Industrial Waste Conference.*

O'Connor, D. J. 1966. "An Analysis of the Dissolved Oxygen Distribution in the East River," *J. Water Poll. Control Fed.* 38(121):1813-1830.

Okubo, A. 1971."Oceanic Diffusion Diagrams,"*Deep-Sea Res.* 18:789-802.

Pielou, E. C. 1969. *An Introduction to Mathematical Ecology* (New York, N.Y.: Wiley-Interscience), 286 pp.

Richardson, L. F. 1926. "Atmospheric Diffusion Shown on a Distance-Neighborhood Graph," *Proc. Roy. Soc., (A),* 110:709-727.

Roache, P. J. 1972. *Computational Fluid Dynamics* (Albuquerque, N.M.: Hermosa Publishers).

Simons, T. J. 1980. "Circulation Models of Lakes and Inland Seas," Canada Centre for Inland Water, Bulletin 203.

Taylor, G. I. 1953. "Dispersion of Soluble Matter in Solvent Flowing Slowly Through a Tube," *Proc. R. Soc. London Ser. A* 219:186–203.

Thomann, R. V. 1963. "Mathematical Model for Dissolved Oxygen," *J. Sanit. Eng. Div. ASCE* 89(SA5):1–30.

Thomann, R. V. 1972. *Systems Analysis and Water Quality Management* (New York: McGraw-Hill), Chapter 3.

Water Resources Engineers. 1969. "Mathematical Models for the Prediction of Thermal Energy Changes in Impoundments," Proj. No. 16130EXT12/69, U.S. Environmental Protection Agency, Washington, D.C.

CHAPTER 13

MODELS OF VERTICAL ASPECTS
OF LAKE WATER QUALITY

As discussed in the last chapter, the primary reason for horizontal gradients in lakes is the interplay between concentrated waste inputs and water movements. Thus, although biological and chemical processes are relevant to modeling these gradients, essential features of their dynamics can be simulated with single-species models. In contrast, because of the effect of gravity on sedimentation, the creation of vertical gradients is greatly influenced by the exchange of matter between settleable and non-settleable forms. Therefore, this chapter focuses on models that discriminate between the solid and dissolved forms of contaminants. These models must be developed for two distinct regions with markedly different physical regimes: the water column and the sediments. The water column is essentially a dilute aqueous solution where thermal stratification plays a major role in dictating pollutant dynamics; the sediments, on the other hand, have a high concentration of solid matter. The different computational frameworks needed to characterize these systems and approaches to calculate the coupled response of the water column and sediments are reviewed and developed.

13.1 SIMULATION OF WATER COLUMN DYNAMICS

On a seasonal time scale, the creation of vertical gradients in the water column is inextricably tied to a lake's biology and chemistry. This is due to the profound effect of thermal stratification on the cycling and partitioning of matter between components of the ecosystem. Because of the importance of temperature, the first part of this section is devoted to thermal modeling. This is followed by descriptions of a number of vertical mass balance models.

13.1.1 Temperature Modeling

A lake's vertical thermal regime has dual significance to the water quality modeler. As mentioned in Chapter 10, temperature has direct importance because it influences the rates of chemical and biochemical reactions. However, it has additional significance as a tracer of mass transport in the water column. In fact, heat balances are a primary tool for estimating mixing rates in the vertical dimension. Before describing heat balance models, we will briefly discuss the seasonal temperature changes in the water column of a lake.

Thermal Regimes in Temperate Lakes

Hutchinson (1957) defines temperate lakes as those "with surface temperature above 4°C in winter, thermal gradients large, two circulation periods in spring and late autumn." Although other lake types can be severely polluted,* this discussion focuses on temperate lakes because many of the world's developed areas are in temperate climates and, consequently, many lakes in these climates have been subject to pollution. Thus, most engineering models have been developed for temperate systems.

The thermal regime of temperate lakes is primarily the result of the interplay of two processes: (1) heat and momentum transfer across the lake's surface and (2) the force of gravity acting on density differences within the lake. Depending on the season of the year, heat transfer tends to either raise or lower the temperature at the lake's surface as a consequence of a number of factors, including the magnitude of solar radiation, air temperature, relative humidity, wind speed and cloud cover. Winds blowing over the lake's surface tend to mix the surface waters and transfer heat and momentum down through the water column. The extent of this mixing is, in turn, inhibited by buoyancy (and sometimes rotational) effects. These relate to the fact that the density of water varies over the range of temperatures encountered in lakes (Figure 13.1a). Therefore, denser waters accumulate at the lake's bottom and are overlaid with lighter waters.

---

*For example, lakes that never mix (*amictic*) or mix incompletely (*meromictic*) can be extremely sensitive to pollutant inputs. In addition, because of growing urbanization and industrialization in the world's tropical regions, many nontemperate lakes are being subjected to severe water quality stress. Although some of the approaches in this section might serve as a starting point for modeling these systems, additional research is needed on development of computational frameworks for nontemperate lakes.

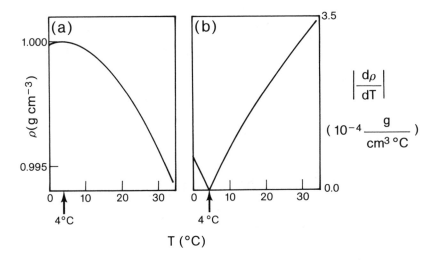

T (°C)

Figure 13.1 Plots of (a) density (g cm^{-3}) and (b) rate of change of density per rate of change of temperature (g cm^{-3} °C^{-1}) versus temperature (°C). Note that the maximum density of water occurs at 4°C.

For example, in Lake Ontario in August (Figure 13.2), surface waters of 18°C with a density of 0.9986 g cm^{-3} overlay deep waters of 4°C with a density of 1.0000 g cm^{-3}. Although these density differences may seem small, considerable work must be expended to mix the entire column (i.e., lift the heavier bottom waters against the force of gravity in order to mix them with the lighter surface waters). During periods of no net heat loss from the surface waters to the atmosphere, the energy to do this work comes from the wind. The result is that buoyancy works against and mitigates wind-induced turbulence. The interplay between these factors can be expressed quantitatively by a dimensionless parameter, the *Richardson number,* that represents the ratio of buoyancy to shear forces as in*

---

*Note that the Richardson number can be formulated in a number of ways. Equation 13.1, which is called the *gradient Richardson number,* can be used to characterize stability at any point in the water column. Another form that is also relevant to the subsequent discussion is the "bulk Richardson number" that characterizes stability of the water column as a whole

$$R_{i,o} = (gL)/(u^2)$$

where L and u are the length and velocity scales imposed by the boundary conditions. See Turner (1973) for a discussion of the various forms and their interpretations.

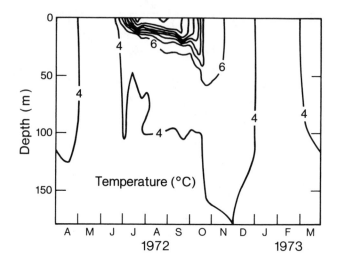

Figure 13.2   Depth-time diagram of isotherms (°C) at a mid-lake station in Lake Ontario, 1972–1973.

$$R_i = \frac{\text{buoyancy}}{\text{shear}} = \frac{g/\rho\,(\partial\rho/\partial z)}{(\partial u/\partial z)^2} \tag{13.1}$$

where z = depth [L], which is positive in the downward direction
  g = the acceleration due to gravity [L T^{-2}]
  ρ = the density of the fluid [ML^{-3}]
  $\partial\rho/\partial z$ = the gradient of density with depth [ML^{-4}]
  $\partial u/\partial z$ = the gradient of horizontal velocity with depth [T^{-1}] or the shear

If R_i is significantly greater than a critical level ($\sim$0.25), a stable flow regime results. If R_i is significantly less than 0.25, connoting strong shear relative to stratification, then shear-induced turbulence is generated. The evolution of turbulent mixing in a stratified fluid is depicted graphically in Figure 13.3. Although this idealized scenario might seem far removed from the natural situation, it can serve as a conceptual basis for discussing the development and degradation of thermal stratification in an actual lake.

Figure 13.2 depicts the seasonal changes in the vertical temperature distribution of Lake Ontario. Although this lake is very deep, its thermal regime has many of the characteristic features of smaller temperate lakes. Some time after the disappearance of any ice cover in spring, temperatures throughout the water column rise to, or within a few degrees of, the maximum density of water (4°C). At this temperature,

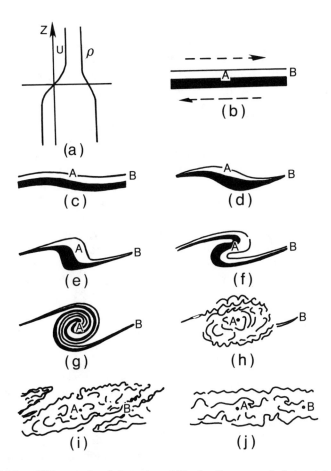

Figure 13.3 The growth of shear instability leading to turbulent mixing in a stratified fluid, subject to shear, with the velocity and density distribution shown in (a). A and B are fixed points, the arrows indicate direction of flow, and the lines represent isopycnals (surfaces of equal density). The gradient Richardson number decreases from (b) through (j) as turbulence is induced. (Redrawn from Mortimer 1975).

heating or cooling of the lake's surface results in very small density differences (Figure 13.1b) and, consequently, only a small amount of wind stress is required to keep the water column well-mixed. In terms of the Richardson number, buoyancy forces (the numerator) are small and, therefore, shear forces (the denominator) of small magnitude are sufficient to reduce R_i below the critical level.

As spring progresses, solar radiation increases, air temperatures rise, and thermal stratification will be established in the near surface waters. However, density gradients are neither large enough nor deep enough to prevent mixing of the water column by major storms.

At the end of spring and the beginning of summer, surface heating increases to the point that mixing is confined to an upper layer called the *epilimnion*. In terms of the bulk Richardson number, the fluid has reached the point where the density gradient is sharp enough that even large storms do not reduce R_i below the stability criterion. At this stage, the lake is said to be stably stratified. The attainment of persistent stratification in a lake leads to the existence of three regimes: the upper and lower (i.e., the *hypolimnion*) layers separated by a narrow region of sharp temperature change—the *thermocline* or *metalimnion*.*

During midsummer, the net daily heat flux at the surface is low and, although the thermocline deepens gradually, the density gradient between the epi- and the hypolimnion remains strong and stable. Although transport of heat and energy across the thermocline occurs, it is at a low level and exchange between the upper and lower layers is at a minimum.

In late summer and fall, loss of heat due largely to falling air temperatures results in a net heat loss from the lake. As surface waters cool, they become more dense than underlying epilimnetic water. Since this is an unstable situation, strong vertical mixing called *convection* occurs. Together with increased winds during fall, the process erodes the metalimnion from above, giving the impression of a sinking thermocline. As the lake cools further, a point is reached at which the deepened surface layer becomes denser than the bottom layer and complete mixing of the column occurs. This episode is called *fall overturn*.

The lake continues to be well-mixed and to lose heat as temperatures drop in winter. In some cases, the surface water cools below 4°C and an inverse stratification results owing to the low density of water below 4°C (Figure 13.1a).

In summary, the seasonal changes in a temperate lake can be idealized in both time and space. Temporally, the cycle consists of two stages: a summer period of strong stratification and a nonstratified period of intense vertical mixing. Spatially, the summer stratified period can be treated as consisting of two layers separated by an interface of minimal

---

*The terms thermocline and metalimnion often are used interchangeably to designate the layer of sharp temperature change. The thermocline also is considered to be the plane passing through the point of maximum decrease in temperature with depth.

vertical mixing. These idealizations form the basis of some efforts to develop engineering models of vertical heat and mass distribution in temperate lakes.

Estimation of Vertical Transport Using Heat Balances

In Section 12.2.1 we showed how gradients of conservative substances, such as chloride, could be used to estimate horizontal diffusion rates. Because of the large seasonal temperature gradients in temperate lakes, heat balances serve an analogous role in vertical models. This implies that water motion has an identical effect on determining heat and mass transport in the water column. Although this analogy does not hold strictly for large particles, it is a good first approximation for most pollutants.

Before discussing heat budgets, we should mention some basic concepts related to their development. *Heat* is a form of energy. *Temperature* is a measure of the amount of heat energy per unit weight of a substance. The two are related by

$$T_a = \frac{H}{\rho CV} \tag{13.2}$$

where T_a = absolute temperature [°K]
   H = the heat energy [cal]
   ρ = the density of the substance [g cm^{-3}]
   V = volume [cm^3]
   C = the heat capacity per unit mass of the substance*
      [cal g^{-1} °K^{-1} (or °C^{-1})]

Because we are dealing with dilute aqueous solutions, the density and heat capacity of water are approximately unity in cgs units and Equation 13.2 can be expressed as

$$T_a \cong \frac{H}{V} \tag{13.3}$$

Recall that in our discussion of Fickian diffusion (Section 12.1.1), we mentioned that heat and temperature are analogous to mass and concen-

---

*The term "specific heat" often is used interchangeably with heat capacity. Although this is not strictly correct, for our purposes we can consider them synonymous.

tration.* Just as concentration is defined as mass per unit volume, Equation 13.3 indicates that, for our purposes, temperature represents heat per unit volume.

We can now write a heat budget in a similar fashion to the mass balance equations derived previously. Consider the simplest case of a temperate lake during the midsummer stratified period. At this time (Figure 13.2), the temperatures in the epi- and hypolimnion are fairly uniform, with the major gradient occurring at the thermocline. Although the thermocline deepens during this period, we assume that the rate of descent is, at most, very gradual. A simple model for this case consists of two well-mixed layers of constant thickness separated by an interface across which diffusive transport occurs. Therefore, the metalimnion is treated as an interface rather than as a distinct region.

With the same approach that we developed previously for embayments (Section 12.2.1), a heat balance for the well-mixed epilimnion can be written as

$$\rho C V_e \frac{dT_{a,e}}{dt} = S + \rho C v_t A_t (T_{a,h} - T_{a,e}) \qquad (13.4)$$

(accumulation)   (sources   (diffusion)
                or sinks)

where V_e = the volume of the epilimnion $[cm^3]$
    $T_{a,e}$ and $T_{a,h}$ = the absolute temperatures of the epi- and hypolimnion $[°K]$, respectively
           t = time [days]
          S = the input (+) or output (−) of heat through the lake's surface $[cal\ d^{-1}]$
         v_t = the vertical heat exchange coefficient across the thermocline $[cm\ d^{-1}]^\dagger$
         A_t = the surface area of the thermocline $[cm^2]$

Since temperatures are typically measured in °C rather than °K, Equation 13.4 can be rewritten as

---

*Quantities such as mass or heat that depend on the size of the system being modeled are usually referred to as *extensive* properties. Quantities such as concentration or temperature that represent properties normalized to system size (e.g., to volume) are called *intensive* quantities.

† It should be noted that exchange across the thermocline also can be parameterized as a vertical diffusion coefficient, E_t, where E_t has units of $cm^2\ d^{-1}$ and is related to the heat exchange coefficient by $v_t = E_t/z_t$ where z_t is the thermocline thickness (cm). This alternative expression is useful in comparing the magnitude of vertical mixing with other processes that are characterized as turbulent processes. However, it has the disadvantage that it requires specification of the thermocline thickness in order to parameterize vertical mixing.

$$V_e \frac{d}{dt}(T_e + 273) = \frac{S}{\rho C} + v_t A_t [(T_h + 273) - (T_e + 273)] \qquad (13.5)$$

where T_e and T_h are temperatures in °C. Note, $T_a = T + 273$. Since the derivative of a constant is zero and the difference between two temperatures measured in °K is the same as the difference measured in °C, Equation 13.5 can be simplifed further to yield

$$V_e \frac{dT_e}{dt} = \frac{S}{\rho C} + v_t A_t (T_h - T_e) \qquad (13.6)$$

In a similar fashion, a hypolimnion balance can be developed,

$$V_h \frac{dT_h}{dt} = v_t A_t (T_e - T_h) \qquad (13.7)$$

The source term represents a variety of mechanisms governing heat transfer across the air-water interface, including solar and atmospheric radiation and evaporation and conduction heat losses. Equations 13.6 and 13.7 imply that these mechanisms only affect the epilimnion. This is a good approximation for most lakes, but it should be noted that radiation in clear lakes can add heat directly to the hypolimnion. In addition, heat transfer with the sediments is not included in the present approach. Although this is a valid approximation for deep lakes, it cannot be disregarded in shallower systems. Hutchinson (1957) summarizes information on the heat budgets of lake sediments.

The model can be used in a number of ways. For example, during the summer stratified period, the hypolimnetic temperature rises at a slow rate. If an average temperature is used to characterize the epilimnion during this period, Equation 13.7 becomes

$$\frac{dT_h}{dt} + \frac{v_t A_t}{V_h} T_h = \frac{v_t A_t}{V_h} \bar{T}_e \qquad (13.8)$$

where $\bar{T}_e$ designates that the epilimnion temperature is assumed to be at a constant level. Equation 13.8 is identical in form to the completely mixed lake model with step input described previously (Section 11.2.1). If the hypolimnion temperature at the beginning of the summer stratified period is $T_{h,i}$, Equation 13.8 can be solved for

$$T_h = T_{h,i} \exp\left(-\frac{v_t A_t}{V_h} t\right) + \bar{T}_e \left[1 - \exp\left(-\frac{v_t A_t}{V_h} t\right)\right] \qquad (13.9)$$

Equation 13.9 can then be arranged to estimate the heat exchange coefficient across the thermocline (Chapra 1980):

$$v_t = \frac{V_h}{A_t t_s} \ln \frac{T_{h,i} - \bar{T}_e}{T_{h,s} - \bar{T}_e} \tag{13.10}$$

where t_s is the time after the onset of stratification at which the hypolimnion temperature, $T_{h,s}$, is measured.

§ § §

Example 13.1. Lake Ontario is strongly stratified from July through September. During this time, the thermocline is at a depth of approximately 15 m. The average epilimnetic temperature over the period is 17.61°C and the surface area of the thermocline is approximately $18,500 \times 10^6$ m^2. The temperature in the hypolimnion (volume = 1380×10^9 m^3) rises from 4.35°C in mid-July to 5.12°C in mid-September (Table 13.1). Use Equation 13.10 to estimate the heat exchange coefficient across the thermocline. In addition, compute the vertical diffusion coefficient if $z_t = 7$ m.

$$v_t = \frac{(1380 \times 10^9)}{18,500 \times 10^6 (60)} \ln \frac{4.35 - 17.61}{5.12 - 17.61} = 0.0744 \text{ m d}^{-1}$$

$$E_t = 0.0744(7)(10^4) \div (86,400) = 0.06 \text{ cm}^2 \sec^{-1}$$

This estimate can then be used to compute mass transfer of substances across the thermocline. For example, in Lake Ontario during the summer the concentrations of soluble reactive phosphorus in the epi- and the hypolimnion are approximately 3.1 and 8.6 mg m^{-3}, respectively. The mass transfer from the hypo- to the epilimnion can be estimated by

$$W_{diffusion} = v_t A_t (p_{s,h} - p_{s,e})$$

where $p_{s,h}$ and $p_{s,e}$ are the soluble reactive phosphorus concentrations in the epi- and the hypolimnion, respectively. Using the appropriate values,

$$W_{diffusion} = 0.0744 (18500 \times 10^6)(8.6 - 3.1)$$

or

$$W_{diffusion} = 7.57 \times 10^9 \text{ mg d}^{-1} = 2762 \text{ mta}$$

Table 13.1   Average Monthly Temperature Data for Surface (0–15 m) and Bottom (15–200 m) Layers of Lake Ontario for the Period from 1967–1972 (Computed estimates of the thermocline diffusion coefficient and the surface heat transfer and flux are also included.)

	Epilimnetic Temperature (°C)	Hypolimnetic Temperature (°C)	Thermocline		Surface	
			Heat Transfer Coefficient (m d^{-1})	Diffusion Coefficient[a] (cm^2 sec^{-1})	Heat Transfer (10^{18} cal d^{-1})	Heat Flux (cal cm^{-2} d^{-1})
Dec.	5.47	5.18			-0.106	-557.2
Jan.	3.18	3.30	32.9	26.7	-0.079	-416.8
Feb.	0.89	2.00	1.41	1.14	0.007	39.1
Mar.	1.55	2.04	-0.101	-0.082	0.004	22.7
Apr.	2.06	2.04	72.1	58.4	0.069	363.3
May	3.91	3.20	3.52	2.85	0.069	426.4
June	8.86	4.05	0.297	0.241	0.081	372.1
July	15.58	4.35	0.062	0.050	0.071	195.7
Aug.	18.56	4.61	0.069	0.056	0.037	86.9
Sept.	17.74	5.12	0.102	0.082	0.017	-161.5

Table 13.1,   continued

		Thermocline		Surface	
Epilimnetic Temperature (°C)	Hypolimnetic Temperature (°C)	Heat Transfer Coefficient (m d^{-1})	Diffusion Coefficient[a] (cm^2 sec^{-1})	Heat Transfer (10^{18} cal d^{-1})	Heat Flux (cal cm^{-2} d^{-1})
Oct.	11.29	5.64	0.123	0.100		
Nov.	7.92	5.68	-0.255	-0.207	-0.027	-140.5
Dec.	5.47	5.18	-10.2	-8.27	-0.044	-230.2
Jan.	3.18	3.30			-0.106	-557.2

[a] Assuming a metalimnion thickness of 7 m.

This estimate can be put into perspective by comparing it to the 12,000 metric tons per year (mta) of total phosphorus that enters the lake from external sources. The fact that diffusive transport to the epilimnion across the thermocline amounts to about 23% of the external load suggests its relative importance in regulating surface production during the growing season.

§ § §

Snodgrass (1974) has summarized estimates of E_t for a number of lakes. The values are positively correlated with mean depth (Figure 13.4) and range over several orders of magnitude from 0.003 to 2.4 cm^2 sec^{-1}. With knowledge of the approximate thickness of the metalimnion, this plot can be used to make a first estimate of the heat exchange coefficient for a lake.

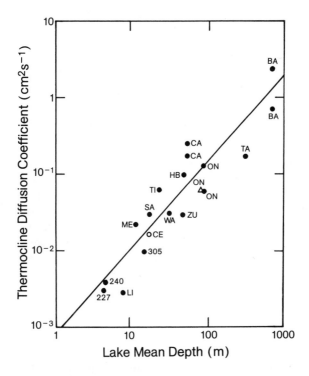

Figure 13.4   Thermocline diffusion coefficient (cm^2 sec^{-1}) versus lake mean depth for a number of temperate lakes. Redrawn from Snodgrass (1974) along with new data from Lake Ontario (Δ) and the central basin of Lake Erie (O).

Aside from estimates during summer stratification, the model can also be used to compute diffusion coefficients throughout the year. Equation 13.7 can be rearranged for this purpose to yield

$$v_t = \frac{V_h(dT_h/dt)}{A_t(T_e - T_h)} \tag{13.11}$$

If the measured temperatures are equally spaced,* a centered-difference approximation can be used to estimate the first derivative

$$\left.\frac{dT_h}{dt}\right|^n = \frac{T_h^{n+1} - T_h^{n-1}}{2\Delta t} \tag{13.12}$$

where Δt is the time interval between measurements. Equations 13.11 and 13.12 can be combined,

$$v_t = \frac{V_h}{2A_t\Delta t} \frac{T_h^{n+1} - T_h^{n-1}}{T_e^n - T_h^n} \tag{13.13}$$

Equation 13.6 can also be used to estimate heat transfer, as in

$$v_t = \frac{V_e \dfrac{T_e^{n+1} - T_e^{n-1}}{2\Delta t} - \dfrac{S}{\rho C}}{A_t(T_h^n - T_e^n)} \tag{13.13a}$$

Note that the use of Equation 13.13a to compute v_t requires an estimate of S. As discussed on page 156, this can be done by back calculation from changes in the lake's heat content or by using models based on meteorological variables and processes. Although both Equations 13.13 and 13.13a yield similar results if temperatures are measured with sufficient accuracy, Equation 13.13a is preferable when measurement error is substantial. Because the temporal rate of change of hypolimnetic temperature is generally much smaller than of the epilimnion, Equation 13.13 is more sensitive in this regard.

§ § §

Example 13.2. Mean monthly temperatures for Lake Ontario for the period from 1967 through 1972 are compiled in Figure 13.5a and Table

---

*For unequally spaced data, a polynomial can be fit to the measurements (Carnahan et al. 1969) and differentiated to estimate the derivative.

13.1. Using Equation 13.13, estimate the thermocline diffusion coefficient over the annual cycle. The hypolimnetic volume is 1380×10^{15} cm^3 and the area and thickness of the thermocline are 18500×10^{10} cm^2 and 700 cm, respectively.

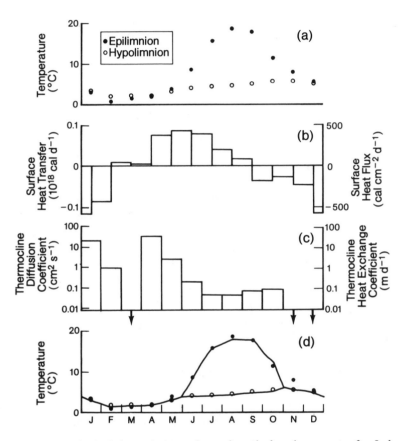

Figure 13.5 Plots of thermal properties and vertical exchange rates for Lake Ontario versus time of year. (a) mean monthly epilimnetic and hypolimnetic temperatures for 1967 from Thomann and Segna (1980), (b) thermocline heat transfer and diffusion coefficients, (c) surface heat transfer and flux and (d) results of simulation of temperature changes using a two-layer heat budget model.

For mid-January, the epi- and hypolimnetic temperatures are 3.18°C and 3.30°C, respectively. The hypolimnetic temperatures in the preceding (December) and following (February) months are 5.18°C and 2.00°C, respectively. The time interval between the measurements is a month, or approximately 30 days.

$$v_t = \frac{(1380 \times 10^{15})}{2(18,500 \times 10^{10})30} \frac{(2.00 - 5.18)}{(3.18 - 3.30)} = 3294.6 \text{ cm d}^{-1}$$

$$E_t = 3,294.6\,(700) = 2.31 \times 10^6 \text{ cm}^2\,\text{d}^{-1} = 26.7 \text{ cm}^2\,\text{sec}^{-1}$$

The computation can be repeated for the other months. The results are compiled in Table 13.1 and plotted in Figure 13.5c.

§ § §

Example 13.2 and Figure 13.5c illustrate features of vertical mixing in Lake Ontario, as well as some limitations of the two-layer, heat exchange approach. Values of the heat transfer coefficients during the stratified period are on the order of the mean summer estimate of 0.0744 m d^{-1} calculated previously in Example 13.1. Heat exchange coefficients for the nonstratified period are much higher (on the order of 10 m d^{-1}), suggesting much higher mixing rates. In addition, for several months (March, November and December), negative diffusion coefficients have been computed. Mathematically, this occurs because during these intervals, the hypolimnion temperature is changing in a manner contrary to what would be expected given the thermal gradient between the surface and bottom waters. For example, the gradient in November suggests a downward transfer of heat, i.e., the temperature of the epilimnion is higher than that of the hypolimnion. However, the hypolimnion temperature during this period is dropping and the combination leads to a negative result in Equation 13.13. Beyond the mathematical explanation, there are physical reasons for such a result. As noted previously, fall cooling is marked by convective mixing that erodes and abruptly lowers the thermocline. A model using a constant layer thickness and diffusive transport is obviously inadequate to simulate this situation. The same is true of periods of intense mixing, such as spring overturn, when the epi- and hypolimnion temperatures are very close. In such cases, a high degree of uncertainty is introduced into an estimate of v_t obtained from Equation 13.13. For these periods, the numerical value of the exchange coefficient becomes meaningless and can only be taken to imply that vertical mixing is intense. In addition, the assumptions of constant thermocline depth and thickness break down for the nonstratified period. As in Figure 13.2 the gradients, if they exist at all, are deeper, more elongated, and more variable than in the summer.

The practical significance of the foregoing is that it leads to the use of a completely mixed vertical model to characterize the winter period and a constant two-layer approach for the summer. Although elaborate models are available for simulating transport and structure during the stratified period, the added detail is usually not justifiable, considering the level of the constructs used to characterize the biology and chemistry in most engineering models. As stated in Chapter 10, the time, space and kinetic scales of a problem are interrelated. As a corollary, it is pointless to develop one aspect of the model to a high degree while other facets are at a low level.

Therefore, for most of the vertical models in this book, a two-layer, two-season segmentation scheme is employed. For summer, the constant heat exchange coefficient method, as in Equation 13.10 and Example 13.1, is used. For winter, the approach is to maintain the two-layer scheme, but use a large enough heat exchange coefficient to ensure complete mixing over the time scale of interest. The magnitude of the winter exchange coefficient can be estimated by trial and error or computed on the basis of the model equations.*

The latter approach is simplified for Lake Ontario by the fact that the epilimnion is much smaller than the hypolimnion. Therefore, the time required for the surface layer to reach a prescribed fraction of a new steady state following a change can be used to determine the necessary diffusion rate. To do this, the heat balance for the epilimnion is written without sources as

$$\frac{dT_e}{dt} + \frac{v_t A_t}{V_e} T_e = \frac{v_t A_t}{V_e} T_h \qquad (13.14)$$

The time to reach 90% of a new steady state for this model (with constant T_h) can be written as (Equation 11.58).

$$t_{90} = \frac{2.3 \, V_e}{v_t A_t} \qquad (13.15)$$

Equation 13.15 can then be solved for the exchange coefficient needed to effect the 90% mixing,

$$v_t \cong \frac{2.3 \, V_e}{A_t t_{90}} \qquad (13.16)$$

---

*A third alternative is to use a single well-mixed volume to model the lake during winter.

§ § §

Example 13.3. If the time scale of interest for Lake Ontario is a day, compute the heat transfer coefficient needed to give complete mixing of the water column. The volume of the epilimnion is 254×10^{15} cm^3. Using Equation 13.16,

$$v_t = \frac{2.3\,(254 \times 10^{15})}{18,500 \times 10^{10}(1)} \cong 3,158 \text{ cm d}^{-1}$$

Note that this value is on the same order as the heat exchange coefficients computed for the nonstratified period in Example 13.2.

§ § §

In order to use Equations 13.6 and 13.7 for calculating the seasonal heat budget, estimates of the sources and sinks of heat are required. One way to obtain these values is to use theoretical and empirical models of air-water heat transfer processes that have been developed for this purpose. These models compute heat flux across the air-water interface as a function of time of year, latitude, meteorological conditions, etc. Although this approach represents a valid option, it requires large amounts of data and fairly elaborate computations. [A report by the Tennessee Valley Authority (1972) provides a good review of available methods.]

A simpler alternative, adequate for many engineering purposes, is to back-calculate the net heat exchange on the basis of temperature changes within the lake. This method is convenient because lake temperature measurements usually are far simpler to obtain than are the meteorological data needed for semitheoretical heat transfer models.

The back-calculation procedure can be developed by adding Equations 13.6 and 13.7 to yield

$$V_e \frac{dT_e}{dt} + V_h \frac{dT_h}{dt} = \frac{S}{\rho C} \qquad (13.17)$$

The first derivatives of temperature can be estimated by simple linear interpolation between temperature readings, and Equation 13.17 can be rearranged to give

$$S_{n,n+1} = \rho C \, \frac{V_e\,(T_e^{n+1} - T_e^n) + V_h\,(T_h^{n+1} - T_h^n)}{t_{n+1} - t_n} \qquad (13.18)$$

where $S_{n,n+1}$ is the net rate of energy transfer over the time period from t_n to t_{n+1} [cal d^{-1}].

§ § §

Example 13.4. Using Equation 13.18 and the data in Table 13.1, estimate the net heat transfer and flux into Lake Ontario over the annual cycle. For mid-January (n) to mid-February (n + 1), the epilimnetic temperature dropped from 3.18°C to 0.89°C and the hypolimnetic temperature dropped from 3.3°C to 2.0°C. The epi- and hypolimnion volumes are approximately 254×10^{15} cm^3 and 1380×10^{15} cm^3. The density and heat capacity of water are approximately 1.0 g cm^{-3} and 1.0 cal g^{-1} °C^{-1}. Substituting these values into Equation 13.18 gives

$$S_{J,F} = 1.0(1.0) \left[\frac{254 \times 10^{15}(0.89 - 3.18) + 1380 \times 10^{15}(2.0 - 3.3)}{30} \right]$$

$$S_{J,F} = -0.079 \times 10^{18} \text{ cal d}^{-1}$$

The flux can be computed by dividing the heat transfer rate by the lake's surface area ($19,000 \times 10^{10}$ cm^2),

$$J_{J,F} = -416.8 \text{ cal cm}^{-2}\text{d}^{-1}$$

This computation can be repeated for the other monthly intervals and is plotted on Fig. 13.5b and summarized in Table 13.1. According to this plot, the maximum heat input is in late spring and early summer and the maximum output is in winter. The transfer in mid- and late summer is close to zero.

§ § §

Example 13.5. Using the results of Examples 13.1 (v_t for summer = 0.0744 m d^{-1}), 13.3 (v_t for winter = 31.6 m d^{-1}), and 13.4 (surface heat transfer), compute the epi- and hypolimnion temperatures over the annual cycle with Equations 13.6 and 13.7.

Examination of Figures 13.2 and 13.5 leads to the specification of the summer period as extending from the beginning of June to the middle of October. A numerical method can be used to integrate Equations 13.6 and 13.7, with the results displayed in Figure 13.5d. The computation and data agree well, with the exception of the fall cooling period.

§ § §

Although the foregoing approach is adequate for many engineering applications, a number of refinements are possible. Where adequate temperature measurements are available, the simplest refinement is to add additional layers. For example, Simons and Lam (1980), and Canada Centre for Inland Waters (1979), added a third well-mixed layer at the top of the hypolimnion (extending from 20 to 40 m) in an effort to account in part for the sinking thermocline during the fall cooling period. As depicted in Figure 13.6, the heat exchange coefficient for the interface at 40 m remains at a low level in mid-October and early November, but the coefficient at 20 m increases markedly at the same time. Thus, the well-mixed surface layer increases from 20 to 40 m deep during this fall cooling period. Simons and Lam's three-layer segmentation scheme also results in a more adequate characterization of mixing during winter inverse stratification when the temperature gradient is deeper and more gradual than in summer.

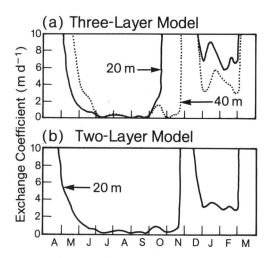

Figure 13.6   Heat exchange coefficients computed by Simons and Lam (1980) using (a) a three-layer and (b) a two-layer heat budget model.

Other possible variations on the present approach include the treatment of the metalimnion as a third layer or the use of a multilayer segmentation scheme to characterize the vertical dimension. The latter approach results in a more continuous profile of diffusion rates with a minimum value in the region of the thermocline (Figure 13.7).

One alternative to adding more segments is to allow the layer thick-

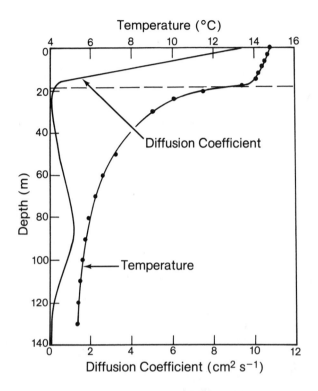

Figure 13.7   Plots of temperature and vertical diffusion coefficient versus depth
for Lake Tahoe. Redrawn from Orlob and Selna (1970). Note the minimum
value of diffusion in the vicinity of the thermocline (dashed line).

nesses to vary. For example, Sweers (1970) used a two-layer approach
that accounts for variations in the thermocline depth during the stratified
period. To do this, he first used temperature readings to determine the
depth of the thermocline.* He then incorporated the change in thermocline depth in his estimate of the heat transfer coefficient. A simple
expression of Sweer's idea, which is directly comparable to our previous
examples, is to rewrite the hypolimnion temperature balance as

---

*In his analysis, Sweers assumed that the location of the 10°C isotherm provided a good
estimate of the depth of the thermocline. Although this is a valid approximation for the
system he modeled (Lake Ontario), an alternative approach is to fit cubic splines to the
temperature data and use the resulting equations to determine the point of maximum
temperature change.

$$\frac{d}{dt}(V_h T_h) = v_t A_t (T_e - T_h) \qquad (13.19)$$

Note that, in contrast to Equation 13.7, the volume of the hypolimnion is not assumed to be constant, but is allowed to vary in time. Using a centered-difference approximation for the derivative, Equation 13.19 can be used to estimate the heat exchange coefficient,

$$v_t = \frac{V_h^n (T_h^{n+1} - T_h^{n-1}) + T_h^n (V_h^{n+1} - V_h^{n-1})}{2 A_t \Delta t (T_e^n - T_h^n)} \qquad (13.20)$$

Equation 13.20 is a simple expression of Sweer's approach. The reader should consult the original publication for additional details and alternative difference formulations for estimating v_t (e.g., Powell and Jassby 1974, Jassby and Powell 1975, Quay et al. 1980).

In addition to back-calculation of exchange coefficients from temperature measurements, more mechanistic heat balance models may be developed. For example, as noted previously, surface heat transfer can be computed on the basis of meteorological variables. The computed sources and sinks of heat can then serve as input to a multilayer heat balance model of the water column. The heat exchange coefficients between layers can then be estimated by making them a function of the density regime as reflected by a relationship such as the Richardson number. Aside from relating the exchange coefficients to density gradients, such a formulation also allows calculation of when and where instabilities occur.

An example of this approach is the work of Sundaram and Rehm (1971, 1973). Information from such a detailed model can then be simplified for use in mass balance models. For example, Scavia (1980) developed an 18-layer vertical temperature model in a fashion similar to Sundaram and Rehm. He then used his results to develop a two-layer model with variable themocline depth (see Figure 13.8) to simulate substance dynamics in the Lake Ontario water column.

Finally, aside from temperature budgets, a number of techniques are available for directly measuring vertical diffusion in lakes. For example, the spreading of a dye patch can be used as a tracer to measure vertical mixing (Kullenberg et al. 1973). In addition, naturally occurring radioisotopes can also be used as tracers (Imboden and Emerson 1978, Quay et al. 1980).

The foregoing is a brief introduction to estimating vertical mixing rates in lakes. The reader is referred to general reviews by Hutchinson (1957)

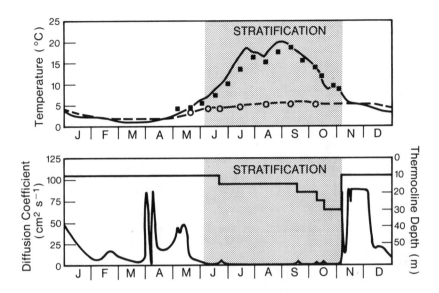

Figure 13.8 (a) Simulated and observed lake-wide averaged temperatures for Lake Ontario and (b) simulated thermocline depth and diffusion coefficients. These computations, developed by Scavia (1980), were simulated using a multi-layer heat balance model. The results of the multilayer model were then used to determine the two-layer version shown in this figure.

and Wetzel (1975). Also, papers and reports by Mortimer (1961), Ryan and Harleman (1971), Orlob and Selna (1970) and Ragotzkie (1978) are recommended for those desiring additional information.

13.1.2 Mass Balance Models

The temperature changes described in the previous section have a profound effect on mass cycling within the water column. The presence of a strong thermocline essentially divides the lake into two vertical layers with markedly different characteristics (Figure 13.9). The surface layer, or epilimnion, is warm and well-illuminated. Consequently, algal photosynthesis leads to transformation of dissolved nutrients into particulate organic matter. Although the thermocline greatly reduces vertical mixing, some of this particulate matter settles and diffuses to the bottom layer, or hypolimnion, where it decomposes and eventually returns to a soluble form. Mixing across the thermocline then reintroduces some of

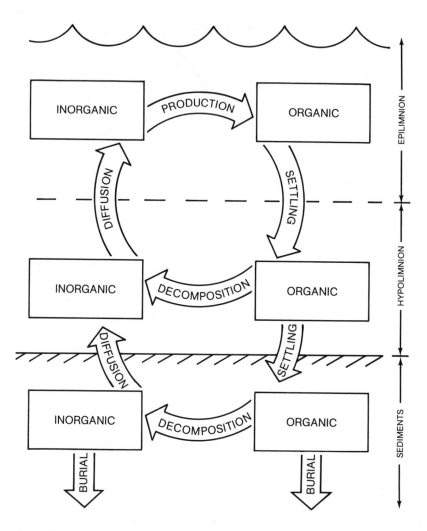

Figure 13.9   Idealized representation of the cycle of production and decomposition that plays a critical role in determining the vertical distribution of matter in stratified lakes.

the dissolved nutrient to the surface water, where it is again taken up by the phytoplankton.

Because many contaminants in lakes are associated with particulate organic matter, this cycle (Figure 13.9) has significance to their transport and fate. This section describes an approach to simulating basic features of this cycle. The key characteristic of the approach is that it partitions the substance being modeled into two fractions. Although the model is specifically developed for phosphorus, this partitioning is basic to many other substances (such as certain toxic compounds), and the approach could serve as a preliminary framework for analysis of the seasonal dynamics of these contaminants. In addition to its use in simulating mass cycling, the model also is used to simulate oxygen concentration in the water column.

The Simplest Seasonal Approach

Most of the models described in earlier chapters of this volume deal with the dynamics of a single substance in a vertically well-mixed lake. As mentioned above, many constituents occur in various chemical and/or biological forms that are subject to transformations due to thermal stratification of the water column. O'Melia (1972), Imboden (1974) and Snodgrass (1974; and O'Melia 1975) have provided a modeling framework that makes a first attempt to simulate some of these changes for the nutrient phosphorus. Simons and Lam (1980) have dubbed this framework the "Simplest Seasonal Approach" or SSA. Although each of their approaches has unique features (for which the reader can refer to the original publications), in general, all the models have the following characteristics:

1. Phosphorus is separated into two components. These conventionally refer to soluble reactive phosphorus (SRP) and phosphorus that is not soluble reactive phosphorus (NSRP).* This breakdown has an operational basis because the two most common phosphorus measurements are for SRP and total phosphorus (TP). NSRP can, therefore, be estimated by the difference of the two quantities as in NSRP = TP − SRP. In the model itself, a further distinction is made in that NSRP is subject to settling losses whereas SRP is not. This is based on the assumption that a significant portion of the NSRP is in particulate form. However, because NSRP also includes nonsettleable dissolved organic phosphorus (DOP), the distinction is not precise. We will return to the subject of the definition and interpretation of the phosphorus fraction and the general question of kinetic segmentation at the end of this section.

2. The lake is segmented spatially into well-mixed upper and lower layers.

3. The year is divided into two seasons representing a summer, strati-

---

*Note that Imboden (1974) treats phosphorus as dissolved P available for bioproduction and particulate P. He, therefore, does not explicitly account for dissolved organic phosphorus on the basis that its role in productivity is somewhat nebulous. The question of kinetic segmentation is explored in further detail at the end of this section.

fied period during which turbulent exchange between the layers is minimal and a winter, circulation period when turbulent transport is intense and the lake is essentially well-mixed vertically.

4. Linear first-order differential equations are used to characterize the transport and kinetics representing the mass exchange between the components. As schematized in Figure 13.10, these exchanges include the following:

- *Waste inputs.* Mass loadings of SRP and NSRP fractions can be input to both the epi- and the hypolimnion.
- *Transport.* Flushing of mass through the lake's outlet is characterized mathematically in a similar fashion to the input-output models (i.e., as flow times concentration), yet differs in that only the surface layer loses mass in this way. Vertical turbulent transfer or diffusion between the layers during the stratified period is formulated as discussed in the previous section. For the winter, the diffusion coefficient is increased to the point where for all practical purposes the lake is well-mixed.
- *Settling.* By definition, only NSRP is removed from the water column using relationships of the form of Equation 11.5 (p. 22). Separate settling velocities can be input for the two layers, as well as for the two seasons.
- *Uptake.* To account for the fact that SRP is transformed into particulate matter via phytoplankton production, uptake of SRP is character-

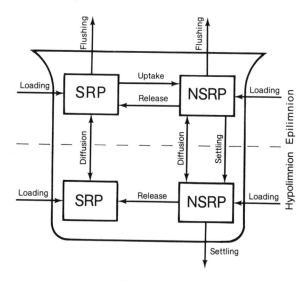

Figure 13.10 Schematic representation of the "Simplest Seasonal Approach" developed by O'Melia, Imboden and Snodgrass.

ized by a first-order reaction. This mechanism is only included in the epilimnion under the assumption that light limitation makes it negligible in the lower layers. In addition, a much higher uptake rate is used during the summer to account for the fact that production is greatest at that time.

- *Release.* A number of mechanisms such as decomposition, respiration, zooplankton grazing, etc., act to return phosphorus from the NSRP to the SRP pool. A first-order reaction dependent on the concentration of NSRP is used to approximate this phenomenon.

To this point, the kinetics of most models in this volume have been characterized as simple first-order decay. With the SSA, we begin to introduce more elaborate representations of substance interactions. As in Figure 13.10, the phosphorus forms are coupled by uptake and release reactions. For example, in the epilimnion, phosphorus is lost from the NSRP compartment or "pool" by a release reaction. This loss, in turn, represents a gain for the SRP pool. Therefore, when writing the mass balance for a particular pool, each arrow in Figure 13.10 represents a term in the resulting differential equation. For example, for the SRP pool in the epilimnion,

$$V_e \frac{dp_{s,e}}{dt} = W_{s,e} - Qp_{s,e} + v_t A_t (p_{s,h} - p_{s,e}) - k_{u,e} V_e p_{s,e} + k_{r,e} V_e p_{n,e}$$

(13.21)

(accumulation) = (loading) − (flushing) + (diffusion) − (uptake) + (release)

Although the reactions in Equation 13.21 are all first order, they could just as easily be more complex formulations. For example, in Chapter 14, nonlinear relationships are used to characterize phytoplankton growth. In addition, if other substances (such as additional forms of phosphorus or other nutrients) were to be included in the model, compartments (each representing a differential equation) and arrows (each representing a term in the differential equation) could be included. The point is that regardless of the complexity of the situation, the conservation of mass, as reflected by the set of differential equations, is a simple bookkeeping exercise to account for how, when and where mass moves within the system.

The mass balances for the three remaining pools are:

$$V_e \frac{dp_{n,e}}{dt} = W_{n,e} - Qp_{n,e} + v_t A_t (p_{n,h} - p_{n,e}) + k_{u,e} V_e p_{s,e} - k_{r,e} V_e p_{n,e} - v_e A_t p_{n,e}$$

(13.22)

$$V_h \, \frac{dp_{s,h}}{dt} = W_{s,h} + v_t A_t (p_{s,e} - p_{s,h}) + k_{r,h} V_h p_{n,h} \qquad (13.23)$$

$$V_h \, \frac{dp_{n,h}}{dt} = W_{n,h} + v_t A_t (p_{n,e} - p_{n,h}) - k_{r,h} V_h p_{n,h} + v_e A_t p_{n,e} - v_h A_t p_{n,h}$$

$$(13.24)$$

where the subscripts n and s designate NSRP and SRP fractions, respectively, and e and h designate epilimnion and hypolimnion, respectively. Definitions and typical values of the parameters are contained in Tables 13.2 and 13.3.

Table 13.2   Typical Ranges of Parameters for the Simplest Seasonal Approach for Modeling Phosphorus[a]

Parameter	Season	Symbol	Range	Units
Epilimnetic uptake rate	Summer	$k_{u,e}$	0.1–5.0	d^{-1}
	Winter	$k_{u,e}$	0.01–0.5	d^{-1}
Epilimnetic release rate	Summer	$k_{r,e}$	0.01–0.1	d^{-1}
	Winter	$k_{r,e}$	0.003–0.07	d^{-1}
Hypolimnetic release rate	Summer	$k_{r,h}$	0.003–0.07	d^{-1}
	Winter	$k_{r,h}$	0.003–0.07	d^{-1}
Settling velocity	Annual	v_e, v_h	0.05–0.6	$m \, d^{-1}$

[a] Values are taken primarily from Imboden (1974) and Snodgrass (1974).

§ § §

Example 13.6. The average annual cycle of phosphorus for Lake Ontario for 1968 through 1976 is contained in Table 13.4. Using these data and the information in Table 13.3, simulate: (a) the seasonal cycle of SRP and NSRP phosphorus in Lake Ontario, (b) the long-term response (i.e., 20 years) if the loading of SRP were totally removed and (c) the long-term response if the NSRP load were reduced by an amount equivalent to that removed in (b).

In order to use the SSA to simulate the seasonal cycle, it is necessary to choose values for the parameters. As summarized in Table 13.2, these parameters have broad ranges and, therefore, some calibration is necessary to obtain the appropriate estimates. One way to do this is by optimization techniques* (e.g., Parker 1973 or Simons and Lam 1980).

---

*Additional discussion of model calibration is included in Chapter 14.

Table 13.3   Information on Lake Ontario in the Early 1970s

Parameter	Symbol	Value	Units
Area			
surface	A_w	19,000	10^6 m^2
thermocline	A_t	18,500	10^6 m^2
Mean Depth			
whole lake	z	86	m
epilimnion	z_e	15	m
hypolimnion	z_h	71	m
Volume			
whole lake	V	1,634	10^9 m^3
epilimnion	V_e	254	10^9 m^3
hypolimnion	V_h	1,380	10^9 m^3
Outflow	Q	212	10^9 m^3 yr^{-1}
SRP Load			
epilimnion	$W_{s,e}$	4,000	10^9 mg yr^{-1}
hypolimnion	$W_{s,h}$	0	10^9 mg yr^{-1}
NSRP Load			
epilimnion	$W_{n,e}$	8,000	10^9 mg yr^{-1}
hypolimnion	$W_{n,h}$	0	10^9 mg yr^{-1}
Primary Production			
annual	Pr	184	gC m^{-2} yr^{-1}
summer	Pr_s	200–250	gC m^{-2} yr^{-1}
winter	Pr_w	50–150	gC m^{-2} yr^{-1}
Oxygen depletion rate			
summer	D_v	0.011	gO$_2$ m^{-3} d^{-1}

These methods can be used to determine the set of parameter values that minimize the sum of the square of the residuals between the data and the model computations. Alternatively, direct measurements of processes can sometimes be used to estimate parameters (e.g., Di Toro et al. 1971). However, in the present case this is complicated by the fact that some of the terms have nebulous physical meaning. For example, since the NSRP is composed of several particulate and dissolved fractions, a settling velocity to characterize the sedimentation of this pool would be difficult, if not impossible, to measure.

For the present example, we use an approach that is intermediate between optimization and direct measurement. We use the latter approach wherever possible to estimate some of the parameters directly. Then, under some simplifying assumptions, we can back-calculate the remaining values on the basis of a calibration to the data.

Table 13.4   Average Monthly Phosphorus Concentrations for
Lake Ontario for the Period from 1968 Through 1976[a]

	Epilimnion[b]			Hypolimnion[b]		
	Total Phosphorus	Soluble Reactive Phosphorus	Non Soluble Reactive Phosphorus	Total Phosphorus	Soluble Reactive Phosphorus	Non Soluble Reactive Phosphorus
Jan.	22.9	13.8	9.1	22.1	13.7	8.4
Feb.	21.4	10.8	10.6	19.9	14.3	5.6
Mar.	24.9	10.8	14.1	23.1	14.1	9.0
Apr.	23.0	9.2	13.8	22.3	10.2	12.1
May	21.0	7.3	13.7	21.0	8.8	12.2
June	20.6	3.8	16.8	20.1	7.3	12.8
July	19.7	4.0	15.7	18.6	7.7	10.9
Aug.	19.7	2.7	17.0	21.4	7.8	13.6
Sept.	19.1	2.7	16.4	22.3	10.2	12.1
Oct.	18.0	4.8	13.2	21.4	9.0	12.4
Nov.	16.3	6.4	9.9	17.4	7.8	9.6
Dec.	20.7	9.6	11.1	21.4	10.7	10.7

[a] From Thomann and Segna 1980.
[b] All values are in mgP m^{-3}.

Direct Measurements

The two direct measurements that can be used for model calibration
are primary production and hypolimnetic oxygen depletion (Table 13.3).
Primary production estimates provide a measure of the uptake of SRP as
defined by the following equation,

$$Pr\, A_w\, a_{pc} = k_{u,e}\, V_e\, p_{s,e} \qquad \text{(i)}$$

where Pr = primary production [gC m^{-2} yr^{-1}]
         A_w = the surface area of the lake [m^2]
         a_{pc} = the ratio of phosphorus to carbon in organic matter
         [mgP gC^{-1}]

Equation i can be solved for

$$k_{u,e} = \frac{Pr\, A_w\, a_{pc}}{V_e\, p_{s,e}} \div 365 \text{ d/yr} \qquad \text{(ii)}$$

The phosphorus to carbon ratio can be computed from the following
general equation for the oxidation of organic matter (Stumm and
Morgan 1981).

$$C_{106}H_{263}O_{110}N_{16}P_1 + 138\ O_2 \qquad\qquad \text{(iii)}$$

According to Equation iii, a_{pc} can be estimated as

$$a_{pc} = \frac{1(31)gP}{106(12)gC} \times \frac{10^3\ mgP}{gP} = 24.4\ \frac{mgP}{gC} \qquad \text{(iv)}$$

(atomic wt. of $P = 31$, atomic wt. of $C = 12$). In summer (July through September), the average value of $p_{s,e}$ is 3.1 mg m^{-3} (Table 13.4). Using the range of estimates of summer primary production in Table 13.3, we can then use Equation ii to determine a range for $k_{u,e}$ from 0.32 to 0.40 d^{-1}. For winter (January through March; $p_{s,e} = 11.8$ mg m^{-3}), the same procedure can be used to estimate a range from 0.021 to 0.064 d^{-1}.

In a similar fashion, the oxygen depletion rate provides an estimate of the hypolimnetic remineralization rate. Before doing this, the measurement must be corrected for diffusive transport of oxygen across the thermocline. This has to be done because the quantity D_v in Table 13.3 was estimated by plotting the average hypolimnetic dissolved oxygen concentration versus time. The slope of this line provided an estimate of the depletion rate. However, since the hypolimnion is not a closed system, the measurement also reflects the transport of oxygen across the thermocline as in

$$D_{v,\,total} = D_{v,\,oxidation} + D_{v,\,diffusion} \qquad\qquad \text{(v)}$$

The part of the total depletion rate due to diffusion can be computed by using a simple relationship of the form,

$$D_{v,\,diffusion} = \frac{v_t A_t}{V_h}\ (DO_h - DO_e), \qquad\qquad \text{(vi)}$$

where DO_e and DO_h are the dissolved oxygen concentrations in the epi- and the hypolimnion, respectively. Therefore,

$$D_{v,\,oxidation} = D_{v,\,total} - \frac{E_t A_t}{z_t V_h}\ (DO_h - DO_e) \qquad \text{(vii)}$$

For summer in Lake Ontario, $DO_e \cong 9.5$ and $DO_h \cong 11.5$ g m^{-3}, and

$$D_{v,\,oxidation} = 0.011 - 0.002 = 0.009\ \frac{gO_2}{m^3\ d} \qquad \text{(viii)}$$

The depletion rate due to oxidation is, in turn, related to the hypolimnetic release rate by

$$D_{v,\,oxidation}\,V_h\,a_{po} = k_{r,\,h}\,V_h\,p_{n,\,h} \qquad (ix)$$

or

$$k_{r,\,h} = \frac{a_{po}\,D_{v,\,oxidation}}{p_{n,\,h}} \qquad (x)$$

where a_{po} is the ratio of phosphorus to oxygen (mgP gO$_2^{-1}$) that can be estimated on the basis of Equation iii,

$$a_{po} = \frac{1(31)\,gP}{138(32)\,gO}\ \frac{10^3\,mgP}{gP} = 7.0\ \frac{mgP}{gO} \qquad (xi)$$

(atomic weight of oxygen = 16). The average value of $p_{n,\,h}$ in the summer is 12.2 mg m^{-3} and, therefore, Equation x can be solved for $k_{r,\,h} = 0.005$ d^{-1}. Since whole-lake conditions in winter are similar to hypolimnion conditions in summer, this value is assumed to apply also to release in both surface and bottom layers during the winter.

Calibration to the Data

The settling velocity is estimated by realizing that an input-output version of the model can be developed by adding Equations 13.21 through 13.24,

$$V_t\,\frac{dp_t}{dt} = W_t - Q\,p_{t,\,e} - v_h\,A_t\,p_{n,\,h} \qquad (xii)$$

where the "t" designates total phosphorus. Although there is some annual variation, the epilimnetic total phosphorus, $p_{t,\,e}$, and the hypolimnetic nonsoluble reactive phosphorus, $p_{n,\,h}$, are at fairly constant levels of 20.6 and 10.8 mg m^{-3}, respectively. If a steady state is assumed, Equation xii can be rearranged to estimate

$$v_h = \frac{W_t - Q\,p_{t,\,e}}{A_t\,p_{n,\,h}} = 0.105\ m\,d^{-1} \qquad (xiii)$$

Finally, the summer release rate in the epilimnion can be estimated by performing a number of seasonal simulations and adjusting $k_{r,\,e}$ (summer) until the model results conform to the general levels of the data.

The complete set of coefficients used in the final calibration are summarized in Table 13.5.

Using a numerical method, Equations 13.21–24 were integrated. The results are displayed in Figure 13.11. As can be seen, the primary feature in the epilimnion is the shift of mass from the SRP and the NSRP fraction during summer due to the large uptake rate. Because of the lack of production, the hypolimnion is generally a more stable system, with concentrations maintained at fairly constant levels throughout the year.

Table 13.5   Values of Parameters Used for Final Calibration
in Lake Ontario

Parameter	Season	Value	Units
$k_{u,e}$	Summer	0.36	d^{-1}
	Winter	0.045	d^{-1}
$k_{r,e}$	Summer	0.068	d^{-1}
	Winter	0005	d^{-1}
$k_{r,h}$	Summer	0.005	d^{-1}
	Winter	0.005	d^{-1}
v_e, v_h	Annual	0.103	$m\ d^{-1}$

The long-term response of the model to load reduction is displayed in Figure 13.12, along with the response of a one-component, total P model. The removal of the SRP fraction results in a slightly greater reduction in the lake's total P level than does removal of the NSRP load. This is because the SRP fraction is cleansed solely by flushing, whereas NSRP is also influenced by sedimentation. This additional cleansing mechanism tends to diminish the effect of the NSRP loading on in-lake levels. Note that the one-component model falls midway between the response curves for the two-component model. Thus, the additional complexity of the latter yields information that could be useful for decision making; i.e., the effect of removing the SRP fraction is greater than is the effect of removing the NSRP. However, since in the present example the differences are slight, the practical value of the additional information is negligible.

In addition to the magnitude of the response, the use of two components has an effect on temporal aspects of the recovery. The SSA model responds slightly more slowly; its 90% response time is 7.4 yr as compared with 7.1 yr for the total P model. This difference is due to the

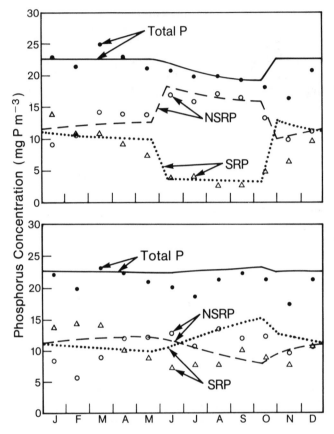

Figure 13.11 Data and simulation results using the simplest seasonal approach for total phosphorus in Lake Ontario. (Top—epilimnion; Bottom—hypolimnion.)

fact that in the two-component model only the surface layer is subject to flushing whereas in the one-component model the entire lake, assumed well-mixed, is subject to flushing. During winter, this effect is minimal since vertical diffusion is intense and hypolimnetic and epilimnetic concentrations are similar. However, during summer stratification, the uptake and sedimentation of particulate P in the surface layer results in a buildup of phosphorus in the bottom layer. Since the hypolimnion is not subject to flushing, this distribution tends to slow the response of the two-component system to changes. Note that, as with the magnitude of the response, the differences between the one- and two-component models are slight. Although there are cases where the use of an SSA

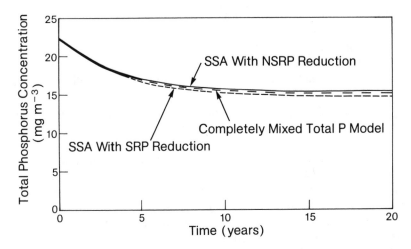

Figure 13.12   Response of Lake Ontario to a step decrease in loading as computed with the simplest seasonal approach (SSA) and a completely mixed total phosphorus model. Simulations with the SSA were made for both nonsoluble reactive phosphorus (NSRP) and soluble reactive phosphorus (SRP) load restrictions.

model might have more of an effect on system response (e.g., shallower lakes, elongated lakes, etc.), the partitioning is usually not critical for long-term computations. It is more useful for the added information that is provided on within-year variability as in Figure 13.11.

§ § §

Although the above framework captures many of the essential features of the seasonal cycle, it has several limitations. In particular, its use of constant coefficients and first-order kinetics limits its general applicability. Many of the processes governing substance interactions in the water column are nonlinear and dependent on factors not accounted for in this model. For example, the epilimnetic uptake rate depends, among other things, on light intensity, temperature and levels of both the phytoplankton and the dissolved nutrient. In addition, the dependence on the nutrient is best described by a nonlinear relationship. Thus, some efforts to refine Equations 13.21–13.24 have focused on more mechanistic characterizations of the kinetic interactions (Imboden and Gachter 1978). Chapter 14 reviews nutrient/food chain models that incorporate sufficient refinements as to constitute an alternative method.

Other ways in which the approach can be modified would be to divide the hypolimnion into several layers to try to resolve vertical gradients in the bottom waters (Imboden and Gachter 1978). In addition, the meta-limnion can be modeled as a third segment.

Likewise, phosphorus can be subdivided into additional components to more realistically define its dynamics. For example, a distinction can be made between living particulate phosphorus and detrital phosphorus or between dissolved organic and dissolved inorganic forms. Figure 13.13 depicts a number of possible kinetic segmentation schemes for phosphorus.

There are three basic rationales underlying kinetic segmentation. First, the division of matter can be based on measurement techniques as in the case with the SRP/NSRP scheme. Similarly, a dissolved/particulate split (Figure 13.13b) is, in part, based on the use of filtration to discriminate between these pools. Second, the segmentation can have a mechanistic basis. For example, the breakdown of matter into pools with similar kinetic characteristics facilitates derivation and measurement of the input-output terms and coupling mechanisms between components. The division of the particulate phosphorus into phytoplankton and detrital components (Figure 13.13h) is illustrative of this rationale since the settling rates of these two pools are different and can be measured separately. The mechanistic division of matter is elaborated in additional detail in our discussion of functional groups in Chapter 14. Finally, the segmentation scheme can have a management basis. For example, the explicit formulation of a phytoplankton pool has informational value for the planner trying to assess the deleterious effects of eutrophication.

A general advantage of adding compartments is that the exchange processes can usually be formulated in a more mechanistic manner based on measurements. A disadvantage is that additional effort must be expended to obtain these measurements. In addition, the more "sophisticated" representations are usually more costly to run on the computer and more difficult to interpret. Further, prediction reliability may actually decrease with additional compartments, because the least understood pools would typically be incorporated last. Therefore, the decision to expand on a basic framework such as Figure 13.10 must be made only after considering these factors.

Oxygen Balance Models

The dissolved oxygen content of a lake is strongly influenced by thermal stratification. The process of uptake and release of phosphorus described in the previous section is accompanied by the production and use of oxygen as represented by Figure 13.14.

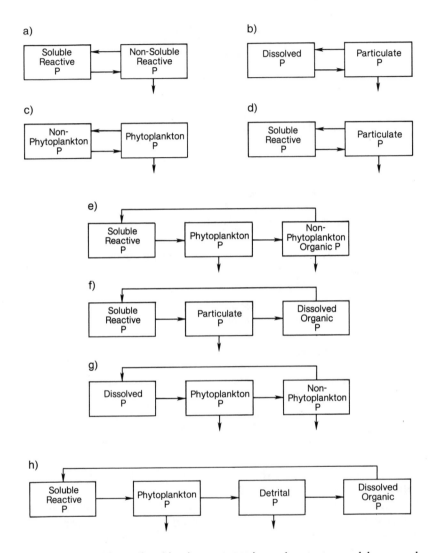

Figure 13.13   Alternative kinetic segmentation schemes to model seasonal phosphorus dynamics.

Thus, during uptake, oxygen is produced and, during release, oxygen is used. Because photosynthesis predominates in the epilimnion and the surface layer is in contact with the atmosphere, the epilimnion is usually saturated or supersaturated with oxygen during summer. In contrast, the hypolimnion is dominated by respiration, which tends to deplete oxygen levels. This situation is compounded by the fact that the bottom layer is

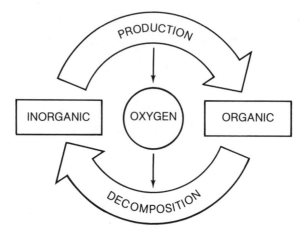

$$106CO_2 + 16NO_3^- + HPO_4^{2-} + 122H_2O + 18H^+ \text{ (+ trace elements; energy)}$$

Photosynthesis ↓ ↑ *Respiration*

$$(C_{106}H_{263}O_{110}N_{16}P_1) + 138O_2$$
algal protoplasm

Figure 13.14 The relationship of oxygen to the production/decomposition cycle in natural waters. As indicated by the equation (Stumm and Morgan 1981), photosynthesis or production creates oxygen, and respiration or decomposition depletes oxygen from a lake.

essentially cut off from atmospheric reaeration by the thermocline. Thus, the hypolimnion typically has an oxygen deficit during summer. In a lake with high productivity and a thin hypolimnion, this can result in complete depletion of oxygen. Such a situation can have a profound effect on the lake's biology and chemistry.

Because of the significance of oxygen to lake water quality, a mass balance model capable of predicting oxygen levels is useful from a management perspective. Since the SSA includes several of the processes (e.g., uptake, release and reduced mixing) that bear on depletion, it can serve as a useful starting point for an oxygen model.* As originally conceived by Imboden (1974), this can be done by assuming a proportionality between phosphorus uptake and oxygen generation and between phosphorus release and oxygen depletion. This was done previously in

---

*Other reactions affecting lake oxygen dynamics (e.g., nitrification) are discussed elsewhere (Wetzel 1974; also Di Toro and Connolly 1980 for details on modeling).

Example 13.6 by using a_{po}, the ratio of phosphorus to oxygen derived from the ideal representation of photosynthesis and respiration in Figure 13.14.

In addition, the movement of oxygen across the air-water interface must be taken into account. The typical way this is done is by a relationship of the form

$$\left(V_e \frac{dDO_e}{dt} \right)_{aeration} = k_l A_w (DO_s - DO_e) \qquad (13.25)$$

where DO_e = the dissolved oxygen concentration in the epilimnion
$[gO_2 \ m^{-3}]$
k_l = an oxygen transfer coefficient across the air-water interface
$[m \ d^{-1}]$
A_w = lake surface area
DO_s = the saturation value of dissolved oxygen $[gO_2 \ m^{-3}]$ that can
be estimated from (Committee on Sanitary Engineering
Research 1960)

$$DO_s = 14.652 - 0.41022 \, T_e + 0.0079910 \, T_e^2 - 0.000077774 \, T_e^3 \quad (13.26)$$

where T_e is epilimnetic temperature (°C). Note that if $DO_e < DO_s$, Equation 13.25 is positive, connoting that the oxygen moves from the atmosphere into the lake. Conversely, if $DO_e > DO_s$, the lake is supersaturated and oxygen exits across the air-water interface.

As discussed in Chapter 15, the oxygen transfer coefficient can be predicted on the basis of variables such as wind speed over the lake's surface. For the present purposes, we will consider it a constant value over the annual cycle. The oxygen mass balances for the epi- and the hypolimnion can, therefore, be written as

$$V_e \frac{dDO_e}{dt} = \frac{k_{u,e} V_e p_{s,e}}{a_{po}} - \frac{k_{r,e} V_e p_{n,e}}{a_{po}} + k_l A_w (DO_s - DO_e)$$

$$+ v_t A_t (DO_h - DO_e) \qquad (13.27)$$

and

$$V_h \frac{dDO_h}{dt} = - \frac{k_{r,h} V_h p_{n,h}}{a_{po}} + v_t A_t (DO_e - DO_h) \qquad (13.28)$$

Along with the SSA (Equations 13.21–13.24), Equations 13.27 and 13.28 can be used to simulate oxygen levels in a lake.

§ § §

Example 13.7. Use Equations 13.27 and 13.28, along with the SSA, to simulate seasonal oxygen concentrations in Lake Ontario. A value of 1 m d^{-1} for the oxygen transfer coefficient is a typical annual average for this lake. Assume constant temperatures of 17.6°C and 3.0°C for the epilimnion during summer and winter, respectively. The simulation results are shown in Figure 13.15.

§ § §

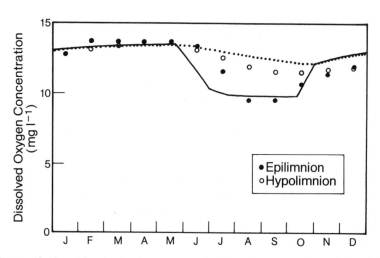

Figure 13.15   Dissolved oxygen concentration measurements and simulation results for Lake Ontario over the annual cycle.

The foregoing oxygen model is a simple representation of the process. Snodgrass (1977) discusses additional aspects of the approach. The reader also can consult more complex efforts to simulate oxygen dynamics in lakes (in particular, Di Toro and Connolly 1980).

13.2   SEDIMENT MODELS

Aside from cycling in the water column, some of the particulate matter in the lake's hypolimnion settles to the bottom sediments (Figure 13.9). Although a portion is buried in the deep sediments, some is reintroduced into the overlying waters. For deep lakes with well-oxygenated hypolimnia, this feedback does not have a strong seasonal component because of the low temperatures and the existence of an oxidized microzone that impedes some chemicals from crossing the sediment-water interface.

However, when the decomposition process is large enough to deplete the hypolimnetic oxygen resources, certain substances can be released in large quantities. In this case, sediment feedback can have a decided effect on the lake's seasonal dynamics.

While feedback is relatively unimportant in determining the seasonal cycling of matter in deep or unproductive lakes, it can have an effect on their long-term dynamics. This relates to the fact that, in contrast to stratification, the sedimentation process is relatively slow. For example, the rate of buildup of a lake's sediments is on the order of 1 to 10 mm yr^{-1}. Since the thickness of the surficial layer is typically on the order of 1 to 10 cm, a rough estimate of the surficial sediment residence time due to burial, τ_m, is approximately

$$\tau_m = \frac{5 \text{ cm}}{0.5 \text{ cm/yr}} = 10 \text{ yr} \tag{13.29}$$

Because other processes contributing to sediment dynamics (oxidation, diffusion across the sediment-water interface, etc.) are also slow, this implies that seasonal approaches would not be needed to model the system. For this reason, the sediment model described in the next section takes a long-term approach. The reader should consult other sources, notably Berner (1980), Di Toro (1978), and Di Toro and Connolly (1980), for an introduction into the literature and techniques on modeling seasonal sediment dynamics.

This section is devoted to simulating substance dynamics within the sediments. In a subsequent section, the sediment model is linked with a mass balance of the water column in order to simulate their coupled response.

13.2.1 Basic Concepts and Processes

All the models developed to this point have been for the liquid phase of the lake. Although solid material is suspended in the water column, its volume is negligible compared to the volume of the water. The sediments are fundamentally different since a significant portion of their volume is in the solid phase. Therefore, in order to model this system, several concepts must be introduced.

Solid Concentration and Porosity

Most lake quality models have been developed for the water column. Because lake water is a dilute solution and water density is approximately unity (in cgs units), water column concentrations are usually based on the normalization of mass to total lake volume as in

$$c_{tt} = \frac{M_t}{V_t} \tag{13.30}$$

where c_{tt} = volume-specific concentration $[\mu g \ m^{-3}]$*
        M_t = the total mass of contaminant in the lake $[\mu g]$
        V_t = total volume $[m^3]$.

There are two basic reasons why Equation 13.30 is not adequate for modeling liquid-solid interactions in lake waters and sediments. First, sorption reaction kinetics, which provide a useful way to represent liquid-solid interactions, are described in terms of the mass of contaminant per unit mass of particulate matter rather than on a volumetric basis. Second, a significant portion of the sediments are in the solid phase. In order to account for these factors, a number of relationships must be defined.

The *porosity* refers to the volume of the sediments that is in the liquid phase and is interconnected (Engelhardt 1977). Strictly speaking, this excludes isolated pore space which is considered part of the solid phase. However, since these are rare in shallowly buried sediments (Berner 1980), the porosity is operationally defined as the fraction of the total volume in the liquid phase,

$$\phi = \frac{V_d}{V_t} \tag{13.31}$$

where V_d = the liquid volume $[m^3]$. Values of ϕ range from 0.4 for well-sorted sands to 0.9–0.95 for sediments with high clay content. In general, porosity is inversely proportional to the grain size of the solid matter constituting the sediments.

For the water column, $\phi \cong 1.0$ and $V_d \cong V_t$. Therefore, we are justified in using Equation 13.30. For the sediments, however, the solid volume must be included, as in

$$V_t = V_p + V_d \tag{13.32}$$

where V_p is the solid volume $[m^3]$.

---

*Note, in the following developments, the quantity of contaminants is measured in μg. In fact, other units such as mg or Ci (for radioactivity) could be used.

Equations 13.31 and 13.32 can be combined to express the solid volume in terms of porosity,

$$V_p = (1 - \phi) V_t \qquad (13.33)$$

The *mass-specific concentration* of contaminant* in the solid phase is defined as the mass of contamination per total mass of solid matter as in

$$\nu_p = \frac{M_p}{m_p} \qquad (13.34)$$

where ν_p is mass-specific concentration [μg g^{-1}], i.e., the quantity of contaminant per unit of particulate matter, M_p is mass of contaminant in the particulate phase [μg] and m_p is the total mass of solid matter [g], which is defined as

$$m_p = V_p \rho_p \qquad (13.35)$$

where ρ_p is the density of particulate matter [g m^{-3}]. Therefore, the mass of contaminant associated with solid matter per total volume, c_{pt}, can be expressed by combining Equations 13.33 through 13.35,

$$c_{pt} = \rho_p (1 - \phi) \nu_p \qquad (13.36)$$

Since the density of water is (in cgs units), by definition, approximately one, the concentration of the liquid phase is conventionally expressed on a volumetric basis as in

$$c_d = \frac{M_d}{V_d} \qquad (13.37)$$

---

*We use the terminology "contaminant" to designate substances that are essentially foreign to the lake ecosystem. Examples are radionuclides from atmospheric weapons testing, pesticides or other synthetic organics. At high enough concentrations, these contaminants can be harmful to the life of the ecosystem. The terminology is intended to differentiate these substances from other more classical water pollutants, such as oxygen-demanding carbonaceous wastewater or eutrophication-causing nutrients. These pollutants represent a water quality problem in that they *overstimulate* rather than directly damage the ecosystem. Although the distinction is sometimes blurred (e.g., although heavy metals occur naturally, we would consider them a contaminant because in most healthy ecosystems they are at low levels, whereas at high levels they directly interfere with life processes), we feel that the distinction has utility from both a management and a modeling perspective. The latter will become evident in the following derivations and in Chapter 15 where we address toxic substance modeling.

where c_d is the volume-specific concentration $[\mu g\ m^{-3}]$ in the dissolved form, and M_d is the mass of contaminant in the dissolved phase $[\mu g]$. Therefore, the mass of contaminant associated with the dissolved phase per unit total volume, c_{dt}, can be expressed as

$$c_{dt} = \frac{M_d}{V_t} = \phi\,c_d \qquad (13.38)$$

Compaction

Within the sediments, the force of gravity squeezes particles together and decreases porosity. This processes, called compaction, is usually greatest near the surface and reaches a limiting level at depth. One equation for describing compaction in terms of porosity is (Athy 1930)

$$\phi(z) = [\phi(0) - \phi']e^{-\beta z} + \phi' \qquad (13.39)$$

where z = depth [m] which is zero at the sediment-water interface* and increases in the downward direction
$\phi(0)$ = the porosity at the top of the sediments
ϕ' = the final porosity
β = an empirically derived parameter $[m^{-1}]$ specifying the rate of compaction with depth.

Burial

Below the surficial sediment layer (where bioturbation, gas movement and mechanical mixing can cause random motion of the bed), the deep compacting sediments can be considered an advective system. Although this region, which we will call the deep sediment, does not actually move, its distance from the sediment-water interface increases as additional material accumulates on the lake bottom. In essence, the sediment-water interface is advecting upward. From the perspective of modeling the sediments, however, it is convenient to conceptualize the process as if the interface were static and the layer were "moving" downward. This motion is influenced by compaction.

For solid matter, a one-dimensional mass balance in the depth dimension can be expressed mathematically as

---

*Note that, if the surficial sediments are well mixed by processes such as bioturbation, the bottom of the well-mixed layer can be specified as $z = 0$ and Equation 13.39 can be used to represent compaction below this interface.

$$\frac{\partial}{\partial t} \rho_p [1 - \phi(z)] = - \frac{\partial}{\partial z} v_p(z) \rho_p [1 - \phi(z)] \qquad (13.40)$$

where $\quad v_p$ = the burial velocity of solid matter [m yr^{-1}]
$\rho_p [1 - \phi(z)]$ = the concentration of solid matter

At steady state, Equation 13.40 is

$$\frac{\partial}{\partial z} v_p(z) \rho_p [1 - \phi(z)] = 0 \qquad (13.41)$$

In other words, the flux is constant with depth. Therefore,

$$v_p(z) \rho_p [1 - \phi(z)] = v_b \rho_p [1 - \phi'] \qquad (13.42)$$

where v_b is the burial velocity [m yr^{-1}] at zero compaction (i.e., at infinite depth). Equation 13.42 can be rearranged to yield

$$v_p(z) = \frac{v_b (1 - \phi')}{[1 - \phi(z)]} \qquad (13.43)$$

In addition to solid sediments, the liquid component or pore water is also buried. In the absence of externally impressed flow, this can be described by

$$\frac{\partial}{\partial t} \rho_w \phi(z) = - \frac{\partial}{\partial z} v_d(z) \rho_w \phi(z) \qquad (13.44)$$

where ρ_w is the density of water [g m^{-3}]. At steady state, flux must be conserved and Equation 13.44 can be rearranged to yield

$$v_d(z) = \frac{v_b \phi'}{\phi(z)} \qquad (13.45)$$

Note the differing effects of compaction on the burial rates of the particulate and the dissolved phases as expressed by Equation 13.43 and 13.45 and as depicted in Figure 13.16. At infinite depth, both are buried at the same, constant rate. At the surface, however, the velocities diverge. The solid phase "moves" quicker at the surface since advection is enhanced as particles move closer together through compaction. The reverse effect is evident for the pore water since the volume displaced by the compacting particles must be compensated for by loss of the liquid phase. This "squeezing" forces some water upward so that the net effect is that pore water burial decreases near the surface.

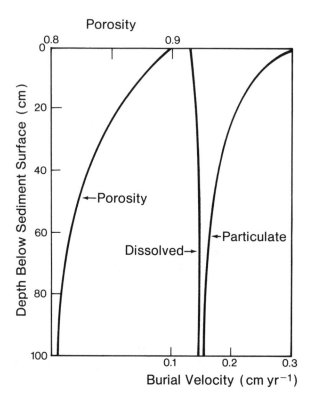

Figure 13.16   Plot of porosity and burial velocity of the particulate and dissolved phases of sediment versus depth.

Pore Water Diffusion

In addition to burial, contaminants are also transported within the sediments by diffusion through the pore water. In the absence of biological mixing, the motion is primarily molecular, with attenuation due to a number of factors, including electrical effects and tortuosity.

Electrical effects are due to the fact that, in addition to its own gradient, an ion's rate of diffusion can also be influenced by gradients of other ions. In addition, ion-pairing can affect diffusion. Although corrections have been developed for both effects (McDuff and Ellis 1979, Lasaga 1979), the impact on most ions is small when compared to attenuation due to tortuosity.

Tortuosity refers to the ratio of the actual path of ions as they move around sediment particles to the straight distance of that path interval. The effect of tortuosity, θ, can be expressed as

$$D_s = \frac{D_m}{\theta^2} \qquad (13.46)$$

where D_s = a whole sediment diffusion coefficient in terms of total area of sediment per unit time [m^2 yr^{-1}]

D_m = the molecular diffusion coefficient of the contaminant in free solution [m^2 yr^{-1}]

Because it is difficult to compute tortuosity for real sediments, the effect is conventionally measured indirectly by resistivity measurements (e.g., Manheim and Waterman 1974). The relationship developed from this technique is

$$\theta^2 = \phi F \qquad (13.47)$$

where F is the formation factor, which is the ratio of the bulk electrical resistivity of the sediment to the resistivity of the pore fluid alone. In the absence of resistivity measurements, an empirical relationship for the formation factor is (Manheim and Waterman 1974)

$$F = \phi^{-n} \qquad (13.48)$$

where n ranges from 1.3 for sands (Archie 1942) to 2.5–5.4 for clays (Manheim and Waterman 1974). A first approximation derived from data compiled by Manheim (1970) is n = 3, whereupon Equations 13.46–13.48 can be combined to yield

$$D_s = D_m \phi^2 \qquad (13.49)$$

Values for D_m as a function of temperature have been compiled by Li and Gregory (1974). As listed in Table 13.6, D_m increases with temperature. For ions diffusing slower than the fluoride ion, the Stokes-Einstein relation can be used to interpolate between temperatures,

$$\left(\frac{D_m \eta}{T_a} \right)_1 = \left(\frac{D_m \eta}{T_a} \right)_2 \qquad (13.50)$$

where η = the viscosity of water [m^2 yr^{-1}]

T_a = the absolute temperature [°K]

For ions diffusing faster than fluoride, the following equation holds

$$(D_m \eta)_1 = (D_m \eta)_2 \qquad (13.51)$$

Figure 13.17 shows the temperature dependence of D_m for a number of ions. Together with porosity measurements for the sediments, Equations 13.49 through and 13.51 provide a procedure for estimating pore water

Table 13.6   Diffusion Coefficients of Ions
at Infinite Dilution[a]

Cation	D_m $(10^{-6}$ cm^2/sec)			Anion	D_m $(10^{-6}$ cm^2/sec)		
	0°C	18°C	25°C		0°C	18°C	25°C
H^+	56.1	81.7	93.1	OH^-	25.6	44.9	52.7
Li^+	4.72	8.69	10.3	F^-	—	12.1	14.6
Na^+	6.27	11.3	13.3	Cl^-	10.1	17.1	20.3
K^+	9.86	16.7	19.6	Br^-	10.5	17.6	20.1
Rb^+	10.6	17.6	20.6	I^-	10.3	17.2	20.0
Cs^+	10.6	17.7	20.7	IO_3^-	5.05	8.79	10.6
NH_4^+	9.80	16.8	19.8	HS^-	9.75	14.8	17.3
Ag^+	8.50	14.0	16.6	S^{2-}	—	6.95	—
Tl^+	10.6	17.0	20.1	HSO_4^-	—	—	13.3
$Cu(OH)^+$	—	—	8.30	SO_4^{2-}	5.00	8.90	10.7
$Zn(OH)^+$	—	—	8.54	SeO_4^{2-}	4.14	8.45	9.46
Be^{2+}	—	3.64	5.85	NO_2^-	—	15.3	19.1
Mg^{2+}	3.56	5.94	7.05	NO_3^-	9.78	16.1	19.0
Ca^{2+}	3.73	6.73	7.93	HCO_3^-	—	—	11.8
Sr^{2+}	3.72	6.70	7.94	CO_3^{2-}	4.39	7.80	9.55
Ba^{2+}	4.04	7.13	8.48	$H_2PO_4^-$	—	7.15	8.46
Ra^{2+}	4.02	7.45	8.89	HPO_4^{2-}	—	—	7.34
Mn^{2+}	3.05	5.75	6.88	HP_4^{3-}	—	—	6.12
Fe^{2+}	3.41	5.82	7.19	$H_2AsO_4^-$	—	—	9.05
Co^{2+}	3.41	5.72	6.99	$H^2SbO_4^-$	—	—	8.25
Ni^{2+}	3.11	5.81	6.79	CrO_4^{2-}	5.12	9.36	11.2
Cu^{2+}	3.41	5.88	7.33	MoO_4^{2-}	—	—	9.91
Zn^{2+}	3.35	6.13	7.15	WO_4^{2-}	4.27	7.67	9.23
Cd^{2+}	3.41	6.03	7.17				
Pb^{2+}	4.56	7.95	9.45				
UO_2^{2+}	—	—	4.26				
Sc^{3+}	—	—	5.74				
Y^{3+}	2.60	—	5.50				
La^{3+}	2.76	5.14	6.17				
Yb^{3+}	—	—	5.82				
Cr^{3+}	—	3.90	5.94				
Fe^{3+}	—	5.28	6.07				
Al^{3+}	2.36	3.46	5.59				
Th^{4+}	—	1.53	—				

[a] From Li and Gregory 1974.

diffusion from tabulated values rather than through direct measurements.

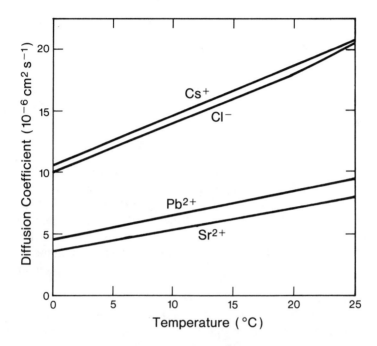

Figure 13.17 Molecular diffusion coefficients in free solution versus temperature for cesium (Cs^+), chloride (Cl^-), lead (Pb^{2+}) and strontium (Sr^{2+}). For details on how these coefficients were determined and additional information on other ions, see Li and Gregory (1974).

§ § §

Example 13.8. Determine the molecular diffusion coefficient of cesium at 4°C.

From Table 13.6, $D_m = 10.6 \times 10^{-6}$ cm² sec⁻¹ at T = 0°C. Since this is faster than the fluoride ion, Equation 13.51 can be used to compute D_m at T = 4°C ($\eta = 1.7923 \times 10^{-2}$ and 1.5676×10^{-2} cm² sec⁻¹ for T = 0°C and 4°C, respectively),

$$D_m(T=4°C) = 10.6 \times 10^{-6} \frac{1.7923}{1.5676} = 12.1 \times 10^{-6} \text{ cm}^2 \text{sec}^{-1}$$

§ § §

The mass flux due to pore water diffusion can be expressed quantitatively by Fick's first law (recall p. 77),

$$J_s = -\phi D_s \frac{\partial c_{di}}{\partial z} \tag{13.52}$$

where J_s = the flux in terms of mass per unit area of total sediment per unit time [$\mu g\ m^{-2}\ yr^{-1}$]
   c_{di} = the concentration of contaminant in the pore water [$\mu g\ m^{-3}$]

Bioturbation

In addition to pore water diffusion, another process that can redistribute contaminants within the sediments is *bioturbation*, the mixing of sediments by organisms. This process is dependent on the types and numbers of organisms and can have advective and diffusive aspects. One type of advective redistribution is accomplished by those benthos that feed at depth and defecate at the surface. Other organisms tend to have a diffusive effect on the sediments because of burrowing, random movement and irrigation (water motion through the burrows due to pumping by organisms).

Bioturbation has been represented mathematically as a diffusional process (e.g., Goldberg and Koide 1962). This characterization differs from pore water diffusion in that both solids and interstitial waters are affected. The flux of solid matter due to the mixing of particles by benthic organisms can be represented as (Berner 1980)

$$J_{B,p} = -E_{B,p} \frac{\partial}{\partial z} \rho_p [1 - \phi(z)] \nu_p \tag{13.53}$$

where $J_{B,p}$ = the flux of solids due to particle mixing expressed in mass per unit area of total sediment per unit time [$\mu g\ m^{-2}\ yr^{-1}$]
   $E_{B,p}$ = a biodiffusion coefficient due to particle mixing expressed in area of total sediment per unit time [$m^2\ yr^{-1}$]

In addition to particle mixing, the pore water is also affected by irrigation by benthic organisms. The total flux due to these processes can be expressed as (Berner 1980)

$$J_{B,d} = -E_{B,p} \frac{\partial}{\partial z} \phi(z) c_{di} - \phi E_I \frac{\partial c_{di}}{\partial z} \tag{13.54}$$

where $J_{B,d}$ = the flux of pore water due to particle mixing and irrigation [$\mu g\ m^{-2}\ yr^{-1}$]

E_I = an irrigation diffusion coefficient expressed as total area per time [m^2 yr^{-1}]

Note that porosity is treated differently for particle mixing and irrigation. The fact that the former includes porosity within the differential connotes that particle mixing affects porosity, whereas irrigation does not.

"Biodiffusion" coefficients for solids have been inferred from profiles of radioactive contaminants in natural sediments (Robbins et al. 1977) and from laboratory studies (Robbins et al. 1979). Results to date indicate values on the order of 10^{-7} cm^2 sec^{-1} (3.15×10^{-4} m^2 yr^{-1}).

Solid / Liquid Sorption

Matter can be transformed by a variety of reactions within the sediments. These range from simple first-order decay to complex, multi-species equilibria. (See Berner 1980 for a review.) Because of its importance in modeling contaminant dynamics, the present section is devoted to the process of sorption.

Sorption is a process whereby a dissolved substance is transferred to and becomes associated with solid material. It includes both the accumulation of dissolved substances on the surface of solids (*adsorption*) and the interpenetration or intermingling of substances with solids (*absorption*). The substance that is sorbed is usually called the *sorbate* and the solid is called the *sorbent*.

The kinetics of sorption can be represented as

$$\text{dissolved} \underset{R_{de}}{\overset{R_{ad}}{\rightleftharpoons}} \text{particulate} \qquad (13.55)$$

where the mass adsorbed per unit time, R_{ad} [μg yr^{-1}], can be represented as

$$R_{ad} = k_{ad} m_p c_d (\nu_{p,max} - \nu_p) \qquad (13.56)$$

where k_{ad} = the mass-specific, volumetric rate of adsorption
             [m^3 μg^{-1} yr^{-1}]
          m_p = the mass of solids [g]
          c_d = the concentration of the dissolved form [μg m^{-3}]
          $\nu_{p,max}$ = the maximum mass-specific concentration of the particles
             [μg g^{-1}]
          ν_p = the mass-specific concentration of the particles [μg g^{-1}]

The mass desorbed per unit time, R_{de} [μg yr^{-1}], can be represented as

$$R_{de} = k_{de} m_p \nu_p \qquad (13.57)$$

where k_{de} is the desorption rate $[yr^{-1}]$.

In a temporal sense, many sorption reactions are rapid and are assumed to reach equilibrium much quicker than the long-term, input-output processes of most lakes. This equilibrium is a dynamic state representing a balance between the rates of adsorption and desorption as in

$$R_{ad} = R_{de} \qquad (13.58)$$

The equilibrium state is typically described using *isotherms* that relate the quantity sorbed per unit of particulate matter to the dissolved concentration. In general, the isotherms increase with increasing solute concentration until available sites approach saturation, i.e., as ν_p approaches $\nu_{p,max}$ (Figure 13.18).

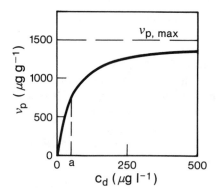

Figure 13.18   A Langmuir isotherm with mass-specific concentration, ν_p, vs dissolved concentration, c_d. Note how the isotherm levels off to a maximum value, $\nu_{p,max}$, with increasing dissolved concentration due to the saturation of available sorption sites on the particles.

There are two isotherms commonly used to characterize sorption equilibria in natural waters (see Travis and Etnier 1981 for a review and comparison of these and other formulations). The *Langmuir* isotherm assumes a monomolecular layer of sorption. It can be derived by substituting Equations 13.56 and 13.57 into Equation 13.58 and rearranging to yield

$$\nu_p = \frac{\nu_{p,max} c_d}{\dfrac{k_{de}}{k_{ad}} + c_d} \qquad (13.59)$$

One flaw of the Langmuir isotherm is that adsorbents often accommodate more than one layer of adsorbate. However, this short-coming does not hold at low concentrations.

The *Freundlich* isotherm, which is an empirical relationship that was, in part, developed to account for the multilayered nature of the sorption mechanism, is expressed as

$$\nu_p = Kc_d^{1/n} \tag{13.60}$$

where K and n are empirically determined constants.

At low concentrations, both the Freundlich and Langmuir isotherms can be approximated as linear functions. For the Langmuir equation, if $c_d \ll k_{de}/k_{ad}$, Equation 13.59 becomes

$$\nu_p = K_d c_d \tag{13.61}$$

where K_d is called a partition (or distribution) coefficient where[*]

$$K_d = \frac{k'_{ad}}{k_{de}} \tag{13.62}$$

where

$$k'_{ad} = k_{ad} \nu_{p, max} \tag{13.63}$$

Since sorption is usually faster than input-output rates, the partition coefficient and the equilibrium assumption often are used to model the process with Di Toro's (1976) local equilibrium solution technique (Section 11.2.3), as discussed in the following section.

---

[*] An alternative formulation for the distribution coefficient is the ratio of mass of contaminant on solids per mass of contaminant in water (e.g., see Lerman and Taniguchi 1972). It is related to the partition coefficient in Equation 13.61 by

$$K'_d = [\rho_p(1 - \phi)/\phi] K_d \tag{13.64}$$

where K'_d might be called the "extensive" distribution coefficient (see footnote on p. 146) since the contaminant masses are neither normalized to solid mass nor water volume as is the case for K_d. We will use the "intensive" distribution coefficient in all of our work but the reader should be cognizant of the existence and use of K'_d in the sediment diagenesis literature. Note further that our use of a prime to denote the "extensive" coefficient is the reverse of the diagenesis literature. They use K'_d and K_d to designate the intensive and extensive coefficients, respectively. We have reversed the convention because it simplifies our nomenclature.

§ § §

Example 13.9. A Langmuir isotherm (Figure 13.18) defining the sorption characteristics of a contaminant and inorganic solids ($\rho_p = 2.5$ g cm^{-3}) has the following characteristics:

$$\nu_{p,\,max} = 1500\ \mu g\,g^{-1}$$

$$a = (k_{de}/k_{ad}) = 50\ \mu g\,l^{-1}$$

$$K_d(Eq.\ 13.62) = 30\ \mu g\,g^{-1}(\mu g\,l^{-1})^{-1}$$

For a closed system (i.e., no inputs or outputs), compute the quantities of contaminant associated with the liquid and solid phases as the contaminant level of the system increases. Perform this computation for: (a) a very dilute system, such as the water column of a lake [$\phi = 0.999995$ and concentration of inorganic suspended solids, $s_i = 12.5$ mg (dry wt) l^{-1}], and (b) a system with a high solids content such as the surficial sediments ($\phi = 0.9$ and $s_i = 250,000$ mg l^{-1}).

Because the system in (b) has a significant fraction of its volume in the solid phase, the concentrations must be adjusted for porosity by using Equations 13.36 and 13.38. The resulting corrections are

$$c_{dt} = \phi c_d \tag{i}$$

and

$$c_{pt} = (1 - \phi)\nu_p \rho_p \tag{ii}$$

where c_{dt} and c_{pt} = concentrations of dissolved and particulate phosphorus, respectively, normalized to the total volume of the system [M L^{-3}]

c_d = the concentration of dissolved contaminant in the pore water [M L^{-3}]

The total concentration of contaminant normalized to the total volume, c_{tt} [M L^{-3}], is defined as

$$c_{tt} = c_{dt} + c_{pt} \tag{iii}$$

These equations can be combined with Equation 13.59, which can be rearranged to yield

$$c_{pt}^2 + \Gamma c_{pt} + \Lambda = 0 \tag{iv}$$

where

$$\Gamma = -[a\phi + c_{tt} + \rho_p(1 - \phi)\nu_{p,\,max}] \tag{v}$$

and

$$\Lambda = \rho_p(1 - \phi)\,\nu_{p,\max}\,c_{tt} \qquad \text{(vi)}$$

and c_{pt} can be solved for

$$c_{pt} = \frac{-\Gamma - \sqrt{\Gamma^2 - 4\Lambda}}{2} \qquad \text{(vii)}$$

and c_{dt} and c_d can be determined using Equations i and iii. The complete form of Equation vii is

$$c_{pt} = \tfrac{1}{2}\{[a\phi + c_{tt} + \rho_p(1 - \phi)\,\nu_{p,\max}]$$

$$- \{[a\phi + c_{tt} + \rho_p(1 - \phi)\,\nu_{p,\max}]^2 - 4\rho_p(1 - \phi)\,\nu_{p,\max}\,c_{tt}\}^{1/2}\} \qquad \text{(viii)}$$

Note that as the contaminant content of the system, c_{tt}, reaches high levels, the quantity associated with the particulate phase approaches a constant, saturated level as in

$$c_{pt} = \rho_p(1 - \phi)\,\nu_{p,\max} \qquad \text{(ix)}$$

When this point is reached, all available sorption sites are effectively filled and additional contaminant goes directly to the dissolved phase. These characteristics are demonstrated in the following computations.

(a) For lake waters with small quantities of suspended solids ($\phi = 0.999995$), Equation viii becomes

$$c_{pt} = \tfrac{1}{2}[(68.75 + c_{tt}) - \sqrt{(68.75 + c_{tt})^2 - 75\,c_{tt}}\,]$$

which can be used to compute the following values

c_{tt} ($\mu g\,l^{-1}$)	c_{pt} ($\mu g\,l^{-1}$)	c_{dt} ($\mu g\,l^{-1}$)
0	0	0
20	4.45	15.55
40	7.40	32.60
60	9.43	50.57
∞	18.75	$\infty - 18.75$

As in Figure 13.19a, the particulate contaminant approaches a saturated level, whereupon the rate of increase of the dissolved fraction becomes equivalent to the rate of increase in the system total contaminant content. Note that, since the contaminant and solids levels are low, the ratio of the dissolved to the particulate concentration is approximately constant. For this reason, models of dilute systems often use partition coefficients rather than isotherms in order to simplify computations.

(b) For a surficial sediment layer, $\phi = 0.9$ and Equation viii becomes

$$c_{pt} = \tfrac{1}{2}\,[(375045 + c_{tt}) - \sqrt{(375045 + c_{tt})^2 - 1.5 \times 10^6\,c_{tt}}\,]$$

which can be used to compute the following values:

c_{tt} $(\mu g\,l^{-1})$	c_{pt} $(\mu g\,l^{-1})$	c_{dt} $(\mu g\,l^{-1})$
0	0	0
200,000	199,949	5 1
400,000	374,343	25,657
600,000	374,925	225,075
800,000	374,960	425,040
∞	375,000	∞ − 375,000

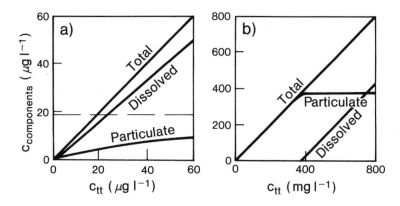

Figure 13.19 Changes in the components of a contaminant with increasing total contaminant content of (a) the water column and (b) the sediments.

The results (Figure 13.19b) are quite different than for the dilute system in (a). For the surficial sediments, there are vast amounts of sorption sites, since the solids' content is four orders of magnitude greater than that of the water column. Consequently, the initial additions of contaminant associate overwhelmingly with the solids. Only upon approaching the saturation point does the contaminant begin accumulating in large quantities in the pore water.

§ § §

13.2.2 General Sediment Mass Balance

The concepts in the previous section can now be used to develop a general mass balance model for lake sediments. For simplicity, we will limit the derivation to the case of a contaminant that is subject to sorption and first-order decay. In addition, it is assumed that: (1) only vertical changes are important, (2) compaction is at a steady state* and (3) no diagenesis, dissolution or precipitation of solid matter occurs.

Because of steady-state compaction, the previous analysis for burial applies. Thus, as in Equations 13.43 and 13.45,

$$v_p(z) = \frac{v_b(1 - \phi')}{[1 - \phi(z)]}$$ (13.65)

and

$$v_d(z) = \frac{v_b \phi'}{\phi(z)}$$ (13.66)

To develop the general model, we will derive separate mass balances for the liquid and solid phases of the contaminant:

Liquid Phase

As in Figure 13.20 there are a number of processes that affect the quantity of contaminant associated with the liquid phase. A general mass balance for a slice of thickness, Δz, over a unit time, Δt, is written as

(accumulation) = (burial in) − (burial out) + (diffusion in) − (diffusion out)

+ (bioturbation in) − (bioturbation out) − (decay)

− (adsorption) + (desorption)

From the relationships introduced in Section 13.2.1 and summarized in Table 13.7, the mass balance can be written as

---

*See Imboden (1975) for a treatment of non-steady-state compaction.

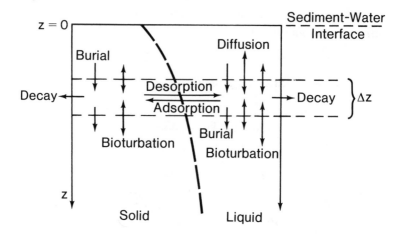

Figure 13.20 Schematic of a finite slice of sediment of thickness, Δz. The arrows designate the processes governing the dynamics of a contaminant undergoing decay and sorption reactions.

$$\frac{\partial}{\partial t}\,\phi(z)\,c_{di} = -v_b\,\phi'\,\frac{\partial c_{di}}{\partial z} + \frac{\partial}{\partial z}\,\phi(z)\,D_s(z)\,\frac{\partial c_{di}}{\partial z}$$

$$+ \frac{\partial}{\partial z}\,E_{B,p}(z)\,\frac{\partial}{\partial z}\,\phi(z)\,c_{di} + \frac{\partial}{\partial z}\,\phi(z)\,E_I(z)\,\frac{\partial c_{di}}{\partial z}$$

$$-k\phi(z)\,c_{di} - k'_{ad}\,\rho_p\,[1-\phi(z)]\,c_{di} + k_{de}\,\nu_p\,\rho_p\,[1-\phi(z)] \qquad (13.67)$$

where c_{di} is the concentration in the pore (or interstitial) water $[\mu g\ m^{-3}]$.

Solid Phase

As in Figure 13.20, the mass balance for the contaminant in the solid phase can be represented as

$$(\text{accumulation}) = (\text{burial in}) - (\text{burial out})$$

$$+ (\text{bioturbation in}) - (\text{bioturbation out})$$

$$- (\text{decay}) - (\text{desorption}) + (\text{adsorption})$$

which can be written in complete form as

$$\frac{\partial}{\partial t}\,[1-\phi(z)]\,\rho_p\,\nu_p = -v_b(1-\phi')\rho_p\,\frac{\partial \nu_p}{\partial z} + \frac{\partial}{\partial z}\,E_{B,p}(z)\,\frac{\partial}{\partial z}\,\rho_p[1-\phi(z)]\,\nu_p$$

Table 13.7   Individual Terms of a Mass Balance for the
Dissolved Phase of a Contaminant in a Lake's Sediments[a]

Accumulation

$$A_m \Delta z \phi(z) \Delta c_{di}$$

Burial input

$$v_b \phi' A_m c_{di} \Delta t$$

Burial output

$$v_b \phi' A_m \left(c_{di} + \frac{\partial c_{di}}{\partial z} \Delta z \right) \Delta t$$

Diffusion input

$$- A_m \phi(z) D_s(z) \frac{\partial c_{di}}{\partial z} \Delta t$$

Diffusion output

$$- A_m \left[\phi(z) D_s(z) + \frac{\partial}{\partial z} \phi(z) D_s(z) \Delta z \right] \left[\frac{\partial c_{di}}{\partial z} + \frac{\partial}{\partial z} \frac{\partial c_{di}}{\partial z} \Delta z \right] \Delta t$$

Bioturbation input

$$- A_m \left[E_{B,p}(z) \frac{\partial}{\partial z} \phi(z) c_{di} + \phi(z) E_I(z) \frac{\partial c_{di}}{\partial z} \right]$$

Bioturbation output

$$- A_m \left[E_{B,p}(z) + \frac{\partial}{\partial z} E_{B,p}(z) \Delta z \right] \left[\frac{\partial}{\partial z} \phi(z) c_{di} + \frac{\partial}{\partial z} \frac{\partial}{\partial z} \phi(z) c_{di} \Delta z \right]$$

$$+ \left[\phi(z) E_I(z) + \frac{\partial}{\partial z} \phi(z) E_I(z) \Delta z \right] \left[\frac{\partial c_{di}}{\partial z} + \frac{\partial}{\partial z} \frac{\partial c_{di}}{\partial z} \Delta z \right] \Delta t$$

Decay

$$k c_{di} \phi(z) A_m \Delta z \Delta t$$

Adsorption

$$k'_{ad} \rho_p [1 - \phi(z)] c_{di} A_m \Delta z \Delta t$$

Desorption

$$k_{de} \nu_p \rho_p [1 - \phi(z)] A_m \Delta z \Delta t$$

[a]The balance is for a slice of thickness, Δz, over a time interval, Δt. Each term represents the amount of mass that enters or leaves the dissolved phase of the slice over the time interval $[MT^{-1}]$. A_m = the area of lake sediment.

$$- k \rho_p [1 - \phi(z)] \nu_p - k_{de} \nu_p \rho_p [1 - \phi(z)]$$

$$+ k'_{ad} \rho_p [1 - \phi(z)] c_{di} \qquad (13.68)$$

By assuming a local equilibrium, Equations 13.67 and 13.68 can be combined to yield

$$\frac{\partial c_t}{\partial t} = -v_b [\phi' + K_d \rho_p (1 - \phi')] \frac{\partial}{\partial z} F_{dp} c_t$$

$$+ \frac{\partial}{\partial z} \phi(z) [D_s(z) + E_I(z)] \frac{\partial}{\partial z} F_{dp} c_t + \frac{\partial}{\partial z} E_{B,p} \frac{\partial c_t}{\partial z} - k c_t$$

(13.69)

where

$$c_t = \phi(z) c_{di} + v_p \rho_p [1 - \phi(z)]$$ (13.70)

and

$$\frac{v_p}{c_{di}} = K_d$$ (13.71)

and

$$c_{di} = F_{dp} c_t$$ (13.72)

where F_{dp} = the fraction of contaminant in the pore water, which is equal to

$$F_{dp} = \frac{1}{\phi(z) + K_d \rho_p [1 - \phi(z)]}$$ (13.73)

Solution Techniques

By making simplifying assumptions, Equation 13.69 can be solved analytically. In particular, Lerman (1971), Lerman and Weiler (1970), and Lerman and Lietzke (1975) have derived a number of solutions. However, for our purposes, numerical solution techniques provide a more general approach. As described in Section 12.3.2, Thomann's (1972) control volume method is particularly useful in this regard because: (1) by definition, it conserves mass, and (2) it is designed to automatically accommodate variable-sized segments.

The former advantage is important because conventional finite difference formulations do not necessarily conserve mass when applied to differential equations with spatially varying coefficients (Roache 1972). The latter advantage—variable-sized segmentation—is useful because, for most cases, finer detail is required near the sediment-water interface than at depth. Aside from the numerical integration technique, boundary conditions are required to solve Equation 13.69. These must be specified at the sediment-water interface and at a lower boundary within the sediments.

For the sediment-water interface, two general approaches can be taken. In the first case, the concentration at $z = 0$ is specified. This is often invoked under the assumption that turbulence causes the concentration at $z = 0$ to equal that in the overlying waters. For this situation, the flux into the first control volume below the sediment-water interface can be formulated as

$$J_{in} = v_b \, [\phi' + K_d \rho_p (1 - \phi')] c_{d,w} + D_s \, \phi(0) \, \frac{c_{d,w} - c_{di,1}}{z_1/2} \qquad (13.74)$$

where $c_{d,w}$ = the contaminant concentration in the dissolved phase for the overlying waters
$\quad\quad\;\; c_{di,1}$ = the pore water concentration in the first control volume
$\quad\quad\;\; z_1$ = the thickness of the first control volume

The second method of formulating the boundary condition is used for cases where the sediments and the water column are being modeled as a coupled system. For this situation, the flux is

$$J_{in} = v_w \, \frac{K_d \, s_w}{1 + K_d \, s_w} \, c_{t,w} + D_s \, \phi(0) \, \frac{c_{d,w} - c_{di,1}}{(z_1 + z_b)/2} \qquad (13.75)$$

where v_w = the settling velocity of particulate matter from the water column to the sediments
$\quad\quad\;\; s_w$ = the concentration of particulate matter in the water column
$\quad\quad\;\; z_b$ = the thickness of the laminar boundary layer just above the sediment-water interface

For the lower boundary, two approaches are also used. Where the concentration at depth is known, the boundary condition is handled by simply writing the mass balance equation for the deepest (i.e., the nth segment) as if an additional segment were below. The concentrations for this segment $n + 1$ would then be set at the prescribed boundary condition.

For the case of a free boundary condition (i.e., unspecified), the simplest approach is to use enough segments so that the bottom boundary flux has negligible effect on the solution in the area of interest. For this case, the flux out of the deepest segment can be specified as

$$J_{out} = -v_b \, c_{t,n} \qquad (13.75a)$$

where $c_{t,n}$ is the total contaminant concentration for the deepest segment. Note that this formulation implies that the gradient at the lower boundary is equal to zero. In a practical sense, this can be accomplished by adding several relatively large segments to the bottom of the segmentation scheme. This ensures that the lower boundary will have negligible effect on the dynamics of the area of interest, the upper sediments.

A final consideration regarding solution techniques is the existence of numerical diffusion as discussed previously on p. 120. In the present context, it is relevant when modeling substances that sorb strongly. For these substances, true diffusive transport is minimal and advective burial is the primary transport mechanism. Thus, numerical diffusion can result in an artificial increase in substance transport for solid-associated contaminants. Using relationships noted previously, numerical diffusion can be estimated. For the general case, an appropriate version for a sediment of constant porosity is (as in Equation 12.112),

$$D_n = \tfrac{1}{2} v_b \, \Delta z \left(1 - \frac{v_b \, \Delta t}{\Delta z} \right) \tag{13.75b}$$

where D_n is a numerical diffusion coefficient (on a whole-sediment basis) and Δz is the thickness of a sediment segment. Equation 13.75b can be directly compared with a relationship such as Equation 13.88 to determine the relative importance of the artificial diffusion. If it has a significant effect on the simulation, two corrective options are available. The first is to decrease the size, Δz, of the segments. The practical problem with this is that it can prove costly due to the increased number of segments needed to characterize the system (see Example 13.14). The second alternative, which is applicable for cases where the contaminant associates overwhelmingly with the solids, is to develop exact, analytical solutions, which are sometimes possible for purely advective systems (see Example 13.11).

§ § §

Example 13.10. Chloride concentrations in Lake Ontario have been increasing since 1900 (Beeton 1965). Lerman and Weiler (1970) have idealized this increase by the following functions:

$$c_{d,w} = 7.68 \qquad\qquad t < 1920$$

$$c_{d,w} = 7.68 + 0.4255 \, (t - 1920) \qquad t > 1920$$

where $c_{d,w}$ is the concentration of chloride in the water of Lake Ontario [g m^{-3}]. With these functions as boundary conditions, use the general sediment model to compute the resulting profile of chloride in the sediments for the cases of (a) constant porosity of 0.85 and (b) porosity varying with depth as

$$\phi(z) = (0.895 - 0.82)e^{-0.07z} + 0.82$$

The burial velocity at depth, v_b, is 0.05 cm yr^{-1}. Assume that bioturbation is negligible.

The temperature of the sediments of a deep system, such as Lake Ontario, is approximately 4°C. A molecular diffusion coefficient of 1.16×10^{-5} cm^2 sec^{-1} can be estimated from Figure 13.17. Using Thomann's control volume approach, Equation 13.69 can be solved numerically with the whole sediment diffusion coefficient related to the molecular diffusivity by Equation 13.49. The results, which are displayed in Figure 13.21, suggest that the diffusion coefficient used in the model is slightly low. Lerman and Weiler (1970) performed the same computation with an exact solution technique and found that values of D_s from 2 to 3 $(\times 10^{-5})$ cm^2 sec^{-1} provided an adequate fit.

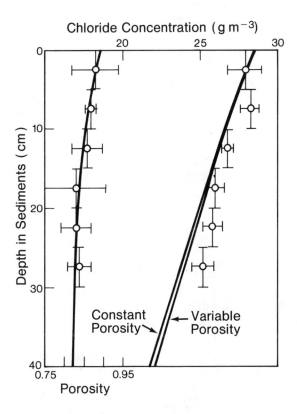

Figure 13.21 Simulation results for chloride in the sediments of Lake Ontario. The profiles correspond to conditions in 1969 due to changes in the overlying water concentration over the previous 49 years.

An important result of the computation is that the effect of variable porosity is negligible. This is generally true for lake sediments with high porosities (i.e., 0.75–0.95). For these cases, a constant porosity model, as described in the next section, can be used. However, for situations such as sandy sediments, where porosities are low, the porosity effect can be more pronounced and should be considered to assess its importance.

§ § §

13.2.3 Simplified Sediment Models

Although the general model described in the previous section can be used to simulate vertical profiles of contaminants in lake sediments, it is too complex and data-demanding for many engineering applications. In particular, the effect of compaction greatly complicates the framework. For this reason, we will develop two simplified versions of the general model that are more compatible with engineering problems. In the first case, we develop a model for contaminants that associate overwhelmingly with the particulate phase. For this situation, the pore water component can be ignored and, for sediments with negligible bioturbation, the model becomes purely advective. Thus, the simulation of the compaction effect is greatly simplified. In the second case, we develop a model for a sediment with negligible compaction. For this situation, porosity is constant with depth and the mathematics are greatly simplified. In both models, bioturbation is accounted for by using a single well-mixed layer at the sediment surface to represent the net effect of biological mixing.

Model of Particulate Distribution

A simple sediment model can be developed for a substance that associates primarily with the solid phase and that decays with first-order kinetics (Robbins and Edgington 1975). In this example, the input from the water column to the surficial (or mixed) layer is assumed to be known *a priori*. In a later section, we present a framework for a computation in which the sediment and water column are coupled. With this in mind, a mass balance for surficial sediment solids would be

$$V_{t,m} \frac{d}{dt} \{\rho_p \nu_{p,m}[1 - \phi(0)]\} = J_{wm} A_w \nu_{p,w} - \nu_m A_m \rho_p \nu_{p,m}[1 - \phi(0)]$$

$$- k_m V_{m,t} \rho_p \nu_{p,m}[1 - \phi(0)] \qquad (13.76)$$

where   subscript m = the surficial sediments
$V_{t,m}$ = the total volume of the surficial sediments [m^3]
J_{wm} = the net flux of solid matter from the water to the sediments [g m^{-2} yr^{-1}]
$\nu_{p,w}$ = the mass-specific concentration of the contaminant for particles in the water column [μg g^{-1}]
v_m = the burial velocity at the interface between the surficial and the deep sediments [m yr^{-1}]
k_m = the decay rate of the contaminant [yr^{-1}]
A_m = the surface area of the sediment-water interface [m^2]

Equation 13.76 can be used as a solids budget as well as a contaminant budget. In this case we use it as a solids budget. At steady-state, Equation 13.76 can be used to estimate v_m, since for solid matter $\nu_{p,w}$ and $\nu_{p,m} = 1.0$ and $k = 0$, and therefore

$$v_m = \frac{J_{wm}}{\rho_p[1 - \phi(0)]} \frac{A_w}{A_m} \qquad (13.77)$$

Once v_m is known, Equation 13.76 can be used as a contaminant budget. For this case (i.e., $\nu_{p,w}$ and $\nu_{p,m} \neq 1.0$), it can be solved for the mass-specific concentration of the constituent in the well-mixed layer

$$\nu_{p,m} = \frac{1}{1 - \phi(0)} \frac{J_{wm} \nu_{p,w}}{v_m \rho_p + k_m z_m \rho_p} \frac{A_w}{A_m} \qquad (13.78)$$

where z_m is the thickness of the surficial sediments [m].

For the deep sediments, an advection equation can be used to compute the profile of the particulate-associated constituent

$$\frac{\partial}{\partial t} \nu_{p,s} \rho_p [1 - \phi(0)] = - \frac{\partial}{\partial z} v_{p,s} \nu_{p,s} \rho_p [1 - \phi(0)] - k_s \nu_{p,s} \rho_p [1 - \phi(0)] \qquad (13.79)$$

where the subscript s refers to the deep sediments. For solid matter ($k = 0$, $\nu = 1.$), Equation 13.79 yields (at steady state)

$$\frac{\partial}{\partial z} v_{p,s} \rho_p [1 - \phi(0)] = 0 \qquad (13.80)$$

In other words, the flux, which is equivalent to the product of velocity, density and $(1 - \phi)$, is constant with depth. Therefore,

$$v_{p,s}(z) \rho_p [1 - \phi(z)] = v_b \rho_p (1 - \phi') \qquad (13.81)$$

Equation 13.39 can be substituted into Equation 13.81 to yield

$$v_{p,s}(z) = \frac{v_b}{1 - \Phi e^{-\beta z}} \qquad (13.82)$$

where

$$\Phi = \frac{\phi(0) - \phi'}{1 - \phi'} \qquad (13.83)$$

Equation 13.82 can be substituted into Equation 13.79

$$\frac{\partial v_{p,s}}{\partial t} = - \frac{v_b}{1 - \Phi e^{-\beta z}} \frac{\partial v_{p,s}}{\partial z} - k_s v_{p,s} \qquad (13.84)$$

Equation 13.84 can be solved for

$$v_{p,s} = v_{p,m} e^{-k\Upsilon} \qquad (13.85)$$

where

$$\Upsilon = \frac{z}{v_b} - \frac{\Phi}{\beta v_b} (1 - e^{-\beta z}) \qquad (13.86)$$

§ § §

Example 13.11. As an example, the above model can be applied to ^{210}Pb in Lake Michigan.* Using the data in Table 13.8, we can compute: (a) the burial velocity at the top of the deep layer, (b) the mass-specific concentration in the surficial layer and (c) the profile in the deep layer.

(a) Equation 13.77 can be used to estimate v_m as in

$$v_m = \frac{92.3}{2.5 \times 10^6 (1 - 0.88)} \frac{53.5}{30} = 5.49 \times 10^{-4} \text{ m yr}^{-1}$$

(b) Equation 13.78

$$v_{p,m} = \frac{1}{1 - 0.88} \frac{92.3(2.1 \times 10^{-11})}{5.49 \times 10^{-4}(2.5 \times 10^6) + 0.0231(2 \times 10^{-2})(2.5 \times 10^6)} \frac{53.5}{30}$$

$$= 11.4 \times 10^{-12} \text{ Ci g}^{-1}$$

---

*Note, that in all our work with radionuclides we use the Curie (Ci) to measure radioactivity. This was done because most of the papers from which we have drawn our examples use that unit. The more acceptable unit, at present, is disintegrations per second (dps or *Becquerels*) that is related to the Curie by 1 Ci = 3.7×10^{10} dps.

Table 13.8   Parameters Used to Compute ^{210}Pb Levels
in Sediments of Lake Michigan

Parameter	Symbol	Value	Units
Solids flux	J_{mw}	92.3	g m^{-2} yr^{-1}
Solids density	ρ_p	2.5×10^6	g m^{-3}
Mixed-layer thickness	z_m	2×10^{-2}	m
Mixed-layer porosity	$\phi(0)$	0.88	
Porosity at depth	ϕ'	0.76	
Rate of compaction	β	19	m^{-1}
Mass-specific concentration of particles in the water	$\nu_{p,w}$	2.1×10^{-11}	Ci g^{-1}
Radioactive decay rate of ^{210}Pb	k, k_m	0.0231	yr^{-1}
Lake surface area	A_w	53.5×10^9	m^2
Mixed sediment surface area	A_m	30×10^9	m^2

(c) Equation 13.85

$$\nu_{p,s}(z) = 11.4 \times 10^{-12} e^{-0.0231\,\Upsilon}$$

where (Equation 13.86)

$$\Upsilon = \frac{z}{2.74 \times 10^{-4}} - \frac{0.5}{19(2.74 \times 10^{-4})}(1 - e^{-19z})$$

since (Equation 13.83)

$$\Phi = \frac{0.88 - 0.76}{1 - 0.76} = 0.5$$

and (Equations 13.82 and 13.83)

$$v_b = v_p(0)[1 - \Phi] = 5.49 \times 10^{-4}(1 - 0.5) = 2.74 \times 10^{-4} \text{ m yr}^{-1}$$

The results of the computation are shown in Figure 13.22 and are compiled in Table 13.9 where depth is measured from the bottom of the surficial sediment layer.

§ § §

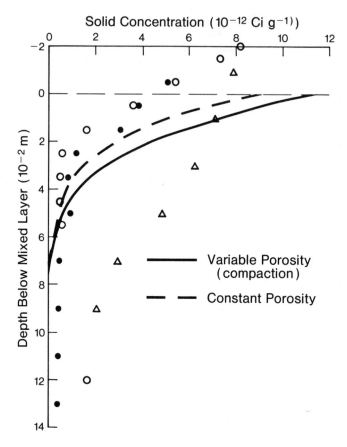

Figure 13.22 Plot of computed profiles of ^{210}Pb in Lake Michigan sediments for models with variable (i.e., compaction) and constant porosity.

Table 13.9   Simulated Values of ^{210}Pb Concentration in the
Deep Sediments of Lake Michigan[a]

$z(10^{-2})$	Υ (yr)	$\nu_{p,s}(10^{-12}\,Ci\,g^{-1})$
0	0.0	11.40
2	42.6	4.26
4	94.9	1.27
6	153.7	0.327
8	216.9	0.076
10	283.3	0.016

[a]Depth is measured downward from the bottom of the surficial layer.

Constant Porosity Model

If porosity can be assumed to be constant, Equation 13.69 can be simplified to yield

$$\frac{\partial c_t}{\partial t} = -v_b \frac{\partial c_t}{\partial z} + D_s' \frac{\partial^2 c_t}{\partial z^2} - kc_t \qquad (13.87)$$

where D_s' is an effective diffusion coefficient defined as

$$D_s' = \frac{\phi D_s}{\phi + K_d \rho_p (1 - \phi)} \qquad (13.88)$$

§ § §

Example 13.12. Compute the effective diffusion coefficient for a contaminant ($D_s = 10^{-5}$ cm^2 sec^{-1}) in a constant porosity sediment ($\phi = 0.85$, $\rho_p = 2.5 \times 10^6$ g m^{-3}). Perform the calculation for the following values of K_d: 0, 10^{-4}, 10^{-3}, 10^{-2}, 10^{-1} and 1.0 m^3 g^{-1}.

Using Equation 13.88, the following values can be computed:

K_d (m^3 g^{-1})	D_s' (cm^2 sec^{-1})
0	10^{-5}
10^{-4}	2.22×10^{-7}
10^{-3}	2.26×10^{-8}
10^{-2}	2.27×10^{-9}
10^{-1}	2.27×10^{-10}
1.0	2.27×10^{-11}

Increasing K_d decreases the effective diffusion coefficient because more of the contaminant is fixed to immobile particles at higher levels of sorption. Consequently, a smaller proportion of the contaminant is dissolved and free to diffuse as K_d is increased. The fact that Equation 13.88 accounts for the reduction of the real diffusion rate, D_s, due to sorption is the reason that D_s' is termed an *effective* diffusion coefficient.

§ § §

Because Equation 13.87 has constant coefficients, its solution is greatly simplified. For example, at steady state, with a boundary condition of $c_t = c_{t,o}$ at $z = 0$, the solution is

$$c_t = c_{t,o} \exp\left(\frac{v_b}{2D_s'} \left[1 - \sqrt{1 + \frac{4D_s' k}{v_b^2}} \right] z \right) \qquad (13.89)$$

For the case of a substance that associates overwhelmingly with the solid phase, Equation 13.87 becomes

$$\frac{\partial \nu_p}{\partial t} = -v_b \frac{\partial \nu_p}{\partial z} - k \nu_p \qquad (13.90)$$

which can be solved at steady state for

$$\nu_p = \nu_o \exp\left(-\frac{k}{v_b} z \right) \qquad (13.91)$$

§ § §

Example 13.13. To illustrate the use of this model we can compute the ^{210}Pb profiles for Lake Michigan assuming constant porosity (Table 13.8). The average porosity from the sediment-water interface to 10 cm in the deep sediments is 0.825. Using Equation 13.77,

$$v_m = \frac{93.2}{2.5 \times 10^{-6}(1 - 0.825)} \frac{53.5}{30} = 3.8 \times 10^{-4} \, \text{m yr}^{-1}$$

Using Equation 13.78

$$\nu_m = \frac{1}{(1 - 0.825)} \frac{92.3(2.1 \times 10^{-11})}{3.8 \times 10^{-4}(2.5 \times 10^{6}) + 0.0231(0.02)2.5 \times 10^{6}} \frac{53.5}{30}$$

$$= 9.38 \times 10^{-12} \, \text{Ci g}^{-1}$$

Using Equation 13.91, the levels in the deep sediment can be computed. The results are shown in Figure 13.22 along with results for the variable porosity computation (Example 13.11). Note that the effect of compaction on the profiles is slight. This suggests that for engineering computations, a constant porosity model represents an adequate approximation.

§ § §

Example 13.14. The sediment model (Equation 13.69) is to be used to simulate contaminant dynamics for a constant porosity system with the following characteristics:

$$
\begin{aligned}
v_b &= 5 \times 10^{-3} \text{ m yr}^{-1} & K_d &= 1 \text{ m}^3 \text{ g}^{-1} \\
\phi &= 0.8 & D_s &= 0.0315 \text{ m}^2 \text{ yr}^{-1} \\
\rho_p &= 2.5 \times 10^6 \text{ g m}^{-3} & k &= 0
\end{aligned}
$$

A control volume approach (Section 12.3.2) with equal-sized segments ($\Delta z = 10^{-2}$ m) and a time step of $\Delta t = 0.1$ yr is to be used to simulate the contaminant distribution in the sediments over a period of twenty years. Determine the numerical diffusion associated with such a computation. Equation 13.75b can be used to estimate the numerical diffusion as in

$$
D_n = \tfrac{1}{2}(5 \times 10^{-3}) 10^{-2} \left[1 - \frac{5 \times 10^{-3}(0.1)}{10^{-2}} \right]
$$

$$
= 2.375 \times 10^{-5} \text{ m}^2 \text{ yr}^{-1}
$$

There are two ways to assess the impact of this level of numerical diffusion on the hypothetical computation. First, it can be compared with the level of real diffusion for the system. Using Equation 13.88, the effective diffusion coefficient can be computed as in

$$
D_s' = \frac{0.8(0.0315)}{0.8 + 1(2.5 \times 10^6)(1 - 0.8)} = 5 \times 10^{-8} \text{ m}^2 \text{ yr}^{-1}
$$

Therefore, artificial diffusion is over two orders of magnitude higher than the real effective diffusion for the system.

Aside from the relationship to real diffusion, numerical diffusion must also be compared with advection to assess its importance. In the absence of the artificial diffusion, the system under consideration is highly advective. If a contaminant were introduced to the sediment-water interface at time zero, it would be transported downward by pure burial. The depth to which it would be buried over the 20 year simulation can be computed as

$$
L_a = t \, v_b = 20(5 \times 10^{-3}) = 10^{-1} \text{ m}
$$

where L_a is the penetration depth of the contaminant due to burial and t is the total time of the computation. Therefore, the contaminant would be buried 10 cm over the 20-year period. This process can be compared with transport due to diffusion by an equation developed by Lerman and Taniguchi (1972)

$$
L_d = \sqrt{D_s t} \tag{i}
$$

where L_d is the penetration depth due to diffusion. This relationship is based on Fickian diffusion models of the kind discussed in Chapter 12 (see Example 12.1 on p. 80). Whereas Fickian models had certain deficiencies with regard to describing large-scale turbulence, they are appropriate and useful in gaining insight into sediment dynamics (see the references of Lerman). For the present example, Equation i can be used to estimate the penetration due to real diffusion for the 20-year period of the computation as in

$$L_d \text{ (real)} = \sqrt{D_s' t} = \sqrt{5 \times 10^{-8} (20)} = 10^{-3} \text{ m}$$

Therefore, penetration by diffusion is negligible in comparison with advective burial. Numerical diffusion, on the other hand, is comparable to burial,

$$L_d \text{ (artificial)} = \sqrt{D_n t} = \sqrt{2.375 \times 10^{-5} (20)} = 2.18 \times 10^{-2} \text{ m}$$

Thus, the numerical scheme will produce spurious transport of the contaminant that will lead to an inaccurate computation. Aside from coming up with an analytical solution (as in Examples 13.11 and 13.13), the only way to remove this error is to use a finer size grid (i.e., smaller segments). A rough estimate of the segment size needed to minimize numerical diffusion can be obtained as 1% of the burial penetration depth as in

$$\Delta z \cong 0.01 L_a = 1 \times 10^{-3} \text{ m}$$

Using this grid size, artificial diffusion would be

$$D_n = \tfrac{1}{2}(5 \times 10^{-3}) 1 \times 10^{-3} = 2.5 \times 10^{-6} \text{ m}^2 \text{yr}^{-1}$$

and the penetration depth would be

$$L_d = \sqrt{(2.5 \times 10^{-6}) 20} = 7.1 \times 10^{-3} \text{ m}$$

which represents about a 10% error. However, the use of the finer segmentation scheme results in 10 times as many segments. This could significantly add to computation costs.

§ § §

13.3 SEDIMENT-WATER MODELS

Now that we have reviewed basic methods for modeling substance dynamics in the water column and in the sediments, we can develop frameworks for computing their coupled response. This development necessitates a choice of time scales. Although some systems show a strong seasonal component owing to hypolimnetic oxygen depletion, we will derive models to resolve year-to-year variations. This choice of an annual time step is based on the assumptions that: (1) the time frame of the sedimentation process in many lakes is on the order of years to decades and (2) although seasonal variations can have profound effects on water quality, it is assumed they do not significantly affect the input-output characteristics of most lakes on an annual time frame.

Because of the annual time scale, the following derivations use partition coefficients to characterize the effect of the seasonal processes on the long-term prediction. First, we review total phosphorus, sediment-water models that have been developed to simulate long-term trends of eutrophication. Then, a sediment-water model that distinguishes between allochthonous and autochthonous solid matter in a deep lake is derived. This model is designed to simulate the dynamics of contaminants; as such, it is a precursor of some of the models developed in Chapter 15 for modeling toxic substances.

13.3.1 Sediment-Water Models for Phosphorus

Lorenzen (1974) and Lorenzen et al. (1976) have developed a simple model of sediment-water interactions for total phosphorus as depicted in Figure 13.23. Mass balances for water column and mixed sediment phosphorus concentrations yield the following coupled differential equations:

$$V_{t,w} \frac{dp_w}{dt} = W_p(t) + v_f A_m p_m - v_p A_w p_w - Q p_w \qquad (13.92)$$

and

$$V_{t,m} \frac{dp_m}{dt} = -v_f A_m p_m + (1 - f_b) v_p A_w p_w \qquad (13.93)$$

where   subscripts w and m = water and surficial sediments, respectively
v_f = velocity of the feedback of phosphorus from the sediments into the water column $(LT^{-1}]$
f_b = the fraction of phosphorus buried directly to the lake's deep sediments*

---

*Lorenzen (1974) interprets f_b as the fraction of the sediment phosphorus that is unavailable for reintroduction into the water column. He calls this unavailable fraction "nonexchangeable phosphorus." The reader should consult Lorenzen's original papers for an accurate representation of his perspective. Our modified version contains most of his approach but is more compatible with the other models in this chapter.

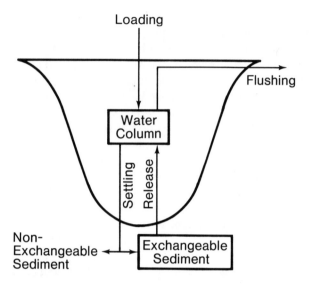

Figure 13.23   Schematic of Lorenzen's long-term sediment/water model for total phosphorus.

If $A_w = A_m$, these equations can be reexpressed as

$$\frac{dp_w}{dt} + \alpha_w \, p_w = \beta_w \, p_m + \Omega_w \qquad (13.94)$$

and

$$\frac{dp_m}{dt} + \alpha_m \, p_m = \beta_m \, p_w \qquad (13.95)$$

where

$$\alpha_w = \frac{Q}{V_{t,w}} + \frac{v_p}{z_w} \qquad (13.96)$$

$$\beta_w = \frac{v_f}{z_w} \qquad (13.97)$$

$$\alpha_m = \frac{v_f}{z_m} \qquad (13.98)$$

$$\beta_m = \frac{(1 - f_b)v_p}{z_m} \qquad (13.99)$$

$$\Omega_w = \frac{W_p(t)}{V_{t,w}} \qquad (13.100)$$

Equations 13.94 and 13.95 are of the same form as Equations 11.57 and 11.70; therefore, the solutions of Equations 11.79–11.82 apply. For example, the steady-state levels are

$$\bar{p}_w = \frac{\overline{W}_p}{Q + f_b v_p A_m} \qquad (13.101)$$

$$\bar{p}_m = \frac{v_p(1 - f_b)}{v_f} \bar{p}_w \qquad (13.102)$$

§ § §

Example 13.15. Lorenzen et al. (1976) applied Equations 13.94 and 13.95 to Lake Washington. Using the coefficients in Table 13.10: (a) calculate the steady-state concentrations of phosphorus in the water and in the exchangeable sediments, and (b) compute the time to reach 90% of a new steady state if the loading is totally removed.

(a) Equations 13.101 and 13.102 can be used to compute the steady-state concentration as in

$$\bar{p}_w = \frac{61000 \times 10^3}{9 \times 10^8 + 0.6(36)(1 \times 10^8)} = 0.02 \text{ g m}^{-3}$$

$$\bar{p}_m = \frac{36(1 - 0.6)}{0.0012} (0.02) = 240 \text{ g m}^{-3}$$

Table 13.10   Data Used by Lorenzen (1976) for His Steady-State Calibration of Lake Washington for the Period from 1941–1950

Parameter	Units	Value
v_p	m yr^{-1}	36
v_f	m yr^{-1}	0.0012
f_b	—	0.6
Q	m^3 yr^{-1}	9×10^8
$\overline{W}_p$	kg yr^{-1}	61,000
A_w	m^2	1×10^8
z_w	m	38
z_m	m	10×10^{-2}

(b) With Equations 11.81 and 11.82 or a fourth-order Runge-Kutta technique (Section 11.3.2), Equations 13.92 and 13.93 can be integrated and plotted as in Figure 13.24. The results show that the lake would take approximately 146 years to reach 90% of the new steady state after the termination of loads. This is in contrast to approximately 3 years as calculated by a single-compartment model for the same system. Thus, according to the model computation, the inclusion of sediment "memory" has a decided effect on the lake's response. It is important to note that these results are a function of a number of factors, including the thickness of the active sediment layer and the assumption that the lake was in equilibrium with the sediments at the beginning of the computation.

§ § §

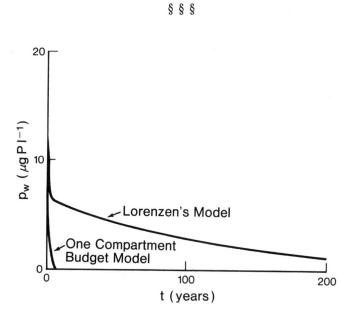

Figure 13.24   The response characteristics of Lorenzen's model and a total phosphorus budget model of Lake Washington to termination of loadings at time = 0. Note, how the one-compartment model responds quickly whereas following a quick initial drop, the Lorenzen model levels off due to sediment feedback of phosphorus.

Although Lorenzen's model represents an important development in phosphorus budget computations, it has a number of shortcomings that limit its general use. Beyond the fact that, as with any long-term approach, it is incapable of simulating the seasonal patterns of sediment release that are quite important in lakes with anoxic hypolimnia, there are two basic problems with the approach.

First, for substances such as phosphorus that accumulate at high concentrations in the pore water, the use of a single well-mixed sediment layer with a one-way loss to the deep sediments is inadequate. For such substances, significant quantities can migrate upward from the deep sediments via pore water diffusion. Because of this, the Lorenzen model is only strictly applicable to substances that associate overwhelmingly with particulate matter. For these cases, diffusive transport would be negligible and the one-way loss to the deep sediments would be a realistic approximation. It should also be noted that for strongly sorbing substances the feedback velocity (v_f) would be due solely to physical resuspension of the sediments.

Second, the mechanistic basis of most of the coefficients is nebulous. For example, the fraction buried in the deep sediments, f_b, is the result of several processes, including the sorption characteristics of the solid sediments and the sedimentation rate. In addition, there is a difficulty in specifying the volume (or thickness) of the exchangeable sediment compartment. This is especially important since the time variable solution to Equations 13.94 and 13.95 is highly sensitive to sediment thickness and adequate guidance for the choice of this parameter is not given.

Lung et al. (1976) have taken a more mechanistic approach by dividing the total phosphorus into particulate and dissolved fractions. In this way they achieve a more realistic representation of processes governing sediment-water interactions. For example, only particulate phosphorus is subject to sedimentation in the water column, whereas only the dissolved fraction is subject to diffusive transport in the sediments. Transformations within the sediments are characterized by a donor-dependent, linear first-order reaction from the particulate to the dissolved form. An additional feature of the approach is that the sediments are treated as a series of thin, well-mixed layers with sedimentation rates and diffusion coefficients used to define interlayer transport. In this way, the somewhat imprecise choice of a thickness for a single sediment layer is avoided.

Kamp-Nielson (1977) has developed an even more mechanistic framework that also distinguishes between dissolved and particulate forms of phosphorus, but divides the latter into exchangeable and nonexchangeable fractions. This model has been used to simulate sediment-water exchange for a single-layer system and uses elaborate, experimentally derived mathematical relationships to represent the kinetic interactions between the various forms of phosphorus. In general, most of the exchanges are donor-dependent reactions. However, diffusion is only used for the anaerobic case and depends on the gradient across the interface. Although Kamp-Nielson's (1977) approach is seasonal and many of the rates are site-specific, his mechanistic orientation allows the rates of processes in the model to be estimated from experimental data.

In subsequent work, Kamp-Nielson (1978) has used a similar model to simulate phosphorus dynamics using a multilayer model in a fashion similar to Lung et al. (1976). An important addition in this model was that, along with nonexchangeable P, exchangeable P and dissolved P, a pool called sorbed P also was included. In contrast to previous work, this pool interacted with the dissolved phase via an equilibrium rather than a kinetic reaction.

In summary, preliminary mathematical frameworks for modeling sediment-water interactions have been developed for the nutrient phosphorus (see Chapter 5 of Volume 1 for additional details). However, most of the significant work has been derived to resolve seasonal processes. The following model differs somewhat in that it is designed to simulate the long-term dynamics of contaminants in lakes and their underlying sediments.

13.3.2 General Long-Term Sediment-Water Model for a Contaminant

As stated at the beginning of this chapter, the partitioning of a substance between settleable and nonsettleable forms is essential to simulating contaminant dynamics in the water column. In Section 13.1, we focused on the seasonal cycle of production and decomposition in order to compute how much of the matter in the water column was in a particulate, settleable form and how much was dissolved and, therefore, nonsettleable. For long-term computations, we again must distinguish between solid and dissolved forms of matter. However, on this time frame, we can ignore stratification and idealize the water column as a completely mixed system. Simple mass balances can then be used to compute the mean annual levels and transfers of solid matter for the lake. In contrast to the seasonal approaches, where the emphasis was on the production and decomposition of organic solids within the lake (i.e., *autochthonous* solids), the long-term model also considers the solid matter delivered to the lake via its tributary streams (i.e., *allochthonous* solids). Once the solids' budgets are determined, simple linear sorption coefficients (similar to those used to model solid-liquid interactions in the sediments) can be used to determine how much of a contaminant associates with the dissolved and solid fractions in the lake and the sediments. Thus, the solid matter represents a transport vehicle for the contaminant between the water column and the sediments.

Solids Budget

Spatial Segmentation. For simplicity, the model is developed for a lake that is deep enough that sediment resuspension is negligible on the long-term time scale.* The system is divided into a well-mixed water column, a well-mixed surficial sediment layer and a one-dimensional deep sediment. The latter idealization is justified because lateral gradients in pore water composition are much smaller than vertical gradients. Also, although there is some lateral motion of solid matter, it is considered to be of minimal importance for depositional zone sediments where wind-induced turbulence is mitigated by the depth of the overlying water.

Because fine-grained sediments typically collect in deposition zones, the segments have different surface areas. Thus, the model has a crude focusing mechanism since mass settles from the larger area of the water to be collected in the smaller surface area of the sediment.

Finally, it is assumed that the solids balance is at a steady state and compaction is negligible (i.e., porosity is constant). Although solids input to the system changes on a year-to-year basis due to variations in erosion, a steady state occurs on a long-term basis in the absence of major modifications of sediment sources. The constant porosity assumption is based on the analysis in the previous chapter demonstrating its negligibility for fine-grained sediments.

Kinetic Segmentation. Because of their differing capacity for sorbing some contaminants, inorganic and organic solids are treated separately in this derivation. Inorganic solids are assumed to be strictly allochthonous, i.e., they originate outside the lake and are transported into the system via tributary streams and the wind. Organic solids are those generated within the lake via primary production. It should be noted that some autochthonous matter is inorganic (e.g., calcite) and some allochthonous matter is organic.

The division into organic and inorganic fractions was done for two

---

*It must be noted that physical resuspension of sediments can be extremely important in determining the water quality of systems such as shallow lakes and near-shore areas. Modifying the models in the present chapter to account for resuspension is relatively straightforward mathematically. Ways to do this are touched on in Chapter 15. Whereas the equations for simulating resuspension can be developed, estimating the rate of resuspension is not a trivial matter. In fact, there are some real problems related to characterizing the process on a long-term time scale. The reader should consult Lam and Jaquet (1976) and Sheng and Lick (1979) for an introduction into the literature on simulating sediment resuspension.

basic reasons. First, the fractions have different physical and chemical characteristics. For example, they could have different settling and sorption rates. Second, the distinction is important because organic solids can be ingested and passed along to higher levels of the food chain.

Aside from the chemical split into organic and inorganic fractions, a physical distinction is made with regard to particle size. Coarse-grained materials such as sands are not included in the computation under the assumption that for systems of large areal extent these particles are deposited rapidly in nearshore zones. The model only considers fine-grained solids that are accessible to the limnetic zone (and, thus, capable of scavenging contaminants from the water column) and accumulate in the lake's depositional basins. Aside from these physical considerations, the size distinction is also useful because many contaminants preferentially associate with fine-grained matter such as clays.

Water Column Balance. A mass balance for inorganic solids in a well-mixed lake can be written as

$$V_{t,w} \frac{ds_{i,w}}{dt} = W_i - Q s_{i,w} - v_i A_w s_{i,w} \qquad (13.103)$$

where   subscript w = the water column
        subscript i = inorganic matter
        s = solids concentration [g(d) m^{-3}] where g(d) designates gram dry weight
        W_i = loading of inorganic solids [g(d) yr^{-1}]
        v_i = settling velocity of inorganic solids [m yr^{-1}]

At steady state, Equation 13.103 can be solved for

$$s_{i,w} = \frac{W_i}{Q + v_i A_w} \qquad (13.104)$$

§ § §

Example 13.16. As an example of the use of Equation 13.104, in the early 1970s, Lake Ontario had the following characteristics:

$W_i = 6 \times 10^{12}$ g yr^{-1}
$Q = 200 \times 10^9$ m^3 yr^{-1}
$A_w = 19000 \times 10^6$ m^2
$V_{t,w} = 1634 \times 10^9$ m^3

The steady-state solids concentration can be computed using Equation 13.104 and a settling velocity of 91.25 m yr^{-1} (0.25 m d^{-1}).

$$s_{i,w} = \frac{6 \times 10^{12}}{200 \times 10^9 + 91.25\,(19000 \times 10^6)} = 3.1\ \mathrm{g\,m^{-3}}$$

§ § §

Just as physical and chemical sorption represents a balance between adsorption and desorption, the process whereby autochthonous matter is produced in the water column can be conceptualized as a balance between uptake and release of a limiting nutrient (in the present case, phosphorus), as in

$$\text{limiting nutrient} \underset{\text{release}}{\overset{\text{uptake}}{\rightleftharpoons}} \text{organic particles} \qquad (13.105)$$

where first-order reactions can be used to characterize the rates of mass transformation

$$R_{\text{uptake}} = k_{\text{up}}\,V_{t,w}\,p_{d,w} \qquad (13.106)$$

and

$$R_{\text{release}} = k_{\text{re}}\,V_{t,w}\,p_{o,w} \qquad (13.107)$$

where k_{up} and k_{re} = first-order coefficients characterizing net annual uptake and release, respectively [$\mathrm{yr^{-1}}$]

$p_{o,w}$ = concentration of particulate organic phosphorus [$\mathrm{mg\ P\ m^{-3}}$]

$p_{d,w}$ = concentration of dissolved phosphorus [$\mathrm{mg\ P\ m^{-3}}$]

Note that these formulations differ from those used to represent sorption where the rate of adsorption was a function of the quantity of mass (and, therefore, sorption sites) in the water. Therefore, for a lake with constant allochthonous loading of exchangeable inorganic matter, the mass available for sorption was fixed and as contaminant is added to the system, the mass-specific concentration increases proportionately.

For autochthonous production, the mass of organic particles is not fixed but grows in direct proportion to the lake's phosphorus level. The mass-specific concentration remains constant and represents the mass of phosphorus per mass of organic matter, i.e., a stoichiometric coefficient. The amount of organic suspended solids can, therefore, be calculated from

$$s_{o,w} = \frac{p_{o,w}}{a_{pd,0}} \qquad (13.108)$$

where $a_{pd,0}$ is the fixed stoichiometric coefficient [$\mathrm{mg\ P\ g(dry\text{-}weight)^{-1}}$].

Using the above concepts, the mass balance for particulate organic and dissolved phosphorus can be written as

$$V_{t,w} \frac{dp_{o,w}}{dt} = -Qp_{o,w} - v_o A_w p_{o,w} + k_{up} V_{t,w} p_{d,w} - k_{re} V_{t,w} p_{o,w} \qquad (13.109)$$

and

$$V_{t,w} \frac{dp_{d,w}}{dt} = W_p(t) - Qp_{d,w} + k_{re} V_{t,w} p_{o,w} - k_{up} V_{t,w} p_{d,w} \qquad (13.110)$$

where v_o is the settling velocity of organic matter [m yr^{-1}]. Because phytoplankton grow and die on time scales of days to weeks, the uptake and release can be assumed to reach a dynamic equilibrium on the long-term time frame and Equations 13.109 and 13.110 can be combined to yield

$$V_{t,w} \frac{dp_{t,w}}{dt} = W_p(t) - Qp_{t,w} - v_o A_w p_{o,w} \qquad (13.111)$$

where

$$p_{t,w} = p_{o,w} + p_{d,w} \qquad (13.112)$$

The particulate and dissolved fractions would then be related by a partition coefficient, Π, as in

$$\frac{p_{o,w}}{p_{d,w}} = \frac{k_{up}}{k_{re}} = \Pi \qquad (13.113)$$

Equations 13.112 and 13.113 can be combined and solved for (recall p. 49)

$$p_{d,w} = \frac{1}{1 + \Pi} p_{t,w} \qquad (13.114)$$

and

$$p_{o,w} = \frac{\Pi}{1 + \Pi} p_t = F'_{ow} p_{t,w} \qquad (13.115)$$

where F'_{ow} is the fraction of the total phosphorus in particulate organic form.

Because of the complexity of lake metabolism, it seems unlikely that such a simple model would describe the generation and decomposition of organic matter in lakes. However, on the long-term time frame, the approach seems to have validity. For example, numerous investigators have demonstrated correlations of total phosphorus and chlorophyll for phosphorus-limited, North Temperate lakes. If chlorophyll is considered an approximate measure of autochthonous particulate matter, Equation 13.115 is a valid expression of these correlations.*

Equations 13.111 and 13.115 can be combined to yield

$$V_{t,w} \frac{dp_{t,w}}{dt} = W_p(t) - Q p_{t,w} - v_o A_w F'_{ow} p_{t,w} \qquad (13.116)$$

which can be solved at steady state for

$$p_{t,w} = \frac{W_p}{Q + v_p A_w} \qquad (13.117)$$

where v_p = an apparent settling velocity of total P [m yr^{-1}] defined as

$$v_p = F'_{ow} v_o \qquad (13.118)$$

With Equation 13.108, the organic solids can then be computed as

$$s_{o,w} = \frac{F'_{ow}}{a_{pd,0}} \frac{W_p}{Q + v_p A_w} \qquad (13.119)$$

§ § §

Example 13.17. Using the same data as for allochthonous solids (Example 13.16), the concentration of total P in Lake Ontario can be computed based on the autochthonous model. Phosphorus/chlorophyll correlations can be used to estimate the partition coefficient between particulate organic matter and dissolved phosphorus. Assuming that chlorophyll provides an estimate of the settleable organic matter in lakes and using our nomenclature, the correlations of a number of investigators (Dillon and Rigler 1974, Schindler 1976, Chapra and Dobson 1981) can be approximated as

$$p_{o,w} = 0.25 p_{t,w} \qquad (13.120)$$

---

*Note that more complex models are developed in Chapter 14 to simulate the seasonal dynamics and levels of autochthonous solids in lakes. Although the present model is simpler, it is more compatible with the long-term time scale used in this section.

With Equation 13.115, the partition coefficient can be computed as $\Pi = 0.33$. If $v_o = 54.8$ m yr^{-1} (0.15 m d^{-1}) and $W_p = 12,000 \times 10^9$ mg yr^{-1}, Equation 13.117 can be solved at steady state for

$$p_{t,w} = \frac{12,000}{200 + 0.25\,(54.8)\,19,000 \times 10^{-3}} = 26.1 \text{ mg m}^{-3}$$

An interesting result of the autochthonous model is that it provides a partial explanation for the discrepancy between settling velocities of total P estimated from budgets and actual settling velocities of organic particles determined from laboratory and in situ measurements. In general, the apparent velocities are approximately half the direct measurements. The fact that Equation 13.120 indicates that 25% of the total P is subject to settling could account, in part, for the difference. For example, if a typical value for a real settling velocity is 0.15 m d^{-1} (Burns and Rosa 1980), the present model can be used to compute an apparent settling velocity of total phosphorus, v_p, as in

$$v_p = F'_{ow} v_o = 0.038 \text{ m d}^{-1}$$

This value falls within the range of average apparent settling velocities (0.027 – 0.044 m d^{-1}) reported for North Temperate, phosphorus-limited lakes (Vollenweider 1975, Chapra 1975, Dillon and Kirchner 1976, etc.). See Thomann (1977) and Section 14.7 for additional efforts to relate long-term and seasonal rate processes. Note also that the above computations are approximate and that other factors, aside from the annual average split between settleable, particulate and nonsettleable, dissolved substances, might be invoked to explain the discrepancies between short- and long-term settling velocities. For example, shorter-term phenomena such as upwelling (Scavia and Bennett 1980) or rapid dissolution and re-suspension of a flocculant benthic boundary layer, certainly influence net settling of velocities in some systems. Nevertheless, the effect of scales on model rates is irrefutable and must be considered when performing longer-term computations.

If the value of $a_{pd,0}$ is approximately 10 mgP g(dry)$^{-1}$, the organic suspended solids can be computed on the basis of Equations 13.108 and 13.115 as

$$s_{o,w} = 0.25(26.1)/10 = 0.65 \text{ g(d) m}^{-3}$$

Together with Equation 13.104, the total suspended solids in the water column is

$$s_{t,w} = s_{i,w} + s_{o,w} \tag{13.121}$$

For Lake Ontario, this results in a total suspended solids concentration of

$$s_{t,w} = 3.1 + 0.65 = 3.75 \text{ g m}^{-3}$$

§ § §

Sediment Balance. The water column solids budget can now be used to estimate parameters within the sediments. For a steady state, constant porosity sediment, the mass transfer of matter settling from the water column must balance the mass transfer due to burial, as in

$$v_i A_w s_{i,w} = v_b A_m \rho_i \phi_i \qquad (13.122)$$

$$v_o A_w s_{o,w} = v_b A_m \rho_o \phi_o \qquad (13.123)$$

where ϕ_i and ϕ_o are the fractions of total sediment volume in inorganic and organic solid form, respectively. If it is assumed that ϕ_o and ϕ_i are constant with depth,

$$1 = \phi_i + \phi_o + \phi \qquad (13.124)$$

Equations 13.122 to 13.124 are a system of three equations with three unknowns v_b, ϕ_i and ϕ_o. They can be solved simultaneously for

$$v_b = \frac{A_w}{A_m(1-\phi)} \left(\frac{v_o s_{o,w}}{\rho_o} + \frac{v_i s_{i,w}}{\rho_i} \right) \qquad (13.125)$$

$$\phi_i = \frac{1-\phi}{1 + \dfrac{v_o s_{o,w} \rho_i}{v_i s_{i,w} \rho_o}} \qquad (13.126)$$

$$\phi_o = 1 - \phi - \phi_i \qquad (13.127)$$

§ § §

Example 13.18. Using the information on allochthonous and autochthonous solids we can now compute v_b, ϕ_o and ϕ_i for Lake Ontario. Porosity is approximately 0.85 and densities of the inorganic and organic solids are approximately 2.5×10^6 and 1.27×10^6 g m^{-3}, respectively. The area of the deposition zone, A_m, is $10,400 \times 10^6$ m^2.
Using Equation 13.125,

$$v_b = \frac{19{,}000}{16{,}000(0.15)} \left[\frac{0.15(365)0.65}{1.27 \times 10^6} + \frac{0.25(365)3.1}{2.5 \times 10^6} \right] = 0.0017 \ \text{m yr}^{-1}$$

$$\phi_i = \frac{1 - 0.85}{1 + \dfrac{0.15(0.65)(2.5 \times 10^6)}{0.25(3.1)(1.27 \times 10^6)}} = 0.12$$

$$\phi_o = 1 - 0.85 - 0.12 = 0.03$$

§ § §

Contaminant Budget

Water Column Balance. Mass balance equations for the various phases of the contaminant in the water column can be written as

$$V_{t,w} \frac{dc_{d,w}}{dt} = W_c(t) - Qc_{d,w} - kV_{t,w}c_{d,w}$$

$$+ \frac{D_s \phi A_m}{(z_b + z_m)/2} (c_{di,m} - c_{d,w}) - k'_{ad,i} m_{i,w} c_{d,w}$$

$$+ k_{de,i} m_{i,w} \nu_{i,w} - k'_{ad,o} m_{o,w} c_{d,w}$$

$$+ k_{de,o} m_{o,w} \nu_{o,w} \tag{13.128}$$

$$m_{i,w} \frac{d\nu_{i,w}}{dt} = -\frac{Q}{V_{t,w}} m_{i,w} \nu_{i,w} - k m_{i,w} \nu_{i,w}$$

$$- \frac{v_i}{z_w} m_{i,w} \nu_{i,w} + k'_{ad,i} m_{i,w} c_{d,w}$$

$$- k_{de,i} m_{i,w} \nu_{i,w} \tag{13.129}$$

$$m_{o,w} \frac{d\nu_{o,w}}{dt} = -\frac{Q}{V_{t,w}} m_{o,w} \nu_{o,w} - k m_{o,w} \nu_{o,w}$$

$$- \frac{v_o}{z_w} m_{o,w} \nu_{o,w} + k'_{ad,o} m_{o,w} c_{d,w}$$

$$- k_{de,o} m_{o,w} \nu_{o,w} \tag{13.130}$$

where $m_{i,w} = s_{i,w} V_{t,w}$
$m_{o,w} = s_{o,w} V_{t,w}$
$W_c(t) =$ rate of mass loading of contaminant [μg yr^{-1}]

Since sorption typically proceeds much faster than input-output processes, a local equilibrium can be assumed and Equations 13.128–13.130 can be combined to yield

$$V_{t,w} \frac{dc_{t,w}}{dt} = W_c(t) - Q c_{t,w} - k V_{t,w} c_{t,w} - \frac{v_i}{z_w} m_{i,w} \nu_{i,w}$$

$$- \frac{v_o}{z_w} m_{o,w} \nu_{o,w} + \frac{D_s \phi A_m}{(z_b + z_m)/2} (c_{di,m} - c_{d,w}) \qquad (13.131)$$

where

$$c_{t,w} = c_{d,w} + c_{o,w} + c_{i,w} \qquad (13.132)$$

where

$$c_{o,w} = \frac{m_{o,w} \nu_{o,w}}{V_{t,w}} \qquad (13.132a)$$

$$c_{i,w} = \frac{m_{i,w} \nu_{i,w}}{V_{t,w}} \qquad (13.132b)$$

and if the assumption for the use of a partition coefficient holds, the dissolved and solid fractions are related by

$$\frac{\nu_{i,w}}{c_{d,w}} = K_{di,w} \qquad (13.133)$$

$$\frac{\nu_{o,w}}{c_{d,w}} = K_{do,w} \qquad (13.134)$$

which can be combined with Equation 13.132 and solved for

$$c_{i,w} = F_{iw} c_{t,w} \qquad (13.135)$$

$$c_{o,w} = F_{ow} c_{t,w} \qquad (13.135a)$$

where F_{iw} and F_{ow} are the fractions of the total contaminant in the water column in particulate inorganic and organic form, respectively, where

$$F_{iw} = \frac{K_{di,w} s_{i,w}}{1 + K_{di,w} s_{i,w} + K_{do,w} s_{o,w}} \qquad (13.136)$$

and

$$F_{ow} = \frac{K_{do,w} s_{o,w}}{1 + K_{di,w} s_{i,w} + K_{do,w} s_{o,w}} \qquad (13.137)$$

F_{dw} is the fraction of the total contaminant in the water column in dissolved form, defined as

$$F_{dw} = \frac{1}{1 + K_{di, w} s_{i, w} + K_{do, w} s_{o, w}} \qquad (13.137a)$$

and

$$c_{d, w} = F_{dw} c_{t, w} \qquad (13.137b)$$

Equations 13.131 to 13.137b can be combined to yield

$$V_{t, w} \frac{dc_{t, w}}{dt} = W_c(t) - Q c_{t, w} - k V_{t, w} c_{t, w} - v_i A_w F_{iw} c_{t, w}$$

$$- v_o A_w F_{ow} c_{t, w} + \frac{D_s \phi A_m}{(z_b + z_m)/2} (c_{di, m} - F_{dw} c_{t, w}) \qquad (13.138)$$

Sediment Balance. Using the concepts previously delineated in Section 13.2, we can now develop mass balance equations for the sediments. For the well-mixed surficial layer, the resulting equation is a balance between inputs, outputs and reactions, as in

$$V_{t, m} \frac{dc_{t, m}}{dt} = v_i A_w F_{iw} c_{t, w} + v_o A_w F_{ow} c_{t, w}$$

$$+ \frac{D_s \phi A_m}{(z_b + z_m)/2} (F_{dw} c_{t, w} - c_{di, m}) - v_b A_m c_{t, m}$$

$$+ \frac{D_s F_{dm} A_m}{(z_m + z_1)/2} (c_{t, 1} - c_{t, m}) - k V_{t, m} c_{t, m} \qquad (13.139)$$

where the subscript 1 refers to the first sediment layer below the mixed layer. The fraction of the total contaminant in dissolved form in the mixed layer *expressed on a total sediment volume basis* (in contrast to a pore water volume basis as in an equation such as 13.73) is

$$F_{dm} = \frac{\phi}{\phi + K_{di, m} \rho_i \phi_i + K_{do, m} \rho_o \phi_o} \qquad (13.139a)$$

where

$$K_{di, m} = \frac{v_{i, m}}{c_{di, m}} \qquad (13.139b)$$

and

$$K_{do,m} = \frac{\nu_{o,m}}{c_{di,m}}$$ (13.139c)

For the deep sediments, Equation 13.87 can be used,

$$\frac{\partial c_t}{\partial t} = D_s' \frac{\partial^2 c_t}{\partial z^2} - v_b \frac{\partial c_t}{\partial z} - kc_t$$ (13.140)

where

$$D_s' = F_{dm} D_s$$ (13.141)

§ § §

Example 13.19. Radionuclides, due primarily to the detonation of nuclear weapons, provide an excellent data base for testing the coupled sediment/water model. The input of fallout peaked in the early 1960s and decreased sharply thereafter (Figure 13.25). Thus, water bodies throughout the world have been subjected to a well-defined loading function of radioactive materials over this time. Because of the large amount of information on in-lake levels, sediment profiles and kinetic properties,

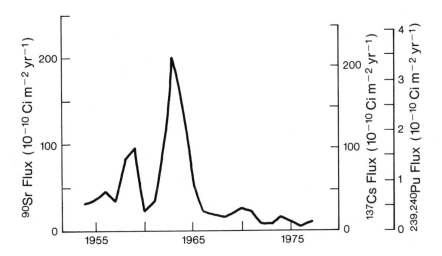

Figure 13.25   Loading flux of ^{90}Sr, ^{137}Cs and ^{239,240}Pu in 10^{-10} Ci m^{-2}yr^{-1} versus time.

three radionuclides—$^{239, 240}$Pu, ^{137}Cs and ^{90}Sr—have been chosen for our test simulations. These substances have additional interest due to their markedly different sorption and decay characteristics (Table 13.11). All computations are done on one or more of the Great Lakes because of the excellent data base for this system.

Table 13.11   Sorption, Decay and Diffusion Coefficients
Used for ^{239,240}Pu, ^{137}Cs and ^{90}Sr Simulations
for the Great Lakes

Parameter	Symbol	Units	^{239,240}Pu	^{137}Cs	^{90}Sr
Distribution coefficient					
Water column					
organic	$K_{do,w}$	$m^3 \, g^{-1a}$	0.1	0.01	2×10^{-4}
inorganic	$K_{di,w}$	$m^3 \, g^{-1}$	0.5	0.5	2×10^{-4}
Mixed sediment					
organic	$K_{do,m}$	$m^3 \, g^{-1}$	0.02	0.02	2×10^{-4}
inorganic	$K_{di,m}$	$m^3 \, g^{-1}$	0.02	0.02	2×10^{-4}
Deep sediment					
organic	$K_{do,s}$	$m^3 \, g^{-1}$	0.02	0.02	2×10^{-4}
inorganic	$K_{di,s}$	$m^3 \, g^{-1}$	0.02	0.02	2×10^{-4}
Decay coefficient					
Water column	k_w	yr^{-1}	1.73×10^{-4}	0.0231	0.0241
Mixed sediment	k_m	yr^{-1}	1.73×10^{-4}	0.0231	0.0241
Deep sediment	k_s	yr^{-1}	1.73×10^{-4}	0.0231	0.0241
Diffusion	D_m	$m^2 \, yr^{-1}$	0.038^b	0.038	0.012
coefficient in free					
solution		$(10^{-6} \, cm^2 \, sec^{-1})$	(12.1)	(12.1)	(3.8)

[a]The dimensionless form of the distribution coefficient can be obtained by multiplying the value in $m^3 \, g^{-1}$ by 10^6.
[b]Assumed to be the same as ^{137}Cs.

The simulation results reflect the differing properties of the radionuclides. The results for ^{90}Sr in Lake Ontario (Figure 13.26) are different from the other computations, primarily due to differences in their sorption characteristics. ^{90}Sr sorbs weakly to particulate matter and thus would be expected to behave in a similar fashion to conservative substances such as chloride. Thus, the bulk of the loading remains in the water column and little is carried to the sediments by particulate matter. This property is further suggested by the "flattened" water column trend due to the fact that flushing is the overwhelming cleansing mechanism for the lake which leads to a slow response time.

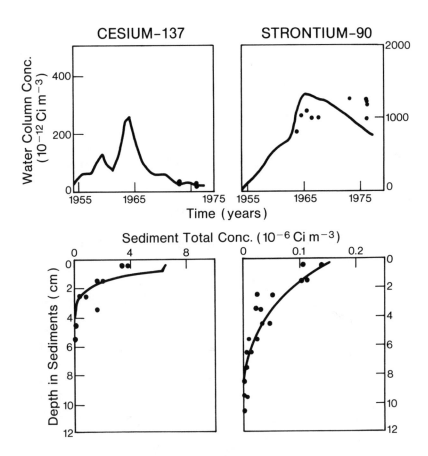

Figure 13.26   Simulation results for ^{137}Cs and ^{90}Sr in the water and sediments of Lake Ontario.

In contrast, the two other radionuclides (^{137}Cs and ^{239,240}Pu in Figure 13.27 and ^{137}Cs in Figure 13.26) display a relatively sharp concentration trend in the water column that closely follows the input signal (Figure 13.25). This is due to the faster response time for these elements because of their strong association with settling particulate matter. Since settling, as well as flushing, acts to purge the contaminants, the lake has a shorter "memory" and the water closely tracks on the load. The additional mechanism also leads to a larger fraction of the contaminant in the sediments.

The sediment profiles themselves indicate differences between the radionuclides. In particular, the ^{90}Sr penetrates further (~ 10 cm) into the sediments than the ^{239,240}Pu and the ^{137}Cs (~ 5 cm). This is due to the

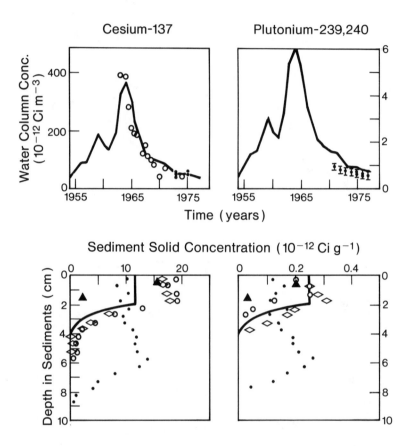

Figure 13.27   Simulation results for ^{137}Cs and ^{239,240}Pu in the water and sediments of Lake Michigan. The open circled data for ^{137}Cs in the water column is actually from Lake Huron but is included because the water column responses of these lakes should be similar for cesium.

greater mobility of ^{90}Sr in the pore waters owing to its weaker sorption characteristics. That is, its effective diffusion is higher.

§ § §

Example 13.20. The time required for a lake to recover following the cessation of contaminant loadings is an important piece of information in lake water quality management (see Chapters 8 and 11). Rainey (1967) derived a simple predictive model to estimate response time of a substance that decays with first-order kinetics that is equivalent to Equation 11.58. Rainey applied his model to the Great Lakes and showed that for highly persistent or conservative substances the recovery of some of the Great Lakes could take centuries. For example, Lakes Michigan and Superior would require approximately 100 and 500 years, respectively, to reach 90% of a new steady state following a step change in loading of a conservative substance. Recovery times for these lakes are this lengthy because conservative substances are purged solely by the mechanism of flushing through the lake's outlet. For Lakes Michigan and Superior which have large volumes and small outflows this results in very high response times. However, Rainey's computation implicitly assumes that the conservative pollutant associates minimally with settling particulate matter. Although this would be a reasonable approximation for substances such as chloride, other contaminants sorb to particles and would, therefore, be purged from the water by incorporation into the lake's bottom sediments.

Several investigators have attempted to account for sedimentation losses. For example, it has been noted (Vollenweider 1969, Sonzogni et al. 1976) that response times for lake eutrophication are greatly accelerated by the association of the limiting-nutrient phosphorus with settling particulate matter. Due to this additional cleansing mechanism, the 90% response time of total phosphorus in Lake Michigan in reduced to approximately 15 years (Chapra 1977, Chapra and Sonzogni 1979). As with Rainey's computation, the total phosphorus response time estimates include an implicit assumption; i.e., that the sedimentation loss is irreversible.

Although the response time estimates for conservative substances and for total phosphorus are valid engineering approximations, they represent relatively simple idealizations of the actual situation. As described in this chapter, the cleansing of most contaminants from lakes is a fairly complicated process whereby substances are carried to the sediments along with particles but can be reintroduced into the water column by diffusion of sediment pore water and by physical resuspension.

In order to gain a more general understanding of the effect of particle/contaminant interactions on lake recovery, we generated a number of test simulations using the model developed in this chapter. These test cases were based on O'Connor and Connolly's (1980) observation that the sorption process is dependent on the solids' content of a solution. They summarized data for a wide variety of contaminants indicating that the distribution coefficient decreases as solids' content increases. As idealized in Figure 13.28, this suggests that contaminants would have a higher distribution coefficient in the dilute water column than in the dense sediments.

In order to estimate the effect of this hypothesis on lake response time, we simulated the response of Lake Ontario to a constant loading of a

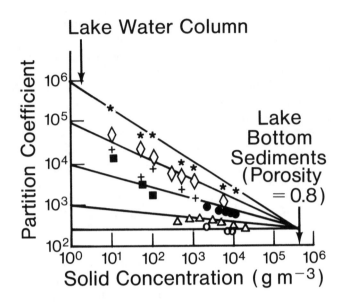

Figure 13.28   Correlation of distribution coefficients and concentration of solids for organic chemicals (from O'Connor and Connolly 1980). Lines represent an attempt to generalize the underlying pattern of data.

conservative contaminant. In all cases, the sediment distribution coefficient ($K_{d,s}$) was held at a constant value of 2×10^2. Five simulations were computed in which the distribution coefficient in the water column was set at increasingly higher levels. In addition, we simulated the response for cases where the distribution coefficient in the sediment was increased along with that in the water column.

Note, that these response calculations are the mirror image of those that would be computed for contaminant subsidence following the termination of loadings if a steady state had been established. Thus, the computed response times can be interpreted as recovery times.

The results, as depicted in Figure 13.29 and summarized in Table 13.12, indicate that decreased sorption in the sediments has a dramatic effect on lake recovery time. As the water distribution is set at higher values, the response time increases markedly up to a value of 222 years for the case of $K_{d,w} = 10^6$. The mechanism underlying this result is that as $K_{d,w}$ is increased, a greater proportion of the contaminant is carried to the lake's sediments by settling particles. However, since $K_{d,s}$ is held at a low level, once the contaminant is in the sediments it is released from the particles into the pore waters. There it is free to diffuse back into the water column along the substantial gradient that is soon established. This

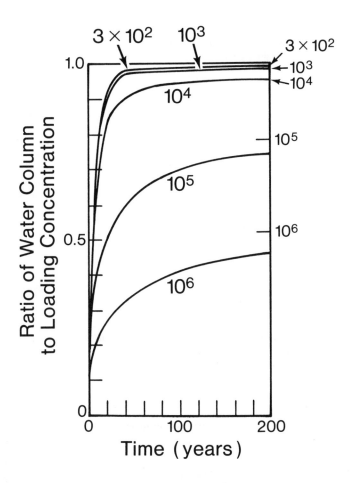

Figure 13.29   Plot of in-lake concentration of contaminant versus time for five magnitudes of the water column distribution coefficient. In all cases, the sediment distribution coefficient is set at the lowest water column value: 2×10^2.

scenario is in contrast to what occurs when both the water and sediment distribution coefficients are increased simultaneously. In these cases ($K_{d,s} = K_{d,w}$), the contaminant that settles to the bottom is held there by the high sediment distribution coefficient. Consequently, as in Table 13.12, t_{90} decreases for these cases.

Aside from response characteristics, the feedback mechanism also influences the magnitude of the ultimate level of contaminant in the lake. We quantify this level by an attenuation coefficient that represents the steady-state concentration of contaminant in the lake water normalized

Table 13.12   Ninety Percent Response Times (t_{90}) and Ratio
of In-Lake to Loading Concentration at Steady-State Due to
a Constant Loading of a Conservative Substance to
Lake Ontario[a]

	t_{90} (years)		Attenuation Coefficient (water column concentration ÷ loading concentration)	
$K_{d,w}$	$K_{d,s} = 2 \times 10^2$	$K_{d,s} = K_{d,w}$	$K_{d,s} = 2 \times 10^2$	$K_{d,s} = K_{d,w}$
2×10^2	18.8	18.8	0.999	0.999
10^3	19.2	18.8	0.987	0.970
10^4	24.5	14.7	0.954	0.778
10^5	111	5.9	0.780	0.321
10^6	222	2.3	0.519	0.126
Conservative ($K_{d,w} = K_{d,s} = 0$)	19.0		1.000	
Total Phosphorus	7.8		0.445	

[a] Values are for different combinations of distribution coefficients in the water column ($K_{d,w}$) and in the sediments ($K_{d,s}$). Values are also shown for a conservative, nonsorbing contaminant and total phosphorus for comparative purposes. Additional information on the attenuation coefficient can be found on pp. 398–400.

to the concentration of contaminant entering the lake from external sources. The loading concentration is defined as the total quantity of contaminant entering the lake per unit time divided by the volumetric rate of water flow through the lake's outlet. As $K_{d,w}$ becomes higher than $K_{d,s}$, the attenuation coefficient decreases as larger portions of the contaminant are carried to the sediments. However, because of the feedback effect, the decrease is much less than for the case of $K_{d,s} = K_{d,w}$ (Table 13.12).

The practical importance of these results is that they caution against the discharge of highly persistent contaminants to lakes. Although natural mechanisms work to purge such contaminants from the water column, the evidence suggests that decreased sorption in the sediments may work to reintroduce these contaminants back to the water at a slow rate. Thus, if lakes are subjected to highly persistent toxic substances for prolonged periods, the resulting health and environmental effects could be of considerable duration.

§ § §

13.4 GENERAL COMMENTS

In summary, we designed this chapter as a broad review of modeling frameworks and techniques for simulating vertical aspects of lake water quality. The key concept throughout the chapter was the effect of solid matter on the vertical distribution of matter in lakes.

For the water column, this involved two major kinetic processes: biological production/decomposition and sorption. From a temporal perspective, both seasonal and long-term time scales were used to characterize the water column. Additional information on simulating seasonal production/decomposition cycles are pursued in Chapter 14.

For the sediments, the emphasis was on sorption and a purely long-term approach was developed. Frameworks for simulating seasonal sediment and sediment-water dynamics were neglected because we consider them somewhat beyond our conception of engineering models. Information on seasonal approaches are described elsewhere (Berner 1980, Di Toro 1978, Di Toro and Connolly 1980).

We devoted considerable space to the mathematics of within-sediment transport and kinetics. This was done because many lake quality engineers are unfamiliar with simulating dynamics of substances in porous media. As should be evident, such computations have properties that make them fundamentally different from the more conventional models of the dilute water column. In addition, since much of our chapter on toxic substance modeling requires familiarity with sorption and sediment mathematics, we chose to emphasize these topics at this time. Further information on sediment-water modeling is contained in Chapter 15.

REFERENCES

Athy, L. F. 1930. "Density, Porosity and Compaction of Sedimentary Rocks," *Am. Assoc. Petrol. Geol. Bull.* 14:1–24.

Beeton, A. M. 1975. "Eutrophication of the St. Lawrence Great Lakes," *Limnol. Oceanogr.* 10:240–254.

Berner, R. A. 1980. *Early Diagenesis* (Princeton, NJ: Princeton University Press), 241 pp.

Burns, N. M., and F. Rosa. 1980. "In Situ Measurement of the Settling Velocity of Organic Carbon Particles and 10 Species of Phytoplankton," *Limnol. Oceanogr.* 25:855–864.

Canada Centre for Inland Waters. 1970. "Assessment of Water Quality Simulation Capability in Lake Ontario," Canada Centre for Inland Waters, Scientific Series No. 111, Burlington, Ontario.

Carnahan, B., H. A. Luther and J. O. Wilkes. 1969. *Applied Numerical Methods* (New York: John Wiley & Sons, Inc.).

Chapra, S. C. 1975. "Comment on 'An Empirical Method of Estimating the Retention of Phosphorus in Lakes,' by W. B. Kirchner and P. J. Dillon," *Water Resources Res.* 11:1033–1034.

Chapra, S. C. 1977. "Total Phosphorus Model for the Great Lakes," *J. Environ. Eng. Div., ASCE* 103:147–161.

Chapra, S. C. 1980. "Application of the Phosphorus Loading Concept to the Great Lakes," in *Phosphorus Management Strategies for Lakes,* R. C. Loehr, C. S. Martin and W. Rast, Ed. (Ann Arbor, MI: Ann Arbor Science Publishers, Inc.).

Chapra, S. C. and H. F. H. Dobson. 1981. "Quantification of the Lake Trophic Typologies of Naumann (Surface Quality) and Thienemann (Oxygen) with Special Reference to the Great Lakes," *J. Great Lakes Res.* 7:182–193.

Chapra, S. C., and W. C. Sonzogni. 1979. "Great Lakes Total Phosphorus Budget for the Mid 1970's," *J. Water Poll. Control Fed.* 51:2524–2533.

Committee on Sanitary Engineering Research. 1960. "Solubility of Atmospheric Oxygen in Water," *J. San. Eng. Div., ASCE,* SA4:41.

Dillon, P. J., and W. B. Kirchner. 1975. "Reply to Chapra (1975)," *Water Resources Res.* 11:1035–1036.

Dillon, P. J. and F. H. Rigler. 1974. "The Phosphorus-Chlorophyll Relationship in Lakes," *Limnol. Oceanogr.* 19:767–773.

Di Toro, D. M. 1976. "Combining Chemical Equilibrium and Phytoplankton Models—A General Methodology," in *Modeling Biochemical Processes in Aquatic Ecosystems,* R. P. Canale, Ed. (Ann Arbor, MI: Ann Arbor Science Publishers, Inc.).

Di Toro, D. M. 1978. "Species Dependent Mass Transport and Chemical Equilibria: Application to Chesapeake Bay Sediments" (unpublished manuscript).

Di Toro, D. M., and J. C. Connolly. 1980. "Mathematical Models of Water Quality in Large Lakes. 2. Lake Erie," U.S. EPA Report EPA-600/3-80-065, (Duluth, MN), 180 pp.

Di Toro, D. M., R. V. Thomann and D. J. O'Connor. 1971. "A Dynamic Model of Phytoplankton Population in the Sacramento–San Joaquin Delta," in *Advances in Chemistry Series 106: Nonequilibrium Systems in Natural Water Chemistry,* R. F. Gould, Ed. (Washington, DC: American Chemical Society), p. 131.

Engelhardt, W. V. 1977. *The Origin of Sediments and Sedimentary Rocks* (New York: Halstead Press), 359 pp.

Fee, E. J. 1976. "The Vertical and Seasonal Distribution of Chlorophyll in Lakes of the Experimental Lakes Area, Northwestern Ontario: Implications for Primary Production," *Limnol. Oceanogr.* 21:767–783.

Goldberg, E. D., and M. Koide. 1962. "Geochronological Studies of Deep-Sea Sediments by the Io/Th Method," *Geochim. Cosmochim. Acta* 26:417–450.

Hutchinson, G. E. 1957. *A Treatise on Limnology, Volume 1, Geography, Physics and Chemistry* (New York: John Wiley & Sons, Inc.), 1015 pp.

Imboden, D. M. 1974. "Phosphorus Models of Lake Eutrophication," *Limnol. Oceanogr.* 19:297–304.

Imboden, D. M. 1975. "Interstitial Transport of Solutes in Non-Steady State Accumulating and Compacting Sediments," *Earth Planet. Sci. Lett.* 27:221–228.

Imboden, D. M., and S. Emerson. 1978. "Natural Radon and Phosphorus as Limnological Tracers: Horizontal and Vertical Eddy Diffusion in Greifensee," *Limnol. Oceanogr.* 23:77–90.

Imboden, D. M., and R. Gachter. 1978. "A Dynamic Lake Model for Trophic State Prediction," *Ecol. Modelling* 4:77–98.

Jassby, A., and T. Powell. 1975. "Vertical Patterns of Eddy Diffusivity During Stratification in Castle Lake, California," *Limnol. Oceanogr.* 20:530–543.

Kamp-Nielson, L. 1977. "Modeling the Temporal Variation in Sedimentary Phosphorus Fractions," in *Proceedings of the Symposium on Interactions between Sediments and Fresh Water,* H. L. Golterman, Ed. (Amsterdam: Junk), 277–285.

Kamp-Nielson, L. 1978. "Modeling the Vertical Gradients in Sedimentary Phosphorus Fractions," *Verh. Internat. Verein. Limnol.* 20:720–727.

Kullenberg, G., C. R. Murthy and H. Westerberg. 1973. "An Experimental Study of Diffusion Characteristics in the Thermocline and Hypolimnion Regions of Lake Ontario," *Proceedings of the 16th Conference on Great Lakes Research,* International Association of Great Lakes Research, pp. 774–790.

Kuznetsov, S. I. 1970. *The Microflora of Lakes and Its Geochemical Activity* (Austin, TX: University of Texas Press).

Lam, D. C. L., and J.-M. Jaquet. 1976. "Computations of Physical Transport and Regeneration of Phosphorus in Lake Erie, 1970," *J. Fish. Res. Board Can.* 33:550–563.

Lasaga, A. C. 1979. "The Treatment of Multi-Component Diffusion and Ion Pairs in Diagenetic Fluxes," *Am. J. Sci.* 271:324–346.

Lerman, A. 1971. "Times to Chemical Steady-States in Lakes and Oceans," in *Advances in Chemistry Series No. 106: Nonequilibrium Systems in Natural Water Chemistry,* R. F. Gould, Ed. (Washington, DC: American Chemical Society), pp. 30–76.

Lerman, A., and T. A. Lietzke. 1975. "Uptake and Migration of Tracers in Lake Sediments," *Limnol. Oceanogr.* 28:497–510.

Lerman, A., and H. Taniguchi. 1972. "Strontium 90–Diffusional Transport in Sediments of the Great Lakes," *J. Geophys. Res.* 77:474–481.

Lerman, A., and R. R. Weiler. 1970. "Diffusion of Chloride and Sodium in Lake Ontario Sediments," *Earth Planet. Sci. Lett.* 10:150-156.

Li, Y.-H., and S. Gregory. 1974. "Diffusion of Ions in Sea Water and in Deep-Sea Sediments," *Geochim. Cosmochin. Acta.* 38:703-714.

Lorenzen, M. W. 1974. "Predicting the Effects of Nutrient Diversion on Lake Recovery," in *Modeling the Eutrophication Process,* E. J. Middlebrooks, D. H. Falkenborg and T. E. Maloney, Ed. (Ann Arbor, MI: Ann Arbor Science Publishers, Inc.).

Lorenzen, M. W., D. J. Smith and L. V. Kimmel. 1976. "A Long-Term Phosphorus Model for Lakes: Application to Lake Washington," in *Modeling Biochemical Processes in Aquatic Ecosystems,* R. P. Canale, Ed. (Ann Arbor, MI: Ann Arbor Science Publishers, Inc.).

Lung, W. S., R. P. Canale and P. L. Freedman. 1976. "Phosphorus Models for Eutrophic Lakes," *Water Res.* 10:1101-1114.

Manheim, F. T. 1970. "The Diffusion of Ions in Unconsolidated Sediments," *Earth Planet. Sci. Lett.* 9:307-309.

Manheim, F. T., and L. S. Waterman. 1974. "Diffusimetry (Diffusion Constant Estimation) on Sediment Cores by Resistivity Probe," *Initial Reports of the Deep Sea Drilling Project* 22:663-670.

McDuff, R. E., and R. A. Ellis. 1979. "Determining Diffusion Coefficients in Marine Sediments: A Laboratory Study of the Validity of Resistivity Techniques," *Am. J. Sci.* 279:666-675.

Mortimer, C. H. 1961. "Motion in Thermocline," *Verh. Internat. Verein. Limnol.* 14:79-83.

Mortimer, C. H. 1975. "Environmental Status of Lake Michigan Region, Volume 2. Physical Limnology of Lake Michigan, Part I. Physical Characteristics of Lake Michigan and Its Response to Applied Forces," Argonne National Laboratory, Argonne, Illinois, ANL/ES-40, Volume 2.

O'Connor, D. J., and J. P. Connolly. 1980. "The Effect of Concentration of Absorbing Solids on the Partition Coefficient," *Water Res.* 14:1517-1524.

O'Melia, C. R. 1972. "An Approach to the Modeling of Lakes," *Schweiz. Z. Hydrol.* 34:1-34.

Orlob, G. T., and L. G. Selna. 1970. "Temperature Variations in Deep Reservoirs," *J. Hydrol. Div., ASCE* 96:361-410.

Parker, R. A. 1973. "Some Problems Associated with Computer Simulation of an Ecological System," in *Mathematical Theory of the Dynamics of Biological Populations.* M. S. Bartlett and R. W. Hiorns, Eds. (London: Academic Press) pp. 269-288.

Powell, T. and A. Jassby. 1974. "The Estimation of Vertical Eddy Diffusivities Below the Thermocline in Lakes," *Water Resources Res.* 10:191-198.

Quay, P. D., W. S. Broecker, R. H. Hesslein and D. W. Schindler. 1980. "Vertical Diffusion Rates Determined by Tritium Tracer Experiments in the Thermocline and Hypolimnion of Two Lakes," *Limnol. Oceanogr.* 25:201-218.

Ragotzkie, R. A. 1978. "Heat Budgets of Lakes," in *Lakes: Chemistry, Geology, Physics.* A. Lerman, Ed. (New York: Springer-Verlag New York, Inc.), pp. 1-19.

Rainey, R. H. 1967. "Natural Displacement of Pollution from the Great Lakes," *Science* 155:1242-1243.

Roache, P. J. 1972. *Computational Fluid Dynamics* (Albuquerque, NM: Hermosa Publishers, Inc.), 434 pp.

Robbins, J., and D. N. Edgington. 1975. "Determination of Recent Sedimentation Rates in Lake Michigan Using Pb-210 and Cs-137," *Geochim. Cosmochim. Acta.* 39:285-301.

Robbins, J. A., J. R. Krezoski and S. C. Mozley. 1977. "Radioactivity in Sediments of the Great Lakes: Post-Depositional Redistribution of Deposit-Feeding Organisms," *Earth Planet. Sci. Lett.* 36:325-333.

Robbins, J. A., P. L. McCall, J. B. Fisher and J. R. Krezoski. 1979. "Effect of Deposit Feeders on Migration of ^{137}Cs in Lake Sediments," *Earth Planet. Sci. Lett.* 42:277-287.

Ryan, P. J., and D. R. F. Harleman. 1971. "Prediction of the Annual Cycle of Temperature Changes in a Stratified Lake or Reservoir: Mathematical Model and User's Manual," Technical Report No. 137, MIT Parsons Laboratory for Water Research and Hydrodynamics.

Scavia, D. 1980. "An Ecological Model of Lake Ontario," *Ecol. Modeling* 8:49-78.

Scavia, D., and J. R. Bennett. 1980. "The Spring Transition Period in Lake Ontario—A Numerical Study of the Causes of the Large Biological and Chemical Gradients," *Can. J. Fish. Aq. Sci.* 37:823-833.

Schindler, D. W. 1976. "Biogeochemical Evolution of Phosphorus Limitation in Nutrient-Enriched Lakes of the Precambrian Shield," in *Environmental Geochemistry,* J. O. Nriagu, Ed. (Ann Arbor, MI: Ann Arbor Science Publishers, Inc.), pp. 647-663.

Sheng, Y. P., and W. Lick. 1979. "The Transport and Resuspension of Sediments in a Shallow Lake," *J. Geophys. Res.* 84:1809-1826.

Simons, T. J., and D. C. L. Lam. 1980. "Some Limitations of Water Quality Models for Large Lakes: A Case Study of Lake Ontario," *Water Resources Res.* 16:105-116.

Snodgrass, W. J. 1974. "A Predictive Phosphorus Model for Lakes—Development and Testing," PhD Dissertation, University of North Carolina at Chapel Hill.

Snodgrass, W. J. 1977. "Relationship of Vertical Transport Across the Thermocline to Oxygen and Phosphorus Regimes: Lake Ontario as a Prototype," in *Transfer Processes in Lakes and Oceans,* R. J. Gibbs and R. P. Shaw, Eds. (New York: Plenum Press), pp. 179–202.

Snodgrass, W. J., and C. R. O'Melia. 1975. "Predictive Model for Phosphorus in Lakes," *Environ. Sci. Technol.* 9:937–944.

Sonzogni, W. C., P. C. Uttormark and G. F. Lee. 1976. "A Phosphorus Residence Time Model: Theory and Application," *Water Research* 10:429–435.

Stumm, W., and J. J. Morgan. 1981. *Aquatic Chemistry* (New York: Wiley-Interscience), 780 pp.

Sundaram, T. R. and R. G. Rehm. 1970. "Formation and Maintenance of Thermoclines in Temperate Lakes," *Am. Inst. Aeronaut. Astronaut. J.* 9:1322–1330.

Sundaram, T. R., and R. G. Rehm. 1973. "The Seasonal Thermal Structure of Deep Temperate Lakes," *Tellus* 25:157–167.

Sweers, H. E. 1970. "Vertical Diffusivity Coefficient in a Thermocline," *Limnol. Oceanogr.* 15:273–280.

Tennessee Valley Authority. 1972. "Heat and Mass Transfer between a Water Surface and the Atmosphere," *TVA Report No. 0–6803,* 127 p. + appendices.

Thomann, R. V., and J. S. Segna. 1980. "Dynamic Phytoplankton-Phosphorus Model of Lake Ontario: Ten-Year Verification and Simulations," in *Phosphorus Management Strategies for Lakes,* R. C. Loehr et al., Eds. (Ann Arbor, MI: Ann Arbor Science Publishers, Inc.), pp. 153–190.

Thomann, R. V. 1977. "Comparison of Lake Phytoplankton Models and Loading Plots," *Limnol. Oceanogr.* 22:370–373.

Travis, C. C., and Etnier, E. L. 1981. "A Survey of Sorption Relationships for Reactive Solutes in Soils," *J. Environ. Qual.* 10:8–17.

Turner, J. S. 1973. *Buoyancy Effects in Fluids* (Cambridge, GB: Cambridge University Press).

Vollenweider, R. A. 1969. Möglichkeiten und Grenzen elementarer modelle der Stoffbilanz von Seen. *Arch. Hydrobiol.* 66:1–36.

Vollenweider, R. A. 1975. "Input–Output Models with Special Reference to the Phosphorus Loading Concept in Limnology," *Schweiz. Z. Hydrol.* 37:53–84.

Wetzel, R. G. 1975. *Limnology* (Philadelphia: W. B. Saunders Company), 743 pp.

SECTION 6

MODELS OF KINETIC RESOLUTION

CHAPTER 14

NUTRIENT/FOOD CHAIN MODELS*

In the previous chapters, physical aspects that contribute to horizontal and vertical gradients in lakes were emphasized. Though detailed spatial resolution was used, the models were designed primarily to simulate dynamics of a single pollutant with simple reaction kinetics. Although these approaches captured essential features of spatial variability, there are a variety of problems and processes that require more sophisticated kinetic characterization.

A case in point is lake eutrophication. Although simple models have been applied successfully to manage the problem (Chapters 8 and 11), there are a variety of questions related to the overenrichment process that demand a more mechanistic treatment of lake biology and chemistry (Shapiro 1979).

Originating with the work of Riley (1946, 1947, 1963) and Riley et al. (1949), a computational framework for simulating production and cycling of matter in natural waters has been developed. This approach is similar to others in this volume in the sense that mass balance equations are written for components of the aquatic ecosystem. The fundamental difference is that nutrient/food chain models represent a concerted effort to express mathematically the cause and effect relationships underlying substance dynamics.

This mechanistic orientation has a number of consequences. First, matter in the lake typically is divided into multiple components. For example, biotic and abiotic substances often are divided into several groups. In addition, more highly mechanistic relationships are used to characterize kinetic interactions between these components than were employed in the simpler models. For example, in the "Simplest Seasonal

---

*This chapter was written by S. C. Chapra, D. Scavia, G. A. Lang and K. H. Reckhow.

Approach'' (Section 13.1.2), a linear, first-order reaction dependent solely on the soluble fraction was used to characterize phosphorus uptake. In reality, this uptake is performed primarily by one component of the particulate matter—phytoplankton. Further, the magnitude of the uptake is a complicated function of both phytoplankton biomass and dissolved nutrients, as well as such factors as light and temperature. Thus, these factors are incorporated into the kinetic formulations of nutrient/food chain models.

As a result, these models tend to be mathematically elaborate and require sophisticated computational software for their solution. In this sense, they might be considered beyond the scope of what we have defined as the engineering approach. However, there are three reasons why they have been included. First, engineers have played an important role in developing, testing and applying these models in management contexts (e.g., Thomann et al. 1974). Second, although there is some controversy surrounding their use for decisionmaking (Schindler 1978), there are many environmental problems that cannot be characterized adequately with simple approaches (Shapiro 1979). Finally, although the present chapter focuses on the problem of eutrophication, the techniques can be used to analyze a variety of other problems. Thus, the following material is presented as an introduction to a general approach for modeling biological, chemical and physical interactions, rather than as a definitive statement regarding lake ecosystem dynamics.

14.1 BASIC CONCEPTS

As in the Simplest Seasonal Approach (SSA), this chapter is concerned with the production and decomposition of matter in lakes. However, in contrast to the SSA, a more mechanistic orientation is used to characterize nutrient/food chain interactions. Therefore, before developing the mathematical model, we will introduce a number of fundamental concepts that bear on its derivation.

14.1.1 Seasonal Nutrient/Food Chain Dynamics in Temperate Lakes

In this section we will describe briefly the seasonal cycling of matter for a stratified lake. Although this description is more detailed than for the SSA, it is still rudimentary and is intended as an introductory overview for those readers who are unacquainted with the basic concepts and nomenclature associated with lake metabolism. Additional and more complete reviews are found elsewhere (e.g., Hutchinson 1957,1967, Wetzel 1975, Parsons et al. 1977).

Production, Decomposition and the Food Chain

The focal point of the nutrient/food chain models developed for lake eutrophication is the photosynthesis/respiration process as represented by (Stumm and Morgan 1981),

$$106CO_2 + 16NO_3^- + HPO_4^{2-} + 122H_2O + 18H^+ \text{ (+ trace elements and energy)}$$

$$\underset{\text{respiration}}{\overset{\text{photosynthesis}}{\rightleftharpoons}} \{C_{106}H_{263}O_{110}N_{16}P_1\} + 138O_2 \qquad (14.1)$$

where CO_2 is dissolved carbon dioxide, NO_3^- is nitrate, HPO_4^{2-} is phosphate, H_2O is water, H^+ is hydrogen ion, $C_{106}H_{263}O_{110}N_{16}P_1$ is algal protoplasm and O_2 is oxygen.

The forward reaction, termed photosynthesis, represents the production of organic matter by aquatic plants. For the limnetic, or deep-water, zone of most lakes, photosynthesis is performed primarily by floating algae called phytoplankton. As in Equation 14.1, these plants synthesize protoplasm from carbon dioxide and dissolved nutrients. The energy for this synthesis comes primarily from solar radiation. Some of the solar energy is stored in chemical form within the plants. All subsequent production of matter within the lake ecosystem stems from this stored energy. For this reason, the photosynthetic process sometimes is referred to as primary production, and the phytoplankton sometimes are referred to as primary producers.* This is in contrast to secondary production, which refers to the generation of organic matter due to the consumption of other organic matter. For example, the generation of biomass due to the consumption of plants by animals is secondary production.

The reverse reaction in Equation 14.1, broadly termed respiration, represents the decomposition of the organic matter to yield the raw materials: carbon dioxide and inorganic nutrients. During this breakdown process, oxygen is consumed and the energy stored in the organic matter is liberated.

---

*Note that there are other autotrophic (self-feeding) organisms, notably certain bacteria, that create food from raw materials. However, in most temperate lakes, their contribution to total primary production is negligible.

Although the breakdown of organic matter is represented as a single reaction in Equation 14.1, it is a complex process involving several pathways. The food chain is critical to this process. After phytoplankton are produced, they can be consumed by tiny animals called zooplankton. These herbivores (plant eaters) and omnivores (plant and animal eaters) are consumed by carnivorous (animal-eating) zooplankton that, in turn, are consumed by higher carnivores such as fish. Thus, the algal protoplasm produced in photosynthesis is passed along a chain of organisms.* Each element of the food chain, including phytoplankton, breaks down some of the organic matter to derive energy. This breakdown process can result in CO_2 and dissolved nutrients, but it also can yield organic compounds intermediate in energy content between the high-energy phytoplankton cells and the basic raw materials. These intermediate compounds can be reutilized by some components of the food chain, as described above, and by other microorganisms such as bacteria as well. The net result of this cycling and recycling of organic matter is its progressive decomposition.

In summary, the cycling of matter and energy in lakes is a balance between the production of energy-rich organic matter by photosynthesis and the decomposition due to food chain metabolism and cycling. As described below, this balance is influenced greatly by the seasonal progression of light and temperature in lakes.

The Seasonal Cycle in a Temperate Lake

In the early spring, temperate lakes typically are cold, well mixed and high in inorganic nutrients (see Section 13.1.1 for a discussion of the temperature cycle). The latter is due in part to the fact that primary production is low during the winter because, at that time, light and temperature are low. Consequently, inorganic nutrient levels build up as the balance between photosynthesis and respiration is tipped in favor of respiration. In addition, inorganic nutrient levels may be elevated due to increased loadings caused by high spring runoff from the watershed.

As spring progresses, water temperatures rise and the lake becomes stratified into a warm, well illuminated upper layer (the epilimnion) and a cold, dark lower layer (the hypolimnion). The combination of increased

---

*Note that the passage of matter along a chain, or series, of progressively larger organisms is a somewhat simplistic representation of the biological cycling of organic matter in lakes. A more realistic framework is a "food web" in which parallel interactions and the complex feedback of organic matter is acknowledged. However, the concept of the food chain is appropriate for the level of this chapter.

light and temperature and the abundance of inorganic nutrients provide all the factors required for the photosynthetic reaction in Equation 14.1. In addition, stratification reduces losses of algae to the lower, unlit waters. Consequently, primary production in the surface layer increases dramatically at this time, and the concentration of phytoplankton reaches high levels. This phenomenon sometimes is called a "bloom." However, with time, this growth is limited by a number of factors, including depletion of the inorganic nutrients, phytoplankton settling, and attenuation of light due to self-shading. Thus, the high growth rates decrease, and phytoplankton concentrations level off and decline. This decrease is enhanced by zooplankton and other consumers that become abundant, graze on the phytoplankton, and depress their levels further.

In contrast, because of low light levels, the hypolimnion is dominated by respiration and decomposition. Thus, inorganic nutrient levels in the bottom water increase as phytoplankton and detritus (nonliving particulate organic matter) settle from the epilimnion and are decomposed. However, because of the diffusion barrier caused by thermal stratification between the upper and lower layers, transfer of nutrient-rich hypolimnetic waters to the epilimnion is limited. In fact, during midsummer, the primary source of inorganic nutrients in the surface waters is often the result of recycling through the food chain.

In autumn, as the thermocline begins to deepen due to falling temperatures and higher winds, some of the nutrient-rich bottom water is entrained into the surface layer. This injection can stimulate a fall bloom. However, growth typically is not of the magnitude of the spring bloom because of decreasing light and temperatures and the lower nutrient levels. Finally, in late fall, the lake becomes well mixed vertically. During winter, the cycle is completed as respiration again dominates, and inorganic nutrient levels slowly grow to the high prestratification concentrations.

Although the above is a simplified representation of seasonal production dynamics in a temperate lake, it includes most of the major features of importance in engineering models. Before developing equations to express this seasonal progression mathematically, we will review some other basic concepts that bear on nutrient/food chain models.

14.1.2 Functional Groups

In the foregoing discussion of the seasonal cycle, we have used a number of collective terms such as "inorganic nutrients," "phytoplankton" and "zooplankton" to represent major components of the lake production/decomposition process. In reality, each of these groups is composed of myriad individual compounds and species. If adequate information were available, mass balance equations could be written for each compound and species; however, because they number in the thousands, such a scheme would be impractical. An alternative is to combine the individual compounds and species into functional groups having similar biological and chemical properties. In so doing, the system is reduced to manageable terms.

The earliest nutrient/food chain models took the simplest approach and divided the system into three components: phytoplankton, zooplankton and a single nutrient. In the following discussion we will briefly review how this basic scheme has been refined for each of these groups.

Nutrients

The importance of simulating nutrient cycles as an integral part of ecosystem models, rather than inputting specified ambient nutrient concentrations, was realized early in the development of model building. Nutrient simulation is necessary because nutrients are the components controlling much of the system behavior, and specifying future nutrient conditions is extremely difficult.

The primary questions concerning the inclusion of nutrients in a model are: How many nutrients should be included, and which are the most important? Although other micronutrients might regulate the growth of certain systems, phytoplankton dynamics of most lakes are governed by macronutrients, which include phosphorus, nitrogen, silicon and carbon.

Modelers have included as few as one of these—for example, nitrogen (Di Toro et al. 1971)—and as many as all four (Scavia 1980c) in simulation models. If the model is to be used to investigate the control of phytoplankton production under varying environmental conditions, then cycles of all of the potentially limiting nutrients must be included because, under future conditions, it is not always clear which nutrients will control phytoplankton growth. If, however, one is interested in the effects of a particular nutrient on the system, it may not be necessary to include calculations for all nutrients. In addition, if the system being modeled presently is limited by a particular nutrient that is to be reduced further through future loading reductions, then the single limiting nutrient can be used. This is typically the case for models designed to simulate the effect of phosphorus reduction programs on phosphorus-limited lakes.

Phosphorus. We broached the subject of kinetic segmentation of phosphorus in our discussion of the Simplest Seasonal Approach (SSA) in Section 13.1.2. In that discussion, we suggested that there are three basic rationales underlying kinetic segmentation schemes: (1) measurement techniques, (2) mechanistic considerations and (3) the management objectives of the modeling effort.

As with all elements of the nutrient/food chain system, the phosphorus subsystem can be compartmentalized with varying degrees of detail. Figure 14.1 represents an effort at a detailed conceptualization of the phosphorus cycling process in a lake ecosystem. On the other extreme, modelers have grouped all nonfood chain phosphorus into a single pool.

Beyond treating all nonfood chain phosphorus as a single compartment, the most commonly used scheme is to divide it into available and unavailable pools (e.g., Thomann and Segna 1980). The available pool, which phytoplankton are capable of utilizing for growth, is approximated analytically by the measurement of soluble reactive phosphorus (SRP). The unavailable pool, which represents all other nonfood chain

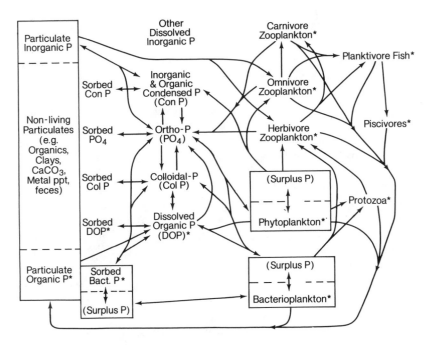

Figure 14.1   Phosphorus flow diagram indicating major components and pathways within the water column. The asterisk indicates several functional groups or life stages within each component. Arrows represent processes (1 - sorption, 2 - death, 3 - excretion/egestion, 4 - uptake, 5 - enzymatic release, 6 - photolysis, 7 - hydrolysis, 8 - precipitation, 9 - feeding, 10 - growth, 11 - microbial colonization). [Reprinted from Scavia (1981)]

phosphorus—for example, detrital P and soluble organic P—is assumed to be unavailable for phytoplankton utilization until conversion to SRP. A further refinement is possible by dividing the unavailable pool into particulate and dissolved components. This division has a number of rationales, including the different physical characteristics of the components (particulates settle, whereas dissolved species do not) and the fact that there are some indications (Herbes 1974, Cowen and Lee 1976) that certain species of soluble unavailable P are made available rapidly for phytoplankton growth.

One important aspect of phosphorus–phytoplankton dynamics and control of the process of eutrophication is nutrient availability. Phosphorus is supplied to lakes in forms ranging from largely undegraded terrestrial litter, which undergoes decomposition and releases nutrients, to dissolved inorganic ions from rainwater, which are immediately available for algal assimilation. Upon reaching the lake, these elements enter complex cycles.

Concern with the availability of phosphorus to phytoplankton generally has been an ill-conceived problem. Simply stated, only the dissolved phosphate ion is immediately available to phytoplankton. The traditional approach to the availability question—observation of phytoplankton response to various phosphorus sources—is fraught with the ambiguity of overlapping and inconsistent time scales. That is, given sufficient time, most forms of limnetic phosphorus will be transformed to phosphate, and thus they eventually become available to phytoplankton. During that "sufficient time," a potentially large set of processes acts to convert a suite of organic and inorganic compounds to the phosphate ion. The important questions are those relating to the relative rates of supply to and removal from the available pool.

Figure 14.2 illustrates both the actual complexity of phosphorus speciation and the relative size and stability of typical limnetic constituents. As for phytoplankton and zooplankton, functional groups of phosphorus compounds must be selected based on similarity of particular attributes. In this case, for example, the relative resistance of specific groups to degradation may be useful for partitioning into available and unavailable forms on a required time frame of analysis.

Nitrogen. The nitrogen cycle in natural waters has been studied in depth [see Brezonik's (1972) review] and has been modeled extensively, particularly in marine environments. The nutrient is divided conventionally into a number of functional groups:

1. Ammonia – This group includes both ammonia [NH_3] and ammonium ion [NH_4^+].

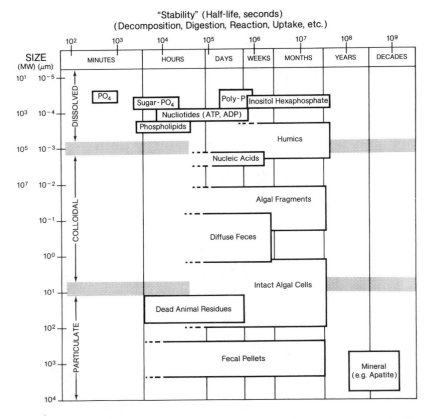

Figure 14.2 Size-stability matrix of nonliving phosphorus components indicating the approximate location of identifiable fractions. [Reprinted from Scavia (1981)]

2. Nitrite – $[NO_2^-]$.
3. Nitrate – $[NO_3^-]$.
4. Organic nitrogen – This group includes a variety of compounds including amino acids, amines, urea and complex higher-molecular-weight organic nitrogen.
5. Elemental or free nitrogen.

In many models, the above scheme is simplified further by combining nitrate and nitrite into a single group. Some of the major processes governing the dynamics of these groups are shown in Figure 14.3. These include:

1. Ammonia and nitrate assimilation: This includes the uptake of inorganic nitrogen by phytoplankton. As described in the next section,

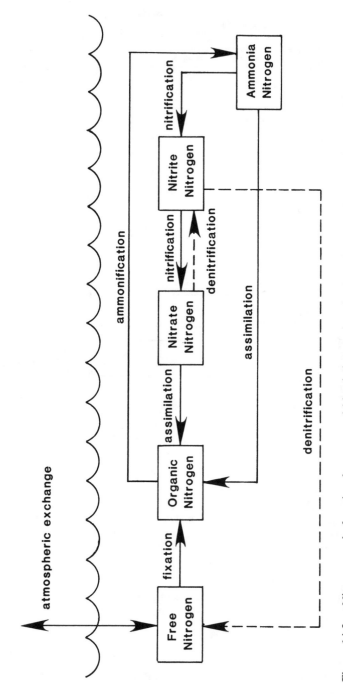

Figure 14.3   Nitrogen cycle functional groups and kinetic interactions in natural waters. Note that both aerobic (solid arrows) and anaerobic (dashed arrows) processes are depicted, although in nature they would not occur simultaneously. [Adapted from Brezonik 1972]

saturating (or Michaelis-Menten) kinetics are used to describe this process mathematically in most nutrient/food chain models. Although phytoplankton utilize both ammonia and nitrate, their preference for the former has been demonstrated (Harvey 1955, Walsh and Dugdale 1972, Bates 1976). Various mathematical constructs have been used to simulate this preference.

2. Ammonification: This is the transformation of organic nitrogen to ammonia. This is a complicated process involving several mechanisms, including bacterial decomposition, zooplankton excretion, and direct autolysis after cell death. Ammonification typically is represented as a first-order reaction in most models.

3. Nitrification: This is the oxidation of ammonia to nitrite and nitrite to nitrate via the action of a select group of aerobic bacteria. This process utilizes oxygen and typically is represented by first-order reactions. The fact that the transformation of nitrite to nitrate is relatively fast supports the use of a single functional group to encompass both nitrate and nitrite in some nutrient/food chain models. For these cases, the nitrification process would be represented kinetically by the oxidation of ammonia.

4. Denitrification: Under anaerobic conditions—for example, in the anoxic hypolimnia of some lakes—nitrate can serve as an electron acceptor for certain bacteria. Nitrite is formed as an intermediate, with the principal end product being free nitrogen.

5. Nitrogen fixation: A number of organisms can fix elemental nitrogen. An important group from the standpoint of nutrient/food chain modeling is blue-green algae possessing heterocysts. These organisms are important because, for lakes with high phosphorus loadings, phytoplankton growth can depress nitrogen levels to the point where nonfixing algae will become nitrogen-limited. The ability of the blue-green algae to utilize free nitrogen gives them a competitive advantage in this situation. The resulting ascendancy of the blue-greens has implications to water quality since many species have objectionable characteristics; for example, they form floating scums. As noted below, this has led some modelers to treat nitrogen-fixing, blue-green algae as a functional group separate from the other phytoplankton.

The foregoing is a brief introduction to the functional groups and processes used to characterize nitrogen in nutrient/food chain models. Other work (Brezonik 1972, O'Connor et al. 1973) can be consulted for additional information.

Silicon. Although it might be considered a minor nutrient, silicon has significance to the dynamics of lake phytoplankton because of its importance as a major structural element in the cells of an important phytoplankton group—the diatoms. These organisms use dissolved reactive silicon (mainly as [Si(OH)$_4$]) to build a frustule that surrounds the cell. Silicon in frustules is not available to other diatoms, and ambient concentrations of available silicon therefore can become low enough to limit further growth of these algae.

In most modeling work to date, silicon has not been simulated. Where it has been included, silicon has been treated as one compartment such as dissolved inorganic silicon (Lehman et al. 1975) or two compartments such as available silicon and unavailable silicon (Scavia 1980c).

Carbon. Modelers usually assume that carbon cannot limit algal growth, although some models (Chen 1970, Chen and Orlob 1975) do allow for potential limitation. Studies dealing with carbon-limited algal cultures raise questions regarding the form of carbon needed for photosynthesis by different algae (Goldman et al. 1974, King and Novak 1974). It also has been suggested that the relative abilities of green and blue-green algae to use various forms of inorganic carbon partially could explain the succession from greens to blue-greens in enriched natural waters (King 1972, Shapiro 1973). These and other developments (see references in Goldman et al. 1974) indicate that control of primary production by carbon limitation could be important in certain systems— particularly soft-water lakes. If this is true, then appropriate mechanisms must be included in multiple-group phytoplankton models, and this will require adding carbonate species calculations (Chen and Orlob 1975, Di Toro 1976, Scavia et al. 1976a). We discuss computational schemes for including inorganic carbon reactions in phytoplankton models in Section 14.4.1 of this chapter.

The Food Chain

Phytoplankton. The development of phytoplankton models has proceeded along two lines. The first group of models simulates phytoplankton as one group represented by chlorophyll *a* (Di Toro et al. 1971, Thomann et al. 1975, Di Toro et al. 1975, Larsen et al. 1973, Canale et al. 1974, Di Toro and Matystik, 1980). The second group simulates several phytoplankton groups, differentiating the phytoplankton according to size (Park et al. 1974, Bloomfield et al. 1973), physiology (Bierman et al. 1973, Bierman 1976, DePinto et al. 1976), or, more recently, size and physiology (Scavia et al. 1976a, Canale et al. 1976, Scavia 1980c).

In the past, the major reasons for representing all phytoplankton as a single group were that quantitative estimates of the species composition of the phytoplankton communities often were not available; and that chlorophyll *a*, which was measured more routinely, was considered to be a good indicator of total phytoplankton biomass. In addition, the management context of many modeling works (Di Toro et al. 1971, Thomann et al. 1975, O'Connor et al. 1975) was such that the interest lay primarily with gross parameters such as chlorophyll *a*.

There are two basic reasons for dividing the phytoplankton community into two or more groups. One reason is that chlorophyll *a* may not be a reliable measure of total algal biomass (Dolan et al. 1978). More important, however, is the fact that certain problems by their very nature dictate the separation of the phytoplankton. For example, the dominance of particular algal species causes taste and/or odor problems in drinking water supplies. Other algae form surface mats and cause filter clogging as well as aesthetic problems. To use models to address problems like these, we must include more than one algal group to simulate or to predict the dominance of the particular algal type of interest.

Mortimer (1975) also has discussed the important of allowing "new actors to come onto the stage" when conditions change in a lake being modeled, and Scavia et al. (1976b) have demonstrated in a modeling exercise for the Great Lakes that, in some circumstances, it probably is important to allow both long-term and seasonal succession of phytoplankton groups to occur in predictive models. To do this, multiple-group phytoplankton models must be implemented. Fortunately, most recent, integrated research programs have included detailed analyses of phytoplankton succession, thus allowing modelers the opportunity to develop and to calibrate these models.

A major concern in many current modeling efforts is the development of criteria for segregating the phytoplankton community. Two criteria have been used: physiological considerations and size.

Physiological Considerations: The most obvious distinction from a physiological standpoint is the difference in nutrient requirements of certain phytoplankton groups. All phytoplankters require carbon, nitrogen and phosphorus, whereas only diatoms require silicon to any significant degree. Certain species of blue-green algae are able to use dissolved nitrogen gas (nitrogen fixation) and therefore are not limited to ammonium and nitrate as nitrogen sources. Thus, an initial segregation could lead to these subdivisions: (1) diatoms, (2) nitrogen-fixing blue-green algae and (3) all other algae. These subdivisions also have been useful categories for grouping species based on other growth-related functions such as light requirements (Ryther 1956), and specific growth rates and temperature effects (Canale and Vogel 1974). The metabolic requirements associated with motility in flagellates (Parsons et al. 1977), as well as their special attributes with regard to searching for optimal light and nutrients and their defenses against sinking, may make it necessary to treat this group separately.

Size: A second way to distinguish groups is by phytoplankton size. Algal size generally is a determining factor in causing filter clogging and similar problems at water intakes. In addition, size categories can be based on feeding preferences of zooplankton; that is, some zooplankton prefer to consume phytoplankton of specific sizes. Some work has been done in an effort to quantify this selectivity by zooplankton (e.g., Poulet 1978, Richman et al. 1981, Vanderploeg 1981). Finally, size is important as it relates to processes affecting phytoplankton transport and kinetics. For example, sinking (Smayda 1970) and photosynthesis/respiration (Banse 1976, Eppley et al. 1969) seem to be related to phytoplankton size.

Zooplankton. Simulating zooplankton dynamics as part of an eco-system model requires consideration of how to form meaningful species aggregations. Riley (1947) included only one zooplankton group in his work, as did most early modelers. Such an approach treats the entire zooplankton community as a single entity and assumes that average process rates adequately represent the community.

The development of a logical basis for separating the zooplankton into functional groups began with a consideration of feeding strategies. One method of separation recognized two categories—carnivorous and herbi-vorous zooplankton (Thomann et al. 1975). A further separation has been made by dividing the herbivorous group into cladocerans and copepods (Bloomfield et al. 1973), based on different feeding strategies and susceptibilities to predation. The most detailed segregation of the zooplankton community is part of a Lake Michigan model developed by Canale et al. (1976). The conceptualization includes two raptors (i.e., zooplankton that actively "grab" their prey), five selective filter feeders, and two nonselective filter feeders. Within each of these three feeding-strategy groups, distinctions are based on the apparent variable suscepti-bilities to predation by higher trophic levels. These distinctions relate in part to size-selection by the predators. The model thus includes nine functional groups: predators, large omnivores, small omnivores, large herbivorous cladocerans, small herbivorous cladocerans, small herbi-vorous copepods and three naupliar groups.

A major component missing from this model, as well as from most other models, is the rotifer group. Because rotifers generally are small, they often are considered unimportant in the food web and thus omitted from models. Hutchinson (1967) refers to this group as "the most impor-tant soft-bodied invertebrates in the freshwater plankton," and, in spite of their small size, their numerical abundance and high production rates suggest an integral role in both nutrient cycling and the food web. The importance of rotifers in food webs should be investigated; however, more work needs to be done to quantify various aspects of rotifer dynamics such as feeding strategies and rates, respiration rates, and assimilation efficiencies as functions of environmental conditions.

14.1.3 Nutrient/Food Chain Mathematics

In the previous chapters of this volume, we have used simple formulations to characterize reactions. For most cases, first-order kinetics were used to represent the decay of a single reactant. In addition, simple linear, first-order formulations were used (Sections 11.2.3 and 13.1.2) to characterize coupled reactions between a pair of substances. For nutrient/food chain computations, the level of kinetic complexity is increased significantly. There are two general aspects to this increase in complexity.

First, many more biological and chemical functional groups are included in nutrient/food chain formulations. Thus, the system will be characterized by many more interconnected differential equations. For example, the "simple" model that we will develop for illustrative purposes in Section 14.2 includes three biological and three nutrient compartments (or state variables) for which a total of 12 differential equations will be written for a two-layer lake. As depicted in Figure 14.6, these compartments are linked by a number of reaction processes. Each of these processes will be characterized by an individual kinetic formulation.

Second, the kinetic formulations themselves are more complex. In previous chapters, the rate of mass transfer due to reactions typically was represented as

$$V\left(\frac{dc}{dt}\right)_{\text{reaction}} = kVc \qquad (14.2)$$

where
V = volume of the system
c = concentration of the reactant
t = time
k = first-order reaction rate

In most cases, k is treated as a constant. For certain situations, however, the constant rate may be inaccurate since, as discussed in Chapter 10, reaction rates are temperature-dependent. By using a constant rate, we implicitly assume that the temperature effect is negligible for the time scale of interest. This might be the case for long-term simulations where year-to-year temperature variations often can be ignored. Similarly, a constant rate approach can be used to simulate conditions during small or sufficiently stable portions of the annual cycle when, for all practical purposes, the temperature can be assumed to be constant. This was the case for Example 12.7, where we simulated summer average bacteria distributions for the near-shore zone of Lake Michigan.

In contrast, when simulating dynamics over periods of time marked by significant temperature changes, such as the seasonal cycle of production in a lake, the effect of temperature on the reaction rates must be included. We took the first step in that direction in the Simplest Seasonal Approach (Section 13.1.2) by dividing the year into two seasons—winter and summer. Although constant coefficients were used to characterize kinetics for this model, different values were used for each season. In so doing, we accounted, in part, for the effect of temperature.

For nutrient/food chain models, we are interested in a more detailed resolution of seasonal kinetics. Consequently, the reaction rates are a function of continuously changing temperature levels (see Figure 14.7). In a similar fashion, because of the dependence of photosynthesis on solar radiation, the phytoplankton growth rate also will be a function of seasonally varying meteorological factors such as light intensity and photoperiod.

Aside from these physical, externally prescribed influences, the kinetic constructs of nutrient/food chain models are complicated further by the fact that they can be formulated as a function of several state variables. For example, phytoplankton growth is dependent not only on available nutrient levels (as was the case for the Simplest Seasonal Approach), but also on the concentration of the phytoplankton themselves. Similarly, zooplankton growth is dependent on both phytoplankton and zooplankton levels. In addition, the rate coefficients for these dependencies are not simple constants but can be functions of other variables.

Although there are a number of ways to express these dependencies, two simple mathematical concepts underlie their formulation: saturation and predator-prey kinetics. In the following section, these concepts are described briefly as a prelude to developing the nutrient/food chain model.

Saturation Kinetics

Monod (1942) originally applied Michaelis-Menten enzyme kinetics to the problem of quantifying the relationship of an organism to its food supply. In the present context, such kinetics have been used to represent the dependency of phytoplankton growth on the quantity of nutrient in a system.

To express these concepts mathematically, we will restrict the discussion to a closed system (i.e., no inputs or outputs) in which there is a single kind of organism and a single type of food. For the purposes of the present example, the organisms are phytoplankton, and the food is available phosphorus. Two mass balances are required to characterize the interactions between the organism and the food:

$$\frac{dp_1}{dt} = k(p_6)p_1 \qquad (14.3)$$

and

$$\frac{dp_6}{dt} = -\frac{1}{a} k(p_6)p_1 \qquad (14.4)$$

where V = system volume (m^3)
p_1 = concentration of phytoplankton [mgP m^{-3}]
p_6 = concentration of available phosphorus [mgP m^{-3}]
$k(p_6)$ = growth rate of the organism [d^{-1}] where (p_6) designates that the rate is a function of the phosphorus concentration

a is a yield (or stoichiometric) constant representing the mass of organism created per mass of food eaten [mg mg^{-1}]. Since both variables are expressed as phosphorus, a equals 1.0 for this example.

The dependence of the growth rate on food is expressed quantitatively by a Michaelis-Menten, or substrate-limiting, kinetic relationship of the form

$$k(p_6) = \frac{k_m p_6}{k_s + p_6} \qquad (14.5)$$

where k_m = maximum growth rate [d^{-1}]
k_s = half-saturation constant [mgP m^{-3}], that is, the concentration at which the growth rate is half the maximum rate

Equation 14.5, which is depicted graphically in Figure 14.4, indicates that, at low food levels (i.e., $p_6 \ll k_s$), the growth of an organism is directly proportional to the food supply.

$$k(p_6) = \frac{k_m}{k_s} p_6 \qquad (14.6)$$

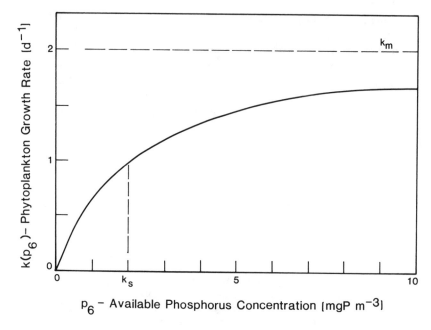

Figure 14.4   Michaelis-Menten curve used to characterize the relationship of the phytoplankton growth rate to the available nutrient concentration. The half-saturation constant, k_s, equals 2 mgP m^{-3} and the maximum growth rate, k_m, equals 2 d^{-1}.

At high substrate levels, however, the growth rate becomes limited by the organism's ability to utilize the food. For this case (i.e., $p_6 \gg k_s$), the growth rate approaches a constant level; that is, it becomes independent of substrate concentration, as in

$$k(p_6) = k_m \qquad (14.7)$$

The introduction of a limit to growth in the Michaelis-Menten formulation is reflective of the fact that unbridled growth is checked and moderated by finite resources in nature. As described next, environmental checks and balances also are reflected in predator-prey formulations that have been developed to quantify the interdependence of an organism and its food.

Predator-Prey Interactions

Interactions between a predator and its prey are fundamental to modeling nutrient/food chain dynamics. For example, phytoplankton serve as prey for predatory herbivorous zooplankton. The herbivores, in turn, are prey for predatory carnivorous and omnivorous zooplankton. Interactions between zooplankton and fish, as well as between species of fish, are other examples of predator-prey relationships.

Linear, Donor-Dependent Model. A variety of mathematical formulations have been developed to represent predator-prey interactions (see Patten 1971). For example, a simple version can be developed using the first-order, donor-dependent (or, in the present case, prey-dependent) constructs that have been used to characterize kinetic interactions in previous chapters (as in Section 13.1.2). Using these constructs, mass balances for phytoplankton, p_1, herbivorous zooplankton, p_2, and available phosphorus, p_6,* can be formulated for a closed system as

$$\frac{dp_1}{dt} = K_{61}p_6 - K_{12}p_1 \qquad (14.8)$$

$$\frac{dp_2}{dt} = K_{12}p_1 - K_{26}p_2 \qquad (14.9)$$

$$\frac{dp_6}{dt} = K_{26}p_2 - K_{61}p_6 \qquad (14.10)$$

where K_{ij} are the first-order transfer rates from compartment "i" to compartment "j."

§ § §

Example 14.1. Integrate Equations 14.8 through 14.10 using the following coefficients: $K_{12} = 0.5$, $K_{26} = 0.5$, $K_{61} = 0.025$ d^{-1}. Initial conditions are $p_1 = 0.1$, $p_2 = 0.1$, and $p_6 = 99.8$ mgP m^{-3}.

The results (Figure 14.5a) indicate that, according to this model, the state variables converge rapidly (on the order of a week) toward stable, steady-state levels.

§ § §

Lotka-Volterra Model. Linear, donor-dependent constructs are appropriate when the predator is abundant and prey is sparse. In such

---

*The nomenclature conforms to the complete nutrient/food chain model that will be developed in Section 14.2. For simplicity, we neglect other state variables included in the complete framework, such as carnivorous zooplankton, p_3, detrital phosphorus, p_4, and unavailable dissolved phosphorus, p_5, that are unnecessary for the present purposes.

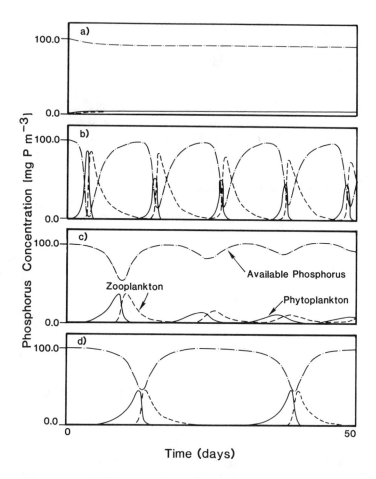

Figure 14.5 Plots of phytoplankton, zooplankton and available nutrient using several models to characterize predator-prey interactions: (a) linear, donor-dependent model, (b) Lotka-Volterra model, (c) Lotka-Volterra model with constant phytoplankton source and (d) Lotka-Volterra model with Michaelis-Menten formulation used to characterize phytoplankton growth rate.

cases, it would be expected that the transfer of mass to the predator would be proportional to the amount of food (i.e., prey) that is present. For the general situation, however, transfer is determined by the levels of both predator and prey. A simple set of equations to describe this case is

$$\frac{dp_1}{dt} = k_m p_1 - C_{12} p_1 p_2 \qquad (14.11)$$

$$\frac{dp_2}{dt} = C_{12}p_1p_2 - K_{26}p_2 \qquad (14.12)$$

$$\frac{dp_6}{dt} = K_{26}p_2 - k_mp_1 \qquad (14.13)$$

where k_m = maximum phytoplankton growth rate [d^{-1}]
        C_{12} = zooplankton feeding rate [m^3 mgP^{-1} d^{-1}]

The first two equations (14.11 and 14.12) are called Lotka-Volterra equations (Lotka 1956). The key features that distinguish them from the linear model (Equations 14.8 through 14.10) are (1) that phytoplankton growth is dependent on phytoplankton concentration (recall that Michaelis-Menten kinetics reduce to this form when nutrients are abundant, as seen in Equation 14.7); and (2) that the interactions between predator and prey are formulated as the product of their respective concentrations. This latter feature, which makes the model nonlinear, has an interesting effect on solutions, as described in the following example.

§ § §

Example 14.2. Repeat the computation in Example 14.1 using Equations 14.11 through 14.13 ($k_m = 0.5$ d^{-1} and $C_{12} = 0.1$ m^3 mgP^{-1} d^{-1}). The results (Figure 14.5b) differ markedly from those obtained with the linear, donor-dependent model. In contrast to a steady state, the solution for the Lotka-Volterra equations is characterized by stable oscillations of the state variables. In essence, with abundant nutrients and the predatory zooplankton at low levels, the phytoplankton grow unchecked. However, because of the increase in phytoplankton, the zooplankton also begin to grow rapidly. Although zooplankton growth at first lags behind the increase of prey, there comes a point where predator feeding outpaces phytoplankton growth and leads to a decline in the amount of prey. Thus, although the zooplankton attain high concentrations, they essentially deplete their food supply. Consequently, in time they also decline. When the predator concentration is reduced to sufficiently low levels, the prey is again free to grow unchecked and the cycle is repeated.

§ § §

Lotka-Volterra Model with Source. The oscillations of the Lotka-Volterra model continue indefinitely. However, Di Toro et al. (1971) have used a perturbation analysis to demonstrate that the oscillations are dampened out if a constant source term is added to the phytoplankton equation, as in

$$\frac{dp_1}{dt} = k_m p_1 - C_{12} p_1 p_2 + W_1/V \qquad (14.14)$$

where W_1 = source of phytoplankton [mgP d^{-1}]
V = volume of the system [m^3]

§ § §

Example 14.3. Repeat Example 14.2 using Equation 14.14 in place of Equation 14.11. Assume a constant volume-specific loading: $W_1/V = 0.3$ mgP m^{-3} d^{-1}.

The results (Figure 14.5c) demonstrate how the oscillations are dampened in the presence of the source. In sufficient time, steady-state levels would be attained. This leads to the conclusion by Di Toro et al. (1971) that mass transport has a stabilizing effect on predator-prey interactions. This is one reason why seasonal nutrient/food chain models of the type described in Section 14.2 do not exhibit the dramatic, high-frequency (with periods on the order of a week) oscillations of the kind in Figure 14.5b.

§ § §

Combined Lotka-Volterra and Michaelis-Menten Kinetics. Recall that the Lotka-Volterra formulation (Equations 14.11 through 14.13) uses a phytoplankton growth formulation ($k_m p_1$) that implicitly assumes an abundance of nutrients. However, as in Figure 14.5b, there are times during the cycle when available phosphorus is reduced to low enough levels that growth might be nutrient-limited. To account for this possibility, Equation 14.5 can be combined with Equations 14.11 through 14.13 to yield

$$\frac{dp_1}{dt} = k_m \frac{p_6}{k_s + p_6} p_1 - C_{12} p_1 p_2 \qquad (14.15)$$

$$\frac{dp_2}{dt} = C_{12} p_1 p_2 - K_{26} p_2 \qquad (14.16)$$

$$\frac{dp_6}{dt} = K_{26} p_2 - k_m \frac{p_6}{k_s + p_6} p_1 \qquad (14.17)$$

§ § §

Example 14.4. Repeat the computation in Example 14.2 using Equations 14.15 through 14.17 ($k_s = 2$ mgP m^{-3}).

The results (Figure 14.5d) still indicate stable oscillations, but with some differences when compared with Example 14.2. In particular, the frequency of the oscillations is decreased (the period increased to approximately three weeks).

§ § §

The foregoing is intended as an introduction to mathematical formulations that are peculiar to nutrient/food chain models. In the next section, they are expanded and developed into a model for a temperate lake.

14.2 A BASIC NUTRIENT/FOOD CHAIN MODEL

Several engineers (notably, Chen 1970 and Di Toro et al. 1971) have applied Riley's theory to the problem context of eutrophication. Because of the complexity of the processes governing the production and cycling of organic matter in aquatic systems, these applications involve a certain amount of idealization to arrive at models that are both tractable and interpretable. These simplifications, to a certain extent, are influenced by the problem context and setting for which the models were developed. The primary factor in this regard has been their "lower food chain" orientation. Since the deleterious effects of eutrophication are associated with nuisance growths of algae, engineering models have tended to focus on these organisms. Thus, as will be seen in the following description, the formulation of phytoplankton kinetics has been fairly elaborate, whereas upper levels of the food chain, such as fish, often have been treated simplistically or even ignored. In the same way, the benthos of deep, unproductive lakes often have been disregarded. This is in contrast to other problems, such as the simulation of bioaccumulating toxic substances, where strong emphasis would have to be placed on fish and the bottom sediments (Chapter 15). In addition, the focus on the primary producers dictates the temporal and spatial scale of the problem since phytoplankton dynamics proceed on a time frame of days to weeks and exhibit strong vertical gradients in stratified temperate lakes. Thus, at the crudest resolution, a seasonal time scale and a two-layer vertical segmentation scheme are required for their adequate characterization.

In the present section, a simple nutrient/food chain model of a two-layer lake is used to introduce the basic approach. The framework is similar to those used in management contexts (e.g., Di Toro et al. 1971, Thomann et al. 1974, 1975, 1976, 1978, Di Toro and Matystik 1980, Di Toro and Connolly 1980), but includes certain refinements to conform to more recent theories of food chain/nutrient cycle interactions. It should be emphasized that the framework described below is but one of a variety of formulations proposed to model nutrient/food chain dynamics in natural waters. Some important refinements and their implications will be discussed in a later section (14.3). The reader also can consult Scavia's (1979a) review of the subject, as well as critical articles by Riley (1963), Steele (1965) and Mortimer (1975).

14.2.1 Spatial Segmentation

The present framework handles physical segmentation (two vertical layers), loadings and transport in the same way as the two-component model (SSA) described in Section 13.1.2. Mass balances for the kth variable (where $k = 1$, 6, as defined in the caption of Figure 14.6) for the layers can be written as:

$$V_e \frac{dp_{k,e}}{dt} = W_{k,e} - Qp_{k,e} + E_t'(p_{k,h} - p_{k,e})$$

$$- v_k A_t p_{k,e} \pm R_{k,e}$$

(14.18)

and

$$V_h \frac{dp_{k,h}}{dt} = W_{k,h} + E_t'(p_{k,e} - p_{k,h}) + v_k A_t p_{k,e}$$

$$- v_k A_t p_{k,h} \pm R_{k,h}$$

(14.19)

where
  e = epilimnion
  h = hypolimnion*
  p_k = concentration of the kth variable [mgP m^{-3}]
  v_k = settling velocity of the kth variable [m d^{-1}]
  R_k = kinetic interactions between the kth and the other variables [mgP d^{-1}]

Note that only nonmotile particulate matter such as phytoplankton and detritus settle; all other variables have $v = 0$.

The method of extending these equations to the case of multiple layers is obvious. Extension to two- or three-dimensional analysis requires the addition of vertical and horizontal advection terms as well as additional

---

*In the subsequent development, if these subscripts are not included it means that the term has the same mathematical form in each layer.

diffusion terms. One also must be concerned in such cases with the particular locations of external loading and outflow, or flushing, terms.*

14.2.2 Kinetic Segmentation

Matter in the lake can be divided into living and nonliving categories, with several functional groups in each, as suggested in Figure 14.6. As described previously in Section 14.1.2, a functional group of chemical constituents or living organisms is a collection of those entities that are similar enough with respect to their roles in the ecosystem such that their dynamics can be adequately described by one representative set of prop-

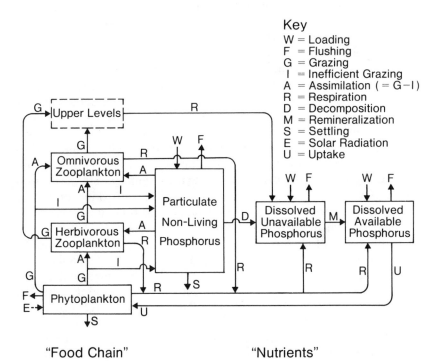

Key
W = Loading
F = Flushing
G = Grazing
I = Inefficient Grazing
A = Assimilation (= G−I)
R = Respiration
D = Decomposition
M = Remineralization
S = Settling
E = Solar Radiation
U = Uptake

"Food Chain"   "Nutrients"

Figure 14.6 Schematic representation of the compartments and interactions of a nutrient/food chain model of a lake. Phytoplankton = 1; herbivores = 2; carnivores = 3; particulate P = 4; unavailable P = 5; available P = 6.

*Note: multilayer, two-dimensional and three-dimensional schemes are discussed in Section 14.3.3.

erties, that is, equations and coefficients. For example, phytoplankton as a functional group principally are responsible for removing dissolved available nutrient from the water column and converting it to particulate organic plant biomass. These plants are grazed by zooplankton, which in turn are grazed by other zooplankton. Thus, two zooplankton functional groups, herbivores and omnivores, are included. While other components of the food chain, such as fish, can be included explicitly, the present model uses a first-order loss from the zooplankton groups to represent the effect of these higher trophic levels.

Dissolved available phosphorus, which is taken up and used by phytoplankton, is an obvious functional group. Dynamics of this group are dictated by balancing uptake by phytoplankton with replenishment by plant and animal excretion, and by remineralization from the dissolved unavailable phosphorus pool. The final nonliving group is the particulate or detrital phosphorus, which is included to differentiate between settleable and nonsettleable fractions. The division of nonliving organic phosphorus into dissolved and particulate fractions also allows the consumption of detritus by the filter-feeding zooplankton and accounts for a chemical functional group that is dissolved but not immediately available for use by the phytoplankton. Transformations from particulate to dissolved unavailable to dissolved available nutrient are described here as first-order rates. While in nature these transformations often are mediated by bacteria, inadequate quantitative descriptions of bacterial processes and the difficulty in measuring their abundance in the environment have precluded including equations for their kinetics per se. Instead, only their effects are considered, as has been done successfully in many stream BOD-oxygen models (e.g., Thomann 1972).

Components of phytoplankton, herbivorous zooplankton and detritus that are grazed but not thoroughly assimilated by zooplankton are egested and contribute to the detrital pool. Dissolved unavailable phosphorus is generated primarily through detrital decomposition. Dissolved phosphorus (both available and unavailable) also is excreted by phytoplankton and zooplankton.

While phytoplankton are the primary driving group in this framework, it becomes apparent that cycling of nutrients through the ecosystem is the critical point of focus. The rates and mechanisms of the cycle largely control phytoplankton dynamics. Most nutrient/food chain models, which simultaneously simulate the cycles of two or more vital plant nutrients—for example, phosphorus, nitrogen or silicon—must be concerned with the calculation of the limiting nutrient at a given instant, as well as with the phenomenon of changing stoichiometric relationships among the nutrients in all groups of organic matter. Some of these matters are discussed in Scavia (1979a), and some are mentioned here in Section 14.3. In the present framework, all forms are expressed as phosphorus. This is done for simplicity and implicitly assumes that phosphorus is the limiting nutrient throughout the year. In addition, it implies constant stoichiometric relationships among certain processes, such as phosphorus uptake and growth by phytoplankton, and nutrient excretion and respiration by zooplankton, which are not entirely accurate. Consideration of potential limitation by other nutrients and the effects of varying stoichiometry certainly are important in many problem contexts. However, they are unnecessary for elaborating the general approach.

14.2.3 Food Chain Equations

Phytoplankton

The kinetic interactions of the phytoplankton consist of growth and loss, as in

$$R_1 = R_{1,\,growth} - R_{1,\,loss} \tag{14.20}$$

where

$$R_{1,\,growth} = G_1 V p_1 \tag{14.21}$$

and

$$R_{1,\,loss} = D_1 V p_1 \tag{14.22}$$

where G_1 and D_1 are growth and loss rates $[d^{-1}]$.

Phytoplankton Growth. Phytoplankton growth is a function of temperature, light and nutrients. Temperature is included by calculating a maximum growth rate for conditions of optimal light and excess nutrients as a function of the temperature of the layer (see Figure 14.7a), as in

$$G_m = G_{m,\,20} \theta_{1,\,g}^{T-20} \tag{14.23}$$

where $\quad G_m$ = maximum growth rate for the temperature of the layer $[d^{-1}]$
$\quad\quad G_{m,\,20}$ = maximum growth rate at 20°C $[d^{-1}]$
$\quad\quad \theta_{1,\,g}$ = a temperature constant (see Equation 10.13)
$\quad\quad T$ = temperature of the layer expressed as °C

This maximum value is then attenuated by functions dependent on the light and nutrient levels of the layer, as in

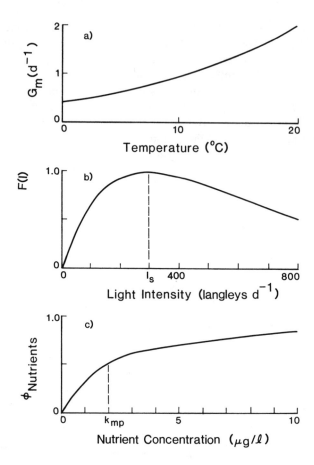

Figure 14.7   Dependency of phytoplankton growth on (a) temperature, (b) light and (c) nutrients.

$$G_1 = G_m \min\{\phi_{\text{light}}, \phi_{\text{nutrients}}\} \qquad (14.24)$$

where ϕ is an attenuation coefficient that ranges from zero at total attenuation to unity at optimal levels. In this framework, phytoplankton are limited by light or nutrients, whichever is in the lowest supply.

Light Attenuation: In general, phytoplankton photosynthesize in proportion to the available light intensity. As depicted in Figure 14.7b, this dependency increases to an optimal value beyond which high light levels tend to inhibit growth. One mathematical expression of the light dependency of phytoplankton, F(I), is (Steele 1965)

$$F(I) = \frac{I}{I_s} \exp\left(-\frac{I}{I_s} + 1\right) \qquad (14.25)$$

where I = light intensity [langleys d^{-1}]
I_s = light intensity at which growth is a maximum [langleys d^{-1}]

For natural waters, the light intensity at a particular depth is a function of the attenuation by water, color and dissolved particles. This attenuation is described theoretically by the Beer-Lambert Law,

$$I(z) = I_0 \exp(-k_e z) \qquad (14.26)$$

where $I(z)$ = light intensity at depth z [langleys d^{-1}]
I_0 = light intensity at the top of the layer [langleys d^{-1}]
k_e = an extinction coefficient that reflects the properties of the water such as color and suspended particles that contribute to light attenuation [m^{-1}]

Equations 14.25 and 14.26 can be combined to yield an equation for the growth rate reduction as a function of light attenuated to a given depth:

$$F[I(z)] = \frac{I_0 \exp(-k_e z)}{I_s} \exp\left[-\frac{I_0 \exp(-k_e z)}{I_s} + 1\right] \qquad (14.27)$$

To use Equation 14.27 in the present mathematical model, it must be averaged in space and time. The former can be done by integrating over the depth of the layer. The temporal averaging must take into account the fact that light varies through the course of a day. This can be approximated as

$$I_0(t) = I_a \qquad o < t < f \qquad (14.28)$$

$$I_0(t) = 0 \qquad f < t < 1 \qquad (14.29)$$

where f = daylight fraction of the day, or photoperiod
I_a = average incident solar radiation during the daylight period [langleys d^{-1}]

The integration over depth and photoperiod can be represented as

$$\phi_{\text{light}} = \frac{1}{z} \int_{z_1}^{z_2} \frac{1}{T} \int_0^f F[I(z)]\, dt\, dz \qquad (14.30)$$

where z_1 = depth of the top of the layer where depth increases downward [m]

z_2 = depth at the bottom of the layer [m]
$\bar{z} = z_2 - z_1$
$I_o = I_a$ in Equation 14.27

The result of the integration for each layer is

$$\phi_{light} = \frac{2.718f}{k_e\bar{z}} [\exp(-\alpha_1) - \exp(-\alpha_0)] \qquad (14.31)$$

where the extinction coefficient can be related to particulate levels by

$$k_e = k_e' + a_p \Sigma p_p \qquad (14.32)$$

and k_e' is the extinction coefficient due to particle-free water [m^{-1}], "a_p" is a factor reflecting the attenuation due to particulate matter [m^2 mgP^{-1}], and Σp_p is the concentration of particulate matter in the appropriate layer [$mgP\ m^{-3}$] = $p_1 + p_2 + p_3 + p_4$ in the present model, and

$$\alpha_1 = \frac{I_a}{I_s} \exp(-k_e z_2) \qquad (14.33)$$

$$\alpha_0 = \frac{I_a}{I_s} \exp(-k_e z_1) \qquad (14.34)$$

Nutrient Attenuation of the Growth Rate: As described in Section 14.1.3, nutrient limitation of growth is given mathematical expression by a Michaelis-Menten formulation, as in

$$\phi_{nutrients} = \frac{p_6}{k_{sp} + p_6} \qquad (14.35)$$

where k_{sp} is a half-saturation constant for growth limitation by phosphorus [$mgP\ m^{-3}$].

Phytoplankton Nutrient Losses. Excretion and grazing by herbivorous and omnivorous zooplankton contribute to phytoplankton phosphorus loss, as in

$$R_{1,loss} = R_{1,excretion} + R_{1,grazing} \qquad (14.36)$$

Phytoplankton excretion is treated as a first-order, temperature-dependent decay, as in

$$R_{1,\,\text{excretion}} = K_1 \theta_{1,r}^{T-20} V p_1 \qquad (14.37)$$

where $\quad K_1 =$ phytoplankton excretion rate at 20°C $[T^{-1}]$
$\theta_{1,r} =$ a temperature constant

This expression is borrowed from similar ones for phytoplankton respiration under the assumption that excretion and respiration are coupled stoichiometrically. Grazing losses via herbivorous and omnivorous zooplankton are described under zooplankton kinetics.

Herbivorous Zooplankton

As with the phytoplankton, herbivorous zooplankton kinetics are a function of their growth and loss, as in

$$R_2 = R_{2,\,\text{growth}} - R_{2,\,\text{loss}} \qquad (14.38)$$

Herbivorous Zooplankton Growth. Growth is based on the conversion of grazed food into new zooplankton biomass. Grazing follows saturation kinetics that allow grazing to be directly proportional to food and zooplankton concentrations at low food concentrations but proportional only to zooplankton concentrations at high food levels. This temperature-dependent (similar to phytoplankton) rate reflects the fact that, above a certain food concentration, zooplankton are limited in their ability to gather and process food. The loss rate of phytoplankton due to herbivorous zooplankton grazing is expressed as

$$D_{1,\,\text{grazing}} = C_m \theta_{2,g}^{T-20} V \frac{\omega_{12} p_1 + \omega_{42} p_4}{k_{sh} + \omega_{12} p_1 + \omega_{42} p_4} p_2 \qquad (14.39)$$

where $\quad k_{sh} =$ half-saturation constant for herbivorous zooplankton grazing on total food (i.e., phytoplankton, p_1, and detritus, p_4) [mgP-herbivores m^{-3}]
$C_m =$ maximum mass-specific grazing rate of the herbivores, p_2 [mgP (mgP d)$^{-1}$]
$\omega_{i2} =$ relative preference factor $(0. - 1.)$ for food source "i"

The portion (f_i) of food taken from each of the potential food groups (in this case phytoplankton and detritus) can be represented as

$$f_i = \frac{\omega_{i2} p_i}{\omega_{12} p_1 + \omega_{42} p_4} \qquad (14.40)$$

In the case of an indiscriminant feeder, all ω_i equal 1 and the fraction of each food in the diet is proportional to the fraction of such food in the water. Thus, the loss term for phytoplankton via herbivore grazing is

$$R_{1,\text{grazing}} = D_{1,\text{grazing}} f_1 = C_m \theta_{2,g}^{T-20} V \frac{\omega_{12} p_1}{k_{sh} + \omega_{12} p_1 + \omega_{42} p_4} p_2 \quad (14.41)$$

Note that a similar phytoplankton loss term also exists to account for grazing by omnivorous zooplankton. Not all of the food grazed can be assimilated. The efficiency of assimilation can vary with, among other things, the amount of food that is present; however, here we assume that the efficiency, ϵ_i, is a food-dependent constant. This constant multiplied by each food grazed (Equation 14.41) determines the rate at which zooplankton biomass is produced:

$$R_{2,\text{growth}} = \sum_i D_{i,\text{grazing}} f_i \epsilon_i \quad (14.42)$$

Food not assimilated is egested, as defined by

$$R_{2,\text{egested}} = \sum_i D_{i,\text{grazing}} f_i (1 - \epsilon_i) \quad (14.43)$$

where the summation is for $i = 1$ and 4. In the present model, it is assumed that the egested food is transferred to the nonliving particulate organic (or detrital) phosphorus pool.

Herbivorous Zooplankton Losses. The loss of herbivore phosphorus is similar to the phytoplankton loss term in the sense that it is a composite of egestion, as described above, plus excretion and grazing by the next level of the food chain, the omnivorous zooplankton, as in

$$R_{2,\text{loss}} = R_{2,\text{excretion}} + R_{2,\text{grazing}} + R_{2,\text{upper}} \quad (14.44)$$

where

$$R_{2,\text{excretion}} = K_2 \theta_{2,r}^{T-20} V p_2 \quad (14.45)$$

and

$$R_{2,\text{grazing}} = C_{gc} \theta_{3,g}^{T-20} \frac{\omega_{13} p_2}{k_{sc} + \omega_{13} p_1 + \omega_{23} p_2 + \omega_{43} p_4} V p_3 \quad (14.46)$$

$$R_{2,\text{upper}} = K_{u,2} V p_2 \quad (14.46a)$$

where $\quad K_2$ = herbivorous zooplankton excretion rate at $20°C$ $[d^{-1}]$

$\theta_{2,r}$ and $\theta_{3,g}$ = temperature coefficients

C_{gc} = maximum mass specific grazing rate of the omnivores, p_3 $[mg\ P\ (mg\ P\ d)^{-1}]$

k_{sc} = half-saturation constant for omnivorous zooplankton grazing on total food (i.e., phytoplankton, p_1, herbivores, p_2, and detritus, p_4) $[mg\ P\text{-omnivores}\ m^{-3}]$

$K_{u,2}$ = first-order loss rate to trophic levels above omnivorous zooplankton $[d^{-1}]$

Omnivorous Zooplankton

The kinetics of the omnivores are expressed as

$$R_3 = R_{3,\text{growth}} - R_{3,\text{loss}} \qquad (14.47)$$

where

$$R_{3,\text{growth}} = R_{3,\text{assimilated}} = \sum_i D_{i,\text{grazing}} f_i \epsilon_i \qquad (14.48)$$

and

$$R_{3,\text{loss}} = R_{3,\text{excretion}} + R_{3,\text{upper}} \qquad (14.49)$$

where

$$R_{3,\text{excretion}} = K_3 \theta_{3,r}^{T-20} V p_3 \qquad (14.50)$$

and

$$R_{3,\text{upper}} = K_{u,3} V p_3 \qquad (14.51)$$

where $\quad \epsilon_i$ = omnivores' assimilation efficiency

K_3 = omnivorous zooplankton excretion rate at $20°C$ $[d^{-1}]$

$\theta_{3,r}$ = temperature coefficient

$K_{u,3}$ = first-order relationship for losses to higher levels of the food chain $[d^{-1}]$

The summation is for $i = 1$, 2 and 4.

As will be seen in the subsequent discussion of the nutrients, the upper food chain loss is input directly to the dissolved unavailable phosphorus pool. Among other things, this assumes a stable population of higher predators with no seasonal variations in feeding pattern except as it relates to the quantity of omnivorous zooplankton present. The mathematical representation is

$$R_{\text{higher predators}} = R_{hp,\text{growth}} - R_{hp,\text{death}} \qquad (14.52)$$

where

$$R_{hp,growth} = R_{hp,death} = K_{u,3}Vp_3 + K_{u,2}Vp_2 \qquad (14.53)$$

14.2.4 Nutrient Equations

Three forms are used to characterize phosphorus. Particulate non-living phosphorus represents detritus. Dissolved unavailable phosphorus includes those organic and inorganic forms that are soluble but unavailable for direct algal assimilation, for example, organic molecules containing phosphorus and condensed phosphates. Dissolved available phosphorus, orthophosphate, is that form available for phytoplankton use.

Particulate Nonliving Phosphorus

The detrital pool is fed by egestion and lost by grazing and decomposition to soluble forms, as in

$$R_4 = R_{4,egestion} - R_{4,decomposition} - R_{4,grazing} \qquad (14.54)$$

The egestion gains relate directly to herbivorous (Equation 14.43) and omnivorous losses, as in

$$R_{4,egestion} = \sum_i (1 - \epsilon_i)D_{i,grazed}f_i + \sum_j (1 - \epsilon_j)D_{j,grazed}f_j \qquad (14.55)$$

where the summations are for $i = 1$ and 4, $j = 1$, 2 and 4. Decomposition is expressed as a first-order, temperature-dependent reaction:

$$R_{4,decomposition} = K_4\theta_{4,r}^{T-20}Vp_4 \qquad (14.56)$$

where K_4 = decomposition rate at 20°C [T^{-1}]
$\theta_{4,r}$ = temperature coefficient

Grazing losses are similar to those calculated for phytoplankton.

Dissolved Unavailable Phosphorus

Dissolved unavailable phosphorus is gained as a result of decomposition of detritus, excretion by organisms, and upper food chain feedback, as in

$$R_{5,\,\text{gains}} = R_{4,\,\text{decomposition}} + \sum_{i=1}^{3} \alpha_i R_{i,\,\text{excretion}} + \sum_{i=2}^{3} R_{i,\,\text{upper}} \qquad (14.57)$$

where α_i represents the fraction of material excreted by each group that is unavailable phosphorus. It is lost by a first-order conversion to the dissolved available form

$$R_{5,\,\text{loss}} = K_5 \theta_{5,\text{r}}^{T\text{-}20} V p_5 \qquad (14.58)$$

where K_5 = remineralization rate 20°C
$\theta_{5,\text{r}}$ = temperature coefficient

Dissolved Available Phosphorus

Dissolved available phosphorus is gained by excretion and remineralization, as in

$$R_{6,\,\text{gains}} = \sum_{i=1}^{3} (1 - \alpha_i) R_{i,\,\text{excretion}} + R_{5,\,\text{loss}} \qquad (14.59)$$

and lost via phytoplankton uptake, as in

$$R_{6,\,\text{loss}} = R_{1,\,\text{growth}} \qquad (14.59a)$$

14.2.5 Total System of Equations

The complete set of equations is written in Table 14.1 for a single layer. Note that most of the terms define internal cycling between compartments. The distinction between internal partitioning and input/output kinetics is discussed in Section 14.7 and is used to relate nutrient/food chain models to simple budget approaches.

The system of food chain equations, written in complete form, is displayed in Table 14.2. This is done to illustrate the increased detail of the relationships at the lower end of the food chain. This detail is an artifact of the problem context that focuses on phytoplankton and their deleterious effects, rather than an expression of an intrinsic complexity of the lower organisms. In fact, other models designed to analyze problems with a higher organism focus would have the opposite result—that is, increased detail at the upper end of the food chain. A case in point is Weininger's (1978) analysis of PCB levels in Lake Michigan trout, which essentially treated the lower end of the food chain as a forcing function for an elaborate bioenergetic model of the trout. This is not meant as a

**Table 14.1   The Differential Equations for the Nutrient/Food
Chain Model in Section 14.2 and Displayed in Figure 14.6.
[For simplicity, the equations are written for a single layer. (a) shows
the complete set of equations for the seasonal computation. The
italicized terms represent internal kinetic interactions and the
nonitalicized are input-output mass transfers. If the internal kinetics
are much faster than the inputs and the outputs, a local equilibrium
assumption can be made and the equations can be combined to yield a
long-term total P model as in (b).]**

(a) COMPLETE SET OF EQUATIONS

$$V \frac{dp_1}{dt} = W_1 - Qp_1 - v_1 A_s p_1 + R_{1,growth} - R_{1,excretion} - \Sigma R_{1,grazed}$$

$$V \frac{dp_2}{dt} = W_2 - Qp_2 + \epsilon_1 R_{1,grazed} + \epsilon_4 R_{4,grazed} - R_{2,excretion} - R_{2,grazed} - R_{2,upper}$$

$$V \frac{dp_3}{dt} = W_3 - Qp_3 + \epsilon_1 R_{1,grazed} + \epsilon_2 R_{2,excretion} + \epsilon_4 R_{4,upper} - R_{3,excretion}$$

$$- R_{3,upper}$$

$$V \frac{dp_4}{dt} = W_4 - Qp_4 - v_4 A_s p_4 + \Sigma (1 - \epsilon_1) R_{1,grazed} + \Sigma (1 - \epsilon_4) R_{4,grazed}$$

$$+ (1 - \epsilon_2) R_{2,grazed} - \Sigma R_{4,grazed} - R_{4,decomposition}$$

$$V \frac{dp_5}{dt} = W_5 - Qp_5 + R_{4,decomposition} - R_{5,remineralization} + \sum_{i=1}^{3} \alpha_i R_{i,excretion}$$

$$+ R_{2,upper} + R_{3,upper}$$

$$V \frac{dp_6}{dt} = W_6 - Qp_6 + R_{5,remineralization} - R_{1,growth} + \sum_{i=1}^{3} (1 - \alpha_i) R_{i,excretion}$$

(b) INPUT-OUTPUT VERSION

$$V \frac{dp_t}{dt} = W_t - Qp_t - v_1 A_s p_1 - v_4 A_s p_4$$

where

$$p_t = \sum_{i=1}^{6} p_i \qquad W_t = \sum_{i=1}^{6} W_i$$

Table 14.2   Kinetic Interactions of the Food Chain for
the Model Described in Section 14.2.
[Note the increased complexity at lower levels of the food
chain. Since such models were developed to simulate
eutrophication, they tend to emphasize the phytoplankton.]

$$R_{\text{upper levels}} = K_{u,2} V p_2 + K_{u,3} V p_3 - K_{u,2} V p_2 - K_{u,3} V p_3$$

$$R_{\text{omnivores}} = \sum_i \epsilon_i C_{gc} \theta_{3,g}^{T-20} \frac{\omega_{i3} p_i}{k_{sc} + \omega_{13} p_1 - \omega_{23} p_2 + \omega_{43} p_4} V p_3 - K_3 \theta_{3,r}^{T-20} V p_3 - K_{u,3} V p_3$$

$$R_{\text{herbivores}} = \sum_i \epsilon_i C_m \theta_{2,g}^{T-20} \frac{\omega_{i2} p_i}{k_{sh} + \omega_{12} p_1 + \omega_{42} p_4} V p_2$$

$$- C_{gc} \theta_{3,g}^{T-20} \frac{\omega_{23} p_2}{k_{sc} + \omega_{13} p_1 + \omega_{23} p_2 + \omega_{43} p_4} V p_3 - K_2 \theta_{2,r}^{T-20} V p_2 - K_{u,2} V p_2$$

$$R_{\text{phytoplankton}} = G_m \theta_{1,g}^{T-20} \min\left(\frac{2.718f}{k_e \bar{z}} \left\{\exp\left[-\frac{I_a}{I_s} \exp(-k_e z_2)\right]\right.\right.$$

$$\left.\left. - \exp\left[-\frac{I_a}{I_s} \exp(-k_e z_1)\right]\right\}, \frac{p_6}{k_{sp} + p_6}\right) V p_1 - K_1 \theta_{1,r}^{T-20} V p_1$$

$$- C_m \theta_{2,g}^{T-20} \frac{\omega_{12} p_1}{k_{sh} + \omega_{12} p_1 + \omega_{42} p_4} V p_2$$

$$- C_{gc} \theta_{3,g}^{T-20} \frac{w_{13} p_1}{k_{sc} + \omega_{13} p_1 + \omega_{23} p_2 + \omega_{43} p_4} V p_3$$

judgment of the superiority of either orientation. The point is that, from an engineering perspective, the problem context partially dictates kinetic resolution. Mechanisms that are unimportant to the problem are disregarded. However, there is a minimal level of resolution required for a credible result. This has special importance in the use of models to make projections of a lake's response to future conditions. Since this minimal level is problem-specific, its definition will not be pursued here. The reader can refer to Mortimer (1975) and Shapiro (1979) for a discussion of some biological factors that relate to adequate system definition. Scavia et al. (1976b) address the same topic from a modeling perspective.

§ § §

Example 14.5. Lake Ontario has the following characteristics:

W_4 = 4000 metric tons yr^{-1}
W_5 = 4000 metric tons yr^{-1}

W_6 = 4000 metric tons yr^{-1}
A_s = 19,000 km^2
z_e = 15 m
z_h = 71 m
Q = 212 km^3 yr^{-1}
k_e = 0.2 m^{-1}

Using the meteorological forcing functions and diffusion and temperature characteristics in Figure 14.8, compute the seasonal cycle of phosphorus components using the nutrient/food chain model described in the
previous section (parameter values are listed in Table 14.3).

As displayed in Figure 14.9, the seasonal cycle of total phosphorus is
similar to that computed previously in Example 13.6 with a two-
component linear model. However, because of the larger number of
components, more information is conveyed by the nutrient/food chain
model. The most striking feature is the epilimnetic phytoplankton peak
that occurs in late spring due to increasing light and temperature levels
and the onset of thermal stratification. The herbivores and omnivores
reach peak values approximately one to two months later. The detrital
and dissolved unavailable phosphorus pools also increase at this time as a
result of respiration and inefficient grazing. In comparison, winter and
hypolimnetic dynamics are relatively stable.

Key
T_e = epilimnetic temperature
T_h = hypolimnetic temperature
I_a = incident solar radiation
f = photoperiod
E_t' = vertical bulk diffusion coefficient

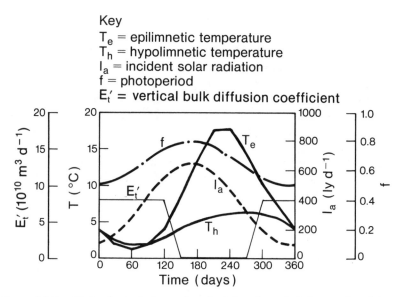

Time (days)

Figure 14.8   Meterological, thermal and mixing characteristics used to drive a
nutrient/food chain model.

Table 14.3   Parameters Used to Simulate Phytoplankton
Dynamics in Example 14.5

Parameter	Symbol	Value	Units
Phytoplankton settling velocity	v_1	0.2	$m\ d^{-1}$
Detrital settling velocity	v_4	0.25	$m\ d^{-1}$
Optimal phytoplankton growth rate at 20°C	$G_{m,20}$	2.0	d^{-1}
Temperature constant for phytoplankton growth	$\theta_{1,g}$	1.08	
Light intensity at which growth is maximum	I_s	300	langleys d^{-1}
Attenuation factor for particulate matter	a_p	0.025	$1\ mgP^{-1}\ m^{-1}$
Half-saturation constant for phosphorus	k_{sp}	2	$mgP\ m^{-3}$
Phytoplankton respiration rate at 20°C	K_1	0.025	d^{-1}
Temperature constant for phytoplankton respiration	$\theta_{1,r}$	1.08	
Herbivorous zooplankton grazing rate at 20°C	C_m	0.86	d^{-1}
Herbivore preference factor for phytoplankton	ω_{12}	1	
Herbivore preference factor for detritus	ω_{42}	1	
Herbivore assimilation efficiency for phytoplankton	ϵ_1	0.7	
Herbivore assimilation efficiency for detritus	ϵ_4	0.1	
Half-saturation constant for herbivore grazing	k_{sh}	10	$mgP\ m^{-3}$
Herbivore respiration rate at 20°C	K_2	0.1	d^{-1}
Temperature constant for herbivore grazing and respiration	θ_2	1.045	
First-order loss for herbivores	$K_{u,2}$	0.002	d^{-1}
Omnivorous zooplankton grazing rate at 20°C	C_{gc}	1.016	d^{-1}
Omnivore preference factor for phytoplankton	ω_{13}	0.85	
Omnivore preference factor for herbivores	ω_{23}	0.5	
Omnivore preference factor for detritus	ω_{43}	0.2	
Omnivore assimilation efficiency for phytoplankton + herbivores	ϵ_1, ϵ_2	0.5	
Omnivore assimilation efficiency for detritus	ϵ_4	0.1	
Half-saturation constant for omnivore grazing	k_{sc}	10	$mgP\ m^{-3}$
Omnivore respiration rate at 20°C	K_3	0.084	d^{-1}
Temperature constant for omnivore grazing and respiration	θ_3	1.045	
First-order loss for omnivores	$K_{u,3}$	0.004	d^{-1}
Detrital decomposition rate at 20°C	K_4	0.005	d^{-1}
Temperature constant for detrital decomposition	$\theta_{4,r}$	1.08	
Fraction of excreted material that is unavailable phosphorus	$\alpha_1, \alpha_2, \alpha_3$	0.2	
Dissolved organic P	K_5	0.075	d^{-1}
Temperature constant for remineralization	$\theta_{5,r}$	1.08	

It must be noted that the model parameters in Table 14.3 were
obtained through a laborious and time-consuming calibration. Although
ranges for most of the parameters can be estimated from the literature or
handbooks (e.g., Jorgensen 1979 or Zison et al. 1978), the exact values

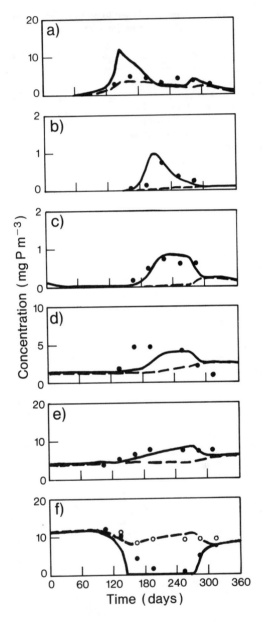

Figure 14.9   Seasonal dynamics of phosphorus components for Lake Ontario as simulated with a nutrient/food chain model: (a) phytoplankton, (b) herbivorous zooplankton, (c) omnivorous zooplankton, (d) detritus, (e) dissolved unavailable phosphorus and (f) dissolved available phosphorus. Note the different scales for the ordinates.

were determined by subjective adjustment of the parameters until an "adequate" fit of the simulation to the data was obtained. This "tuning" process is discussed in further detail in Section 14.5.1.

§ § §

Although the foregoing approach has been designed to resolve seasonal variability, it also can be used to simulate long-term trends. However, prior to such an application, the model would have to be calibrated and tested with several years of data. This is due to the fact that for long residence time systems such as Lake Ontario, in-lake response can lag loading changes by several years. A single, seasonal simulation of the type in Example 14.5 therefore is dictated more by the initial conditions in the lake than by the inputs and outputs. Thus, the fact that a single seasonal simulation mimics a single year of data gives no assurance that the multiple-year trajectories, which are determined by inputs and outputs, would be computed accurately.

14.3 GENERAL ISSUES OF IMPORTANCE TO NUTRIENT/FOOD CHAIN MODELING

Because of the simplicity of the model described in the foregoing section, we have disregarded a number of issues related to possible refinements of the approach. The present section addresses some of these issues.

14.3.1 Multiple Nutrient Limitation

The model described in Section 14.2 dealt strictly with phosphorus. This was done not only for simplicity, but also because in many lakes phosphorus is the primary nutrient limiting phytoplankton growth. However, in some systems, human and natural perturbations can induce limitation by another nutrient. For example, if large quantities of phosphorus are introduced into a phosphorus-limited lake, eventually some other nutrient such as nitrogen may come into short supply. Such a shift could then give a competitive advantage to nitrogen-fixing algae. Phosphorus models—both of the input-output and nutrient/food chain varieties—are not capable of simulating these shifts. For this reason, many nutrient/food chain models include compartments for several (typically N and P and sometimes Si and/or C) nutrients.

As in Section 14.2, most models use a Michaelis-Menten formulation to relate phytoplankton growth rate, $k(p_6)$, to a single external nutrient concentration, p_6, and the maximum rate, k_m. Equation 14.5 can be reformulated as the fractional limitation of the maximum growth rate, as in (note: R is equivalent to $\phi_{nutrients}$ in Equation 14.35)

$$R = \frac{k(p_6)}{k_m} = \frac{p_6}{k_s + p_6} \qquad (14.60)$$

where R equals the fractional limitation term. If there is more than one potentially limiting nutrient, a formulation is required to compute R as a function of the limitation terms for the individual nutrients, R_i. Some constructs that have been proposed for this purpose are:

$$R = R_1 \times R_2 \times R_3 \times \ldots R_i \quad \text{(Chen 1970, Di Toro et al.} \qquad (14.61)$$
$$\text{1971, Thomann et al. 1975)}$$

$$R = \text{Min}(R_1, R_2, \ldots R_i) \quad \text{(Larsen et al. 1973, Scavia} \qquad (14.62)$$
$$\text{1980c, Bierman 1976)}$$

$$R = \frac{n}{\sum\limits_{i=1}^{n} (1/r_i)} \quad \text{(Bloomfield et al. 1973, Park} \qquad (14.63)$$
$$\text{et al. 1974)}$$

$$R = \frac{1}{n} \sum\limits_{i=1}^{n} R_i \quad \text{(Patten et al. 1975)} \qquad (14.64)$$

where n is the total number of potentially limiting nutrients. The first three constructs produce similar values of R if one nutrient is significantly more limiting than others and the number of potentially limiting nutrients is low. Large discrepancies arise when several nutrient concentrations are close to limiting levels.

§ § §

Example 14.6. Given four individual nutrient reduction terms— $R_1 = 0.8$, $R_2 = 0.7$, $R_3 = 0.6$ and $R_4 = 0.5$—compute the overall reduction using Equations 14.61 through 14.64.

R (Equation 14.61) = $0.8(0.7)0.6(0.5) = 0.168$

R (Equation 14.62) = $\text{Min}(0.8, 0.7, 0.6, 0.5) = 0.500$

$$R \text{ (Equation 14.63)} = \frac{4}{(1/0.8) + (1/0.7) + (1/0.6) + (1/0.5)} = 0.630$$

R (Equation 14.64) = $\frac{1}{4}$ (0.8 + 0.7 + 0.6 + 0.5) = 0.650

These large discrepancies in R may result in different standing crop estimates, depending on the timing of other processes controlling phytoplankton dynamics.

§ § §

Di Toro et al. (1971), using phosphorus uptake rates as a function of phosphorus and nitrogen concentrations (Ketchum 1939), produced a good fit to uptake rates with Equation 14.61. Rhee (1978), however, found Equation 14.62 to be better than Equation 14.61 in relating the growth rate of *Scenedesmus* spp. to intracellular concentrations of nitrogen and phosphorus. (The question of relating growth rates, uptake rates, intracellular nutrients and extracellular nutrients will be discussed below.) More work is needed to determine the best construct for describing multiple-nutrient limitation because both of the above studies were conducted with individual species, whereas many recent models include groups of species. We must use a construct that describes competition among the modeled groups, while allowing implicit adaptation and/or succession of species within each group.

It can be shown (Scavia and Chapra 1977) that for phosphorus-limited lakes, input-output and nutrient/food chain models yield similar long-term predictions. This suggests that, because of their low cost and ease of application, the simpler input-output approaches are preferable for such predictions. However, as indicated above, there are cases where the assumption of phosphorus-limitation breaks down. It is for simulating these cases that nutrient/food chain models using multiple nutrients have the greatest potential value for planning.

14.3.2 Variable Stoichiometry

In Section 14.2, the uptake of a nutrient by phytoplankton and their subsequent growth were assumed implicitly to be equivalent. The two processes, in fact, are quite distinct. An imbalance in their respective rates causes the amount of nutrient per phytoplankton biomass (the stoichiometry) to vary considerably. It is only when these two rates are equal that Equation 14.59a is strictly valid.

The two-step process can be modeled explicitly (in this case, for phosphorus) with separate equations (e.g., Droop 1974) for uptake, v [mol cell^{-1} d^{-1}]:

$$v = \frac{v_m p_6}{k_{su} + p_6} \qquad (14.65)$$

and growth, μ:

$$\mu = \mu_m(1 - q_o/q) \qquad (14.66)$$

where v_m = maximum uptake rate [mol cell^{-1} d^{-1}]
k_{su} = half-saturation constant for uptake [mgP m^{-3}]
μ_m = maximum growth rate [d^{-1}]
q = cell quota (the amount of phosphorus per phytoplankton cell) [mol cell^{-1}]
q_o = minimum cell quota ($q = q_o$ when $\mu = 0$) [mol cell^{-1}]

Recent research also has indicated that both v_m and k_{su} can also be functions of q (e.g., Gotham and Rhee 1981, Auer 1979). If it is assumed (1) that uptake is independent of the cell quota and (2) that the processes of uptake and growth are at steady state, then uptake must be balanced by growth and

$$v = \mu q \qquad (14.67)$$

For this case, Equations 14.65 through 14.67 can be combined and rearranged to yield Equation 14.5 (Droop 1973):

$$\mu = k(p_6) = k_m \frac{p_6}{k_s + p_6} \qquad (14.68)$$

where the model coefficients now are defined in terms of more fundamental parameters, as in

$$k_m = \frac{v_m \mu_m}{v_m + q_o \mu_m} \qquad (14.69)$$

and

$$k_s = \frac{k_{su}}{1 + v_m/(q_o \mu_m)} \qquad (14.70)$$

In cases where the assumption of equilibrium between uptake and growth is invalid, one additional differential equation describing the time-dependent balance of the internal nutrient quota, q, must be included. The kinetics associated with the dynamics of this internal pool are often much faster than the other processes discussed so far. This leads to the solution of slow and fast differential equations simultaneously, that is, a stiff system of equations. Therefore, this additional equation has not been included in most models of whole systems. (Examples where it has been included are Grenney et al. 1973, Huff et al. 1973, Lehman et al. 1975, Bierman 1976). It often is included in models of phytoplankton cultures.

Di Toro (1980) discusses and demonstrates calculations illustrating modification to the standard Michaelis-Menten expression for growth that take into account control of growth and uptake by the internal store of nutrient. This approach, which also has been derived and verified for steady-state phytoplankton culture experiments (Goldman 1977), assumes nutrient uptake is rapid enough so that q can be considered to be in equilibrium with external nutrient concentrations, even for moderately fast changes in p_6. The computational approach, which is similar to that described in Section 14.4 for coupling fast (equilibrium) reactions of the carbonate system to slower kinetics of phytoplankton growth, greatly reduces the computational burden of following internal pool kinetics explicitly.

We must be cautious in the application of this equilibrium assumption, for it only applies when the nutrient under consideration, in fact, is limiting growth. If limitation switches seasonally from one nutrient to another, or spatially from one nutrient to light, then uptake of the non-limiting nutrient will become out of balance with algal growth such that actual q can become tremendously large with respect to the equilibrium q.

At this point in the development of phytoplankton models, it is not clear whether explicit formulations for the kinetics of q are necessary for predicting seasonal phytoplankton succession. There are, however, other reasons to encourage at least the implicit inclusion of q kinetics through the equilibrium assumption. If long-term storage of various nutrients does occur and is simulated, then the nutrient status or physiological state of the population can be determined at any particular point in time. The internal nutrient status (i.e., the actual amount of nutrients in the cell relative to the minimum amount needed for growth) can then be used to aid in simulating the regulation of respiration, sinking and cell death (cf. Lehman et al. 1975). It also may be very important for proper simulation of the transport of particulate nutrients since both the related physical processes and nutrient status will vary spatially and temporally.

14.3.3 Space/Time Scale Considerations

To this point we have considered only the simplest segmentation scheme: a two-layer, horizontally homogeneous model for seasonal eutrophication simulations. Problems, both research- and management-oriented, also arise for which more spatial or temporal resolution is required. These problems may require two- or three-dimensional models. It is well known that physical processes such as diffusion are scale-dependent; that is, as one views a system from larger space scales, more advective processes appear as random diffusive processes (see pp. 81–83). Therefore, as the space scale increases, so does the diffusion coefficient. Also evident from these considerations of scale-dependent physical processes is the tight coupling of space and time scales (see Figure 10.5). In general, large space scale phenomena are important on large time scales (e.g., hydraulic washout of lakes), and small space scale phenomena are important on small time scales (e.g., molecular diffusion).

In an excellent article, Harris (1980) emphasizes that ecological processes also can be scale-dependent. This scale dependency is illustrated in Figure 14.10, where phytoplankton responses to a spectrum of environmental fluctuations are illustrated. The important concept here is to recognize that for any given time scale of observations (for example, weeks), phenomena at longer time scales (the long-term average or "climatology") will appear constant, phenomena at smaller time scales (physiology) will appear to be in equilibrium with ambient conditions, and only phenomena (ecology) at the observed time scales will appear kinetic. It is this relationship that allows one simulating seasonal eutrophication phenomena to model the carbonate system at equilibrium and to treat lake volume as a constant.

Also evident from this scale analysis is that, in a fashion similar to physical phenomena, small space-scale phenomena (e.g., algal physiology) are important on small time scales. Thus, careful matching of space and time scales for models is important, and their selection must be dictated by the problem under consideration.

A typical suite of models at varying time and space scales is illustrated in Figure 14.11. These conceptualizations dictate the important physical phenomena to consider in obvious ways. However, we also must consider scale-dependent ecological phenomena. For example, if the two-dimensional transect model was selected to address a particular problem, then vertical and horizontal advection and turbulent diffusion must be considered. In addition, by reference to the 10-km region in Figure 14.10 (this figure is for horizontal scales), it is clear that chlorophyll production and seasonal community changes will be important kinetic properties. Alternatively, if the nearshore three-dimensional model were needed, then phytoplankton processes on the 1-km horizontal scale would have to be considered.

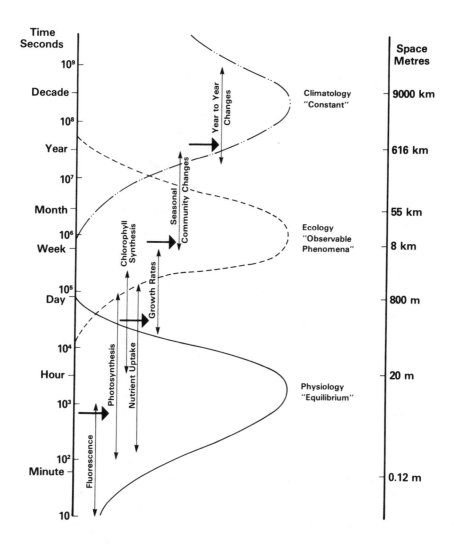

Figure 14.10   A summary of the hierarchy of the various algal responses to the spectrum of environmental fluctuations [reprinted from Harris (1980)]. The temporal and spatial scales are linked by the processes of horizontal turbulent diffusion. The three bell curves roughly define the scales of interest to physiologists, ecologists and climatologists. The horizontal arrows are meant to show that higher-frequency (lower level) processes collapse into higher-level responses. For more details and references, see Harris (1980).

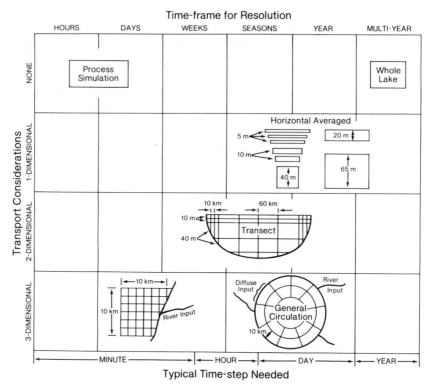

Figure 14.11   Relationship of time and space scales for a variety of model segmentation schemes.

§ § §

Example 14.7. The spatial distribution of biological and chemical properties in the Great Lakes is determined by variations of water depth, sunlight and temperature, by the locations of rivers, and by currents. Separating these physical factors from in situ transformations is a difficult problem, which numerical simulation can help to solve. Scavia and Bennett (1980) focused on the transition period between spring and summer for this problem because both vertical mixing and large-scale circulation are important. In addition, the temperature and current patterns of Lake Ontario are relatively two-dimensional (i.e., small longshore gradients). Therefore, variations along the long axis of the lake are negligible. They simulated the flow, temperature, biology and chemistry for a north-south transect of the lake. The approach was as follows.

The temperature calculations of a hydrodynamic model (Bennett 1971, 1974) were compared to observations, and the model was adjusted until computed and observed temperature contours were in general agreement. The calculations then were repeated together with the chemical and biological processes from an ecological model (Scavia et al. 1976; Scavia 1980c) and compared with observations.

Physical Properties. During the spring transition period, a combination of strong heating and low wind speeds causes the thermocline to form. Because the lake water at the beginning of spring is colder than 4°C, the temperature of maximum density, this process starts in the shallow water. Thus, the lake is divided into two hydrodynamic regimes—a deep region where the water temperature is less than 4°C and where surface heating causes vertical mixing, and a shallow region near the coast with temperatures greater than 4°C which may stratify. In Figure 14.12 the simulated temperatures are compared with observations. The model correctly simulates this general spring temperature pattern and the depth of the thermocline.

Wind and buoyancy combine to cause simple but interesting flow patterns. The wind tends to drive a one-cell pattern, with upwelling at the shore to the left of the wind and downwelling near the opposite shore. Heating drives a two-cell pattern, with the warm water rising near both shores and colder water sinking in the deep region.

Ecological Properties. Using the ecological equations and parameters unchanged from an original lakewide average, two-layer version (Scavia 1980c) resulted in good qualitative comparisons between observations and computations for nutrients (phosphorus, nitrogen, silica) and estimates of biomass (chlorophyll *a*, particulate organic carbon).*

By the end of May, distinct offshore gradients had developed; nutrients, especially phosphorus and silica, were depleted severely in the regions within 10 km of both shores (Figure 14.13). In addition, at this time, no strong vertical gradients were obvious in either the model output or the data. At the end of the period of simulation (corresponding to the June 20–22 cruise), the symmetry of the north and south shore contours was lost. The region of nutrient depletion along the north increased to greater than 25 km, and vertical stratification was not as strong there. The spatial and temporal progression of the region of nutrient depletion is demonstrated for phosphorus in Figure 14.13.

Biomass parameters (chlorophyll *a* and particulate organic carbon) in April were relatively homogeneous vertically, with higher nearshore values. Patterns in May generally showed offshore gradients and little

---

*In the original paper (Scavia and Bennett 1980), the authors state that the sinking rate has to be adjusted for a good fit to data. Actually, no coefficient changes were necessary.

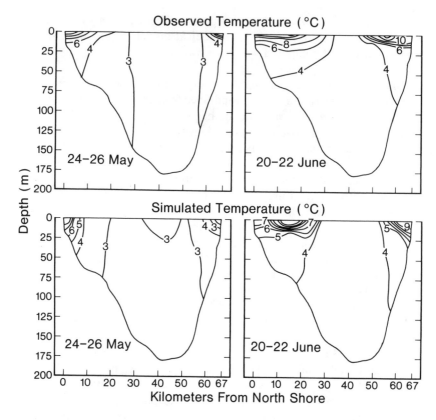

Figure 14.12   Comparison of observed (upper) and calculated (lower) temperatures (°C) corresponding to May and June cruises in Lake Ontario. [Reprinted from Scavia and Bennett (1980)]

vertical structure (Figure 14.14), except for evidence of nearshore subsurface chlorophyll peaks, which the model did not reproduce. The simulations indicated that between the May and June cruises, upwelling moved higher nearshore concentrations offshore, creating a lens of high biomass about 15 km from the north shore. By the time of the June cruise, increased nearshore production apparently created higher biomass again close to shore. A similar structure was produced along the south shore with the exception that, like the nutrient contours, the biomass contours were constrained closer to shore by the wind-driven flow.

Hydrodynamic Transport Vs In Situ Production. During spring, there are several physical mechanisms that influence the distribution of chemical and biological parameters. Differences in surface temperature

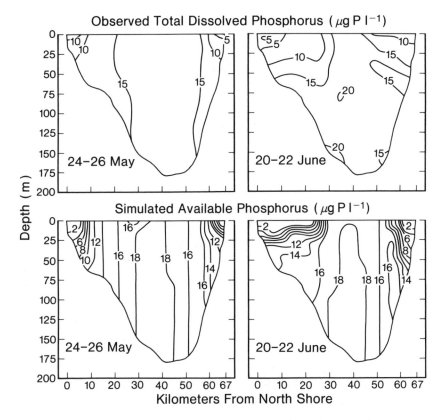

Figure 14.13 Comparison of observed (upper) and calculated (lower) concentrations of phosphorus (μgP l^{-1}) corresponding to May and June cruises in Lake Ontario. Observed phosphorus is total dissolved phosphorus, and calculated phosphorus is that considered available for phytoplankton growth. [Reprinted from Scavia and Bennett (1980)]

can stimulate different rates of biomass production and nutrient cycling. Differences in vertical temperature gradients can produce different intensities of vertical mixing. Currents driven by density differences or wind stress can bring nutrients into the photic zone.

Some numerical experiments were performed to find out which of the physical mechanisms were most important. In these experiments, two simulations were run and the results were compared to the original calculations discussed above (henceforth, the normal case). In the first simulation, mass transport by advection and diffusion were eliminated. In the second simulation, only vertical diffusion was included. In all cases, in situ biological and chemical processes and sinking were included, and

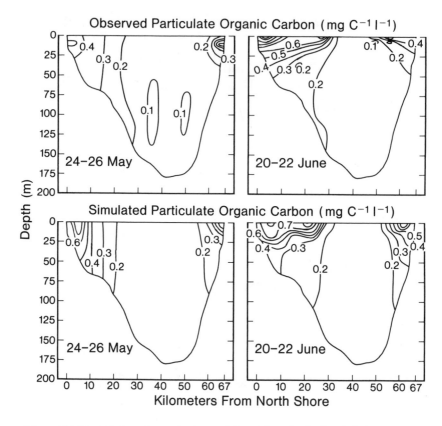

Figure 14.14   Comparison of observed (upper) and calculated (lower) concentrations of particulate organic carbon (mgC l^{-1}) corresponding to May and June cruises in Lake Ontario. Calculated carbon is the sum of simulated phytoplankton, zooplankton and detrital carbon. [Reprinted from Scavia and Bennett (1980)]

temperature distributions were kept the same as in the normal case. The results of these experiments are summarized in Figure 14.15 for available phosphorus and particulate organic carbon.

The simulation with no advection or diffusion showed that phytoplankton production in the cold offshore waters, although reduced when compared to inshore waters, is sufficient to deplete nutrients from the surface layer within the 72-day simulation (Figure 14.15a). Therefore, temperature-controlled in situ production alone was not sufficient to produce the persistent offshore gradients.

The second simulation illustrates that vertical mixing, together with in situ production, is sufficient to reproduce the observed biological and

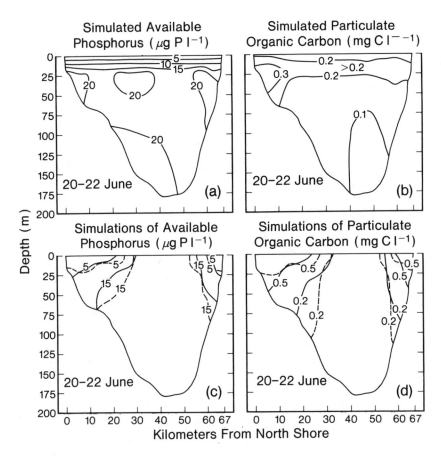

Figure 14.15   Contours of model output demonstrating the relative effects of physical and biological processes on the distribution of available phosphorus (μgP l^{-1}) and particulate organic carbon (mgC l^{-1}): a, b—contours of model output generated with no advection or diffusion included; c, d—broken lines represent normal case (i.e., all processes included); solid lines represent simulation without vertical or horizontal advection. [Reprinted from Scavia and Bennett (1980)]

chemical patterns. The major effect of vertical and horizontal advection is to smooth the nutrient gradients through increased mixing caused by repeated reversals in flow direction. The same was true for plankton along the relatively dilute, cold-water boundary (Figure 14.15d).

It appears that the distribution of chemical and biological properties in the vicinity of the 4°C isotherm is controlled primarily by the interaction of in situ processes and the differences in vertical mixing on either side of the isotherm. Shoreward, vertical stratification of the water mass is weak. This reduces the mixed depth and allows increased biomass production and subsequent nutrient depletion. Lakeward, deep vertical mixing keeps a significant portion of the phytoplankton removed from the sunlit surface layers and therefore inhibits their growth.

§ § §

14.4 THE COUPLING OF NUTRIENT/FOOD CHAIN MODELS WITH FAST REACTION PROCESSES

Kinetic interactions of the model described in Section 14.2 proceed on time scales of days to weeks. However, there are processes related to nutrient cycling that move on shorter time frames. For example, many chemical reactions go to completion in minutes to hours. Analysis of the effect of acid rain on the ecology of a soft-water lake would require the coupling of such fast reactions with the slower kinetics of the food chain. Another quick process is sorption, which typically takes place on scales of hours. Since a large fraction of the phosphorus loading in some lakes is associated with particulate matter carried into the lake via its tributaries, the coupling of a nutrient/food chain approach with sorption interactions would be necessary to simulate the effect of inorganic particles on such systems.

In the present section, Di Toro's (1976) local equilibrium technique (see pp. 48–49) is used to combine a simple chemical equilibrium model of inorganic carbon with the nutrient/food chain model. In addition, an example is used to demonstrate the coupling of fast sorption reactions with slow phytoplankton kinetics. The river-run system is chosen for the sorption analysis because much of the effect of allochthonous matter on a lake's nutrient cycling occurs in the nearshore zone. As demonstrated in Chapter 12, the river-run model is an ideal example of an incompletely mixed system since it has the general characteristics of most nearshore areas (loading at one boundary, advective-diffusive transport), yet its one-dimensional transport structure simplifies interpretation of the kinetic interactions.

14.4.1 Coupling Fast Chemical Reactions with Food Chain Models

Up to this point, we have focused on the effect of biological processes on the cycling of nutrients within a lake. Although a host of chemical reactions contribute to this cycling, we have not modeled them directly, but have represented their net affect via empirically derived kinetic constructs. Although this is a reasonable approach for simulating nutrient/ food chain dynamics, there are other interactions whereby biochemical processes affect and are affected by chemical reactions. Many of these interactions require a more explicit treatment of lake chemistry.

To demonstrate techniques for accomplishing this objective, we have chosen the problem of lake acidity. This problem has practical relevance because of the recent devastating effect of "acid rain" on certain lake ecosystems. In addition, because photosynthesis and respiration affect lake acidity, the context is ideally suited to demonstrate how chemical and biological processes can be coupled. Before presenting the method, a number of key concepts related to lake acidity must be elaborated.

Acidity and pH

Pure water dissociates to yield a hydrogen (or more properly, hydrated protons; see Stumm and Morgan 1981), H^+, and a hydroxyl ion, OH^-,

$$H_2O \underset{k_2}{\overset{k_1}{\rightleftharpoons}} H^+ + OH^- \tag{14.71}$$

where k_1 = reaction rate for the dissociation of the water into the ions (sec^{-1})

         k_2 = reaction rate for the formation of water from the ions $(1 \; mol^{-1} \; sec^{-1})$

If the reaction goes to completion, the rates of dissociation and reaction are in balance. The properties of reactants and products at this equilibrium state are defined by (see p. 9)

$$K = \frac{k_1}{k_2} = \frac{[H^+][OH^-]}{[H_2O]} \tag{14.72}$$

where $[H_2O]$ = molar concentration* of water $(mol \; l^{-1})$

         $[H^+]$ = hydrogen ion $(mol \; l^{-1})$

---

*A molar concentration is the number of gram molecular weights, or moles, of a compound per unit volume of water. A gram molecular weight (GMW) refers to the molecular weight of a compound expressed in grams. For example, for elemental phosphorus, the molecular (actually atomic) weight is 31 and the GMW is 31 g. Therefore, a total phosphorus concentration of 20 $\mu g \; l^{-1}$ would be equivalent to 20 $\mu g \; l^{-1} \div 31 \; g \; mol^{-1} = 0.645$ $\mu mol \; l^{-1}$. See a basic chemistry book such as Sawyer and McCarty (1967) for additional details.

$[OH^-]$ = hydroxyl ion (mol l^{-1})

K = equilibrium constant

Because the concentration of water in dilute aqueous solutions is so much greater than the ions and is decreased so little by the ionization, it may be assumed to be at a constant level. Therefore, the equilibrium relationship is conventionally reexpressed as

$$K_w = [H^+][OH^-] \qquad (14.73)$$

where K_w is known as the *ion,* or *ionization, product of water,* which at 25°C is equal to approximately 10^{-14} (see Table 14.4).*

For pure water, equal amounts of $[H^+]$ and $[OH^-]$ are formed and, therefore, the concentration of either is equal to approximately 10^{-7} mol l^{-1}. When an acid is added to the water, it ionizes and increases the hydrogen ion concentration. Consequently, for Equation 14.73 to hold, the hydroxyl concentration must decrease so that the product of the ions equals 10^{-14}. For example, if the addition of an acid to pure water raises $[H^+]$ from 10^{-7} to 10^{-5}, then $[OH^-]$ must decrease to 10^{-9}.

Because it is somewhat cumbersome to work in terms of negative powers of 10, the pH was defined as

$$pH = -\log_{10}[H^+] \qquad (14.74)$$

Due to the negative sign and the logarithmic transformation of $[H^+]$, a high pH represents a low hydrogen ion activity, whereas a low pH represents a high hydrogen ion activity. Consequently, the pH scale is taken to express the intensity of the acidic or basic (or alkaline) condition of the water. As in Figure 14.16, low pH connotes acidic and high pH connotes alkaline waters with a neutral condition at pH of 7.0. The pH of lakes ranges from 1.7 for volcanic lakes to 12.0 for closed alkaline systems (Hutchinson 1957). However, the typical range is from 6.0 to 9.0.

The tendency of natural waters to remain within a relatively restricted range of hydrogen ion activity is due to the presence of substances called buffers that resist changes in pH as acids or bases are increased or are formed within the water. They do this by scavenging H^+ or OH^- ions as

---

* To be precise, equilibrium constants are expressed in terms of activities. The convention used is that the activity of water equals 1.0, and that the activities of dissolved species approach their molar concentration as ionic strength approaches zero. Because this book deals primarily with dilute, fresh waters, we assume that the use of molar concentrations is a valid approximation. The reader can consult Stumm and Morgan (1981) for information regarding activity corrections.

Table 14.4   Temperature Dependence of Equilibrium
Constants for the Inorganic Carbon System as Computed by
the Relationships in Table 14.5 [a]

T(°C)	pK_w	pK_1	pK_2	pK_H
0	14.94	6.58	10.63	1.11
5	14.73	6.52	10.56	1.19
10	14.53	6.46	10.49	1.27
15	14.35	6.42	10.43	1.34
20	14.17	6.38	10.38	1.40
25	14.00	6.35	10.33	1.46
30	13.84	6.33	10.29	1.52

[a] $K = 10^{-pK}$

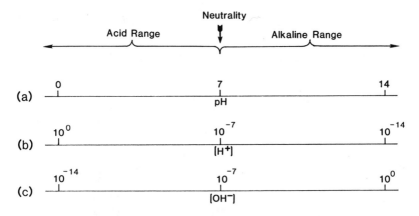

Figure 14.16   Three scales showing the relationship of (a) pH to the concentrations of (b) hydrogen ion and (c) hydroxyl ion in water.

they are released from acids or bases. In most lakes, much of the buffering is related to the dissolved inorganic carbon species: carbon dioxide
(CO_2), bicarbonate ion (HCO_3^-) and carbonate ion (CO_3^{2-}). The inorganic carbon buffering system, in turn, is influenced and enhanced
greatly by a number of heterogeneous reactions that occur in nature. We
may recall that heterogeneous reactions are those that occur between
phases, as opposed to homogeneous reactions that occur within a single
phase. For the inorganic carbon system, the heterogeneous reactions
include atmospheric exchange of CO_2, dissolution/precipitation of carbonate minerals such as calcium carbonate ($CaCO_3$) and photosynthesis/
respiration. The major objective of the present section is to demonstrate

how the fast homogeneous reactions governing the interaction between the dissolved inorganic carbon species can be coupled with the relatively slower heterogeneous reactions.

The Inorganic Carbon system

Figure 14.17 depicts interactions between inorganic carbon and the food chain. Carbon dioxide enters and leaves the inorganic carbon pool via two major pathways: atmospheric and biological exchange processes. Note that other heterogeneous reactions such as calcium carbonate dissolution and precipitation are neglected.

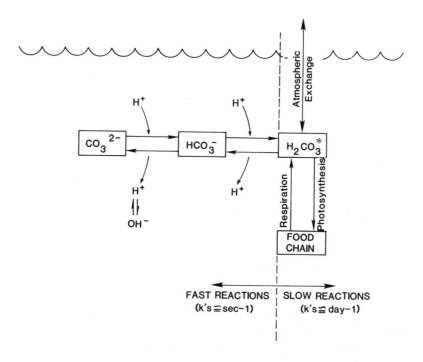

Figure 14.17 A simplified representation of the inorganic carbon system and its relationship with the food chain. The carbonate species shown are carbonate ion (CO_3^{2-}), bicarbonate ion (HCO_3^-) and dissolved carbon dioxide and carbonic acid ($H_2CO_3^*$). The reactions between these species are relatively fast, with reaction rates on the order of seconds to minutes. In contrast, the heterogeneous reactions with the food chain and the atmosphere are typically much slower, with rates on the order of days.

Atmospheric Exchange. The atmospheric exchange can be quantified via

$$W_{atm} = k_l A_w \{ [CO_2(aq)]_s - [CO_2(aq)] \}$$ (14.75)

where W_{atm} = rate of mass transfer of CO_2 across the air-water interface (10^3 mol d^{-1})
k_l = mass transfer coefficient (m d^{-1})
A_w = lake surface area (m^2)
$[CO_2(aq)]_s$ = concentration of dissolved carbon dioxide at saturation
(mol l^{-1})
$[CO_2(aq)]$ = concentration of dissolved carbon dioxide in the lake

The mass transfer coefficient, k_l, is a function of a number of factors,
including wind speed. For low to moderate wind conditions, the CO_2
exchange coefficient is on the order of 0.1 to 1 m d^{-1}. Section 15.1 contains additional information regarding estimates of this coefficient.
The saturation concentration, $[CO_2(aq)]_s$, is the level that the lake
would reach under steady-state conditions for a given temperature. The
level can be estimated on the basis of Henry's Law:

$$[CO_2(aq)]_s = K_H p_{CO_2}$$ (14.76)

where K_H = Henry's constant [mol (1 atm)$^{-1}$]
p_{CO_2} = partial pressure of CO_2 (atm)

Figure 14.18 shows the relationship of carbon dioxide saturation with
temperature for lake water at a typical partial pressure. Values for K_H are
summarized in Table 14.4.

Photosynthesis/Respiration. In addition to reaeration, CO_2 is
introduced and removed from a lake via biological reactions. As discussed in Section 14.1.1, photosynthesis and respiration can be represented by Equation 14.1.
According to the stoichiometry of Equation 14.1, 3.419×10^{-3} mol of
CO_2 ($= 106 \div 31 \div 10^3$) are consumed during the synthesis of 1 mgP of
algal protoplasm. Therefore, using Equation 14.21, the CO_2 consumed
during photosynthesis can be computed as

$$W_{phot} = -3.419 \times 10^{-6} R_{l, growth}$$ (14.77)

where W_{phot} = rate of mass of CO_2 consumed during photosynthesis (10^3
mol d^{-1})
$R_{l, growth}$ = rate of mass growth of phytoplankton (mgP d^{-1}), as
computed in the nutrient/food chain model (Equation
14.21)

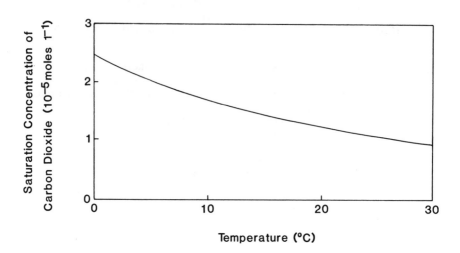

Figure 14.18   Saturation concentration of carbon dioxide (10^{-5} mol l^{-1}) vs temperature (°C) for an atmospheric partial pressure of CO_2 gas of $10^{-3.5}$ atm.

Conversely, 3.419×10^{-3} mol CO_2 per mgP is produced during respiration, as in

$$W_{resp} = 3.419 \times 10^{-6} R_{6,\,gains} \qquad (14.78)$$

where W_{resp} = rate of mass of CO_2 produced during respiration (10^3 mol d^{-1})

          $R_{6,\,gains}$ = gains of the dissolved available pool (mgP d^{-1}) due to excretion and remineralization of unavailable P, as calculated by Equation 14.59

The excretion gain is assumed to approximate CO_2 production due to respiration. The remineralization gain is assumed to reflect CO_2 production by bacteria during the decomposition process.

The heterogeneous reactions with the atmosphere and the food chain proceed on time scales of hours to days and serve to introduce and to remove CO_2 from lake water. In turn, the carbon dioxide takes part in a number of fast reactions (e.g., half-lives ~ seconds to minutes) with other inorganic carbon species as delineated below. In essence, Equations 14.77 and 14.78 are the links between the nutrient/food chain model and the inorganic carbon system.

Dissociation of Carbon Dioxide. When carbon dioxide is introduced into an aqueous solution, it combines with water to form carbonic acid:

$$CO_2 + H_2O \rightleftharpoons H_2CO_3 \tag{14.79}$$

where $[H_2CO_3]$ is the molar concentration of carbonic acid. The carbonic acid, in turn, dissociates into ionic form, as in

$$H_2CO_3 \rightleftharpoons H^+ + HCO_3^- \tag{14.80}$$

Because the equilibrium constant for the hydration of carbon dioxide (Equation 14.79) is so small, the proportion present as carbonic acid is negligible and

$$[CO_2(aq)] \cong [CO_2(aq)] + [H_2CO_3] \tag{14.81}$$

Therefore, the processes of hydration and dissociation conventionally are treated as a single reaction:

$$H_2CO_3^* \underset{k_4}{\overset{k_3}{\rightleftharpoons}} H^+ + HCO_3^- \tag{14.82}$$

where $[H_2CO_3^*] = [CO_2(aq)] + [H_2CO_3] \cong [CO_2(aq)]$
k_3 and k_4 = reaction rates

The equilibrium constant for the combined reaction is

$$K_1 = \frac{[H^+][HCO_3^-]}{[H_2CO_3^*]} \tag{14.83}$$

where K_1 is called the composite acidity constant of $H_2CO_3^*$, or the first dissociation constant of carbonic acid. Values of K_1 are summarized in Table 14.4.

Dissociation of Bicarbonate Ion. The bicarbonate ion, in turn, also dissociates to yield a hydrogen ion and a carbonate ion,

$$HCO_3^- \underset{k_6}{\overset{k_5}{\rightleftharpoons}} H^+ + CO_3^{2-} \tag{14.84}$$

The equilibrium constant for this reaction is

$$K_2 = \frac{[H^+][CO_3^{2-}]}{[HCO_3^-]} \tag{14.85}$$

where K_2 is the second dissociation constant of carbonic acid (see Table 14.4).

Temperature Dependence of Equilibrium Constants. The inorganic carbon equilibrium constants for a number of temperatures are displayed in Table 14.4. Relationships that are useful for computing values at temperatures in the normal range (0 to 35°C) for natural waters are contained in Table 14.5. Stumm and Morgan (1981) summarize equations that also account for the effect of dissolved ions on the constants.

Equilibrium Solutions. Before combining the above relationships with a nutrient/food chain model, we should note that a number of useful analytical and graphical techniques are available for determining the inorganic carbon levels of a natural water at equilibrium (Stumm and Morgan 1981). The following development demonstrates how the foregoing relationships can be applied for this purpose.

The inorganic carbon system delineated above consists of five unknowns: $[H_2CO_3^*]$, $[HCO_3^-]$, $[CO_3^{2-}]$, $[H^+]$ and $[OH^-]$. For the steady-state case, five simultaneous equations are needed to solve for these unknowns. Three of the five are provided by the equilibrium relationships defined by Equations 14.73, 14.83 and 14.85. Since we have assumed equilibrium conditions, the system would be at a balance with the atmosphere, and Equation 14.76 provides a fourth equation.

Finally, a fifth equation results from the fact that the solution must be electrically neutral. This can be expressed as a charge balance, or *electro-*

Table 14.5   Equations to Compute Temperature Dependence of Equilibrium Constants for the Inorganic Carbon System[a]

Harned and Hamer (1933):

$$pK_w = 4787.3/T_a + 7.1321 \log_{10} T_a + 0.010365T_a - 22.801$$

Harned and Davis (1943):

$$pK_1 = 3404.71/T_a + 0.032786T_a - 14.8435$$

Harned and Scholes (1941):

$$pK_2 = 2902.39/T_a + 0.02379T_a - 6.498$$

Edmond and Gieskes (1970):

$$pK_H = -2385.73/T_a - 0.0152642T_a + 14.0184$$

[a] All temperatures as °K (= °C + 273); note, K = 10^{-pK}.

neutrality equation, which specifies that the total number of positive charges must equal the total number of negative charges. For a pure carbonate system, this can be formulated as

$$C_A + [H^+] = [HCO_3^-] + 2[CO_3^{2-}] + [OH^-] + C_B \qquad (14.86)$$

where C_B and C_A are the amounts of base and acid that have been added to the system, respectively. By defining a new quantity alkalinity [Alk], as $C_B - C_A$, Equation 14.86 can be reformulated as

$$[Alk] = [HCO_3^-] + 2[CO_3^{2-}] + [OH^-] - [H^+] \qquad (14.87)$$

Thus, alkalinity is defined as the acid-neutralizing capacity of the system.* If [Alk] is known, Equation 14.87 is the fifth equation needed to solve for the five unknowns.

§ § §

Example 14.8. Use the above relationships to determine the relationship of pH and alkalinity for a lake in equilibrium with atmospheric CO_2.

A sixth equation defining mass conservation for the system is

$$C_T = [H_2CO_3^*] + [HCO_3^-] + [CO_3^{2-}] \qquad (14.88)$$

where C_T is the concentration of total inorganic carbon in the system. Equations 14.83 and 14.85 can be used in conjunction with Equation 14.88 to solve for (Stumm and Morgan 1981)

$$[H_2CO_3^*] = \alpha_0 C_T \qquad (14.89)$$

$$[HCO_3^-] = \alpha_1 C_T \qquad (14.90)$$

$$[CO_3^{2-}] = \alpha_2 C_T \qquad (14.91)$$

where

$$\alpha_0 = \frac{[H^+]^2}{[H^+]^2 + K_1[H^+] + K_1 K_2} \qquad (14.92)$$

---

*Note: Our definition of alkalinity is only applicable to systems in which other buffers are at negligible levels. Other reactions contribute to alkalinity in lake waters but these often are ignored because of the importance of inorganic carbon in many systems.

$$\alpha_1 = \frac{K_1[H^+]}{[H^+]^2 + K_1[H^+] + K_1K_2} \tag{14.93}$$

$$\alpha_2 = \frac{K_1K_2}{[H^+]^2 + K_1[H^+] + K_1K_2} \tag{14.94}$$

The motivation for formulating the system in terms of α's and C_t is due to the fact that the equilibrium equations specify the relationship of one inorganic species to another and to H^+. However, measurements typically are made of C_t and H^+. Equations 14.89 through 14.91 provide a way to compute the species in terms of the measurable quantities.

Equations 14.76 and 14.89 through 14.91 can be substituted into Equation 14.87 to yield

$$[\text{Alk}] = \frac{K_H p_{CO2}}{\alpha_0}(\alpha_1 + 2\alpha_2) + [OH^-] - [H^+] \tag{14.95}$$

Using Equation 14.73 and 14.92 through 14.94, the relationship can be reexpressed as

$$[\text{Alk}] = \frac{K_H p_{CO2}}{[H^+]^2}\{K_1[H^+] + 2K_1K_2\} + \frac{K_w}{[H^+]} - [H^+] \tag{14.96}$$

With Equation 14.74, $[H^+]$ values can be determined for various pH levels and substituted into Equation 14.96 to compute alkalinity. The results, using equilibrium constants (Table 14.4) for a temperature of 4°C, are shown in Figure 14.19 along with other components of the inorganic carbon system.

Note that dissolved carbon dioxide, $[H_2CO_3^*]$, is at a constant level since the system is at equilibrium with the atmosphere. In the normal range of natural waters ($6.0 < \text{pH} < 9.0$), pH increases along with alkalinity. According to Figure 14.19, Lake Ontario ($[\text{Alk}] \cong 1.95$ meq l^{-1}) should have a pH of approximately 8.5 when at equilibrium with atmospheric CO_2. Since the average annual temperature of the lake is approximately 4°C (actually, 4.6°C according to Table 13.1), the value of 8.5 will be used as a reference point when computing the effect of photosynthesis/respiration on pH in the next section.

§ § §

Mass Balance Model for pH

Whereas equilibrium solutions such as in Example 14.8 are extremely useful, our goal in the present section is to compute nonequilibrium solu-

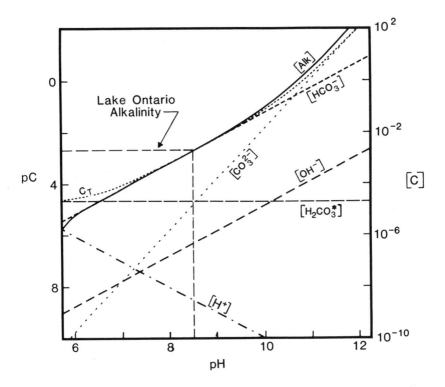

Figure 14.19 Plot of the concentration (expressed as $pC = -\log_{10}C$) of components of the inorganic carbon system vs pH for a water body at equilibrium with atmospheric carbon dioxide ($p_{CO_2} = 10^{-3.5}$ atm) at a temperature of 4°C.

tions by coupling the inorganic carbon system with dynamic nutrient/food chain computations. The key to this coupling is that the homogeneous reactions governing the interrelationships between the inorganic carbon species and water are typically much faster than the rates of reaeration and photosynthesis/respiration. Therefore, the computational strategy (as originally devised by Di Toro 1976) is to use a dynamic, differential equation to compute the effect of the heterogeneous reactions on the total inorganic carbon level of the system with a time step on the order of days. Because they are much more rapid, the homogeneous reactions always can be assumed to be at equilibrium on this time scale. Thus, algebraic solution techniques of the sort used in Example 14.8 can be employed to solve for pH and the individual inorganic carbon species at each time step.

Using the principles of mass conservation and the law of mass action presented in Chapter 10, mass balances can be developed for all the species involved in the inorganic carbon system. For example, Equations

14.75, 14.77, 14.78 and 14.82 can be used to develop the following balance for carbon dioxide:

$$V \frac{d[H_2CO_3^*]}{dt} = W_{atm} - W_{phot} + W_{resp} - k_3 V[H_2CO_3^*]$$
$$+ k_4 V[H^+][HCO_3^-] \qquad (14.97)$$

In a similar fashion, equations for the other species can be developed, such as the bicarbonate ion:

$$V \frac{d[HCO_3^-]}{dt} = k_3 V[H_2CO_3^*] - k_4 V[H^+][HCO_3^-] - k_5 V[HCO_3^-]$$
$$+ k_6 V[H^+][CO_3^{2-}] \qquad (14.98)$$

and the carbonate ion:

$$V \frac{d[CO_3^{2-}]}{dt} = k_5 V[HCO_3^-] - k_6 V[H^+][CO_3^{2-}] \qquad (14.99)$$

Since the reactions between the inorganic carbon species are much faster than the gains and losses due to atmospheric and biotic exchange, a local equilibrium assumption can be made (Di Toro 1976; Section 11.2.3) and Equations 14.97 through 14.99 can be combined to yield

$$V \frac{dC_T}{dt} = W_{atm} - W_{phot} + W_{resp} \qquad (14.100)$$

where C_T is the concentration of total inorganic carbon as defined by Equation 14.88. Equation 14.100 allows computation of the dynamics of total inorganic carbon as a function of biotic and atmospheric interactions. As such, it effectively connects the inorganic carbon system with the food chain.

§ § §

Example 14.9. Compute the seasonal changes of pH in Lake Ontario using the nutrient/food chain model developed in Section 14.2. Assume that the lake chemistry is dominated by the inorganic carbon system. Also assume that aside from atmospheric exchange, the lake is a closed system; that is, no precipitation/dissolution reactions occur. The alkalinity remains constant at approximately 1.95 meq l^{-1}.

As stated above, the computational strategy is to use Equation 14.100

(in conjunction with the nutrient/food chain model described in Section 14.2) to compute total inorganic carbon, C_T, dynamically. Then, at each time step, the equilibrium relationships (Equations 14.73, 14.83, 14.85, 14.87 and 14.88) can be solved simultaneously for the five unknowns— $[H^+]$, $[OH^-]$, $[H_2CO_3^*]$, $[HCO_3^-]$ and $[CO_3^{2-}]$. This can be accomplished with numerical methods designed to solve sets of nonlinear simultaneous equations. A simpler and less costly alternative is to solve the equations directly. Park (1969) has done this by assuming that hydrogen and hydroxyl ions have a negligible affect on alkalinity. This is a very good assumption for the alkalinity and pH levels encountered in Lake Ontario. The alkalinity of 1.95×10^{-3} eq l^{-1} dwarfs $[H^+]$ and $[OH^-]$ levels, which are on the order of $10^{-8.5}$ and $10^{-5.5}$, respectively. For such cases, the electroneutrality equation can be replaced by

$$[A_c] = [HCO_3^-] + 2[CO_3^{2-}]$$

where $[A_c]$ is carbonate alkalinity [eq l^{-1}], which is assumed to be $\cong [Alk]$. The equilibrium equations can then be solved algebraically for

$$[H_2CO_3^*] = \frac{[A_c]k - [C_T]k - 4[A_c] + \sqrt{(4[A_c] + [C_T]k - [A_c]k)^2 + 4(k-4)[A_c]^2}}{2(k-4)}$$
$$+ [C_T] - [A_c]$$
(14.101)

$$[HCO_3^-] = \frac{[C_T]k - \sqrt{(4[A_c] + [C_T]k - [A_c]k)^2 + 4(k-4)[A_c]^2}}{(k-4)}$$
(14.102)

$$[CO_3^{2-}] = \frac{[A_c]k - [C_T]k - 4[A_c] + \sqrt{(4[A_c] + [C_T]k - [A_c]k)^2 + 4(k-4)[A_c]^2}}{2(k-4)}$$
(14.103)

where $k = K_1/K_2$ (Park 1969).

Since $[A_c]$ is constant for this example and Equation 14.100 can be solved along with the nutrient/food chain model to obtain values of $[C_T]$ over the seasonal cycle, we can calculate carbonate speciation via Equations 14.101–14.103 and thus pH via Equation 14.83 or 14.85 at each time step. The results are displayed in Figure 14.20. Note how the summer, epilimnetic pH rises as temperature increases and primary production removes carbon dioxide from the surface waters.

§ § §

For additional details regarding aquatic chemistry, the reader can consult Stumm and Morgan (1981). In addition, Snoeyink and Jenkins (1980) and Butler (1982) provide informative descriptions of carbonate chemistry.

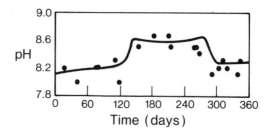

Figure 14.20   Seasonal pH computations for Lake Ontario. Data are for the epilimnion. Note that at the average annual temperature of $4°C$, a pH of 8.5 would be computed for the lake at equilibrium with atmospheric CO_2 in the absence of photosynthesis/respiration and precipitation/dissolution reactions.

14.4.2 The Effect of Allochthonous Solids on the Phosphorus Dynamics of a River-Run Lake

One objection to the use of total phosphorus loading as a determinant of lake eutrophication is that a portion of such input is associated with particulate matter that settles rapidly upon entering a lake and thus never influences mid-lake productivity. In addition, allochthonous matter (matter originating outside the lake) can influence productivity by shading the phytoplankton. To analyze these phenomena, models are needed which (1) differentiate between the various forms of phosphorus, (2) incorporate light limitation effects and (3) compute gradients that occur between the loading point and mid-lake. In the present section, we develop such a model for a river-run system.

The kinetic characterization for phosphorus involves two particulate and two dissolved fractions (Figure 14.21). Inorganic particulate phosphorus (i.e., associated with inorganic particles such as fine-grained suspended sediments) adsorbs and desorbs dissolved inorganic phosphorus via equilibrium relationships. Phytoplankton phosphorus, on the other hand, is modeled kinetically and takes up dissolved available phosphorus according to Michaelis-Menten kinetics and releases phosphorus to the dissolved unavailable pool via a first-order reaction. Dissolved unavailable phosphorus, in turn, is recycled to the dissolved available pool by a first-order reaction. In addition, the particulate fractions are lost by sedimentation, with the inorganic matter settling at a somewhat higher rate.

In essence, the framework is a synthesis of the river-run model (Section 12.2.2), the allochthonous sorption model (Section 13.3.2), and the nutrient/food chain model (Section 14.2), using the control volume approach (Section 12.3.2) and the numerical integration techniques (Section 11.3.1) to obtain solutions.

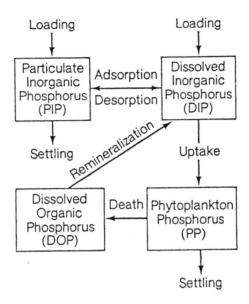

Figure 14.21   Schematic of a multispecies phosphorus model. One-way arrows designate mass transfer mechanisms that are modeled kinetically. The two-way arrow specifies that sorption is treated as an equilibrium reaction (i.e., it is modeled using a partition coefficient).

The results of the simulation are shown in Figure 14.22. Note that the inorganic particles are at a high level at the beginning of the lake, but eventually are removed from the water column (along with considerable quantities of adsorbed phosphorus) via sedimentation. In addition, the solids affect productivity by light attenuation, with the result that phytoplankton growth is suppressed for most of the lake. Thus, while inorganic particles carry phosphorus into the system, their tendency to diminish water clarity and to remove phosphorus from the water by sedimentation tends to inhibit productivity.

The importance of these factors to remedial control measures is demonstrated in Figure 14.23 where the effect of two alternative phosphorus abatement strategies is simulated. In the first, phosphorus loading is controlled by lowering the dissolved available fraction with no effect on the incoming solids, as might be the case for point source treatment. The result (Figure 14.23a) is that phytoplankton levels are decreased in proportion to the load reduction. Figure 14.23b, on the other hand, shows the results if the solids loading is removed along with the phosphorus, as might be the case if land runoff control were being implemented. In this simulation, the peak phytoplankton level is higher

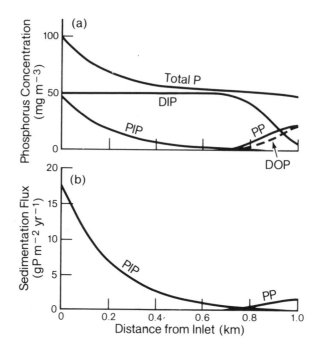

Figure 14.22 Plots of (a) simulated phosphorus concentration (mg m^{-3}) and (b) simulated phosphorus sedimentation flux (g P m^{-2} yr^{-1}) vs distance downstream from the inlet of a river-run lake.

than in Figure 14.23a because less phosphorus is removed from the water by sedimentation of inorganic particles. Additionally, the extent of phytoplankton growth increases to encompass most of the lake because of the absence of light attenuation by the inorganic solids. Thus, from the standpoint of productivity, the latter control measure results in a more highly degraded lake than before treatment.

It must be stressed that these computations are hypothetical simulations. They are merely intended to demonstrate how a mathematical model can be used to synthesize and analyze complex physical, biological and chemical interactions. For an actual lake, the approach would have to be verified and/or modified on the basis of measurements and experiments.

14.5 CALIBRATION AND VERIFICATION

14.5.1 Calibration

By far the most common method of calibration (parameter estimation) for aquatic ecosystem models is subjective variation of parameter values

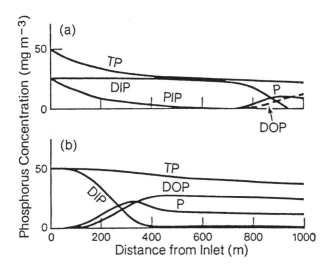

Figure 14.23   Plots of simulated phosphorus concentration vs distance downstream from the inlet of a river-run lake where (a) the phosphorus loading is reduced by 50% with no solids control and (b) the phosphorus loading is reduced by 50% with all particulate inorganic solids removed.

and qualitative comparison between resulting model solutions and observations. This technique has definite heuristic advantages and provides a medium for human intervention during model development and testing— an intervention that is most essential in other than strictly empirical models. However, it does not provide error bounds or guarantee global optimality in the selected parameter values.

One method of obtaining optimal parameter values is to minimize a chosen error criterion with respect to those values. The most common criterion is the sum of squares of differences between model predictions and observations (see Chapter 6). For linear models, the optimal set of parameter values is the uniquely defined solution of the normal equations (Draper and Smith 1966). However, in the case of nonlinear systems, the problem becomes more one of optimization, response surface searching, and iteration, because the normal equations have many solutions. In both linear and nonlinear cases, generally all available data are processed simultaneously (batch processing) and, in practice, the observations usually are assumed to be error-free, or at least to be of uniform variance, and uncorrelated.

Various methods of parameter optimization for nonlinear models have been developed (Fletcher and Powell 1963, Draper and Smith 1966, Himmelblau 1970, Benson 1979). Yih and Davidson (1975) presented a good accounting of the algorithms often used in water resource problems and compared those methods by estimating the longitudinal dispersion coefficient in an estuarine water quality model. Powers and Canale (1975) demonstrated the use of some other parameter optimization techniques for typical water quality problems. Rinaldi et al. (1979) used a least-squares approach to optimize deoxygenation and reoxygenation rate constants of a Streeter-Phelps stream model. Chapra and Reckhow (1979) used a nonlinear, least-squares approach to estimate two parameters in one of the empirical phosphorus models presented in Chapter 8. Chapra (1975) and Dillon and Kirchner (1975) also used least-squares techniques for evaluating the apparent settling velocity of phosphorus for these loading models. In fact, the least-squares approach also is imbedded in many other systems approaches to model identification and parameter estimation (e.g., Bargmann and Halfon 1977, Halfon 1979). In Chapter 6, we discuss least-squares and other parameter estimation techniques for linear models.

Another method of parameter estimation falls under the broad category of nonlinear optimal estimation. In general, "An optimal estimator is a computational algorithm that processes measurements to deduce a minimum error estimate of the state of a system by utilizing: knowledge of system and measurement dynamics, assumed statistics of system noises and measurement errors, and initial condition information" (Gelb 1974). These estimators are different from those employed in nonlinear regression in that they usually process data (measured state variables) iteratively rather than simultaneously (as in regression analysis). Under the iterative procedure, individual data points are incorporated sequentially into the analysis, and after each data addition, new parameter estimates are calculated. Resulting parameter estimates thus are allowed to take on different values at each measurement time. In this way, we not only obtain optimal estimates (in the sense of a specified error criterion, as discussed in Chapter 1), but also test the validity of assumed constant coefficients.

Probably the most common nonlinear, time-dependent, optimal estimator used on water resources problems is the Kalman Filter. Description of this algorithm is beyond the scope of this text; its derivation and applications can be found in Gelb (1974), Jazwinski (1970), and Chiu (1978). Calibration, or parameter estimation, is accomplished through augmentation of the state-variable system with differential equations describing the dynamics of the parameters. The most common and simplest approach has been to assume constant parameter dynamics (that is, $dA/dt = 0$, where A is a model parameter) with an uncertain initial value (mean and variance). When observations are processed and state-variable values are estimated, the algorithm treats the augmented parameters as state variables and estimates their values as well. The estimates are based on the differences between modeled and observed state variables and on relationships between state variables and parameters. The estimating procedure is analogous to weighted least-squares estimation including measurement errors; the selection of the optimal Kalman gain matrix (the weights assigned to observations) is based on minimizing the sum of the diagonal elements of the covariance matrix.

The most common water resource application of the Kalman Filter in this context has been in estimating parameters of the DO-BOD stream models (Beck 1976, Beck and Young 1976, Koivo and Phillips 1976); however, more recently, Bowles and Grenney (1978a,b) applied the technique to a more complicated river model including algae and a detailed nitrogen cycle. In all of these applications, the filter was reasonably successful in estimating stable parameter values, resulting in good fits to observations. The reader should consult Moore (1973) regarding important requirements and limitations of the algorithm.

14.5.2 Verification or Confirmation

The mechanistic models presented in this chapter should be developed according to standard procedures of model specification, calibration and confirmation as discussed in Chapter 1. Confirmation of water quality simulation models in principle should involve several candidate models as hypotheses and should be based on objective statistical tests with an independent data set. Few, if any, models have undergone this type of analysis, but the modeler must realize that, in the absence of confirmation of this nature, there is incomplete assurance that the model will perform as desired. This problem is discussed in detail in Chapter 16.

Often, complete confirmation of a mechanistic model is not possible by objective statistical techniques because we do not have a complete and independent data set. This is because sampling of many of the properties simulated in more mechanistic models is difficult and expensive—for example, zooplankton biomass.

Even when a data set is available for confirmation of a mechanistic model, we often are left with serious questions concerning reliability because there are increased degrees of freedom in these generally non-linear models. Increased degrees of freedom, in this context, means that more than one set of coefficient values may satisfy tests for calibration and confirmation. The basis for increased degrees of freedom is the cyclic nature of mechanistic models. Since these models generally simulate ecosystem cycles, we would not expect material to accumulate excessively in one particular component, but rather to flow among all of the components. Then, because of the principles of mass conservation, we could expect that, if the rate of flow were increased or decreased proportionately, the state-variable concentrations would not be affected significantly, or at least not within the variability usually inherent in the field data.

Several of the statistical methods presented in Volume 1 and in Chapter 16 of this volume may be used to compare two sets of "data" (predictions and observations) for calibration or confirmation. As an example, Scavia and Chapra (1977) demonstrated a way to test a mechanistic model in terms of gross properties. In this test, the model output was treated like lake data to see if it conformed to an empirical correlation known to be applicable for a wide variety of lakes. In other words, the model was subjected to the same statistical analysis that has been used on actual observations, and the results were compared. The correlation (Dillon and Rigler 1974) relates ($r = 0.95$) summer average chlorophyll a (chl a) to spring total phosphorus (p_v) for a data set of 46 lakes, each with a nitrogen-to-phosphorus ratio greater than 12:

$$\log_{10}[\text{chl a}] = 1.449 \log_{10} p_v - 1.136 \qquad (14.104)$$

It is reasonable to assume that Equation 14.104 well represents a large cross section of lakes. For model comparison, the mechanistic model was run under a number of conditions, and for each year that N:P > 12, spring total phosphorus concentrations and summer average chlorophyll a concentrations were calculated. These results then were plotted (Figure 14.24) along with Equation 14.104. The agreement between model output and the empirical curve was good up to a point. Beyond about 75 mgP m^{-3}, the model output diverged consistently from the line. Thus, in this case, confidence in the model could be assessed objectively with a statistical test comparing observations and predictions. The model failed to function consistently under extremely eutrophic conditions. Scavia and Chapra (1977) suggest causes for the failure, but the important point here is that this evaluation procedure provided a test of confidence and also set a possible limit on the model's applicability.

Internal Dynamics. Evaluation of mathematical models also may yield insight regarding the internal dynamics of the mechanistic model.

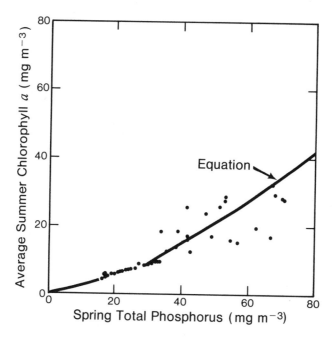

Figure 14.24   Comparison of nutrient/food chain model results (points) with Dillon and Rigler's (1974) correlation (line) between average summer chlorophyll a and spring total phosphorus. [Reprinted from Scavia and Chapra (1977)]

One of the most important reasons for using mechanistic models is to examine the controls of the system. For example, a mechanistic model can be used to examine the controls of phytoplankton production (Figure 14.25a) and phosphorus cycling (Figure 14.25b). In this context, model output is used to estimate the timing and relative magnitude of the influence of specific processes on state-variable dynamics. One important question concerning this use of the model is whether the simulated process rates are accurate representations of real processes. As mentioned above, compensating errors at the process level might lead to a successful calibration at the state-variable level. Thus, if models are to be used at the process level and we are to have faith in the dynamics that produce the state variables, we must look closely at the modeled processes (Scavia 1980b). The following example demonstrates one method of evaluating process models and the way in which compensating errors at the process level can lead to erroneous conclusions regarding system controls.

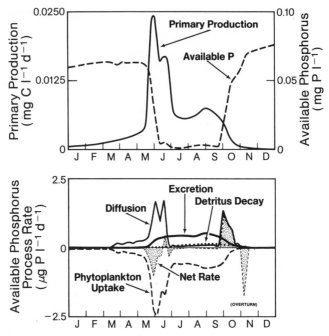

Figure 14.25   (Top) Simulated concentration of available phosphorus and rates of gross primary production in the epilimnion of Lake Ontario. (Bottom) Rate plots indicating control of available phosphorus dynamics. Stippled area represents the net rate of change. [Reprinted from Scavia (1979b)]

§ § §

Example 14.10. After initial calibration of the state variables in a mechanistic model of Lake Ontario, simulated process rates were compared to actual measurements. For this comparison, an averaged phosphorus flow diagram for summer (July–Sept.) was constructed (Figure 14.26a) from aggregated model output. The flow (or transfer) rates then were compared to measurements and calculations from Lake Ontario and to other, more theoretical estimates. Many of the simulated process rates were very low (as much as three to seven times lower) compared to actual rates, with the most serious discrepancies in transfers among available phosphorus, phytoplankton and zooplankton, yet the state variables compared successfully with field observations! The model was calibrated again, keeping the process rates in mind and most coefficient values still within acceptable ranges (Zison et al. 1978, Jorgensen 1979). The new calibration is shown in Figure 14.26b. The interesting point here is that the state variables are close to the values originally calibrated and still

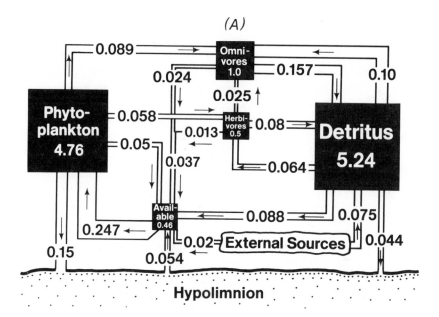

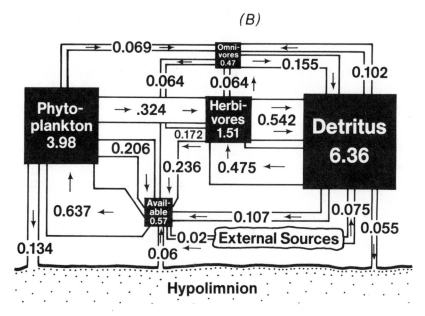

Figure 14.26   Phosphorus flow diagrams for epilimnion of Lake Ontario. Concentrations in boxes are in $\mu g\ l^{-1}$ and in pipes are in $\mu g\ l^{-1}\ d^{-1}$. These values are averaged over the period from July–September. (A) for state-variable calibration only and (B) for state-variable and process calibration. [Reprinted from Scavia (1979b)]

can be considered to be calibrated; however, the process rates are much higher and, in fact, much closer to observed values (Scavia, 1979b). This example demonstrates that if the model were calibrated only in terms of state variables and then used to examine control of the phosphorus cycle, then the relative importance of certain processes would be incorrectly estimated. For example, bacterial regeneration of available phosphorus (detritus to available P) is relatively more important in Figure 14.26b than in Figure 14.26a, and the relative importance of external loads and of transport into and out of the epilimnion is exaggerated in Figure 14.26a.

§ § §

14.6 UNCERTAINTY ANALYSIS

Mathematical models of the type described in this chapter have become relatively common tools in management contexts. In many cases, they also have become useful for suggesting research needs, synthesizing extant information, and analyzing ecosystems in ways that are not tractable through field and laboratory studies alone (see Section 14.8). The mechanistic models used most often in these contexts have similar attributes; they are generally time-dependent, often nonlinear, ordinary differential equation models based on parameterized physiological processes and mass conservation.

These models, whether from the management or the research milieu, have another common thread: they generally are deterministic. That is, although it is often recognized that initial conditions, parameters, and forcing functions of the model have stochastic properties, they are seldom accounted for. Moving beyond acknowledgment of variances of these elements to assessment of their effects is important because these stochastic properties affect the confidence that can be placed in the model output; that is, confidence generally is inversely related to variance.

Analysis of this variability is important in a management context to establish error bounds on predictions. As we note in Chapter 2, the prediction errors indicate the value of the information provided by the model. Eutrophication models have been developed to generate deterministic predictions of water quality based on present and expected scenarios of system inputs (Di Toro et al. 1971; Chen and Orlob 1975; Thomann et al. 1975, 1976, 1979; Canale et al. 1976; Bierman 1976). Output from these deterministic models can influence decisions that affect many thousands of people socially and economically (e.g., Vallentyne and Thomas 1978); yet quantitative limits of confidence are lacking for these models, unlike many of their simpler counterparts (Chapra and Reckhow 1979, Reckhow 1979, Lettenmaier and Richey 1979, Reckhow and Simpson 1980). In particular, only qualitative evaluations of calibration and confirmation results have been carried out to date, and experience with even these tests is limited. Because eutrophication models are crude representations of highly variable, stochastic systems, to ignore such important attributes often results in naive confidence or unwarranted disbelief in the models' solutions. For these models to become more generally accepted and effectively used, they must be placed in the proper perspective. Evaluating the effects of input (forcing function and parameter) variability on model output provides some of the needed perspective.

Two important methods have been used for estimating errors (or variances) in water quality models (see Chapter 2): first-order error analysis and Monte Carlo analysis. For example, Reckhow (1979) and Lettenmaier and Richey (1979) used first-order error analyses for total phosphorus, mass balance lake models, whereas Tiwari and Hobbie (1976), O'Neill and Gardner (1979), O'Neill et al. (1980), and Gardner et al. (1980) used Monte Carlo analyses for estimating errors in more complicated food web models. Occasionally, both methods have been used in the same study (Burges and Lettenmaier 1975, Montgomery et al. 1980). Assumed implicitly in these latter studies and suggested explicitly elsewhere (Gelb 1974) is the notion that Monte Carlo represents "truth" and that it can be used to check the accuracy of approximations in the first-order variance propagation analysis. The work presented in Scavia et al. (1981a) suggests that Monte Carlo and first-order variance propagation do not necessarily quantify the same type of variability. Suggestions based on these results indicate the conditions for which each method should be used and when they should be expected to agree.

14.6.1 Monte Carlo Simulation

Two types of Monte Carlo analysis generally are used. In the first type, a single simulation is performed, and at regular (or variable) intervals during the simulation, parameter values and/or forcing functions are varied randomly about their deterministic value. In the second type of analysis, the model equations are solved repeatedly. Each solution is performed with new values for initial conditions, parameters, and/or forcing functions that are selected randomly from some distribution but held constant through each simulation. From these repeated model executions, state-variable means, variances, and other statistics are calculated at given intervals throughout the period of simulation. The analysis is terminated after many (often as many as 1000) simulations when state-variable means and variances are converging on constant values. Further details on Monte Carlo simulations in general can be found in McGrath and Irving (1973). That publication also provides useful information for generating distributions of input variables.

The first type of analysis results in a single trajectory for each state variable that often displays a vacillation due to alterations in parameter and forcing values. The second type of analysis results in a family of trajectories and summary statistics (i.e., mean, model variance, quartiles) for each state variable. This latter technique is most applicable to the examination of model output uncertainty based on inputs with error. The former technique addresses directly the influence of a varying environment on model output.

We must be cautious when calculating summary statistics from Monte Carlo analysis of these typically nonlinear eutrophication models. For example, Scavia et al. (1981a) demonstrated that for a model similar to the one described in Section 14.2, distributions of state-variable values changed dramatically from symmetric to asymmetric during the course of the simulation period (Figure 14.27). Use of "standard" statistics that usually assume normal, or at least symmetric, distributions could be misleading and ambiguous.

14.6.2 Variance Propagation

The familiar first-order variance propagation formula for a scalar, time-invariant model is (Cornell 1972)

$$\sigma_y^2 = \left[\frac{\partial g(z)}{\partial z} \right]^2 \sigma_z^2 \qquad (14.105)$$

where σ_y^2 and σ_z^2 are the variances of y, the dependent variable, and z, the independent variable of the nonlinear algebraic model, $y = g(z)$. The partial derivative usually is evaluated at the mean value of z. Chapter 2 contains a derivation and graphical description of Equation 14.105 and a simple, single-equation example.

The more general case includes correlated independent variables (z_i) and a system of nonlinear equations

$$y_1 = g_1(z_1, \ldots, z_j, \ldots z_m)$$

$$y_i = g_i(z_1, \ldots, z_j, \ldots z_m) \qquad (14.106)$$

$$y_n = g_n(z_1, \ldots, z_j, \ldots z_m)$$

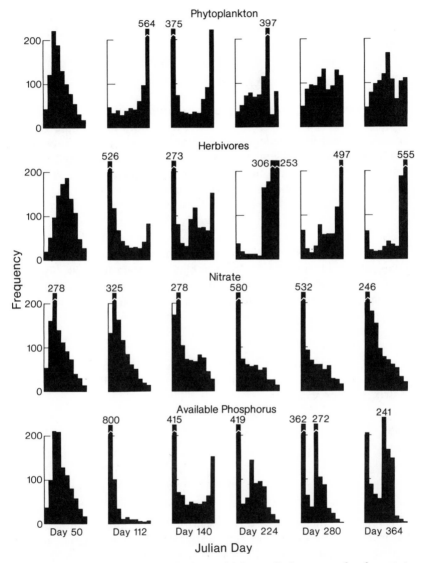

Figure 14.27   Frequency distributions of Monte Carlo output for four state variables at selected time slices during annual simulation. Day 50 distributions are initial distributions. 1000 cases are used. [Reprinted from Scavia et al. (1981a)]

represented by the first-order Taylor series approximation (in matrix notation):

$$y = A Z \qquad (14.107)$$

where $A_{ij} \equiv [\partial g_i / \partial z_j]$ is evaluated at the mean values of Z.

The covariance matrix of the dependent variables (P_y) can be estimated as a function of the independent variable covariance matrix (P_z) from a generalization of Equation 14.105

$$P_y = A P_z A^T \qquad (14.108)$$

where superscript T represents matrix transpose.

The time propagation of covariance, from both initial state variable covariance and independent variable (or parameter) covariance, for a nonlinear time-dependent model $[Y_{k+1} = g(Y_k)]$ can be accomplished in a similar fashion. Given a linearized system of equations describing the transition of the dependent variables from time k to k + 1

$$Y_{k+1} = \Theta_k Y_k \qquad (14.109)$$

where Θ_k represents a first-order approximation of the dependent variables' time-transition matrix for a nonlinear system $[\Theta_{ij} \equiv \partial g_i / \partial y_j]$. We may augment those equations with a set of equations describing the deterministic portion of the uncertain parameters, β,

$$\beta_{k+1} = \Delta_k \beta_k \qquad (14.110)$$

where Δ_k in this case for constant parameters is equal to the identity matrix I. Combining Equations 14.109 and 14.110 and writing them in matrix notation yields

$$X_{k+1} = \phi_k X_k \qquad (14.111)$$

where

$$X \equiv \begin{bmatrix} Y \\ \cdots \\ \beta \end{bmatrix} \quad \phi \equiv \begin{bmatrix} \partial g/\partial y & \vdots & \partial g/\partial \beta \\ \cdots & \vdots & \cdots \\ 0 & \vdots & I \end{bmatrix} \qquad (14.112)$$

The upper left quadrant of ϕ represents a linear approximation of nonlinearities among dependent state variables; the upper right quadrant represents a linear approximation of nonlinearities between the state variables and parameters. By analogy to Equations 14.107 and 14.108, it can be seen that the covariance matrix of $X(P)$ will propagate discretely in time from k to k + 1 as

$$P_{k+1} = \phi_k P_k \phi_k^T \qquad (14.113)$$

where P_k includes variances and covariances of both dependent variables and uncertain parameters at time k.

Further, this discrete-time variance propagation equation can be rewritten in continuous matrix form as

$$P = AP + PA^T \qquad (14.114)$$

by employing the definition of the derivative and performing the proper limiting operations (Gelb 1974). The initial conditions for this matrix differential equation are the elements of P at time zero, which are the variances and covariances of the vector X (see Equation 14.109) at time zero. In this particular application, these represent the variances and covariances of both the model initial conditions (Y) and uncertain parameters (β). A more complete discussion of this approach can be found in Scavia (1980a), and formal derivations can be found in Gelb (1974) and Jazwinski (1970).

§ § §

Example 14.11. This technique has been applied to a model of Saginaw Bay, Lake Huron, similar to the one described in Section 14.2. In that application (Scavia et al. 1981b), dependent variables Y are those illustrated in Figure 14.28a, and the augmented uncertain parameters β are those listed in Table 14.6. The functions g_i ($z_1 \ldots z_j \ldots z_m$) are nonlinear, simultaneous, ordinary differential equations described in Thomann et al. (1975) and Scavia (1980a). Partial derivatives of those functions with respect to state variables and uncertain parameters (elements of A in Equation 14.111) were derived analytically.

In this particular application, the following were assumed as sources of variance: (1) seven of the 22 parameters, (2) all of the eight initial conditions, (3) all of the five nutrient loads, and (4) the mixing parameter at the boundary between inner and outer Saginaw Bay segments. It was assumed that the remaining 15 parameters and the model equations were perfect deterministic functions. These input variances are listed in Tables 14.6 through 14.8.

Treating input errors, as done herein, allows estimation of model variance that corresponds to the variance of the natural system. It does not strictly estimate the error associated with the ability of the model to predict. To do this, we certainly must examine errors introduced by the equations themselves and perform the analysis over the time frame of the prediction, as has been done for some empirical and simpler lake models (e.g., Reckhow 1979).

From the model input statistics and variance propagation technique described above, state-variable variance estimates were made for an annual simulation based on variances of the initial conditions and given

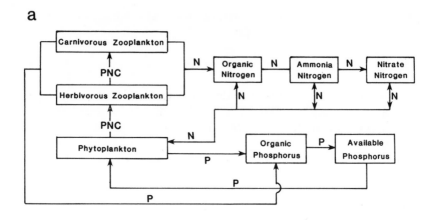

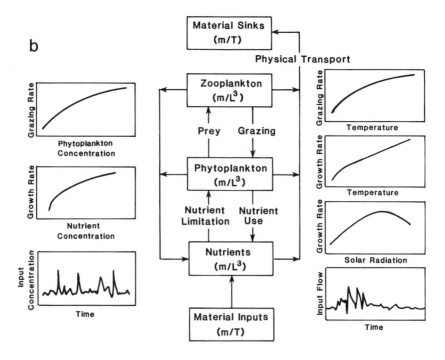

Figure 14.28   (a) Conceptual model of Saginaw Bay eutrophication dynamics. P, N and C show flux of phosphorus, nitrogen and carbon, respectively. [Redrawn from Richardson and Bierman 1976.] (b) Conceptual illustration of inputs and nonlinear relationships in Saginaw Bay model. [Redrawn from Richardson and Bierman 1976.]

Table 14.6   Variances and Values of Parameters Assumed
Uncertain in Saginaw Bay Model

Parameter	Mean	Variance	Coefficient of Variation	Unit	Definition
KIC	0.58	0.08	48	day^{-1}	maximum phytoplankton specific growth rate
KMP	0.005	6×10^{-6}	49	$mgP\ l^{-1}$	Michaelis constant for phosphorus
CGT	0.06	0.002	75	$1\ mg\ C^{-1}\ day^{-1}\ °C^{-1}$	herbivorous zooplankton filter rate
CCHL	30	1000	105	$mgC\ mgChl^{-1}$	carbon-to-chlorophyll ratio
KMPL	0.02	0.00027	82	$mg\ l^{-1}$	Michaelis constant for phytoplankton
K4T	0.006	2×10^{-5}	75	$(day\ °C)^{-1}$	herbivore respiration rate
PCHL	0.6	0.1	53	$mgP\ mgChl^{-1}$	phosphorus-to-chlorophyll ratio

Table 14.7   Statistics Used for State-Variable Initial Conditions

Variable	Mean	Variance	Coefficient of Variation (%)
Phytoplankton	$0.0092\ mg\ Chl\ l^{-1}$	2.98×10^{-5}	59
Herbivores	$0.0075\ mg\ C\ l^{-1}$	2.0×10^{-5}	60
Organic N	$0.14\ mg\ N\ l^{-1}$	3.8×10^{-3}	44
Ammonia	$0.031\ mg\ N\ l^{-1}$	2.6×10^{-3}	164
Nitrate-Nitrite	$0.75\ mg\ N\ l^{-1}$	1.0×10^{-1}	42
Organic P	$0.02\ mg\ P\ l^{-1}$	4.0×10^{-4}	100
PO_4	$0.0084\ mg\ P\ l^{-1}$	1.44×10^{-4}	143
Carnivores	$0.032\ mg\ C\ l^{-1}$	3.0×10^{-4}	54

parameters. Resulting variances are represented as model output plus or minus its standard deviation in Figure 14.29 and are normalized as coefficients of variation (CV; standard deviation/state-variable value) in Table 14.9.

Peaks in variance estimates occurred at times when the state variables were changing fastest. Gardner et al. (1980b) found this property to be

Table 14.8   Statistics for Volume-Specific
State-Variable Loads[a]

Variable	Mean	Variance	Coefficient of Variation (%)
Day 50–115			
Organic N	3.1×10^{-3}	2.3×10^{-5}	155
Ammonia	4.7×10^{-4}	2.6×10^{-7}	102
Nitrate-Nitrite	8.2×10^{-3}	5.8×10^{-5}	93
Organic P	8.2×10^{-5}	1.0×10^{-6}	122
PO_4	1.6×10^{-4}	1.9×10^{-8}	87
Day 165–365			
Organic N	4.6×10^{-4}	7.8×10^{-8}	60
Ammonia	2.1×10^{-4}	1.1×10^{-8}	51
Nitrate-Nitrite	2.7×10^{-4}	3.4×10^{-8}	68
Organic P	6.9×10^{-5}	1.2×10^{-8}	159
PO_4	9.4×10^{-5}	3.7×10^{-9}	65

[a]Units are mg l^{-1} day^{-1}.

common among several predator-prey models. Maximum CV (generally in late spring) ranged between 148 and 772%; however, the average CV during summer ranged between 33 and 40%. While these values are large, they are in many cases comparable to the variability within the bay itself (Table 14.9, Figure 14.29). Gardner et al. (1980b) also observed that summer is the most predictable period of simulation and, from that perspective, suggested that sampling during summer is not particularly useful for model confirmation. Moore (1973) and Moore et al. (1976) have presented excellent strategies for design of water quality sampling programs based on estimation and subsequent reduction of variances.

If it is of interest to determine the most significant sources of variability in this model, then the analysis can be repeated with initial condition, parameter, load and mixing parameter variances used singly or in simple combinations. This amounts to a sensitivity analysis for various model characteristics.

§ § §

The major assumption required for use of this analysis technique is that the effects on the model of variations in uncertain properties are linear within a region determined by the magnitude of variability in the uncertain property (Chapter 2). This assumption often is quite valid for small perturbations; however, when the variance of the uncertain inputs

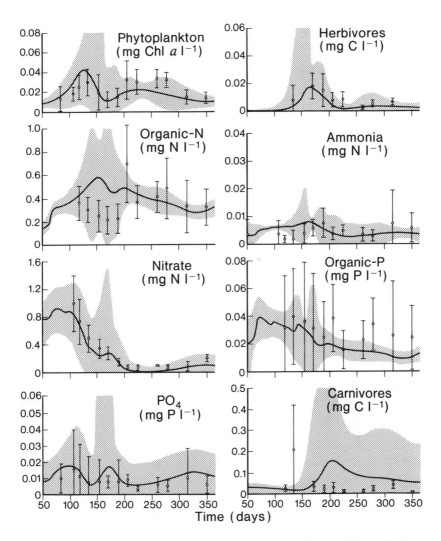

Figure 14.29   Plots of eight variable trajectories (smooth curve) from Saginaw Bay model. Model error estimates are represented as ±1 standard deviation bands (shaded) from first-order analysis. Data (circles with error bars) are represented by baywide mean plus or minus standard deviation of all samples. [Reprinted from Scavia et al. (1981b)]

becomes large, the assumption becomes invalid. Gardner et al. (1981) found the validity of the linear approximation deteriorated rapidly when the coefficient of variation for the parameter of a simple but highly non-linear function increased above 30%. They also demonstrated, for a non-

Table 14.9. Maximum and Mean of Summer Coefficients
of Variation (%) Calculated by the First-Order Analysis From
Uncertain Initial Conditions and Parameters Compared to
Coefficients of Variation From Measured Variables

Variable	Maximum	Summer Mean[a]	Observations[b]
Phytoplankton	593	78	52
Herbivores	772	206	65
Organic N	148	33	48
Ammonia	201	155	92
Nitrate-Nitrite	550	407	40
Organic P	163	48	96
PO$_4$	552	186	115
Carnivores	707	266	67

[a] Summer: July–September
[b] Calculated coefficient of variation of spatially averaged values from all sampling dates

linear stream ecosystem model with input errors typically near 50%
(range of coefficients of variation equals 1 to 3000%), that the linear
approximation for sensitivity analysis also is questionable. For these
cases, higher-order propagation techniques may help (see Athans et al.
1968); however, their implementation often is quite difficult.

14.7 RELATIONSHIP OF SIMPLE AND COMPLEX EUTROPHICATION MODELS

Lake eutrophication models generally can be divided into two categories: (1) budget, or input-output, models and (2) nutrient/food chain
approaches. The primary rationale underlying budget models is to predict a system's component concentrations by determining mass transfer
of the substance across its boundaries. Because of the emphasis on these
transfers, the models typically use simple mathematical idealizations
(e.g., first-order reactions, partition coefficients, complete mixing) to
represent the contaminant's kinetics and internal transport. The input-
output approach usually is designed for management predictions and is
suited for long-term or steady-state computations (see Chapters 8 and 11).

In contrast, the nutrient/food chain models discussed in this chapter
are attempts to express cause-and-effect relationships underlying substance dynamics in mathematical terms. They typically represent a synthesis of available information gleaned from laboratory and field studies
and can be developed for parts or for the whole ecosystem. While they
can be used in a management context, they have primary value as analy-

tical tools. Because of their process orientation, they usually are mathematically elaborate and best suited for short-term, or seasonal, computations.

Since these models address the same basic process, albeit from different scale perspectives, it is important that they yield consistent predictions regarding lake eutrophication. Thomann (1977) has performed an interesting derivation that provides insight into the theoretical basis for this consistency. In essence, he wrote nutrient/food chain equations similar to those in Table 14.1a. He then combined them to derive a differential equation for total phosphorus (Table 14.1b) in a fashion similar to that used by Di Toro to model fast and slow reactions simultaneously (Section 11.2.3). As with Di Toro's technique, Thomann's derivation depends on the kinetic interactions of the phosphorus components within the lake being substantially more rapid than the time scale on which the input-output calculation is performed. Since the processes that govern the partitioning of phosphorus in the water column, such as phytoplankton growth and sorption reactions, are rapid (hours to days) in comparison to the annual time frame of most budget models, this prerequisite holds. Aside from allowing the consolidation of the individual equations into a single total phosphorus model, the rapid internal kinetics imply that the internal reactions are at dynamic equilibria from the perspective of the longer time scale of the input-output fluxes. Thus, Thomann demonstrates that the equivalence of the simple and complex models hinges on the existence of a predictable, linear partitioning between the internal forms of phosphorus. In particular, he suggests that the phytoplankton-to-total-phosphorus ratio should be constant. Since evidence (Dillon and Rigler 1974, Schindler 1976) suggests that this is statistically valid for phosphorus-limited lakes, a theoretical basis for the equivalance of simple and complex models is implied.

14.8 USE OF NUTRIENT/FOOD CHAIN MODELS AS RESEARCH TOOLS

Models of the type described in this chapter, as well as more complicated descriptions of interactions among aquatic ecosystem components, have begun to be tested only recently in the management arena. Continued development and testing in that context eventually should lead to models with quantified and acceptable error bounds. However, as we have mentioned several times in this chapter, these models also have immediate utility in research studies. Coupling numerical modeling analyses with experimental and field investigations provides a framework for analysis of aquatic systems in ways intractable or impossible by either means alone. Such models have been useful tools for analysis of large-scale, physically driven systems (Example 14.7) as well as biologically dominant systems (see Example 14.12, Lehman et al. 1975, Lehman 1978 and Robertson and Scavia 1979). Since these models attempt to collect and to synthesize interdisciplinary information that bears on a given limnological setting, they also are useful for identifying particularly important ecosystem aspects requiring further experimental analysis (see Scavia 1979a). In that context, Steele (1974) addressed this point succinctly in describing his model:

> ... It does not in any sense produce new facts, but merely permits the evaluation of laboratory experiments carried out on different components in isolation. By forcing one to produce formulas to define each process and put numbers to the coefficients, it reveals the lacunae in one's knowledge. Although the output of the model can be tested against existing field observations and experimental results, the main aim is to determine where the model breaks down and use it to suggest further field or experimental work.

Riley (1946) introduced this concept of assuming mathematical formulations for individual biological processes and then synthesizing the formulations in a model. He suggested:

> ... developing the mathematical relationships on theoretical grounds and then testing them statistically by applying them to observed cases of growth in the natural environment. At present this can be done only tentatively, with over-simplification of theory and without the preciseness of mathematical treatment that might be desired. It is not expected that any marine biologist, including the writer, would fully believe all the arbitrary assumptions that will be introduced.

Mortimer (1975) also has recently reemphasized the "two-pronged approach" to systems studies, which involves an interaction between modeling efforts and experimental investigations.

The rationale behind this use of models is based on two assumptions: (1) that we actually can represent isolated biological and chemical processes or events with mathematical equations (process constructs) and (2) that combining these expressions results in a whole system model that represents the actual structure of the real world. The quantification of processes by Riley et al. (1949) and the formulation of more recent process constructs indicate the general acceptance of the first assumption—for example, for nutrient uptake and phytoplankton growth (Munk and Riley 1952, Droop 1968, Eppley and Thomas 1969, Fuhs 1969,

Dugdale 1975, 1977), for photosynthetic light limitation (Steele 1962, Vollenweider 1965, Jassby and Platt 1976a,b, Platt et al. 1977), and for zooplankton and fish processes (McAllister 1970, Mullin et al. 1975, Steele and Mullin 1977, Ivlev 1966, Ursin 1967). The validity of the second assumption has begun to be investigated only recently for ecological models. To prove that combinations of process equations indeed can simulate the dynamics of ecological systems, model output must be compared to nature. This has been done for a wide range of models differing in orientation, complexity and utility. One example, consisting of one phytoplankton group, one zooplankton group and total inorganic nitrogen, is the model of Di Toro et al. (1971), which was applied to an estuary system to assess nutrient loads for management purposes. Since that time, other models have been developed that simulate variations in several phytoplankton and zooplankton groups, as well as cycles of nitrogen, phosphorus, silicon, carbon and oxygen in lakes for research purposes. There also exists a spectrum of models, both engineering- and research-oriented, with varying degrees of complexity. A number of recent examples are identified in Table 14.10. Most of these models have been reasonably successful in describing the dynamics of the systems for which they were built and, therefore, lend credence to the second assumption; however, final acceptance of this assumption can be brought about only by continued success in modeling efforts. It is important to note here that validation of both assumptions is not a sufficient criterion for model application for predictive purposes. This validation only demonstrates the model's capability of describing (i.e., simulating) important biological and chemical processes simultaneously. The confirmation procedures necessary before proceeding with predictions are far more rigorous (Orlob 1975, O'Connor et al. 1975).

If one accepts the two assumptions, then the models can be considered to be mathematical representations of existing knowledge concerning the modeled processes and interactions. Therefore, systematic investigation of the model can be used to identify obstacles to developing better models and to obtain a clearer understanding of the system and thus to determine specific research areas needing further study. The following example demonstrates how such a model analysis can lead to information on the functioning of the system that may be very difficult and expensive to obtain experimentally.

§ § §

Example 14.12. Because of its size, Lake Ontario has been studied through discrete and often isolated research programs. Over the past decade, several excellent studies have been conducted illuminating the

Table 14.10   Examples of Varying Model Complexity

References	System	Primary Producers	Herbivores	Carnivores	Nutrient Cycles	Physical Segments	Compartments per Segment
Di Toro et al. 1971	San Joaquin River	1	1	0	1	1	3
Bloomfield et al. 1973	Lake Wingra, WI	2	2	2	0	1	8
Larsen et al. 1973	Shagawa Lake, MN	1	0	0	2	1	3
Thomann et al. 1974	Potomac Estuary	1	1	0	3	38	9
MacCormick et al. 1974	Lake Wingra, WI	1	1	2	0	1	8
Park et al. 1974	Lake George, NY	2	4	4	0	1	28
Scavia et al. 1974	Lake George, NY	2	2	3	1	1	11
Steele 1974	North Sea	1	1	0	1	1	4
Thomann et al. 1975	Lake Ontario	1	1	3	2	2	10
Chen and Orlob 1975	Lake Washington	2	1	0	3	33	17
Chen and Orlob 1975	San Francisco Bay	2	1	0	3	67	17
Di Toro et al. 1975	Lake Erie	1	1	0	2	7	7
Lehman et al. 1975	Linsley Pond, CT	4	0	0	2	1	6
Thomann et al. 1976	Lake Ontario	1	1	3	2	67	10
Bierman 1976	Saginaw Bay, Lake Huron	3	2	1	3	1	14
Canale et al. 1976	Lake Michigan	4	6	3	3	2	25
DePinto et al. 1976	Stone Lake, MI	3	2	1	2	1	11
Di Toro and Matystick 1980	Saginaw Bay, Lake Huron	1	1	2	2	5	9
Scavia et al. 1976a	Lake Ontario	4	5	1	3	3	17
McNaught and Scavia 1976	Lakes Ontario and Michigan	2	3	0	0	1	6
Steele and Mullin 1975	None	1	1	0	1	12	3
Walsh 1977	Several Marine Systems	1	2	0	3	?	9
Scavia 1980c	Lake Ontario	5	6	1	4	2	20

controls and mechanisms of several important ecological and physical processes. However, there have been few attempts to examine simultaneously several of these processes through field or laboratory experiments. Where combinations of processes have been examined, it has been done, by necessity, for only one or two stations. Information from these studies is important for understanding ecosystem controls. However, because Lake Ontario is neither homogeneous horizontally nor simple hydrodynamically, it is not possible to extrapolate information from one or two stations to estimate lakewide conditions. Thus, a comprehensive view of whole-lake processes for Lake Ontario has not been possible.

Because it is unlikely that a large field program designed to investigate important processes on a lakewide scale is tractable for Lake Ontario, some other method of synthesizing and analyzing the available information is needed to generate insight into whole-lake processes. One method of synthesis is to develop some mathematical representation of the ecosystem and the interactions among its components, and thereby to produce some quantitative, yet theoretical, information on the processes.

This example illustrates the use of a model of the Lake Ontario ecosystem, based on theoretical concepts of nutrient cycles and food web ecology as well as data collected on Lake Ontario to examine two aspects of the lake ecosystem: (1) the factors controlling the dynamics of phytoplankton biomass, and (2) the seasonal dynamics of available phosphorus, including the relationship of these dynamics to the control of phytoplankton production (Scavia 1979b).

The model (Figure 14.30) includes phytoplankton and zooplankton; cycles of phosphorus, nitrogen, silicon and carbon; an oxygen balance; and calculations of the carbonate equilibrium system. A sediment compartment includes benthic invertebrates as well as cycles of carbon, phosphorus, nitrogen and silicon.

Each model compartment is represented by a differential equation composed of important biological, chemical and physical processes. For example, the phytoplankton equation includes terms for gross primary production, respiration, excretion, grazing, sinking and vertical mixing, and the zooplankton equation includes terms for grazing, assimilation, respiration, excretion, defecation and production. Justification and rationale for the process equations used, as well as detailed documentation of the overall model, are presented in Scavia (1980c).

Phytoplankton Dynamics. The simulated processes controlling the seasonal dynamics of the "Large Others" phytoplankton group in the epilimnion are shown in Figure 14.31. The stippled area indicates the net

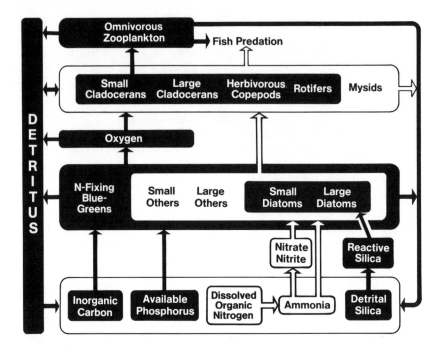

Figure 14.30   Conceptualization of Lake Ontario ecological model. [Reprinted from Scavia (1979b)]

rate of change of the population biomass. In winter and early spring, this algal group, as well as the others, is controlled primarily by the balance between gross primary production and two physical processes, sinking and vertical mixing. During this time, phytoplankton gross production is limited mainly by the availability of light, which is controlled both by the amount of incoming solar radiation and the depth of the entire water column. This loss to the dark, deeper layers prevents substantial increases in algal biomass. Significant increases in algal biomass occur only after mid-spring, when the surface waters in Lake Ontario begin to warm and the lake begins to stratify vertically. At this time (early June), phytoplankton populations increase rapidly, and the concentrations of the nutrients they assimilate begin to decrease. The concentrations of nutrients decrease because they also become relatively isolated from the nutrient-rich lower strata.

At this time, production becomes limited by the availability of phosphorus. During late summer, grazing stress exerted by zooplankton becomes most intense. This time-history of simulated grazing pressure reflects the general seasonal pattern of crustacean zooplankton biomass.

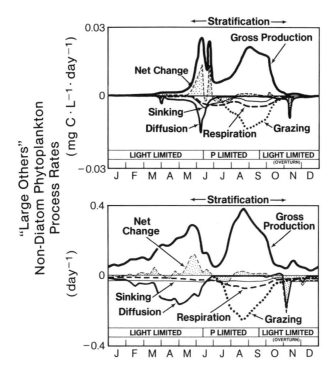

Figure 14.31 Rate plots indicating simulated controls of epilimnion phytoplankton dynamics in Lake Ontario during 1972. "Large Others" represent nondiatoms greater than 20 μ. Top: rates as mg $C^{-1} l^{-1} d^{-1}$, bottom: rates as d^{-1}. Stippled area represents net growth rate. [Reprinted from Scavia (1979b)]

In late September, the thermocline deepens, and nutrient-rich, hypolimnetic water is mixed with epilimnetic water. Because of this increase in nutrient concentrations and the simultaneous increase in mixing depth, the algae again become limited by light. In early November, the lake overturns and becomes vertically homogeneous and phytoplankton concentrations begin to approach winter values. This, of course, is a simplification of the three-dimensional effects discussed by Simons (1976); however, in a one-dimensional model, all advective and diffusive processes are parameterized as vertical mixing.

Phosphorus Cycling. Although it is clear from the above analysis that nutrient limitation does not solely control phytoplankton dynamics, the role of nutrients, especially phosphorus and silicon, certainly is critical during the period of stratification. The dominant phytoplankters during the summer months in Lake Ontario are limited primarily by phosphorus, as demonstrated in the simulations discussed above. Therefore, to understand better the control of phytoplankton dynamics in Lake Ontario, we must investigate the processes influencing the cycling of phosphorus.

Figure 14.25 illustrates the seasonal changes in the simulated concentration of available phosphorus and the rate of gross primary production in the epilimnion. As discussed above, after spring, the phytoplankton become limited by nutrients and thus the production rate decreases sharply. It is interesting to note that, although the production rate has decreased considerably, it does not approach low winter values and, in fact, after the initial drop, the rate increases gradually. This sustained production proceeds at the same time that available phosphorus concentrations, both actual and simulated, are extremely low. We might expect that, with phosphorus concentrations this low (<1 μgP l^{-1}) and sustained phytoplankton production, phosphorus assimilation by algae would rapidly drive the concentration of phosphorus to virtually zero and thus severely limit further phytoplankton productivity. However, this is not the case. It appears that the supplies of phosphorus during this time period are sufficient to balance phytoplankton assimilation. The sum of the rates of detritus remineralization, phytoplankton and zooplankton excretion, and the diffusion input from the hypolimnion, is approximately equal to the rate of assimilation by phytoplankton. This analysis suggests that decomposer input is about one-fourth of the excretion input from algae and zooplankton during the summer stratification and that phosphorus input from the lower strata is important only before and after stratification.

To examine more closely the relationship among the various processes in this conceptual phosphorus cycle, a phosphorus flow diagram was constructed (Figure 14.26b) from the model output averaged over the period of July to September and the results compared with available information. The sizes of the five phosphorus compartments, as well as the rates of flow of phosphorus among the compartments, are representative of Lake Ontario during this period of time (Scavia 1979b, 1980c).

Figure 14.26b shows that it would take less than one day in the summer epilimnion for the phytoplankton to deplete the available phosphorus pool if there were no recycling, and that external sources and hypolimnetic sources alone could not meet this algal phosphorus demand. In fact, this analysis indicates that 86% of the assimilated phosphorus is recycled within the epilimnion. These results suggest that, for this five-compartment conceptualization, zooplankton excretion and the direct release by photoplankton are approximately equal and are the most important processes supplying phosphorus to the available pool. The rate of remineralization of detrital phosphorus is somewhat slower. The role of zooplankton in the phosphorus cycle must be emphasized. While the zooplankton have an obvious role in applying pressure to reduce algal concentrations (Figure 14.31), they also appear to play a dual role in recycling phosphorus. Not only do the zooplankton input directly to the available nutrient pools through excretion, but they also serve as suppliers of detrital material (feces), which undergoes additional degradation by the decomposers and eventually adds to the available nutrient supply. Thus, it may well be that the zooplankton are principally responsible for the high recycling rates estimated by Stadelmann and Fraser (1974) in Lake Ontario.

§ § §

14.9 GENERAL COMMENTS

In conclusion, the foregoing material is a brief introduction to the basic mathematical techniques and pertinent issues concerning the modeling of physical, chemical and biological interactions within lake systems. Although we have focused on the seasonal cycling of matter between organic and inorganic forms in temperate lakes, the general methodology should be useful in other systems and problem contexts.

It must be stressed, however, that the reader should not come away from this chapter with the impression that he or she is expert at "ecosystem modeling." As stated in this volume's preface, the material herein hopefully will acquaint the reader with the vocabulary and some of the major organizing concepts connected with lake modeling. However, particularly with regard to this chapter, proficiency only can be gained by experience. For example, the arduous task of calibrating a nutrient/food chain model to a new data base (which was glossed over in Example 14.5) can be a sobering and highly instructive experience. The reader is urged to apply the techniques presented in this chapter to a number of lakes in order to truly appreciate the powers and limitations of the approach.

REFERENCES

Athans, M., R. P. Wishner and A. Bertolini. 1968. "Suboptimal State Estimation for Continuous-Time Nonlinear Systems for Discrete Noisy Measurements," *IEEE Transactions Automatic Control* Oct.:504–414.

Auer, M. T. 1979. "The Dynamics of Fixed Inorganic Nitrogen Nutrition in Two Species of Chlorophycean Algae." PhD Dissertation, University of Michigan.

Banse, K. 1976. "Rates of Growth, Respiration and Photosynthesis of Unicellular Algae as Related to Cell Size—A Review," *J. Phycol.* 12:135-140.

Bargmann, R. E., and E. Halfon. 1977. "Efficient Algorithms for Statistical Estimation in Compartmental Analysis: Modelling Kinetics in an Aquatic Microcosm," *Ecol. Modelling* 3:211-226.

Bates, S. S. 1976. "Effects of Light and Ammonium on Nitrate Uptake by Two Species of Estuarine Phytoplankton," *Limnol. Oceanog.* 21:212-218.

Beck, M. B. 1976. "Identification and Parameter Estimation of Biological Process Models," in *System Simulation in Water Resources,* C. C. Vansteenkiste, Ed. (Amsterdam: North-Holland Publishing Co.), pp. 19-43.

Beck, M. B., and P. C. Young. 1976. "Systematic Identification of DO-BOD Model Structure," *J. Environ. Eng. Div. (ASCE)* 102(EE5):909-927.

Bennett, J. R. 1971. "Thermally Driven Lake Currents during the Spring and Fall Transition Periods," in *Proc. 14th Conf. Great Lakes Res.,* Ann Arbor, MI, pp. 535-544.

Bennett, J. R. 1974. "On the Dynamics of Wind-Driven Lake Currents," *J. Phys. Oceanog.* 4:400-414.

Benson, M. 1979. "Parameter Fitting in Dynamic Models," *Ecol. Modeling* 6:97-116.

Bierman, V. J. 1976. "Mathematical Model of the Selective Enrichment of Blue-Green Algae by Nutrient Enrichment," in *Modeling of Biochemical Processes in Aquatic Ecosystems,* R. P. Canale, Ed. (Ann Arbor, MI: Ann Arbor Science Publishers, Inc.), p. 1.

Bierman, V. J., F. H. Verhoff, T. L. Paulson and M. W. Tenny. 1973. "Multi-Nutrient Dynamic Models of Algal Growth and Species Competition in Eutrophic Lakes," in *Modeling the Eutrophication Process,* E. J. Middlebrooks, D. H. Falkenborg and T. E. Maloney, Eds. (Ann Arbor, MI: Ann Arbor Science Publishers, Inc.), p. 89.

Bloomfield, J. A., R. A. Park, D. Scavia and C. S. Zahorcak. 1973. "Aquatic Modeling in the EDFB, US-IBP," in *Modeling the Eutrophication Process,* E. J. Middlebrooks, D. H. Falkenborg and T. E. Maloney, Eds. (Ann Arbor, MI: Ann Arbor Science Publishers, Inc.), p. 139.

Bowles, D. S., and W. J. Grenney. 1978a. "Estimation of Diffuse Loading of Water Quality Pollutants by Kalman Filtering," pp. 581-598, in *Application of Kalman Filter to Hydrology, Hydraulics, and Water Resources,* C. L. Chiu, Ed. (Pittsburgh, PA: University of Pittsburgh).

Bowles, D. S., and W. J. Grenney. 1978b. "Steady State River Quality Modeling by Sequential Extended Kalman Filters," *Water Resources Res.* 14:84-96.

Brezonik, P. L. 1972. "Nitrogen: Sources and Transformations in Natural Waters," in *Nutrients in Natural Waters,* H. E. Allen and J. R. Kramer, Eds. (Ann Arbor, MI: Ann Arbor Science Publishers, Inc.), pp. 1–50.

Burges, S. J., and D. P. Lettenmaier. 1975. "Probabilistic Methods in Stream Quality Management," *Water Resources Bull.* 11:115–130.

Butler, J. N. 1982. *Carbon Dioxide Equilibria and Their Applications* (Reading, MA: Addison-Wesley Publishing Co.).

Canale, R. P., D. F. Hinemann and S. Nachippan. 1974. "A Biological Production Model for Grand Traverse Bay," University of Michigan Sea Grant Program, Technical Report No. 37 (Ann Arbor, MI: University of Michigan Sea Grant Program).

Canale, R. P., and A. H. Vogel. 1974. "Effects of Temperature on Phytoplankton Growth," *J. Env. Eng. Div., ASCE* 100(EEI):231–241.

Canale, R. P., L. M. DePalma and A. H. Vogel. 1976. "A Plankton-Based Food Web Model for Lake Michigan," in *Modeling Biochemical Processes in Aquatic Ecosystems,* R. P. Canale, Ed. (Ann Arbor, MI: Ann Arbor Science Publishers, Inc.), p. 33.

Chapra, S. C. 1975. "Comment on an Empirical Method of Estimating the Retention of Phosphorus in Lakes by W. B. Kirchner and P. J. Dillon," *Water Resources Res.* 11:1033–1036.

Chapra, S. C., and K. H. Reckhow. 1979. "Expressing the Phosphorus Loading Concept in Probabilistic Terms," *J. Fish. Res. Bd. Can.* 36:225–229.

Chen, C. W. 1970. "Concepts and Utilities of Ecologic Models," *J. San. Eng. Div. ASCE* 96(SA5):1085–1086.

Chen, C. W., and G. T. Orlob. 1975. "Ecological Simulation for Aquatic Environments," in *Systems Analysis and Simulation in Ecology, Vol. III,* B. C. Patton, Ed. (New York: Academic Press, Inc.), p. 475.

Chiu, C. L. (Ed.). 1978. "Applications of Kalman Filter to Hydrology, Hydraulics, and Water Resources," Stochastic Hydraulics Program, Dept. of Civ. Eng. (Pittsburgh, PA: University of Pittsburgh),783 pp.

Cornell, C. A. 1972. "First-Order Analysis of Model and Parameter Uncertainty," paper presented at the International Symposium on Uncertainty in Hydrologic and Water Resource Systems, University of Arizona, Tucson.

Cowen, W. F., and G. F. Lee. 1976. "Algal Nutrient Availability and Limitation in Lake Ontario during IFYGL Part 1. Available Phosphorus in Urban Runoff and Lake Ontario Tributary Waters," U.S. Environmental Protection Agency, Corvallis, Oregon, EPA-600/3-76-094a.

DePinto, J. V., V. J. Bierman and F. H. Verhoff. 1976. "Seasonal Phytoplankton Succession as a Function of Species Competition for Phosphorus and Nitrogen," in *Modeling Biochemical Processes in Aquatic Ecosystems,* R. P. Canale, Ed. (Ann Arbor, MI: Ann Arbor Science Publishers, Inc.), p. 141.

Dillon, P. J., and W. B. Kirchner. 1975. "Reply to Chapra," *Water Resources Res.* 11:1035–1036.

Dillon, P. J., and F. H. Rigler. 1974. "The Phosphorus-Chlorophyll Relationship in Lakes," *Limnol. Oceanog.* 19:767–773.

Di Toro, D. M. 1976. "Combining Chemical Equilibrium and Phytoplankton Models-A General Methodology," in *Modeling Biochemical Processes in Aquatic Ecosystems,* R. P. Canale, Ed. (Ann Arbor, MI: Ann Arbor Science Publishers, Inc.), p. 233.

Di Toro, D. M. 1980. "Applicability of Cellular Equilibrium and Monod Theory to Phytoplankton Growth Kinetics," *Ecol. Modelling* 8:201–218.

Di Toro, D. M., and J. C. Connolly. 1980. "Mathematical Models of Water Quality in Large Lakes. 2. Lake Erie," U.S. EPA Report EPA-600/3-80-065, Duluth, MN, 180 pp.

Di Toro, D. M., and W. F. Matystik, Jr. 1980. "Mathematical Models of Water Quality in Large Lakes. 1. Lake Huron and Saginaw Bay" U.S. EPA Report EPA-600/3-80-056, Duluth, MN, 249 pp.

Di Toro, D. M., D. J. O'Connor, R. V. Thomann and J. L. Mancini. 1975. "Phytoplankton-Zooplankton Nutrient Interaction Model for Western Lake Erie," in *Systems Analysis and Simulation in Ecology, Vol. III,* B. C. Patton, Ed. (New York: Academic Press, Inc.), p. 423.

Di Toro, D. M., R. V. Thomann and D. J. O'Connor. 1971. "A Dynamic Model of Phytoplankton Population in the Sacramento-San Joaquin Delta," in *Advances in Chemistry Series 106: Nonequilibrium Systems in Natural Water Chemistry,* R. F. Gould, Ed. (Washington, DC: American Chemical Society), p. 131.

Dolan, D., V. J. Bierman, M. H. Dipert and R. D. Geist. 1978. "Statistical Analysis of the Spacial and Temporal Variability of the Ratio of Chlorophyll *a* to Phytoplankton Cell Volume in Saginaw Bay, Lake Huron," *J. Great Lakes Res.* 4:75–83.

Draper, N. R., and H. Smith. 1966. *Applied Regression Analysis* (New York: John Wiley and Sons, Inc.), 407 pp.

Droop, M. R. 1968. "Vitamin B_{12} and Marine Ecology, IV. The Kinetics of Uptake, Growth and Inhibition in *Monochrysis lutheri,*" *J. Mar. Biol. Assoc.* (U.K.) 48:689–733.

Droop, M. R. 1973. "Some Thoughts on Nutrient Limitation in Algae," *J. Phycol.* 9:264–272.

Droop, M. R. 1974. "The Nutrient Status of Algal Cells in Continuous Culture." *J. Mar. Biol. Assoc.* (U.K.) 54:825–855.

Dugdale, R. C. 1975. "Biological Modeling I," in *Modeling of Marine Systems, Oceanography Series, Vol. 10,* J. C. J. Nihoul, Ed. (New York: Elsevier), 187 pp.

Dugdale, R. C. 1977. "Nutrient Modeling" in *The Sea, Vol. 6: Marine Modeling,* E. D. Goldberg, I. N. McCave, J. J. O'Brien and J. H. Steele, Eds. (New York: Wiley-Interscience), 789 pp.

Edmond, J. M., and J. A. T. M. Gieskes. 1970. "On the Calculation of the Degree of Saturation of Sea Water with Respect to Calcium Carbonate Under *In Situ* Conditions," *Geochim. Cosmochim. Acta.* 34:1261–1291.

Eppley, R. W., J. N. Rogers and J. J. McCarthy. 1969. "Half-Saturation Constants for Uptake of Nitrate and Ammonia by Marine Phytoplankton," *Limnol. Oceanog.* 14:912–920.

Eppley, R. W., and W. H. Thomas. 1969. "Comparison of Half-Saturation Constants for Growth and Nitrate Uptake of Marine Phytoplankton," *J. Phycol.* 5:375–379.

Fletcher, R., and M. J. Powell. 1963. "A Rapidly Convergent Descent Method for Minimization," *Comput. J.* 6:163–168.

Fuhs, G. W. 1969. "Phosphorus Content and Rate of Growth in the Diatoms *Cyclotella nana* and *Thalassiosira fluviatilis,*" *J. Phycol.* 5:312–321.

Gardner, R. H., R. V. O'Neill, J. B. Mankin and J. Jones. 1980a. "Application of Error Analysis to a Marsh Hydrology Model," *Water Resources Res.* 16:659–664.

Gardner, R. H., R. V. O'Neill, J. B. Mankin and D. Kumar. 1980b. "Comparative Error Analysis of Six Predator-Prey Models," *Ecology* 61:323–332.

Gardner, R. H., R. V. O'Neill, J. B. Mankin and J. H. Carney. 1981. "A Comparison of Sensitivity Analysis and Error Analysis Based on a Stream Ecosystem Model," *Ecol. Modelling* 12:173–190.

Gelb, A. 1974. *Applied Optimal Estimation* (Cambridge, MA: MIT Press), 374 pp.

Goldman, J. C. 1977. "Steady State Growth of Phytoplankton in Continuous Culture: Comparison of Internal and External Nutrient Equations," *J. Phycol.* 13:251–258.

Goldman, J. C., W. J. Oswald and D. Jenkins. 1974. "The Kinetics of Inorganic Carbon Limited Algal Growth," *J. Water Poll. Control Fed.* 46:554–573.

Gotham, I. J., and G. Y. Rhee. 1981. "Comparative Kinetic Studies of Phosphate Limited Growth and Phosphate Uptake in Phytoplankton in Continuous Culture," *J. Phycol.* 17:257–265.

Grenney, W. J., D. A. Bella and H. C. Curl, Jr. 1973. "A Mathematical Model of the Nutrient Dynamics of Phytoplankton in a Nitrate-Limited Environment," *Biotech. Bioeng.* 15:331–358.

Halfon, E. 1979. "Mathematical Modeling of Phosphorus Dynamics Through Integration of Experimental Work and System Theory," in *Perspectives on Lake Ecosystem Modeling,* D. Scavia and A. Robertson, Eds. (Ann Arbor, MI: Ann Arbor Science Publishers, Inc.), pp. 75–83.

Harned, H. S., and R. Davis, Jr. 1943. "The Ionization Constant of Carbonic Acid in Water and the Solubility of Carbon Dioxide in Water and Aqueous Salt Solutions from 0 to 50°C," *J. Am. Chem. Soc.* 65:2030-2037.

Harned, H. S., and W. J. Hamer. 1933. "The Ionization Constant of Water," *J. Am. Chem. Soc.* 51:2194.

Harned, H. S., and S. R. Scholes. 1941. "The Ionization Constant of HCO_3^-," *J. Am. Chem. Soc.* 63:1706-1709.

Harris, G. P. 1980. "Temporal and Spatial Scales in Phytoplankton Ecology. Mechanisms, Methods, Models, and Management," *Can. J. Fish Aquat. Sci.* 37:877-900.

Harvey, H. S. 1955. *The Chemistry and Fertility of Seawater* (Cambridge, England: Cambridge University Press), 240 pp.

Herbes, S. E. 1974. "Biological Utilization of Dissolved Organic Phosphorus in Natural Waters," PhD Thesis, University of Michigan, Ann Arbor, MI.

Himmelblau, D. M. 1970. *Process Analysis by Statistical Methods* (New York: John Wiley and Sons, Inc.).

Huff, D. D., J. F. Koonce, W. R. Ivanrson, P. R. Weiler, E. H. Dettman and R. F. Harris. 1973. "Simulation of Urban Runoff, Nutrient Loading, and Biotic Response of a Shallow Eutrophic Lake," in *Modeling the Eutrophication Process,* E. J. Middlebrooks, D. H. Falkenborg and T. E. Maloney, Eds. (Ann Arbor, MI: Ann Arbor Science Publishers, Inc.), p. 33.

Hutchinson, G. E. 1957. *A Treatise on Limnology: Vol. 1. Geography, Physics and Chemistry* (New York: Wiley-Interscience), 1015 pp.

Hutchinson, G. E. 1967. *A Treatise on Limnology. Vol. 2. Introduction to Lake Biology and the Limnoplankton* (New York: Wiley-Interscience), 1115 pp.

Ivlev, V. S. 1966. "The Biological Productivity of Waters," *J. Fish Res. Bd. Can.* 23:1727-1759.

Jassby, A. D., and T. Platt. 1976a. "Mathematical Formulation of the Relationship between Photosynthesis and Light for Phytoplankton," *Limnol. Oceanog.* 21:540-547.

Jassby, A. D., and T. Platt. 1976b. "The Relationship between Photosynthesis and Light for Natural Assemblages of Coastal Marine Phytoplankton," *J. Phycol.* 12:421-430.

Jazwinski, A. H. 1970. *Stochastic Processes and Filtering Theory* (New York: Academic Press).

Jorgensen, S. E. (Ed.) 1979. *Handbook of Environmental Data and Ecological Parameters* (Copenhagen: International Society for Ecological Modelling), 1162 pp.

Ketchum, B. H. 1939. "The Absorption of Phosphate and Nitrate by Illuminated Cultures of *Nitzschia closterium*," *Am. J. Bot.* 26:399-407.

King, D. L. 1972. "Carbon Limitation in Sewage Lagoons," in *Nutrients and Eutrophication Special Symposia, Vol. I* (Am. Soc. Limnol. and Oceanog.), pp. 98-112.

King, D. L., and J. T. Novak. 1974. "The Kinetics of Inorganic Carbon-Limited Algal Growth," *J. Water Poll. Control Fed.* 46:1812-1816.

Koivo, A. J., and G. Phillips. 1976. "Optimal Estimation of DO, BOD, and Stream Parameters Using a Dynamic Discrete Time Model," *Water Resources Res.* 12:705-711.

Larsen, D. P., H. T. Mercier and K. W. Malueg. 1973. "Modeling Algal Growth Dynamics in Shagawa Lake, Minnesota, with Comments Concerning Projected Restoration of the Lake," in *Modeling the Eutrophication Process,* E. J. Middlebrooks, D. H. Falkenborg and T. E. Maloney, Eds. (Ann Arbor, MI: Ann Arbor Science Publishers, Inc.), p. 15.

Lehman, J. T. 1978. "Aspects of Nutrient Dynamics in Freshwater Communities," PhD dissertation, University of Washington, Seattle.

Lehman, T. D., D. B. Botkin and G. E. Likens. 1975. "The Assumptions and Rationales of a Computer Model of Phytoplankton Population Dynamics," *Limnol. Oceanog.* 20:343-364.

Lettenmaier, D. P., and J. E. Richey. 1979. "Use of First-Order Analysis in Estimating Mass Balance Errors and Planning Sampling Activities," in *Theoretical Systems Ecology,* E. Halfon, Ed. (New York: Academic Press), pp. 80-106.

Lotka, A. J. 1956. *Elements of Mathematical Biology* (New York: Dover Publications, Inc.)

MacCormick, A. S. A., O. L. Loucks, J. F. Koonce, J. F. Kitchell and P. R. Weiler. 1974. "An Ecosystem Model for the Pelagic Zone of Lake Wingra," Eastern Deciduous Forest Biome (IBP) Report EDFB-IBP-7-47.

McAllister, D. C. 1970. "Zooplankton Rations, Phytoplankton Mortality, and Estimating Marine Production," in *Marine Food Chains,* J. H. Steele, Ed. (Berkeley, CA: University of California Press), p. 419.

McGrath, E. J., and D. C. Irving. 1973. "Techniques for Efficient Monte Carlo Simulation," Office of Naval Res. Resp. AD 762 721-723 (3 volumes) (Springfield, VA: Natl. Tech. Inform. Serv.), 408 pp.

McNaught, D. C., and D. Scavia. 1976. "Applications of a Model of Zooplankton Composition to Problems of Fish Introduction to the Great Lakes," in *Modeling of Biochemical Processes in Aquatic Ecosystems,* R. P. Canale, Ed. (Ann Arbor, MI: Ann Arbor Science Publishers, Inc.), pp. 281-304.

Monod, J. 1942. "Recherches sur la Croissance des Cultures Bacteriennes," (Paris: Hermann)

Montgomery, R. H., V. D. Lee and K. H. Reckhow. 1980. "A Comparison of Uncertainty Analysis Techniques: First-Order Analysis vs. Monte Carlo

Simulation," paper presented at 1980 Conference on Great Lakes Research, Int. Assoc. for Great Lakes Res., Queens College, Kingston, Ont.

Moore, S. F. 1973. "Estimation Theory Applications to Design of Water Quality Monitoring Systems," *J. Hydrol. Div. ASCE* 99(Hy5):815-831.

Moore, S. F., G. C. Dandy and R. J. DeLucia. 1976. "Describing Variance with a Simple Water Quality Model and Hypothetical Sampling Programs," *Water Resources Res.* 12:795-804.

Mortimer, C. H. 1975. "Modeling of Lakes as Physico-Biochemical Systems— Present Limitations and Needs," in *Modeling of Marine Systems,* J. C. J. Nihoul, Ed. (New York: Elsevier), p. 217.

Mullin, M. M., E. F. Stewart and F. J. Foglister. 1975. "Ingestion of Planktonic Grazers as a Function of Concentration of Food," *Limnol. Oceanog.* 20:259-262.

Munk, W. H., and G. A. Riley. 1952. "Adsorption of Nutrients by Aquatic Plants," *J. Mar. Res.* 11:215-240.

O'Connor, D. J., D. M. Di Toro and R. V. Thomann. 1973. "Dynamic Water Quality Forecasting and Management," U.S. EPA Report, Washington, DC: U.S. Environmental Protection Agency, EPA-660/3-73-009.

O'Connor, D. J., D. M. Di Toro and R. V. Thomann. 1975. "Phytoplankton Models and Eutrophication Problems," in *Ecological Modeling in a Resource Management Framework,* Clifford S. Russell, Ed. (Washington, DC: Resources for the Future, Inc.), pp. 149-210.

O'Neill, R. V., and R. H. Gardner. 1979. "Sources of Error in Ecological Models," in *Methodology in Systems Modeling and Simulation,* B. D. Zeigler, M. S. Elzas, G. J. Klir, and T. I. Oren, Eds. (Amsterdam: North-Holland), pp. 447-463.

O'Neill, R. V., R. H. Gardner and J. B. Mankin. 1980. "Analysis of Parameter Error in a Nonlinear Model," *Ecol. Model.* 8:297-312.

Orlob, G. T. 1975. "Present Problems and Future Prospects of Ecological Modeling," in *Ecological Modeling in a Resource Management Framework,* C. S. Russell, Ed. (Washington, DC: Resources for the Future, Inc.), pp. 215-233.

Park, K. 1969. "Oceanic CO_2 System: An Evaluation of Ten Methods of Investigation," *Limnol. Oceanog.* 14:179-186.

Park, R. A., R. V. O'Neill, J. A. Bloomfield, H. H. Shugart, R. S. Booth, R. A. Goldstein, J. B. Mankin, J. F. Koonce, D. Scavia, M. S. Adams, L. S. Clesceri, E. M. Colon, E. H. Dettmann, J. Hoopes, D. D. Huff, S. Katz, J. F. Kitchell, R. C. Kohberger, E. J. LaRow, D. C. McNaught, J. Peterson, J. Titus, P. R. Weiler, J. W. Wilkinson and C. S. Zahorcak. 1974. "A Generalized Model for Simulating Lake Ecosystems," *Simulation* 23(2):33-50.

Parsons, T., M. Takahashi and B. Hargrave. 1977. *Biological Oceanographic Processes,* 2nd ed. (New York: Pergamon Press), 332 pp.

Patten, B. C. 1971. "A Primer for Ecological Modeling and Simulation with Analog and Digital Computers," in *Systems Analysis and Simulation in Ecology, Vol. I*, B. C. Patton, Ed. (New York: Academic Press, Inc.), pp. 3–121.

Patten, B. C., et al. 1975. "Total Ecosystem Model for a Cover in Lake Taxoma," in *Systems Analysis and Simulation in Ecology, Vol. III*, B. C. Patton, Ed. (New York: Academic Press, Inc.), p. 206.

Platt, T., K. L. Denman and A. D. Jassby. 1977. "Modeling the Productivity of Phytoplankton," in *The Sea, Vol 6: Marine Modeling*, E. D. Goldberg, I. N. McCave, J. J. O'Brien and J. H. Steele, Eds. (New York: John Wiley and Sons, Inc.), p. 807.

Poulet, S. A. 1978. "Comparison Between Five Coexisting Species of Marine Copepods Feeding on Naturally Occurring Particulate Matter," *Limnol. Oceanog.* 23:1126–1143.

Powers, W. F., and R. P. Canale. 1975. "Some Applications of Optimization Techniques to Water Quality Modeling and Control," *IEEE Trans. Syst., Man, Cybernetics* 5:312–321.

Reckhow, K. H. 1979. "Empirical Lake Models for Phosphorus Development: Applications, Limitations, and Uncertainty," in *Perspectives on Lake Ecosystem Modeling*, D. Scavia and A. Robertson, Eds. (Ann Arbor, MI: Ann Arbor Science Publishers, Inc.), pp. 183–222.

Reckhow, K. H., and J. T. Simpson. 1980. "A Procedure Using Modeling and Error Analysis for the Prediction of Lake Phosphorus Concentration from Land Use Information," *Can. J. Fish. Aquat. Sci.* 37:1439–1488.

Rhee, G. Y. 1978. "Effects of N:P Atomic Ratios and Nitrate Limitations in Algal Growth, Cell Composition, and Nitrate Uptake," *Limnol. Oceanog.* 23:10–25.

Richardson, W. L., and V. J. Bierman, Jr. 1976. "A Mathematical Model of Pollutant Cause and Effects in Saginaw Bay, Lake Huron," in *Water Quality Criteria Research of the U.S. Environmental Protection Agency, Proceedings of a Symposium on Marine, Estuarine and Fresh Water Quality* (Corvallis, OR: U.S. EPA), pp. 138–158.

Richman, S., S. A. Bohon and S. E. Robbins. 1981. "Grazing Interactions Among Freshwater Calanoid Copepods." pp. 219–233. In *Evolution and Ecology of Zooplankton Communities*, W. C. Kerfoot, Ed. (Hanover, NH: University Press of New England).

Riley, G. A. 1946. "Factors Controlling Phytoplankton Population on Georges Bank," *J. Mar. Res.* 6:54–73.

Riley, G. A. 1947. "A Theoretical Analysis of the Zooplankton Population of Georges Bank," *J. Mar. Res.* 6:104–113.

Riley, G. A. 1963. "Theory of Food-Chain Relations in the Ocean," in *The Sea* M. N. Hill, Ed. (New York: Interscience), pp. 438–463.

Riley, G. A., H. Stommel and D. F. Bumpus. 1949. "Quantitative Ecology of the Plankton of the Western North Atlantic," *Bull. Bingham Oceanog. Coll.* 12:1-169.

Rinaldi, S., P. Romano and R. Soncini-Sessa. 1979. "Parameter Estimation of Streeter-Phelps Models," *J. Environ. Eng. Div. ASCE* 105(EE1):75-88.

Robertson, A., and D. Scavia. 1979. "The Examination of Ecosystem Properties of Lake Ontario Through the Use of an Ecological Model," in *Perspectives on Lake Ecosystem Modeling,* D. Scavia and A. Robertson, Eds. (Ann Arbor, MI: Ann Arbor Science Publishers, Inc.), pp. 281-292.

Ryther, J. H. 1956. "Photosynthesis in the Ocean as a Function of Light Intensity," *Limnol. Oceanog.* 1:61-70.

Sawyer, C. N., and P. L. McCarty. 1967. *Chemistry for Sanitary Engineers.* (New York: McGraw-Hill Book Company) 518 pp.

Scavia, D. 1979a. "The Use of Ecological Models of Lakes in Synthesizing Available Information and Identifying Research Needs," in *Perspectives on Lake Ecosystem Modeling,* D. Scavia and A. Robertson, Eds. (Ann Arbor, MI: Ann Arbor Science Publishers, Inc.), p. 109.

Scavia, D. 1979b. "Examination of Phosphorus Cycling and Control of Phytoplankton Dynamics in Lake Ontario with an Ecological Model," *J. Fish. Res. Board Can.* 36:1336-1346.

Scavia, D. 1980a. "Uncertainty Analysis of a Lake Eutrophication Model," PhD dissertation, University of Michigan, Ann Arbor.

Scavia, D. 1980b. "The Need for Innovative Verification of Eutrophication Models," in *Proceedings of National Workshop on Verification of Water Quality Models,* R. V. Thomann and T. O. Barnwell, Jr., Eds. (Athens, GA: U.S. Environmental Protection Agency), pp. 214-225.

Scavia, D. 1980c. "An Ecological Model for Lake Ontario." *Ecol. Model.* 8: 49-78.

Scavia, D. 1981. "Conceptual Model of Phosphorus Cycling," in *Nutrient Cycling in the Great Lakes: A Summarization of Factors Regulating the Cycling of Phosphorus,* D. Scavia and R. Moll, Eds. Great Lakes Research Division Special Report No. 83, University of Michigan, Ann Arbor, MI. 119 pp.

Scavia, D., J. A. Bloomfield, J. S. Fisher, J. Nagy and R. A. Park. 1974. "Documentation of CLEANX: A Generalized Model for Simulating the Open-Water Ecosystems of Lakes," *Simulation* 23:51-56.

Scavia, D., B. J. Eadie and A. Robertson. 1976a. "An Ecological Model of Lake Ontario: Model Formulation, Calibration, and Preliminary Evaluation," NOAA, Technical Report ERL 371GLERL 12, Ann Arbor, MI: National Oceanic and Atmospheric Administration.

Scavia, D., B. J. Eadie and A. Robertson. 1976b. "An Ecological Model for the Great Lakes," in *Environmental Modeling and Simulation,* W. R. Ott,

Ed. EPA 600/9-76-016 (Washington, DC: U.S. Environmental Protection Agency, 1976), pp. 629-633.

Scavia, D., and J. R. Bennett. 1980. "The Spring Transition Period in Lake Ontario—A Numerical Study of the Causes of the Large Biological and Chemical Gradients," *Can. J. Fish Aquat. Sci.* 37:823-833.

Scavia, D., and S. C. Chapra. 1977. "Comparison of an Ecological Model of Lake Ontario and Phosphorus Loading Models," *J. Fish. Res. Board Can.,* 34:286-290.

Scavia, D., W. F. Powers, R. P. Canale and J. L. Moody. 1981a. "Comparison of First-Order Error Analysis and Monte Carlo Simulation in Time-Dependent Lake Eutrophication Models," *Water Resources Res.* 17:1051-1059.

Scavia, D., R. P. Canale, W. F. Powers and J. L. Moody. 1981b. "Variance Estimates for a Dynamic Eutrophication Model of Saginaw Bay, Lake Huron," *Water Resources Res.* 17:1115-1124.

Schindler, D. W. 1976. "Biochemical Evolution of Phosphorus Limitation in Nutrient-Enriched Lakes of the Precambrian Shield," in *Environmental Biogeochemistry,* J. O. Nriagu, Ed. (Ann Arbor, MI: Ann Arbor Science Publishers, Inc.), pp. 647-664.

Schindler, D. W. 1978. "Predictive Eutrophication Models," *Limnol. Oceanog.* 23:1080-1081.

Shapiro, J. 1973. "Blue-Green Algae: Why They Became Dominant," *Science* 179:382-384.

Shapiro, J. 1979. "The Need for More Biology in Lake Restoration," in *Lake Restoration,* U.S. EPA Report-440/5-79-001 (Washington, DC: U.S. Environmental Protection Agency), pp. 161-167.

Simons, T. J. 1976. "Analyses and Simulation of Spatial Variations of Physical and Biochemical Processes in Lake Ontario," *J. Great Lakes Res.* 2:215-233.

Smayda, T. J. 1970. "The Suspension and Sinking of Phytoplankton in the Sea," *Oceanog. Mar. Biol. Ann. Rev.* 8:353-414.

Snoeyink, V. L., and D. Jenkins. 1980. *Water Chemistry* (New York: John Wiley & Sons, Inc.).

Stadelmann, P., and A. Fraser. 1974. "Phosphorus and Nitrogen Cycle on a Transect in Lake Ontario During the International Field Year for the Great Lakes (IFYGL)," p. 92-107 in Proc. 17th Conf. Great Lakes Res. Internat. Assoc. Great Lakes Res.

Steele, J. H. 1962. "Environmental Control of Photosynthesis in the Sea," *Limnol. Oceanog.* 7:137-150.

Steele, J. H. 1965. "Notes on Some Theoretical Problems in Production Ecology," in *Primary Production in Aquatic Environments,* C. R. Goldman, Ed. (Berkeley, CA: University of California Press).

Steele, J. H. 1974. *The Structure of Marine Ecosystems* (Cambridge, MA: Harvard University Press), 128 pp.

Steele, J. H., and M. M. Mullin. 1975. "Zooplankton Dynamics," in *The Sea Vol. 6: Marine Modeling,* E. D. Goldberg, I. N. McCave, J. J. O'Brien and J. H. Steele, Eds. (New York: Wiley-Interscience), p. 857.

Stumm, W., and J. J. Morgan. 1981. *Aquatic Chemistry* (New York: Wiley-Interscience), 780 pp.

Thomann, R. V. 1972. *Systems Analysis and Water Quality Management* (New York: McGraw-Hill Book Company), 286 pp.

Thomann, R. V. 1976. "On the Verification of a Three Dimensional Phytoplankton Model of Lake Ontario," in *Environmental Modeling and Simulation,* W. T. Ott, Ed. EPA-600/9-76-016 (Washington, DC: U.S. Environmental Protection Agency), pp. 568-572.

Thomann, R. V. 1977. "Comparison of Lake Phytoplankton Models and Loading Plots," *Limnol. Oceanog.* 22:370-373.

Thomann, R. V., and T. O. Barnwell, Jr. 1980. "Workshop on Verification of Water Quality Models," U.S. Environmental Protection Agency Report No. EPA-600/9-80-016, 274 pp.

Thomann, R. V., D. M. Di Toro, R. P. Winfield and D. J. O'Connor. 1975. "Mathematical Modeling of Phytoplankton in Lake Ontario. 1. Model Development and Verification," EPA-600/3-75-005, Corvallis, OR: U.S. Environmental Protection Agency.

Thomann, R. V., and J. S. Segna. 1980. "Dynamic Phytoplankton-Phosphorus Model of Lake Ontario: Ten Year Verification and Simulations," in *Phosphorus Management Strategies for Lakes,* R. C. Loehr, Ed. (Ann Arbor, MI: Ann Arbor Science Publishers, Inc.), pp. 153-205.

Thomann, R V., R. P. Winfield and D. M. Di Toro. 1974. "Modeling of Phytoplankton in Lake Ontario (IFYGL)," in *Proceedings of 17th Conference on Great Lakes Research* (Ann Arbor, MI: International Association Great Lakes Research), pp. 135-149.

Thomann, R. V., R. P. Winfield and D. M. Di Toro. 1976. "Mathematical Modeling of Phytoplankton in Lake Ontario. 2. Simulations Using Lake 1 Model," U.S. EPA Report EPA-600/3-76-065, Duluth, MN: U.S. Environmental Protection Agency.

Thomann, R. V., R. P. Winfield and J. J. Segna. 1979. "Verification Analysis of Lake Ontario and Rochester Embayment Three-Dimensional Eutrophication Models," U.S. Report EPA-600/3-79-094, Washington, DC: U.S. Environmental Protection Agency.

Thomann, R. V., R. P. Winfield and D. S. Szumski. 1978. "Estimated Responses of Lake Ontario Phytoplankton Biomass to Varying Nutrient Levels," *J. Great Lakes Res.* 3:123-131.

Tiwari, J. L., and J. E. Hobbie. 1976. "Random Differential Equations as Models of Ecosystems: Monte Carlo Simulation-Approach," *Math. Biosci.* 28:25–44.

Ursin, E. 1967. "A Mathematical Model of Some Aspects of Fish Growth, Respiration and Mortality," *J. Fish. Res. Board Can.* 24:2355–2392.

Vallentyne, J. R., and N. A. Thomas. 1978. "Fifth Year Review of Canada-United States Great Lakes Water Quality Agreement Report of Task Group III, a Technical Group to Review Phosphorus Loadings," U.S. Department of State, Washington, DC, 86 pp.

Vanderploeg, H. A. 1981. "Seasonal Particle-Size Selection *Diaptomus sicclis* in Offshore Lake Michigan," *Can. J. Fish. Aquat. Sci.* 38:504–517.

Vollenweider, R. A. 1965. "Calculation Models of Photosynthesis-Depth Curves and Some Implications Regarding Day Rate Estimates in Primary Production Measurements," in *Primary Productivity in Aquatic Environments,* C. R. Goldman, Ed. (Berkeley, CA: University of California Press), p. 425.

Walsh, J. J. 1977. "A Biological Sketchbook for an Eastern Boundary Current," in *The Sea Vol. 6: Marine Modeling,* E. D. Goldberg, I. N. McCave, J. J. O'Brien and J. H. Steele, Eds. (New York: Wiley-Interscience), p. 923.

Walsh, J. J., and R. C. Dugdale. 1972. "Nutrient Submodels and Simulation Models of Phytoplankton Production in the Sea," in *Nutrients in Natural Waters,* H. E. Allen and J. R. Kramer, Eds. (New York: John Wiley and Sons, Inc.), p. 171.

Weininger, D. 1978. "Accumulation of PCB's by Lake Trout of Lake Michigan," PhD Thesis, University of Wisconsin, Madison, WI.

Wetzel, R. G. 1975. *Limnology* (Philadelphia, PA: W. B. Saunders Company), 743 pp.

Yih, S. M., and B. Davidson. 1975. "Identification in Nonlinear, Distributed Parameter Water Quality Models," *Water Resources Res.* 11:693–704.

Zison, S. W., W. B. Mills, D. Deimer and C. W. Chen. 1978. "Rates, Constants, and Kinetics Formulations in Surface Water Quality Modeling." U.S. EPA Report EPA-600/3-78-105, Athens, GA: U.S. Environmental Protection Agency.

CHAPTER 15

TOXIC SUBSTANCE MODELS

Over the past 50 years, engineers have developed a variety of mathematical models to predict a water body's response to pollutant inputs. The earliest formulations used first-order kinetics to characterize the effect of municipal sewage on the levels of aquatic oxygen and bacteria. Most of the models developed in the first chapters of this volume are related to that work. In the early 1970s, interest in eutrophication and the growing availability of digital computers stimulated more mechanistic characterizations of the biology and chemistry of aquatic systems. Consequently, as reviewed in Chapter 14, these models were much more complex than oxygen and bacteria models. Today, contamination of natural waters by toxic wastes necessitates another broadening of the scope of water quality modeling.

At first glance, this need for broadening might be perceived as a need for greater complexity. In contrast to classical water quality issues, such as oxygen depletion and eutrophication, the toxic substance problem does not address a single process. In fact, the label "toxic substance" itself represents myriad compounds, with the major unifying feature that they are life-threatening. This broad umbrella encompasses everything from heavy metals to synthetic organic chemicals (Table 15.1). This diversity could hinder the development of an easily implemented and unified approach to modeling these substances. On the other hand, the overwhelmingly large number of potential toxicants underscores the need for simple methods to identify the contaminants posing the greatest threat to the ecosystem and to human health.

This dilemma is reminiscent of that faced by limnologists and engineers when they first approached the problem of modeling lake trophic state. Although eutrophication does not encompass the sheer numbers of pollutants included in the toxic substance problem, it is just as complex kinetically. As described in Chapter 14, one school of modelers attempted

Table 15.1   Some Toxic Substances Found in the Environment (CEQ 1978)

Pollutant	Characteristics	Sources	Remarks
Pesticides: generally chlorinated hydrocarbons	Readily assimilated by aquatic animals, fat-soluble, concentrated through the food chain (biomagnified), persistent in soil and sediments	Direct application to farm and forest lands, runoff from lawns and gardens, urban runoff, discharge in industrial wastewater	Several chlorinated hydrocarbon pesticides already restricted by EPA; aldrin, dieldrin, DDT, DDD, endrin, heptachlor, lindane and chlordane
Polychlorinated Biphenyls (PCBs): used in electrical capacitors and transformers, paints, plastics, insecticides, other industrial products	Readily assimilated by aquatic animals, fat-soluble, subject to biomagnification, persistent, chemically similar to the chlorinated hydrocarbons	Municipal and industrial waste discharges disposed of in dumps and landfills	TOSCA ban on production after 6/1/79 but will persist in sediments; restrictions on many freshwater fisheries as result of PCB pollution (e.g., lower Hudson, upper Housatonic, parts of Lake Michigan)
Metals: antimony, arsenic, beryllium, cadmium, copper, lead, mercury, nickel, selenium, silver, thallium and zinc	Not biodegradable, persistent in sediments, toxic in solution, subject to biomagnification	Industrial discharges, mining activity, urban runoff, erosion of metal-rich soil, certain agricultural uses (e.g., mercury as a fungicide)	
Other Inorganics			
Asbestos	May cause cancer when inhaled; aquatic toxicity not well understood	Manufacture and use as a retardant, roofing material, brake lining, etc.; runoff from mining	
Cyanide	Variably persistent; inhibits oxygen metabolism	Wide variety of industrial uses	
Halogenated Aliphatics: used in fire extinguishers, refrigerants,	Largest single class of ''priority pollutants;'' can cause damage	Produced by chlorination of water, vaporization during use	Large-volume industrial chemicals, widely dispersed, but

propellants, pesticides, solvents for oils and greases, and in dry cleaning	to central nervous system and liver; not very persistent		less threat to the environment than persistent chemicals
Ethers: used mainly as solvents for polymer plastics	Potent carcinogen; aquatic toxicity and fate not well understood	Escape during production and use	Although some are volatile, ethers have been identified in some natural waters
Phthalate Esters: used chiefly in production of polyvinyl chloride and thermoplastics as plasticizers	Common aquatic pollutant, moderately toxic but teratogenic and mutagenic properties in low concentration; aquatic invertebrates are particularly sensitive to toxic effects; persistent and can be biomagnified	Waste disposal vaporization during use (in nonplastics)	
Monocyclic Aromatics (excluding phenols, cresols and phthalates): used in the manufacture of other chemicals, explosives, dyes and pigments, and in solvents, fungicides and herbicides	Central nervous system depressant; can damage liver and kidneys	Enter environment during production and by-product production states by direct volatization, wastewater	
Phenols: large-volume industrial compounds used chiefly as chemical intermediates in the production of synthetic polymers, dyestuffs, pigments, pesticides and herbicides	Toxicity increases with degree of chlorination of the phenolic molecule; very low concentrations can taint fish flesh and impart objectionable odor and taste to drinking water; difficult to remove from water by conventional treatment; carcinogenic in mice	Occur naturally in fossil fuels; wastewater from coking ovens, oil refineries, tar distillation plants, herbicide manufacturing and plastic manufacturing; can all contain phenolic compounds	

Table 15.1, continued

Pollutant	Characteristics	Sources	Remarks
Polycyclic Aromatic Hydrocarbons; used as dye-stuffs, chemical intermediates, pesticides, herbicides, motor fuels and oils	Carcinogenic in animals and indirectly linked to cancer in humans; most work done on air pollution; more is needed on the aquatic toxicity of these compounds; not persistent and are biodegradable, although bioaccumulation can occur	Fossil fuels (use, spills and production), incomplete combustion of hydrocarbons	
Nitrosamines: used in the production of organic chemicals and rubber; patents exist on processes using these compounds	Tests on laboratory animals have shown the nitrosamines to be some of the most potent carcinogens	Production and use can occur spontaneously in food cooking operations	

to incorporate this complexity into its computational schemes. However, as summarized in Chapter 8, other modelers developed simple methods to predict trophic state on the basis of a minimal number of independent variables. Although the best work usually resulted when the approaches were applied in tandem (Bierman 1980), the simple methods have proven more valuable in actual management contexts. In most cases, the complex models are too data-demanding and costly for broad-scale application. Needless to say, the great variety of toxic substances that have been (and will be) discharged into water bodies makes complex models even less practical for management purposes.

For this reason, and because of our predisposition toward simple engineering methods, we have approached the toxic substance problem with a mind toward developing screening models similar to those derived for broad-scale evaluation of trophic state. To do this, we must identify initially some underlying concepts and assumptions upon which this endeavor will be based.

First, we must acknowledge the critical role of solid matter in the transport and fate of toxicants. Classical water quality problems such as oxygen depletion and eutrophication deal with pollutants that occur naturally. The management question usually is: to what extent does the human contribution exaggerate the natural process? Algal blooms and oxygen depletion are examples of this overstimulation of life by classical pollutants. Toxic substances, on the other hand, are usually foreign to the aquatic environment and are concentrated at levels that can in fact be life-threatening. For these substances, the management question becomes not the total quantity present, but the percentage associated with living (i.e., organic) solid matter.

The association with solid matter has ancillary significance as a transport vector within and through the ecosystem. For example, the association of contaminants with settling and resuspending particles is a key mechanism controlling their transport and fate. Models that account for this "scavenging" (e.g., Section 13.3.2) will form an important component of our present effort to develop simple toxicant models. Further, small organic particles, such as phytoplankton and detritus, can be ingested and passed along to higher organisms. Such transfer up the food chain is significant because of the consumption of certain species of fish by humans.

Second, this chapter will focus on toxicants that are persistent and chronic. By persistent we mean that the contaminant has a kinetic time scale on the order of years. By chronic, we mean that the problem is the result of routine societal practices. This is in contrast to catastrophic pollution—such as nuclear reactor leaks or oil spills—which poses short-term, intense threats that require a totally different control strategy and are beyond our defined engineering approach.

Finally, a long-term or annual approach will be taken. This perspective originates, in part, from our interest in persistent pollutants. In addition, the toxic substance problem typically focuses on higher organisms, such as fish, because of their potential inclusion in human diet. This is in contrast to eutrophication, where the emphasis is on phytoplankton and the lower levels of the food chain. Because large fish mature on time scales of several years, the deleterious effects of pollution from toxic substances likely would exhibit a strong, long-term component. The use of a long-term time scale is reinforced by the potential impact of the lake's bottom sediments on toxic substance cycling, because sediments are by nature a slowly responding system (Chapter 13).

In the first part of this chapter, mechanisms influencing contaminant dynamics are reviewed. A number of computational frameworks for modeling toxicant dynamics are then described. Because toxic substances have only recently become a focus of interest, the state of the art of toxicant modeling is less developed than for other areas treated herein. Since the field is in a state of development, this chapter is intended as a survey of the key processes and frameworks that have emerged during this evolution and that could provide a basis for an engineering approach to this problem.

15.1 KINETICS

A number of different processes act to transform contaminants in natural waters. For example, some toxic substances exit a lake's surface via vaporization or volatilization. Some decompose due to exposure to sunlight (photolysis), through chemical reactions (e.g., hydrolysis) or by bacterial degradation. Thus, the net rate of transformation, R $[MT^{-1}]$, is a composite of these individual mechanisms,

$$R = R_v + R_p + R_h + R_b \qquad (15.1)$$

where R_v, R_p, R_h and R_b are the rates of volatilization, photolysis, hydrolysis and bacterial decomposition, respectively. Still other reactions might be included for particular contaminants (e.g., free radical oxidation), but the point is that a variety of processes contribute to the total rate.*

---

*In addition, the process of "scavenging," whereby a contaminant is removed from the lake by sorbing to settling particulate matter, is often treated as a kinetic process. The mathematics of sorption were reviewed in Chapter 13 and will not be pursued here.

In the initial chapters of this volume, simple first-order reactions were used to characterize such kinetics. Then, in Chapter 14, more complex formulations were developed to model nutrient food chain interactions. The toxic substance problem would also appear to require a complex approach due to the variety of kinetic processes that potentially transform contaminants in lake water. However, although complex approaches can be used, first-order expressions have also been developed for many of these processes. Because such constructs are more compatible with simple engineering estimates, first-order expressions are emphasized in the following discussion of the mechanisms governing toxicant dynamics.

15.1.1 Vaporization

Certain toxic compounds move across a lake's surface by evaporative transfer. This process can be quantified by Whitman's two-film, or two-resistance, theory (Whitman 1923, Lewis and Whitman 1924).* As schematized in Figure 15.1, the bulk or main body of the gaseous and liquid phases is assumed to be well-mixed and, therefore, homogeneous. A contaminant moving between the phases encounters maximum resistance in two boundary layers at the air-water interface, where mass transfer is via molecular diffusion. The fluxes through these layers, which at steady state would be equal, can be represented by Fick's first law and approximated as

$$J = k_l(c_i - c_l) \tag{15.2}$$

and

$$J = \frac{k_g}{RT_a}(p_g - p_i) \tag{15.3}$$

where J = flux [gmole m^{-2} d^{-1}]
k_l, k_g = mass transfer coefficients in the liquid and gaseous phases, respectively [m d^{-1}]
c_l, c_i = liquid concentrations in the bulk fluid and at the air-water interface, respectively [gmole m^{-3}]
R = universal gas constant [8.2×10^{-5} m^3 atm gmole^{-1}°K^{-1}]
T_a = absolute temperature [°K]
p_g, p_i = partial pressures of the gas in the bulk and at the interface, respectively [atm]

---

*The two-film theory is but one of several models that have been developed to characterize gas transfer. For example, see Dankwertz (1970) and Froment and Bischoff (1979) for additional discussion.

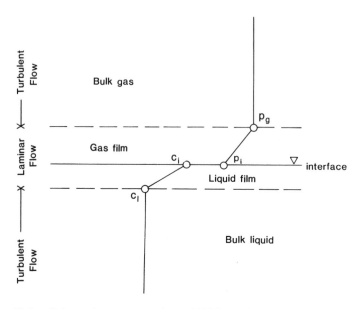

Figure 15.1   Schematic representation of Whitman's two-film theory of gas transfer. Liquid and gas concentration at the interface are assumed to be at an equilibrium as defined by Henry's Law (Equation 15.5). Gradients in the films control the rate of gas transfer between the bulk fluids.

Note that a negative flux indicates a loss of contaminant from the liquid to the gaseous phase. Also note that partial pressure and concentration are related by the ideal gas law

$$c = \frac{p}{RT_a} \tag{15.4}$$

The key assumption in Whitman's theory is that, at the air-water interface, the two phases are at an equilibrium as expressed by Henry's law

$$p_i = Hc_i \tag{15.5}$$

H is a distribution coefficient [atm m^3 gmole^{-1}] specific to each contaminant. The distribution coefficient is sometimes expressed in dimensionless form (Stumm and Morgan 1981) as

$$H' = \frac{H}{RT_a} \tag{15.6}$$

where H' is the dimensionless distribution coefficient. It is also directly related to Henry's constant (recall Equation 14.76) by

$$H = \frac{1}{K_H} \times \left(\frac{m^3}{10^3 l} \right) \tag{15.7}$$

where K_H is Henry's constant [moles $(1 \text{ atm})^{-1}$].

§ § §

Example 15.1. Henry's constant for oxygen at 25°C is approximately 1.263×10^{-3} moles $(1 \text{ atm})^{-1}$. The partial pressure of atmospheric oxygen is approximately 0.203 atm. On the basis of this information and Equation 15.7, the distribution coefficient can be computed as:

$$H = 1/(1.263 \times 10^{-3} \times 10^3) = 0.79177 \text{ atm m}^3 \text{ gmole}^{-1}$$

The dimensionless form is (Equation 15.6):

$$H' = 0.79177/(8.2 \times 10^{-5} \times 298) = 32.4$$

At this atmospheric pressure, Equation 15.5 indicates that the dissolved oxygen concentration of water should tend toward

$$c_i = p_i/H = 0.203/0.79177 = 0.2564 \text{ gmole m}^{-3}$$

or in mass units

$$c_i = 0.2564 \text{ gmole m}^{-3} (32 \text{ g O}_2 \text{ gmole}^{-1}) = 8.2 \text{ g m}^{-3}$$

This saturation value is consistent with that computed using Equation 13.26.

§ § §

Equation 15.5 can be substituted into Equation 15.3, which can be solved for:

$$c_i = \frac{1}{H} \left[p_g - \frac{JRT_a}{k_g} \right] \tag{15.8}$$

and Equation 15.2 can be rearranged to yield

$$c_i = \frac{J}{k_l} + c_l \tag{15.9}$$

These equations can be set equal and solved for flux in terms of the levels in the bulk fluids,

$$J = \frac{K_g}{RT_a}(p_g - Hc_1) \tag{15.10}$$

where K_g is related to the mass transfer coefficients for the individual phases by

$$\frac{1}{K_g} = \frac{H}{RT_a k_1} + \frac{1}{k_g} \tag{15.11}$$

Similarly, Equations 15.2, 15.3 and 15.4 can be combined and expressed as

$$J = K_1\left(\frac{p_g}{H} - c_1\right) \tag{15.12}$$

where

$$\frac{1}{K_1} = \frac{RT_a}{Hk_g} + \frac{1}{k_1} \tag{15.13}$$

§ § §

Example 15.2. Typical values of k_1 and k_g for large lakes are 1.5 and 300 m d^{-1}. Using the value of H computed in Example 15.1 (H = 0.79177 atm m^3 gmole^{-1}), K_g can be calculated as (Equation 15.11):

$$\frac{1}{K_g} = \frac{0.79177}{8.2 \times 10^{-5}(298)1.5} + \frac{1}{300} = 21.6 \text{ d m}^{-1}$$

$$K_g = 0.0463 \text{ m d}^{-1}$$

and K_1 can be calculated as (Equation 15.13):

$$\frac{1}{K_1} = \frac{8.2 \times 10^{-5}(298)}{0.79177(300)} + \frac{1}{1.5} = 0.667 \text{ d m}^{-1}$$

$$K_1 = 1.5 \text{ m d}^{-1}$$

If the lake's oxygen concentration is supersaturated due to photosynthesis ($c_1 = 16.0$ g m^{-3} = 0.5 gmole m^{-3}), compute the flux at the lake's surface.

Recall from Example 15.1 that p_g is approximately equal to 0.203 atm. The flux can be computed using Equation 15.10:

$$J = \frac{0.0463}{8.2 \times 10^{-5}(298)}[0.203 - 0.79177(0.5)] = -0.365\,\text{gmole m}^{-2}\text{d}^{-1}$$

Thus, the lake would lose oxygen at this rate. A similar result would be obtained from Equation 15.12,

$$J = 1.5(0.203/0.79177 - 0.5) = -0.365\,\text{gmole m}^{-2}\text{d}^{-1}$$

§ § §

As in Equation 15.13, the total resistance $(1/K_1)$ is a function of the individual resistances in the gaseous $[RT_a/(Hk_g)]$ and the liquid $(1/k_1)$ layers. The interrelationships between the three coefficients (H, k_1, k_g) that determine mass transfer can be illustrated by using Equation 15.13 to develop (Mackay 1977):

$$R_1 = \frac{(1/k_1)}{RT_a/(Hk_g) + 1/k_1} = \frac{H}{H + RT_a(k_1/k_g)} \qquad (15.14)$$

R_1 is the ratio of the liquid layer resistance to the total resistance. For lakes, k_g varies from approximately 100 to 1000 m d^{-1} and k_1 from 0.1 to 10 m d^{-1} (Liss 1975, Emerson 1975). The ratio of k_1 to k_g generally ranges from 0.001 to 0.01, with the higher value (due primarily to lower k_g because of sheltering from winds) in small lakes. A plot of R_1 vs H for the range indicates where liquid or gas or both films govern transport for contaminants of differing solubility (Figure 15.2). In general, the mass transfer of some compounds are liquid-controlled (e.g., benzene), some are gas-controlled (e.g., lindane), whereas others are controlled by both phases (e.g., DDT). Note, that larger lakes tend to be more liquid-controlled.

§ § §

Example 15.3. Use Equation 15.14 to estimate which film limits resistance for oxygen transfer in a large lake.

Using results and parameters from Examples 15.1 and 15.2, the ratio of liquid to total resistance can be computed with Equation 15.14,

$$R_1 = \frac{0.79177}{0.79177 + 8.2 \times 10^{-5}(298)1.5/300} = 0.99985$$

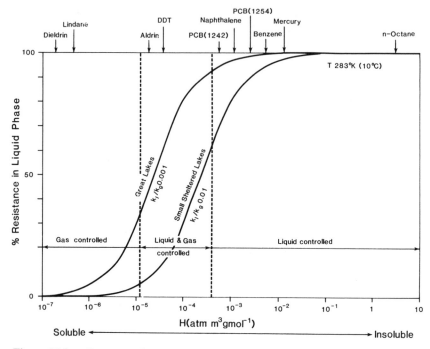

Figure 15.2 Percent resistance to gas transfer in the liquid phase as a function of H, the distribution coefficient. Values of H for some toxic substances are indicated (modified from Mackay 1977).

Therefore, for this case, resistance in the liquid film determines transfer.

§ § §

In cases where a single phase controls vaporization, there are a number of ways in which Equations 15.10 or 15.12 may be simplified. For example, very soluble compounds are gas controlled and the flux can be represented as:

$$J = \frac{k_g H}{RT_a}\left(\frac{p_g}{H} - c_l\right) = \frac{k_g H}{RT_a}(c_g - c_s) \qquad (15.15)$$

where c_s is the saturation concentration, which is the equivalent of the vapor pressure of the water. For certain highly soluble compounds with low vapor pressure (i.e., $p_g = 0$), Equation 15.15 can be simplified further to give

$$J = - \frac{k_g H}{RT_a} c_1 \tag{15.16}$$

Equation 15.16 represents the volatilization process as a first-order loss. In cases where the liquid phase controls, the flux reduces to

$$J = k_1 \left(\frac{p_g}{H} - c_1 \right) \tag{15.17}$$

This relationship is appropriate for very insoluble substances. For gases that are abundant in the atmosphere, such as oxygen, p_g/H represents a constant saturation concentration, c_s, that the liquid tends toward at equilibrium,

$$J = k_1 (c_s - c_1) \tag{15.18}$$

§ § §

Example 15.4. Because oxygen is liquid controlled, Equation 15.18 can be used to estimate flux. For the same case as in Examples 15.1 through 15.3,

$$J = 1.5(0.2564 - 0.5) = -0.365 \, \text{gmole m}^{-2} \, \text{d}^{-1}$$

which is identical to the result obtained previously in Example 15.2.

§ § §

For less abundant compounds, p_g/H can sometimes be negligible and Equation 15.17 reduces to a first-order loss

$$J = -k_1 c_1 \tag{15.19}$$

or in terms of the rate of mass transfer

$$R_v = -k_1 A_w c_{d,w} \tag{15.20}$$

where $c_{d,w} = c_1$ and A_w is lake surface area. Equation 15.19 can be used to characterize vaporization for some hydrophobic organic compounds. However, many other chemicals of environmental concern lie in the intermediate range where both resistances are important. For these cases, the complete flux equations must be used and knowledge of Henry's constant and the gas and liquid transfer coefficients is required. Methods for estimating these quantities will be explored after the next example.

§ § §

Example 15.5. Polychlorinated biphenyls (PCBs) are a class of compounds used primarily as coolant insulation fluids in electrical transformers and capacitors (see Table 15.1). PCBs are highly toxic to animals and man. Unfortunately, quantities have leaked or been discharged to the environment. For example, possibly dangerous levels have been found in freshwater fish, particularly in the Great Lakes.

Doskey and Andren (1981) have summarized information for two PCB compounds in Lake Michigan. Use this information (Table 15.2) to (1) determine which phase controls volatilization of these compounds and (2) determine the flux and rate of mass transfer for the lake (surface area = 53.5×10^9 m^2, $k_l/k_g = 0.005$ and T = 25°C).

Equation 15.14 can be used to compute

$$R_l(1242) = \frac{5.7 \times 10^{-4}}{5.7 \times 10^{-4} + 8.2 \times 10^{-5}(298)0.005} = 0.82$$

$$R_l(1254) = \frac{2.8 \times 10^{-3}}{2.8 \times 10^{-3} + 8.2 \times 10^{-5}(298)0.005} = 0.96$$

Therefore, Aroclor 1254 is predominantly liquid-controlled, whereas Aroclor 1242 is somewhat influenced by the gas film.

Equation 15.13 can be used to compute K_l for Aroclor 1242 (with $k_g = 300$ and $k_l = 1.5$ m d^{-1})

$$\frac{1}{K_l} = \frac{8.2 \times 10^{-5}(298)}{5.7 \times 10^{-4}(300)} + \frac{1}{1.5} = 0.8096$$

$$K_l = 1.235$$

and for Aroclor 1254

$$\frac{1}{K_l} = \frac{8.2 \times 10^{-5}(298)}{2.8 \times 10^{-3}(300)} + \frac{1}{1.5} = 0.6958$$

$$K_l = 1.437$$

Equation 15.12 can be used to estimate a flux for Aroclor 1242

Table 15.2   Information on Two Types of PCB (Doskey and
              Andren 1981) for Lake Michigan

	Aroclor 1242	Aroclor 1254
Air Concentration, p_g (atm)	5.6×10^{-14}	1.5×10^{-14}
Water Concentration, c_l (gmole m^{-3})	7.7×10^{-9}	2.6×10^{-8}
Distribution Coefficient, H (atm m^3 gmole^{-1})	5.7×10^{-4}	2.8×10^{-3}

$$J = 1.235 \left(\frac{5.6 \times 10^{-14}}{5.7 \times 10^{-4}} - 7.7 \times 10^{-9} \right) = -9.39 \times 10^{-9} \, \text{gmole m}^{-2} \, \text{d}^{-1}$$

and for Aroclor 1254

$$J = 1.437 \left(\frac{1.5 \times 10^{-14}}{2.8 \times 10^{-3}} - 2.6 \times 10^{-8} \right) = -3.74 \times 10^{-8} \, \text{gmole m}^{-2} \, \text{d}^{-1}$$

Mass loss (if molecular weights are 256 and 324 for Aroclors 1242 and 1254, respectively) can then be computed by

$$R_v(1242) = -9.39 \times 10^{-9}(256)(53.5 \times 10^9) = -1.29 \times 10^5 \, \text{g d}^{-1}$$

and

$$R_v(1254) = -3.74 \times 10^{-8}(324)(53.5 \times 10^9) = -6.5 \times 10^5 \, \text{g d}^{-1}$$

Now, use Equation 15.19 to make the same estimate as in

$$J(1242) = -1.5(7.7 \times 10^{-9}) = -1.2 \times 10^{-8} \, \text{gmole m}^{-2} \, \text{d}^{-1}$$

and

$$J(1254) = -1.5(2.6 \times 10^{-8}) = -3.9 \times 10^{-8} \, \text{gmole m}^{-2} \, \text{d}^{-1}$$

Thus, using the simplified method (Equation 15.19) results in a negligible error (4%) for the liquid controlled Aroclor 1254, whereas a significant discrepancy (28%) is introduced into the estimate for Aroclor 1242.

§ § §

Distribution Coefficient. H is conventionally determined by measuring the partial pressure and aqueous concentration of a compound at equilibrium between the two phases. However, because accuracy is greatest at high concentration and pressures, values contained in handbooks often differ from those in the environment. Therefore, direct measurements under environmental conditions are preferable.

For compounds that are relatively insoluble, H can be estimated from vapor pressure and aqueous solubility as in

$$H = \frac{P}{S} \qquad (15.21)$$

where P = vapor pressure [atm], which is approximately equal to the partial pressure in the air at equilibrium
   S = aqueous solubility [gmole m^{-3}]

Research is presently underway to develop and refine estimates of H. The reader is referred to work by Mackay and his colleagues for details (e.g., Mackay and Wolkoff 1973, Mackay and Leinonen 1975, Mackay and Shiu 1977, Mackay et al. 1979, 1980, 1982).

Exchange Coefficients. According to the Whitman model, mass transfer across the liquid or gas boundary layers is represented by exchange coefficients k_l or k_g, which are related to molecular diffusivity in the layers by

$$k = \frac{D_m}{z_f} \qquad (15.22)$$

where D_m = molecular diffusion coefficient [m^2 d^{-1}]
   z_f = thickness of the film [m]

In Equation 15.22, the exchange coefficient varies due to the amount of turbulence in the bulk phases as reflected by the film thickness. For example, high winds tend to decrease both gas and liquid boundary layers and, thus, increase both exchange coefficients. However, since the film thicknesses are very thin and, consequently, difficult to measure, development of predictive equations has focused on correlating the exchange coefficients directly with environmental conditions.

For lakes, the primary force influencing exchange is wind speed.* Air motion directly affects exchange through the gas film and indirectly affects the liquid boundary layer by inducing turbulence in the water. Formulas based on information summarized by Mackay (1980) after Liss

---

*This is in contrast to rivers and sheltered estuaries, where turbulence due to flowing water can dominate.

and Slater (1974), Cohen et al. (1978) and Deacon (1977) can be used to relate the transfer coefficients to wind speed and a compound's molecular weight, as in:

$$k_l = 0.56 \frac{W^{3/2}}{\sqrt{M}}$$ (15.23)

and

$$k_g = 1200 \frac{W}{\sqrt{M}}$$ (15.24)

where k_l and k_g are in [m d^{-1}], W is wind speed [m s^{-1}] and M is molecular weight of the compound.

15.1.2 Photolysis

Photolysis refers to the breakdown of chemicals due to the radiant energy of light. In natural waters, the rate of photodecomposition depends on the surface light intensity, which varies temporally (e.g., diurnal and seasonal changes) and spatially (e.g., latitude and elevation). Within a lake, the surface light intensity is attenuated due to the absorption of light energy by dissolved and particulate substances as well as by water itself. Photolysis in a quiescent, turbid lake might be limited to a thin surface layer, whereas it could extend to great depths in relatively clear water. Finally, the hydrodynamics or mixing characteristics of the lake can affect the extent of photodegradation, as it determines what fraction of a lake's water resides in the photic zone for what duration.

Light transforms toxicants by two general modes. The first, called direct photolysis, occurs through absorption by the compound itself. The second, called indirect or sensitized photolysis, represents a group of processes that are initiated through light absorption by intermediary compounds. Direct decomposition predominates in systems with little extraneous dissolved or particulate matter such as clear lakes. In more turbid or highly colored systems, sensitized photolysis could be of comparable or greater significance.

The following is a brief review of mathematical frameworks developed to model photolysis. The reader is referred elsewhere (Zepp and Cline 1977, Zepp 1980) for additional details. In general, the rate of photolysis can be represented as

$$\text{Rate} = -\phi I'$$ (15.25)

where ϕ = quantum yield
$\quad\quad$ I' = rate of absorption of light $[T^{-1}]$

The quantum yield is a measure of the efficiency of the reaction and represents the number of molecules photolyzed per light quanta absorbed. Because of the low concentrations of contaminants found in most natural waters, the light absorption rate is proportional to the amount of toxicant present

$$I' = k_a c \qquad (15.26)$$

where   c = concentration of the contaminant
$\quad\quad$ k_a = specific light absorption rate $[T^{-1}]$

On the basis of this proportionality, the rate of disappearance of contaminant due to photolysis can be represented as a first-order reaction

$$\frac{dc}{dt} = -k_{pr}c \qquad (15.27)$$

where

$$k_{pr} = \phi k_a \qquad (15.28)$$

Both direct and sensitized photolysis can be represented in this way as in

$$\frac{dc}{dt} = -(k_d + k_s)c \qquad (15.29)$$

where the subscripts d and s denote the direct and sensitized processes.

Direct photolysis. As in Equation 15.28, the direct photolysis rate constant can be represented, for a particular wavelength of light, λ, as

$$k_{d,\lambda} = \phi_d k_{a,\lambda} \qquad (15.30)$$

Note that ϕ_d is assumed to be independent of wavelength. The specific light absorption rate can be related to more fundamental quantities by

$$k_{a,\lambda} = \frac{I_\lambda \epsilon_{\lambda,d}}{j} \qquad (15.31)$$

where I_λ = light intensity [photons cm^{-2} s^{-1}]
$\quad\quad$ $\epsilon_{\lambda,d}$ = molar absorptivity at λ [1 (m mole)$^{-1}$], which represents the probability that the toxicant will absorb light at λ

j = constant that converts intensity units into mass concentration
units $[= 6.02 \times 10^{20}$ photons 1 cm^{-2} mole^{-1} m$^{-1}]$

The first-order decay rate at a particular wavelength can, therefore, be developed by combining Equations 15.30 and 15.31 to yield

$$k_{d,\lambda} = \frac{\phi_d I_\lambda \epsilon_{\lambda,d}}{j} \qquad (15.32)$$

Indirect Photolysis. Sensitized photolysis was discovered when it was observed that some compounds photolyzed more rapidly in nature than in distilled water. This increase has been ascribed to the presence of other compounds. A number of processes have been identified as contributing to sensitized photolysis, including the formation of excited state complexes, energy transfer from a sensitizer to the contaminant and reaction of the toxicant with a sensitizer. Because of the variety of processes that are potentially involved, indirect photodecomposition is more difficult to quantify than direct photolysis. Nevertheless, attempts (e.g., Zepp 1980) have been made to develop formulations to model sensitized reactions. The formulations are similar to those used for direct photolysis in that they require information regarding the available light spectrum. However, they differ in that they include the magnitude and absorbance characteristics of the sensitizer. In cases where the sensitizer concentration is constant, the rate of decay reduces to a constant, and a first-order expression (Equation 15.28) can be used to model the reaction kinetics.

Light Attenuation in the Water. To this point, we have presented equations that do not account for the fact that, aside from the contaminant, radiant energy is also absorbed by water, dissolved compounds and particulate matter. These competing energy losses must be determined in order to compute how much net radiation is delivered to contaminant molecules at various depths in the water column. The Beer-Lambert law provides a framework for quantifying total attenuation as in

$$I_\lambda(z) = I_\lambda(0)e^{-\eta_\lambda z} \qquad (15.33)$$

where $I_\lambda(z)$ = light intensity of a particular wavelength at a depth z below the water surface

η_λ = total extinction coefficient for wavelength $\lambda[L^{-1}]$, which is a composite of a number of factors as in

$$\eta_\lambda = \eta_{w,\lambda} + \eta_{p,\lambda} + \eta_{d,\lambda} + \epsilon_\lambda c \qquad (15.34)$$

where $\eta_{w,\lambda}, \eta_{p,\lambda}, \eta_{d,\lambda}$ = extinction coefficients for water, particles and dissolved matter, respectively

$\epsilon_\lambda c$ = extinction due to the contaminant being modeled

For a well mixed system, the average irradiance from depth = 0 to z is obtained by integrating Equation 15.33 to yield

$$I_\lambda \Big|_0^z = \frac{I_\lambda(0)}{\eta_\lambda z} [1 - \exp(-\eta_\lambda z)] \qquad (15.35)$$

Equation 15.35 can be combined with Equation 15.32 to obtain a depth-averaged rate for direct photolysis. The result is

$$k_{d,\lambda} \Big|_0^z = \frac{\phi_d}{j} \frac{I_\lambda(0)}{\eta_\lambda z} [1 - \exp(-\eta_\lambda z)] \epsilon_{\lambda,d} \qquad (15.36)$$

Equation 15.36 can then be substituted into Equation 15.29 to determine photolysis losses.

Implementation. The foregoing theory requires considerable information to estimate the effects of photolysis. Among other things, spectra (i.e., information across a range of wavelengths) of light intensity and absorbance as well as an estimate of the quantum yield are required. In addition, factors not treated in the present review, such as the angle of incidence of radiation, should be considered in a complete predictive scheme. For this reason, fairly complicated computer algorithms have been developed (e.g., Zepp and Cline 1977) to compute photolysis decay rates.

The problem of implementation is further compounded by the fact that decay rates exhibit strong diurnal and seasonal periodicities. As in Figure 15.3, photolysis rates vary considerably over these cycles. Thus, a variety of factors, such as date, time and latitude, should accompany particular estimates to place them in proper perspective. In addition, the development of long-term rates such as mean annual half-lives requires considerable averaging.

Aside from computer programs, some effort has been made to simplify the estimation of photolysis rates. However, problems such as the differential attenuation in water of portions of the light spectrum somewhat detract from their use for finer-scale predictions.

In summary, a first-order theory exists for estimating photolysis in lakes. However, the application of this theory to compute actual rates in the environment is a complicated process that in many cases requires laboratory work and computer programs for implementation.

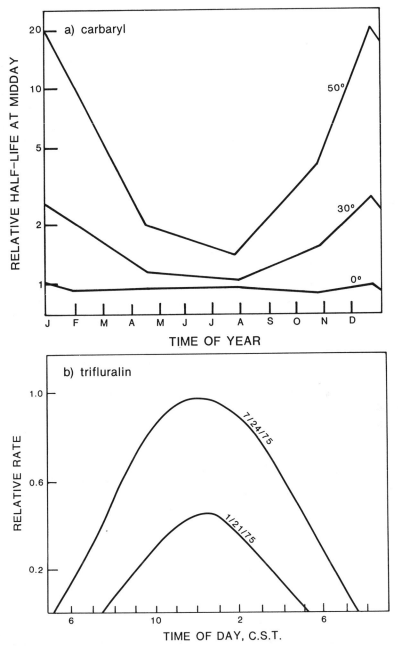

Figure 15.3 Plots showing a) seasonal and b) diurnal variations in photolysis rates for toxic substances (redrawn from Zepp and Cline 1977). The seasonal plot shows variations for three latitudes and the diurnal plot shows variations for a day in summer and a day in winter.

15.1.3 Hydrolysis

Hydrolysis refers to reactions in which the bond of a molecule is cleaved and a new bond is formed with the hydrogen and hydroxyl components of a water molecule. Hydrolytic reactions may be catalyzed by acids or bases and, to a more limited extent, by reactions with water. These catalytic effects depend on the type of reaction and the chemical structure of the compound. The pH and temperature of the solution have an influence on the rate of reaction.

The kinetics of hydrolysis can be expressed as (Smith et al. 1977)

$$R_h = -k_h V_{t,w} c_{t,w} \qquad (15.37)$$

k_h is a first-order rate constant where

$$k_h = k_B[OH^-] + k_A[H^+] + k_N \qquad (15.38)$$

where k_B, k_A and k_N are constants representing basic, acidic and neutral effects on the reaction. From Equation 15.38, it is evident that if k_A and/or $k_B \neq 0$, then k_h depends on pH. If the equilibrium relationship for the dissociation of water

$$K_w = [H^+][OH^-] \qquad (15.39)$$

is substituted into Equation 15.38, the result can be rewritten as

$$k_h = \frac{k_B K_w}{[H^+]} + k_A[H^+] + k_N \qquad (15.40)$$

This equation can be plotted as in Figure 15.4 where it can be seen that three general regions exist:

1. An acidic region, where

$$k_A[H^+] > k_N + \frac{k_B K_w}{[H^+]} \qquad (15.41)$$

 and consequently

$$\log k_h = \log k_A - pH \qquad (15.42)$$

 In this region, the acid-catalyzed reaction is dominant and a slope of -1 characterizes the effect of pH on $\log k_h$.

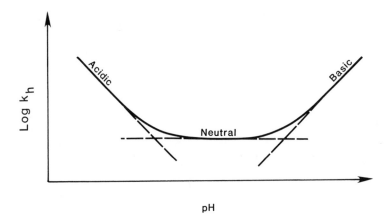

Figure 15.4   Effect of pH on hydrolysis rate.

2. A neutral region, where

$$k_N > k_A[H^+] + \frac{k_B K_w}{[H^+]} \qquad (15.43)$$

and consequently,

$$\log k_h = \log k_N \qquad (15.44)$$

In this region, the reaction is independent of pH.

3. A basic region, where

$$\frac{k_B K_w}{[H^+]} > k_N + k_A[H^+] \qquad (15.45)$$

and consequently,

$$\log k_h = \log k_B K_w + pH \qquad (15.46)$$

In this region, the base-catalyzed reaction is dominant and k_h is linearly dependent on pH.

When performing simulations within the neutral range, the effect of hydrolysis can be represented as a first-order reaction as in

$$R_h = -k_h V_{t,w} c_{t,w} \qquad (15.47)$$

However, for the acid and basic range, the approach is not valid for systems with fluctuating pH. Although the practical significance of this fact for long-term computations is not clear, the effect could be important in seasonal calculations where productivity and decomposition can influence pH (recall Figure 14.20). Additional information on hydrolysis can be found in Wolfe (1979) and Wolfe et al. (1976).

15.1.4 Biodegradation

The effect of microorganisms on aquatic toxicants is generally called biodegradation. The label encompasses a number of distinctly different processes including (Alexander 1979):

1. mineralization: the conversion of an organic compound to inorganic products;
2. detoxication: the conversion of a toxicant to innocuous by-products;
3. cometabolism: the metabolism of a compound that the organisms cannot use as a nutrient (which does not result in mineralization, and organic metabolites remain);
4. activation: a substance is made toxic or increased in toxicity by microbial action; and
5. defusing: the conversion of a potential toxicant into a harmless metabolite before the potential is realized.

For cases where the contaminant is the sole source of nourishment, a Monod, or Michaelis-Menten, relationship can be used to model the rate as in

$$\frac{ds}{dt} = -\frac{k_m XS}{k_s + S} \qquad (15.48)$$

and

$$\frac{dx}{dt} = -a\frac{ds}{dt} \qquad (15.49)$$

where X = concentration of the bacteria
a = yield of bacterial biomass per unit of substrate utilized
k_m = maximum utilization rate
S = is the substrate concentration
k_s = half-saturation constant

Although Equations 15.48 and 15.49 are sometimes appropriate for the laboratory, they do not hold for most natural cases, since contaminant levels are usually low and the bacteria usually have abundant, more preferable carbon sources. Further, since bacteria grow rapidly relative to other higher organisms, their population usually exists at a fairly stable level in the environment, particularly when viewed from the long-term perspective. For this reason, the process is often modeled as a simple first-order decay as in

$$R_b = -k_b V_{t,w} c_{t,w} \qquad (15.50)$$

where k_b is the first-order degradation rate constant. It should be noted that aside from degradation, explicit computation of bacterial biomass could be important as it relates to the lake sediments where microorganisms are a critical link between detritus and higher levels of the benthic food chain and where bacterial biomass is not necessarily constant.

The differences between laboratory and field conditions that influence the choice of a mathematical model also have a bearing on interpretation of the research in this area. For example, many laboratory degradation studies are performed using microbial populations that have been acclimated to a particular organic compound. Whether such species would tend to behave similarly in the lake environment is questionable and makes it difficult to apply some of the laboratory work to natural situations. The reader is referred to Alexander (1979, 1981) and Baughman et al. (1980) for additional information regarding biodegradation.

15.1.5 Summary

Equations 15.20, 15.29, 15.37 and 15.47 can be combined with Equation 15.1 and used to develop the following first-order representation of long-term contaminant kinetics,

$$R = -k_{t,w} V_{t,w} c_{t,w} \qquad (15.51)$$

where $k_{t,w}$ is the total contaminant decay rate which is equal to

$$k_{t,w} = k_1 F_{d,w}/z_w + (k_d + k_s) + k_h + k_b \qquad (15.52)$$

where $F_{d,w}$ = fraction of the contaminant in the dissolved phase
z_w = lake depth

Note that Equation 15.52 implies that the processes of photolysis, hydrolysis and biodegradation have the same effect on both dissolved and particulate phases of the contaminant. If this were not true, Equation 15.52 would have to be modified to include different rates for each of the phases. For instance, in a subsequent example (15.6), it is assumed that these processes solely act on the dissolved phase of the contaminant.

As should be evident from the above review, the mathematics of certain of the processes governing toxicant dynamics are not as well developed as others. In spite of this, these mechanisms were included to acquaint the reader with the present level of understanding. Hopefully, in the near future, the mathematics and measurements needed to estimate these process rates will be developed further.

15.2 MODELS

As stated in the introduction to this chapter, the transport, fate and significance of many toxic substances are determined, in large measure, by their association with solid matter in lakes. These solids can be divided conceptually into two categories: the biota, or food chain solids, and particles (Figure 15.5).

The biota have direct importance because of our interest in contamination of higher organisms, such as fish, that may enter the human diet. Additionally, transfer along the food chain should be considered in a complete characterization of toxicant dynamics. As described in Chapter 14, computational schemes are available to simulate the cycling of matter through the biota.

Second, contaminants associate in varying degrees with both organic and inorganic particles. The transport and fate of the toxicant are, therefore, partially dictated by the dynamics of these particles. A large portion of Chapter 13 was devoted to simulating such particle/contaminant interactions. In addition, particulate matter and the biota are linked directly by the fact that the base of the food chain consists of small organic particles.

The models developed in this chapter deal with both types of solid matter as well as with their combined effect. The first part of the chapter employs modifications of computational schemes derived in Chapter 13 to simulate particle/contaminant interactions. Then, simplified food chain models are developed to predict contaminant levels in the biota. Finally, the two components are combined in a model that computes toxicant levels in the food chain as a function of a lake's external loadings.

15.2.1 Input-Output Models of Particle/Contaminant Interactions

If mass balances were written for each component in Figure 15.5, six differential equations would result. In addition, equations would

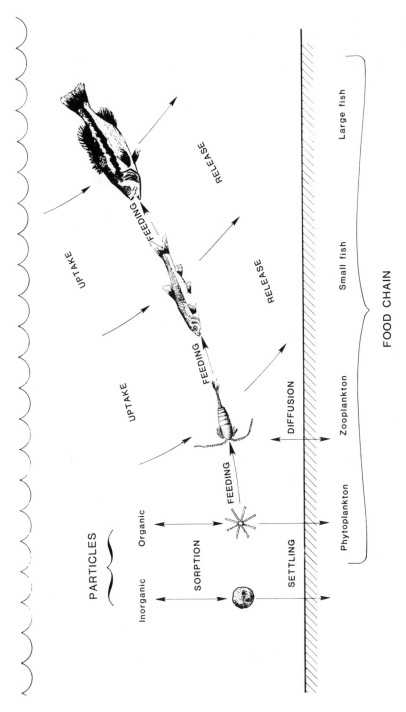

Figure 15.5   Schematic of the interactions between a dissolved contaminant and solid matter in a lake. The solid matter is divided into two categories: particles and a simple linear food chain.

also be required to simulate contaminant dynamics within the lake's bottom sediments. Although such large systems of equations can certainly be solved, the computational burden and expense might discourage their widespread application. Simplifications could increase their utility in this regard.

One simplification is to decouple and exclude the upper food chain (i.e., zooplankton, and small and large fish) from the computation. This assumption can usually be justified on the premise that a negligible fraction of the lake's total contaminant inventory may be associated with the upper food chain. In addition, higher organisms are assumed to be self-propelled or motile; as such, they are not passive subjects of processes such as sedimentation and flushing that act to transport particles out of the water column. Consequently, they do not figure directly in the input and output mass transfers that determine the long-term trends of contaminants in the lake.

A Dynamic Input-Output Model

By dealing strictly with the dissolved and small particulate forms, the model can be greatly simplified. For example, if sediment-water interactions are excluded, the models presented in Chapter 13 (e.g., those in Section 13.3.2) can be simplified to yield the following contaminant mass balance for the water column,

$$V_{t,w} \frac{dc_{t,w}}{dt} = W_c(t) - Qc_{t,w} - k_{t,w}V_{t,w}c_{t,w} - v_wF_{pw}A_wc_{t,w} \quad (15.53)$$

where
$V_{t,w}$ = lake volume [m³]
$c_{t,w}$ = total contaminant concentration [μg m⁻³]
t = time [yr]
$W_c(t)$ = rate of mass loading of contaminant [μg yr⁻¹]
Q = outflow [m³ yr⁻¹]
v_w = apparent particulate settling velocity [m yr⁻¹]
A_w = lake surface area [m²]
F_{pw} = fraction of contaminant in particulate form as in

$$F_{pw} = \frac{K_{d,w}s_w}{1 + K_{d,w}s_w} \quad (15.54)$$

where
$K_{d,w}$ = partition coefficient [m³ g⁻¹]
s_w = total suspended solids [g m⁻³]
$k_{t,w}$ = decay rate for the total contaminant [yr⁻¹], which can be related to the dissolved and particulate fractions by

$$k_{t,w} = F_{pw}k_{p,w} + F_{dw}k_{d,w} \quad (15.55)$$

where $\quad k_{p,w}, k_{d,w}$ = the decay rates for the particulate and the dissolved fractions, respectively

$\quad\quad\quad F_{dw}$ = fraction of contaminant in dissolved form = $1 - F_{pw}$

§ § §

Example 15.6. Bierman and Swain (1982) used a modified version of Equation 15.53 to analyze DDT trends in Lakes Michigan and Superior. Their modification consisted of assuming that particulate fraction decay was negligible ($k_{p,w} = 0$). Under this assumption, Equation 15.53 becomes

$$V_{t,w} \frac{dc_{t,w}}{dt} = W_c(t) - Qc_{t,w} - k_{d,w}F_{dw}V_{t,w}c_{t,w} - v_wF_{pw}A_wc_{t,w} \quad (15.56)$$

which can be rewritten as (note $k' = \alpha$ on p. 25)

$$\frac{dc_{t,w}}{dt} + k'c_{t,w} = \frac{W_c(t)}{V_{t,w}} \quad (15.57)$$

where k' is a first-order rate coefficient [yr^{-1}] that accounts for all losses of contaminant from the lake as in

$$k' \quad = \quad 1/\tau_w \quad + \quad k_{d,w}F_{dw} \quad + \quad v_pF_{pw}/z_w \quad (15.58)$$
$$\begin{array}{ccccc} \text{total loss} & = & \text{flushing} & + & \text{decay} & + & \text{sedimentation} \\ \text{rate} & & \text{rate} & & \text{rate} & & \text{rate} \end{array}$$

where $\quad \tau_w$ = water residence time [yr] = $V_{t,w}/Q$

$\quad\quad\quad z_w$ = water depth [m]

After 1969, DDT use was banned in the United States. If it is assumed that DDT loadings to the Great Lakes ceased after that year, $W_c(t) = 0$ and Equation 15.57 can be solved for (recall p. 27)

$$c_{t,w} = c_{t,w,i}e^{-k't} \quad (15.59)$$

where $c_{t,w,i}$ is the initial concentration at $t = 0$ in 1969. Thus, the contaminant would be expected to be purged from the water at an exponential rate. Dividing Equation 15.59 by $c_{t,w,i}$ and taking the natural logarithm yields

$$\ln(c_{t,w}/c_{t,w,i}) = -k't \quad (15.60)$$

If the model is a correct representation of DDT dynamics, a plot of $\ln(c_{t,w}/c_{t,w,i})$ vs time should yield a straight line with a slope of $-k'$. Unfortunately, sufficient water concentration data for DDT did not exist to test this hypothesis. However, DDT concentrations in small fish were available. By assuming that total water and fish concentration were directly proportional, Bierman and Swain used the fish data to test Equation 15.60. Figure 15.6 shows the result for Lake Michigan. Such analyses were used to determine values of 0.330 and 0.279 yr^{-1} for k' in Lakes Michigan and Superior, respectively.

Bierman and Swain then used this information along with the data in Table 15.3 and Equation 15.58 to back-calculate values for v_w. Their results along with apparent particulate settling velocities for other substances are contained in Table 15.4. Two observations can be made with regard to this table:

1. There is considerable variability of v_w between substances. For example, the settling velocity for plutonium is almost an order of magnitude higher than phosphorus. This may in part be due to factors such as sediment-water exchange that are not accounted for in the simple model.
2. The ratio of the values for Lake Superior to those for Lake Michigan are quite similar: a mean of 1.72 with a range of 1.6 to 1.8.

§ § §

Bierman and Swain's (1982) study is an excellent example of an engineering approach to the toxic substance problem. Aside from gaining insight into the relative importance of the various mechanisms governing contaminant levels in lakes, Equations 15.53 or 15.56 can also be used to compute directly the dynamics of a toxic substance in a single lake due to changing loading rates.

§ § §

Example 15.7. Use the data in Table 15.5 along with Equation 15.53 to simulate PCB dynamics in Lake Michigan from 1940 to 1980.

In order to perform this simulation, an estimate of PCB inputs, $W_c(t)$, is required. This is complicated by the fact that measurements have only recently been made for the lake. In order to simulate levels over the past 50 years, historical industry production figures were used to determine the growth rate of inputs in a fashion similar to Whitmore (1977). Using this rate in conjunction with measurements of the present loadings (Whitmore 1977, PLUARG 1978, Murphy and Rzeszutko 1978,

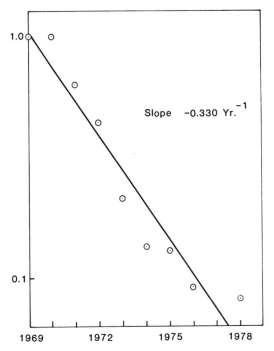

Figure 15.6 Plot of ln (ν/ν_i) vs time for DDT in small fish in Lake Michigan. The slope of the line provides an estimate of the total loss rate of DDT from the water.

Table 15.3   Parameters Used by Bierman and Swain (1982) to Analyze DDT Trends in Lakes Michigan and Superior

Parameter	Lake Michigan		Lake Superior
z_w (m)	85		145
$V_{t,w}$ (m³)	4.91×10^{12}		1.19×10^{13}
τ_w (yr)	69		177
s_w (g m⁻³)	1.0		0.75
$k_{d,w}$ (yr⁻¹)		0.069	
$K_{d,w}$ (m³ g⁻¹)		0.5	
k' (yr⁻¹)	0.330		0.279

Strachan and Huneault 1979), the following loading function was developed and used for the PCB simulation,

$$W_c(t) = 2.47 \times 10^7 (t - 1930)^{3.5} \qquad 1930 < t < 1970 \qquad (15.61)$$

Table 15.4   Comparison of Apparent Particulate Settling
Velocities for Lakes Michigan and Superior from Bierman
and Swain (1982)

	Settling Velocity (m yr^{-1})		
Constituent	Lake Michigan	Lake Superior	Lake Superior / Lake Michigan
Phosphorus	24.5	39.2	1.60
Phytoplankton	73		
Plutonium	210	369	1.76
DDT			
With $W_c = 0$ after 1970	68.8	118	1.72
With $W_c \neq 0$ after 1970	84.0	151	1.80

Table 15.5   PCB Parameters for Lake Michigan

Parameter	Value
Apparent Particulate Settling Velocity, v_w (m yr^{-1})	84[a]
Partition Coefficient, $K_{d,w}$ (m^3 g^{-1})	0.1
Decay Rate, $k_{t,w}$ (yr^{-1})	0[b]

[a] Assumed to be the same as DDT.
[b] Decay assumed to be negligible.

$$W_c(t) = 0 \qquad t > 1970 \qquad (15.62)$$

where $W_c(t)$ is PCB loading (μg yr^{-1}). As in Equation 15.62 and Figure 15.7, the loading is terminated in 1970 to coincide with the PCB ban imposed on the Great Lakes system at that time. Although PCB still enters the system from external sources, this idealization represents a first approximation of the effect of the ban on the loading function.

Equations 15.61 and 15.62 can be combined with Equation 15.53 to yield an equation that is appropriate from 1940 to 1970,

$$\frac{dc_{t,w}}{dt} + k'c_{t.w} = \frac{2.47 \times 10^7}{V_{t,w}}(t - 1930)^{3.5} \qquad (a)$$

and after 1970,

$$\frac{dc_{t,w}}{dt} + k'c_{t,w} = 0 \qquad (b)$$

where

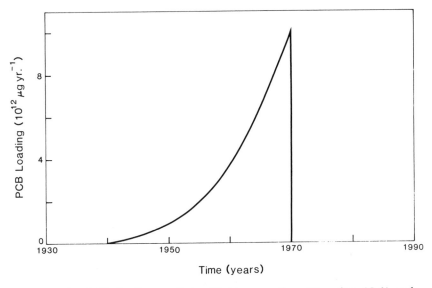

Figure 15.7   PCB loading to Lake Michigan vs time (Equation 15.61 and 15.62). The abrupt drop corresponds to the ban on the toxicant that went into effect in 1970.

$$k' = 1/\tau_w + k_{t,w} + v_w F_{p,w}/z_w \qquad (c)$$

Using the appropriate parameters from Table 15.3 and the PCB parameters from Table 15.5, these equations can be solved numerically and the results are as in Table 15.6 and Figure 15.8. Note that PCB builds up exponentially until 1970, when elimination of the loads results in an exponential decrease. The rate of this decrease can be quantified by

$$t_{90} = \frac{2.3}{k'} = 22\,yr$$

Therefore, in the absence of loads, the model computation indicates that approximately two decades would be required for a 90% reduction in Lake Michigan's PCB concentration.

§ § §

Steady-State Screening: A Contaminant Loading Model

Lake models can be developed from longitudinal or cross-sectional perspectives. The former approach is designed to predict changes in a single lake over time, whereas the latter addresses differences between

Table 15.6   Values of Loading, $W_c(t)$, and Total
Contaminant Concentration, $c_{t,w}$, for Dynamic PCB Simulation
for Lake Michigan

Year	$W_c(t)$ $(10^{12} \ \mu g \ yr^{-1})$	$c_{t,w}$ $(\mu g \ m^{-3})$
1930	0.00	0.00
1935	0.01	0.00
1940	0.08	0.03
1945	0.32	0.17
1950	0.88	0.57
1955	1.93	1.45
1960	3.65	3.09
1965	6.27	5.79
1970	10.00	9.93
1975	0.00	5.90
1980	0.00	3.50
1985	0.00	2.08
1990	0.00	1.23

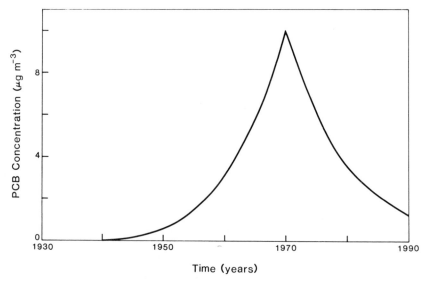

Figure 15.8   Simulation of PCB concentration in Lake Michigan vs time, as calculated in Example 15.7.

lakes. The application of the particle/contaminant model to Lake Michigan in Example 15.7 represents a longitudinal analysis. Although such applications have obvious value, cross-sectional approaches could be of equal or greater utility in managing toxic substance pollution.

The situation is akin to lake eutrophication where both longitudinal and cross-sectional models have been developed to predict trophic state as a function of phosphorus loading. Although dynamic models have served as useful management tools in specific lakes (e.g., Thomann et al. 1974, Chapra 1977) cross-sectional loading plots have found much broader application (see Chapter 8 of Volume 1). This is due to their ease of implementation as well as to the fact that they are designed for broad-scale analysis. A manager in a state or federal agency faced with the prospect of computing loading guidelines for 100 or so lakes would be predisposed and well advised to use simple loading models for first estimates.

For toxic substances, cross-sectional models would be even more useful, since, for this problem context, two cross sections are involved. In eutrophication, only one pollutant—phosphorus—is controlled. For toxics, not only must managers deal with lake-to-lake differences, but they must also discriminate among the myriad contaminants that are introduced to these lakes. Thus, cross-sectional models could answer two basic questions: (1) which of a group of substances poses the greatest threat to a particular lake and (2) which of a group of lakes is most sensitive to the loading of a particular pollutant.

To date, a number of investigators (e.g., Thomann 1979, 1981; Mackay 1980; Schnoor 1981; Bierman and Swain 1982) have begun to develop analytical frameworks that collectively are the beginning of a "toxicant loading concept." It seems reasonable to expect that the experience and techniques derived from the phosphorus loading concept might contribute to this endeavor. In this section, we do this by developing a steady-state solution for the particle/contaminant model (Chapra 1982). This solution can be used to determine in-lake levels of a contaminant as a function of loading and can be used to derive parameter groups, such as retention coefficients, that have proven useful in eutrophication management. Before doing this we will briefly review aspects of phosphorus loading models that will bear on our derivation. Additional information on the phosphorus loading concept is reviewed in Volume 1.

Brief Review of Phosphorus Loading Models. The theoretical basis of the phosphorus loading concept is a mass balance for a well mixed lake as proposed by Vollenweider (1969), with modification by Chapra (1975).

$$V_{t,w} \frac{dp_{t,w}}{dt} = W_p(t) - Qp_{t,w} - v_a A_w p_{t,w} \qquad (15.63)$$

where $V_{t,w}$ = volume of the water column [m³]
$p_{t,w}$ = concentration of total phosphorus in the water column [mg P m⁻³]

$W_p(t)$ = rate of mass loading of total phosphorus [mg P yr^{-1}]
Q = outflow [m^3 yr^{-1}]
v_a = apparent settling velocity of total phosphorus [m yr^{-1}]
A_w = lake's surface area [m^2]

This model is typically solved at steady state to yield

$$P_{t,w} = \frac{W_p}{Q + v_a A_w} \qquad (15.64)$$

Thus the model can be used to compute in-lake levels as a function of external loading rate. Equation 15.64 may be reexpressed as

$$R_a = \frac{P_{t,w}}{L_p} = \frac{1}{q_s + v_a} \qquad (15.65)$$

where R_a = assimilation coefficient for areal loading [mg P m^{-3} (mg P m^{-2} yr^{-1})$^{-1}$] that represents the in-lake concentration that results from a unit areal loading of phosphorus
L_p = areal loading rate of phosphorus to the lake [mg P m^{-2} yr^{-1}]
q_s = areal water loading [m yr^{-1}] = $Q\,A_s^{-1}$

Equation 15.65 is the basis of nomographs that can be used to estimate the loading needed to attain a desired in-lake concentration of phosphorus (Vollenweider 1976, Chapra and Tarapchak 1976).

Equation 15.65 is designed to evaluate the relative ability of lakes to assimilate loadings that enter as a flux across the surface. An alternative expression, which is more generally applicable, is

$$R_a' = \frac{P_{t,w}}{W_p} = \frac{1}{Q + v_a A_w} = \frac{1}{\P_p} \qquad (15.66)$$

where R_a' = assimilation coefficient for unit loading rate [mg P m^{-3} (mg P yr^{-1})]
$\P_p$ = assimilation factor discussed in Chapter 10

Equations 15.65 and 15.66 are related by

$$R_a' = R_a / A_w \qquad (15.67)$$

An additional formulation that has proven useful in eutrophication analysis is Dillon and Rigler's (1974) retention coefficient, which can be defined in terms of Equation 15.64 as (Chapra 1975)

$$R_p = \frac{v_a}{q_s + v_a} \qquad (15.68)$$

This parameter group is useful in that it provides a measure of the fraction of the external loading that is incorporated into the lake's bottom sediments. Vollenweider (1976) and Larsen and Mercier (1976) have also shown that the quantity $1 - R_p$ (which we will call the attenuation coefficient, R_i) represents the ratio of the in-lake phosphorus concentration to that of the inflow. It therefore provides a measure of the decrease in phosphorus due to the net effect of removal mechanisms.

Before proceeding to the toxic substance budget, two properties of the phosphorus loading concept that have a bearing on its application to contaminants must be noted. First, in the above models, total phosphorus is treated as a conservative substance, i.e., it is not subject to removal processes other than sedimentation and flushing. In contrast, many contaminants are lost from aquatic systems via processes such as photolysis, vaporization, hydrolysis and microbial degradation. Second, Equation 15.63 does not include sediment feedback in an explicit fashion. It is usually assumed, for lakes with perennially oxic hypolimnia and minimal sediment resuspension, that feedback is negligible. This assumption cannot be made of some toxicants and is accounted for explicitly in the following derivation.

Steady-State Contaminant Budget Model. The model is identical to the contaminant/particle model derived previously in Section 13.3.2 with the exception that only allochthonous solids are simulated and resuspension is included (Figure 15.9). For this case, a mass balance for suspended solids can be written as

$$V_{t,w}\frac{ds_{t,w}}{dt} = W_s - Qs_{t,w} - v_w A_w s_{t,w} + v_r A_m(1 - \phi)\rho_p \qquad (15.69)$$

where $s_{t,w}$ = concentration of solids in the water column [g m^{-3}]
W_s = rate of mass loading of solid matter [g yr^{-1}]
v_w = settling velocity of solids [m yr^{-1}]
v_r = resuspension velocity of solids from the sediments to the overlying waters [m yr^{-1}]
A_m = surface area of the mixed sediment layer (i.e., the area of the deposition zone)
ϕ = porosity of the sediments
ρ_p = density of solids [g m^{-3}]

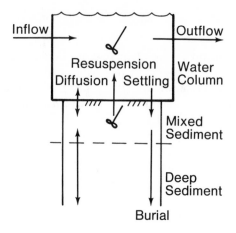

Figure 15.9   Three zone idealization of a lake.

At steady state, Equation 15.69 can be solved for

$$s_{t,w} = \frac{W_s + v_r A_m (1 - \phi)\rho_p}{Q + v_w A_w} \qquad (15.70)$$

For the mixed sediment layer, the balance is

$$V_{t,m}\rho_p \frac{d(1 - \phi)}{dt} = v_w A_w s_{t,w} - (v_r + v_b)A_m(1 - \phi)\rho_p \qquad (15.71)$$

where v_b = burial velocity [m yr^{-1}].

At steady state, Equation 15.71 can be solved in two ways. If the resuspension velocity is known, it can be used to estimate the burial velocity as in

$$v_b = \frac{v_w A_w s_{t,w}}{A_m (1 - \phi)\rho_p} - v_r \qquad (15.72)$$

Alternatively, if the burial velocity is known, Equations 15.70 and 15.71 can be combined and solved for the resuspension velocity:

$$v_r = \frac{v_w W_s A_w / A_m - v_b(Q + v_w A_w)(1 - \phi)\rho_p}{Q(1 - \phi)\rho_p} \qquad (15.73)$$

Note that in the above budget the solids are strictly allochthonous, i.e., they originate outside the lake. Methods of including autochthonous solids in such schemes have been discussed in previous sections. Limiting the analysis to the allochthonous case does not modify the general conclusions drawn in the present exercise.

Mass balances for contaminant in the three zones (Figure 15.9) can be written as:

1. water column:

$$V_{t,w}\frac{dc_{t,w}}{dt} = W_c(t) - Qc_{t,w} - F_{pw}v_wA_wc_{t,w} - k_wV_{t,w}c_{t,w}$$

$$+ \frac{\phi D_s A_m}{z_b'}(F_{dp}c_{t,m} - F_{dw}c_{t,w}) + v_rA_mc_{t,m} \qquad (15.74)$$

2. mixed sediment:

$$V_{t,m}\frac{dc_{t,m}}{dt} = F_{pw}v_wA_wc_{t,w} + \frac{\phi D_s A_m}{z_b'}(F_{dw}c_{t,w} - F_{dp}c_{t,m}) - v_rA_mc_{t,m}$$

$$- v_bA_mc_{t,m} - k_mV_mc_{t,m} + \phi F_{dp}D_sA_m\frac{dc_{t,s}}{dz} \ (@z_s = 0)\ (15.75)$$

3. deep sediment:

$$\frac{\partial c_{t,s}}{\partial t} = \phi F_{dp}D_s\frac{\partial^2 c_{t,s}}{\partial z^2} - v_b\frac{\partial c_{t,s}}{\partial z} - k_sc_{t,s} \qquad (15.76)$$

where $c_{t,w}, c_{t,m}, c_{t,s}$ = concentrations of contaminant in the water, the mixed sediment and the deep sediments, respectively [$\mu g\ m^{-3}$]

W_c = rate of mass loading of contaminant [$\mu g\ yr^{-1}$]
k = first-order decay rate for the contaminant [yr^{-1}]
D_s = diffusion rate for the contaminant in the sediment pore water [$m^2\ yr^{-1}$]
z_b' = $(z_b + z_m)/2$ = thickness defining the gradient between the mixed sediment layer and the overlying water [m]

In addition, the following quantities are also defined to specify the partitioning of contaminant between particulate and dissolved forms,

$$F_{pw} = \frac{K_{d,w}s_{t,w}}{1 + K_{d,w}s_{t,w}} \qquad (15.77)$$

$$F_{dw} = 1 - F_{pw} = \frac{1}{1 + K_{d,w}s_{t,w}} \qquad (15.78)$$

$$F_{dp} = \frac{1}{\phi + (1-\phi)\rho_p K_{d,s}} \qquad (15.79)$$

where $K_{d,w}, K_{d,s}$ = partition coefficients in the water and sediments, respectively $[m^3 \, g^{-1}]$

F_{pw} = fraction of contaminant in particulate form in the water column

F_{dw} = dissolved fraction in the water column

F_{dp} = fraction dissolved in the pore water

Note that it is assumed that $K_{d,m} = K_{d,s}$; therefore Equation 15.79 holds for both the mixed and the deep sediments.

At steady state, Equation 15.76 can be solved for

$$c_s = B_1 \exp(\lambda_1 z) + B_2 \exp(\lambda_2 z) \tag{15.80}$$

where

$$\lambda_1 = \frac{v_b}{2\phi D_s F_{dp}} \left[1 + \sqrt{1 + \frac{4\phi F_{dp} D_s k_s}{v_b^2}} \, \right] \tag{15.81}$$

$$\lambda_2 = \frac{v_b}{2\phi D_s F_{dp}} \left[1 - \sqrt{1 + \frac{4\phi F_{dp} D_s k_s}{v_b^2}} \, \right] \tag{15.82}$$

and B_1 and B_2 are arbitrary constants that can be evaluated via boundary conditions. For example, as z_s approaches infinity, dc_s/dz would approach zero and therefore $B_1 = 0$ and Equation 15.80 becomes

$$c_s = B_2 \exp(\lambda_2 z) \tag{15.83}$$

An additional boundary condition is that concentration be continuous at the interface between the mixed and deep sediments. Therefore, $B_2 = c_{t,m}$ and

$$c_{t,s} = c_{t,m} \exp(\lambda_2 z) \tag{15.84}$$

Equation 15.84 can now be substituted into Equation 15.75, which can be solved at steady state for

$$c_{t,m} = \frac{F_{dw}}{F_{dp}} R_{df} c_{t,w} \tag{15.85}$$

where R_{df} is a diffusive feedback ratio, i.e., the ratio of contaminant concentration in the pore water to that dissolved in the water column where

$$R_{df} = \frac{\phi(D_s/z_b') + K_{d,w} s_{t,w} v_w (A_w/A_m)}{\phi(D_s/z_b') + s_{t,w} v_w (A_w/A_m)\{K_{d,s} + \phi/[(1-\phi)\rho_p]\} + (k_m z_m/F_{dp}) - \phi D_s \lambda_2} \tag{15.86}$$

Equation 15.85 can be substituted into Equation 15.74, which can be solved for

$$c_{t,w} = \frac{W_c}{Q + k_w V_{t,w} + v_a A_w} \tag{15.87}$$

where v_a is defined as

$$v_a = F_{pw} v_w + \phi \frac{D_s}{z_b'} \frac{A_m}{A_w} F_{dw}(1 - R_{df}) - v_r \frac{A_m}{A_w} \frac{F_{dw}}{F_{dp}} R_{df} \tag{15.88}$$

Equation 15.87 can be used in conjunction with Equations 15.84 and 15.85 to compute contaminant concentration in the three zones depicted in Figure 15.9. In essence, Equation 15.87 is a toxicant loading model that is directly comparable to the steady-state phosphorus loading model derived previously (Equation 15.64), except that it accounts for decay and includes feedback effects in the apparent settling velocity (Equation 15.88). The model can be used to compute steady-state contaminant levels in a lake. However, a number of additional parameter groups can be developed to gain insight into lake contaminant dynamics.

Parameter Groups. As described previously, parameter groups, such as the retention coefficient, have proven useful in eutrophication management. A number of groups that are derived from the present analysis are summarized in Table 15.7.

Diffusive Feedback Ratio. The parameter group R_{df} (Equation 15.86) provides a measure of the magnitude of the diffusive transport between the sediments and the overlying waters. If $R_{df} = 1$, the dissolved concentration in the sediments and the water column would be equivalent and no diffusive transport would occur. For $R_{df} > 1$, the gradient would be out of the sediments and feedback would occur. For $R_{df} < 1$, the gradient would be into the sediments and penetration or intrusion would result. It is interesting to note that for the case where $K_{d,w} = K_{d,m} = K_{d,s}$, Equation 15.86 indicates that $R_{df} \geq 1$ (since λ_2 is always ≤ 0). This leads to the general conclusion that for the steady-state case, diffusive sediment feedback can only occur if $K_{d,w} > K_{d,m}$.

Apparent Settling Velocity. The apparent settling velocity was originally proposed (Chapra 1975) to parameterize the net loss of total phosphorus to a lake's sediments on an annual basis. It was empirically derived from whole-lake phosphorus budget data and was called "apparent" since it represented the net effect of the various processes affecting sediment-water interactions. The present approach differs in that it relates the apparent settling velocity to measurable quantities. As in

Table 15.7 Parameter Groups Used to Quantify Sediment-Water Interactions and Assimilative Capacity for Steady-State Model (Chapra 1982)

Description	Interpretation	Symbol	Formula
Diffusive feedback ratio: ratio of contaminant concentration in pore water to dissolved concentration in the water column; provides a measure of diffusive transport of contaminant between the sediments and the overlying waters	$R_{df} < 1.0$: diffusive penetration $R_{df} = 1.0$: no diffusive transport $R_{df} > 1.0$: diffusive feedback	$R_{df} =$	$\dfrac{\phi \dfrac{D_s}{z_b'} + K_{d,w} S_{t,w} v_w \dfrac{A_w}{A_m}}{\phi \dfrac{D_s}{z_b'} + s_{t,w} v_w \dfrac{A_w}{A_m}\left\| K_{d,s} + \dfrac{\phi}{(1-\phi)\rho_p} \right\| + \dfrac{k_m z_m}{F_{dp}} - \phi D_s \lambda_2}$
Apparent settling velocity: provides a measure of the net transfer rate of contaminants from the water to the sediments via the integrated effect of settling, diffusion and resuspension	$v_a = 0.0$: no net sedimentation loss $v_a = F_{pw} v_w$: maximum sedimentation loss	$v_a =$	$F_{pw} v_w + \phi \dfrac{D_s}{z_b'} \dfrac{A_m}{A_w} F_{dw}(1 - R_{df}) - v_r \dfrac{A_m}{A_w} \dfrac{F_{dw}}{F_{dp}} R_{df}$
Retention coefficient: provides a measure of the fraction of the external loading that is retained within the lake; includes burial and decay losses	$R_p = 0.0$: no retention of contaminant $R_p = 1.0$: total retention	$R_p =$	$\dfrac{v_a + k_w z_w}{q_s + v_a + k_w z_w}$
Attenuation coefficient: ratio of contaminant in the water column to the concentration of the loading; provides a measure of the decrease in contaminant due to the net effect of the lake's removal process	$R_i = 0.0$: water column concentration equals zero $R_i = 1.0$: water column concentration equivalent to concentration of loading; no removal	$R_i =$	$1 - R_p = \dfrac{q_s}{q_s + v_a + k_w z_w}$
Assimilation factor: ratio of loading of contaminant into the lake to water column concentration	$\P_c = \infty$: complete assimilation $\P_c = Q$: minimal assimilation	$\P_c =$	$Q + v_a A_w + k_w V_{t,w}$
Internal loading ratio: ratio of sediment feedback to loading; provides a comparison of internal to external loadings of contaminant to the water column; internal loads are defined as feedback due to resuspension and diffusive transport across the sediment-water interface	$R_{iw} < 0.0$: penetration $R_{iw} = 0.0$: no feedback $R_{iw} < 1.0$: feedback < loading $R_{iw} > 1.0$: feedback > loading	$R_{iw} =$	$\dfrac{v_r A_m \dfrac{F_{dw}}{F_{dp}} R_{df} + \phi \dfrac{D_s A_m}{z_b'} F_{dw}(R_{df} - 1)}{Q + F_{pw} v_w A_w + k_w V_{t,w} - \phi \dfrac{D_s A_m}{z_b'} F_{dw}(R_{df} - 1) - v_r A_m \dfrac{F_{dw}}{F_{dp}} R_{df}}$

Equation 15.88, v_a is a composite of the processes of sedimentation, diffusion and resuspension.

If v_a were equal to zero, it would indicate that net transfer to the sediments is nonexistent. This could result from the individual transfer processes being small, as would be the case for substances that sorb weakly to particles. Alternatively, the processes could be large but cancel each other. For example, a lake where large resuspension balanced the sedimentation of strongly sorbed substances would result in a net apparent settling velocity approaching zero.

At high values, v_a approaches the product of the particle settling velocity, v_w, and the fraction of contaminant in particulate form in the water column, F_{pw}. Thus, at the limit (high $K_{d,w} = K_{d,m} = K_{d,s}$ and no resuspension) the toxicant would associate overwhelmingly with particles and settle accordingly.

Retention and Attenuation Coefficients and the Assimilation Factor. As described earlier, retention and attenuation coefficients grew out of phosphorus budget modeling. The assimilation factor was introduced in Equation 10.15.

Versions for the contaminant model are presented in Table 15.7 with the major modification again being the inclusion of first-order decay and a mechanistic apparent settling velocity. As with phosphorus modeling, their interpretation is the same. For example, high values of R_p (i.e., approaching 1) indicate that a large fraction of the load is trapped, whereas low R_p signifies that little of the contaminant is retained within the lake. However, it should be noted that for the contaminant, retention includes the first-order decay as well as trapping losses.

Internal Loading Ratio. The internal loading ratio is a dimensionless number that represents the ratio of internal to external loadings to a lake's water column. Internal loadings are defined as feedback due to resuspension and diffusive transport across the sediment-water interface. This parameter group is particularly interesting, since it provide a criterion for judging where sediment feedback must be considered or may be neglected. This would be particularly useful when developing estimates of the temporal response of lakes to changes in contaminant loadings. As discussed in Sections 11.2.3 and 13.3.1, analytical solutions for the dynamics of coupled systems consist of a pair of exponentials. Consequently, they cannot be solved explicitly for response time as is possible for single isolated segments (pp. 42–44). If we can neglect feedback (say for lakes where feedback is less than 10% of the external loading, $R_{fw} < 0.10$), the t_{90} for the contaminant can be approximated as (using Equation 11.58)

$$t_{90} \cong \frac{2.3}{(Q/V_{t,w}) + (F_{pw}V_w/z_w) + k_w} \tag{15.89}$$

For cases with significant feedback ($R_{fw} > 0.10$), the coupled response would have to be computed numerically as in Example 13.20.

Use of the Model for Screening Purposes. Simple bivariate plots have proven extremely useful in lake eutrophication management (Vollenweider 1968, 1975, 1976). These plots are generally based on an assimilation coefficient as in Equation 15.65. Since a relationship of similar form has been developed for toxicants, it would seem reasonable to use this model as the basis of a loading plot. Although this can be done, the introduction of contaminant-specific processes such as sorption and decay complicates the task. Therefore, for most evaluations the equations in Table 15.7 should be used directly as described below.

§ § §

Example 15.8. The Great Lakes are an ideal setting to demonstrate the model's use for screening purposes. As summarized in Table 15.8, the lakes have a broad range of physical characteristics from the deep, slow-flushing Lake Superior to the shallower, fast-flushing Lake Erie. In addition to morphologic and hydrologic characteristics, the lakes also have distinct sedimentation regimes. In particular, Lake Erie differs from the other lakes in having a large sediment load and sedimentation rate as well as being the only deep-water (i.e., excluding near-shore areas and embayments) region where sediment resuspension is substantial.

Nine contaminants of varying sorption and decay characteristics were chosen for the screening analysis. As ordered in Table 15.9, the contaminants range from substances that would be expected to have a short half-life in the water column (i.e., high sorption and decay rates) to those that would be expected to persist for long periods. A hypothetical contaminant that associates overwhelmingly with the solid phase (labeled "Strong Sorber" in the tables) is included for comparative purposes.

The screening procedure consists of computing values of the parameter groups for each contaminant in each lake. The results, displayed in Tables 15.10 through 15.13, can then be interpreted to determine which of the contaminants would have the greatest effect on which of the lakes.

Diffusive Feedback Ratio. Table 15.10 shows the diffusive feedback ratio, R_{df}, which indicates the importance of diffusive transport between the sediments and the water column. Both the "strong sorber" and chloride have $R_{df} = 1$, which indicates no diffusive transport (i.e., pore

Table 15.8 Physical Parameters for the Great Lakes

	Superior	Michigan[a]	Huron[b]	Ontario	Erie
Surface Area					
Water Column, A_w (10^6 m²)	82,100	53,537	43,806	18,960	25,212
Deposition Zone, A_m (10^6 m²)	38,600	18,200	18,500	10,400	17,150
Mean Depth, z_w (m)	145	90	66	86	18.6
Mixed Sediment Thickness, z_m (10^{-2} m)	1	2	2	3	5
Volume					
Water Column, $V_{t,w}$ (10^9 m³)	11,905	4,818	2,891	1,631	469
Mixed Layer, $V_{t,m}$ (10^9 m³)	0.386	0.364	0.370	0.312	0.858
Solids Loading, W_s (10^{12} g yr⁻¹)	6.1	3.8	4.7	5.3	18.7
Resuspension Velocity, v_r (10^{-3} m yr⁻¹)	0	0	0	0	7.2
Outflow, Q (10^9 m³ yr⁻¹)	67	60	161	212	182
Suspended Solids Concentration (Equation 15.70), $s_{t,w}$ (g m⁻³)	0.81	0.77	1.15	2.73	20.0
Burial Velocity (Equation 15.72), v_b (10^{-3} m yr⁻¹)	0.63	0.83	0.98	1.8	3.5
Sedimentation Flux, J_b (g m⁻² yr⁻¹)	158	208	245	450	875
Residence Time, τ_w (yr)	178	80	18	7.7	2.6

[a] Excluding Green Bay.
[b] Excluding Saginaw and Georgian Bays.

Table 15.9   Contaminant Parameters for the Great Lakes

	Water Column Partition Coefficient, $K_{d,w}$ [m³ g⁻¹ (dimensionless)]	Sediment Partition Coefficient, $K_{d,m}, K_{d,s}$ [m³ g⁻¹ (dimensionless)]	Water Column Decay Rate, k_w [yr⁻¹]	Sediment Decay Rate, k_m, k_s [yr⁻¹]	Vaporization Coefficient, k_1 [m yr⁻¹]	Diffusion Rate, D_s [m² yr⁻¹ (cm² sec⁻¹)]
Strong Sorber	∞	∞	0	0	0	0.0128 (5×10^{-6})
^{210}Pb	10.0 (10^7)	10.0 (10^7)	0.0311	0.0311	0	0.0120 (4.7×10^{-6})
^{137}Cs	0.5 (5×10^5)	0.02 (2×10^4)	0.0231	0.0231	0	0.0309 (12.1×10^{-6})
^{239,240}Pu	0.5 (5×10^5)	0.02 (2×10^4)	1.73×10^{-5}	1.73×10^{-5}	0	0.0309 (12.1×10^{-6})
DDT	0.5 (5×10^5)	0.01 (1×10^4)	0.1	0.01	0	0.0128 (5×10^{-6})
PCB	0.01 (1×10^5)	0.01 (1×10^4)	0	0	2.5	0.0128 (5×10^{-6})
Dieldrin	3×10^{-3} (3000)	3×10^{-4} (300)	0.1	0.01	0	0.0128 (5×10^{-6})
^{90}Sr	2×10^{-4} (200)	2×10^{-4} (200)	0.0241	0.0241	0	0.0097 (3.8×10^{-6})
Chloride	0 (0)	0 (0)	0	0	0	0.0284 (4.1×10^{-6})

Table 15.10   Comparison of Diffusive Feedback Ratios, R_{df}, for Contaminants in the Great Lakes

	Superior	Michigan	Huron	Ontario	Erie
Strong Sorber	1.00	1.00	1.00	1.00	1.00
^{210}Pb	0.67	0.57	0.61	0.66	0.87
^{137}Cs	10.29	11.72	12.86	16.00	22.16
$^{239,240}Pu$	13.71	17.55	18.39	21.80	24.59
DDT	25.35	30.00	32.13	38.37	47.07
PCB	6.18	7.56	7.84	8.98	9.87
Dieldrin	1.27	1.52	1.63	2.47	6.66
^{90}Sr	0.90	0.85	0.86	0.83	0.87
Chloride	1.00	1.00	1.00	1.00	0.99

Table 15.11   Apparent Settling Velocities, v_a (m yr^{-1}), for Contaminants in the Great Lakes

	Superior	Michigan	Huron	Ontario	Erie
Strong Sorber	91.25	91.25	91.25	91.25	29.96
^{210}Pb	81.21	80.75	83.84	88.03	37.51
^{137}Cs	17.58	20.45	27.01	47.82	32.30
$^{239,240}Pu$	14.40	17.79	24.25	45.95	26.76
DDT	16.84	19.86	26.50	47.66	29.36
PCB	4.22	4.92	7.27	17.58	19.69
Dieldrin	0.08	0.07	0.10	0.28	1.43
^{90}Sr	0.06	0.04	0.06	0.09	0.17
Chloride	0.00	0.00	0.00	0.00	0.00

Table 15.12   Attenuation Coefficients, R_i, for Contaminants in the Great Lakes

	Superior	Michigan	Huron	Ontario	Erie
Strong Sorber	0.01	0.01	0.04	0.11	0.19
^{210}Pb	0.01	0.01	0.04	0.11	0.16
^{137}Cs	0.04	0.05	0.11	0.18	0.18
$^{239,240}Pu$	0.05	0.06	0.13	0.20	0.21
DDT	0.03	0.04	0.10	0.17	0.19
PCB	0.16	0.19	0.34	0.39	0.27
Dieldrin	0.05	0.11	0.35	0.56	0.69
^{90}Sr	0.19	0.34	0.69	0.84	0.92
Chloride	1.00	1.00	1.00	1.00	1.00

Table 15.13   Internal Loading Ratio, R_{fw}, for Contaminants
in the Great Lakes

	Superior	Michigan	Huron	Ontario	Erie
Strong Sorber	0.00	0.00	0.00	0.00	1.65
[210]Pb	−0.00	−0.00	−0.00	−0.00	1.18
[137]Cs	0.40	0.21	0.18	0.08	1.27
[239,240]Pu	0.78	0.40	0.31	0.12	1.65
DDT	0.29	0.18	0.18	0.07	1.39
PCB	0.52	0.26	0.18	0.07	1.53
Dieldrin	0.01	0.01	0.02	0.02	0.35
[90]Sr	−0.01	−0.01	−0.01	−0.00	0.02
Chloride	−0.00	−0.00	−0.00	−0.00	−0.00

water = dissolved concentration in the water column). Diffusive feedback is only important ($R_{df} > 1$) for those contaminants such as ^{137}Cs, [239,240]Pu and DDT, where sorption in the sediments ($K_{d,s}$) is significantly less than in the water column ($K_{d,w}$).

Apparent Settling Velocity. As in Table 15.11, v_a decreases with decreasing sorption, since less contaminant is associated with settling particulate matter. Note, however, that reduced sorption in the sediments for ^{137}Cs, [239,240]Pu and DDT tends to diminish this effect, since diffusion tends to reintroduce contaminant back into the water column and decrease the net settling velocity. Also note the pronounced effect of sediment resuspension on the apparent settling velocity of the "strong sorber" and ^{210}Pb for Lake Erie. This indicates that Lake Erie would be particularly sensitive to inputs of contaminants associated strongly with particulate matter.

Attenuation Coefficient. Table 15.12 contains results for R_i (which equals $1 - R_p$). This coefficient is particularly useful for screening purposes, since it reflects the diminution of loading due to in-lake cleansing processes. Thus, $R_i = 1$ indicates that the resulting in-lake concentration equals the loading concentration. This implies that in-lake cleansing is nonexistent, as would be the case for a conservative substance like chloride. At the other end of the spectrum are substances (such as the "strong sorber" and ^{210}Pb) that sorb strongly in both the water column and the sediments and have R_i's approaching zero. Such values indicate that self-cleansing would have a significant impact on ambient levels.

Internal Loading Ratio. In general, the highest levels of internal feedback are for sorbing substances in Lake Erie (Table 15.13). This is primarily due to resuspension. In addition, contaminants with $K_{d,w} > K_{d,s}$ (e.g., ^{137}Cs, $^{239,240}Pu$, DDT and PCB) have substantial diffusive feedback that results in significant internal loading for all the lakes.

On the basis of the above analysis, it can be concluded that of the five Great Lakes, Lake Erie is the most susceptible to toxic contamination because of sediment resuspension. In addition, weakly sorbing contaminants pose a threat because of the absence of sedimentation as a cleaning mechanism. The larger lakes with small outflows (Superior and Michigan) are particularly sensitive in this regard. Finally, contaminants that sorb strongly in the water and weakly in the sediments are also maintained at relatively high levels in the water column due to reintroduction through diffusive feedback.

§ § §

15.2.2 Models of Food Chain/Contaminant Interactions

In the previous section we decoupled the food chain from the system in Figure 15.5 to simplify the computation of particle/contaminant interactions. Now we will review models that calculate contaminant levels along the food chain as a function of prescribed concentrations in the water and in the organic particles.

This volume deals with the movement and distribution of matter along temporal, spatial and kinetic (or ecological) dimensions. Two basic approaches have been used to characterize changes in time and space: exact and approximate methods. The former treats the dimensions as continuous, whereas the latter divides them into discrete time steps or spatial compartments. In general, the continuous approaches were preferred because of their greater efficiency, i.e., they encompass more information for the effort. However, approximate approaches were useful because of their broader applicability.

In Chapter 14, we developed a discrete method for the kinetic dimension where ecological "space" was divided into groups or compartments of organisms. In the next section, we will discuss a continuous approach that is the analog of the compartmentalized food chain. Then, we will review attempts to develop long-term food chain/contaminant models based on a compartmentalized approach.

The Food Chain as a Continuum

A fundamental problem of simulating toxic substance dynamics in aquatic systems is that large numbers of differential equations are needed for their adequate characterization. This is because most conventional approaches divide ecological and spatial coordinates into numerous compartments for which individual differential equations are required. In addition, at least two sets of these equations (and more, if different forms of the contaminant are considered) are needed for the toxicant, as well as for some measure of the mass level of each compartment. For a system with m ecological and n spatial segments, the resulting set of $m \times n \times 2$ equations can often be expensive to solve and difficult to interpret.

Thomann (1978, 1979) has attempted to circumvent this problem by representing ecological space as a continuous rather than a compartmentalized dimension. By choosing organism length as the metric for this coordinate, a single differential equation can be used to characterize regions of the food chain with homogeneous source, sink and transfer characteristics. In essence, Thomann's continuous food chain is analogous to a nondispersive river model, where uptake of a toxicant is similar to waste sources uniformly distributed along the river bank; release is akin to losses such as settling to the stream bottom; and transfer up the food chain is analogous to the movement of matter downstream with the river's flow. In fact, since his equation is of the same mathematical form as a stream equation, the well developed theory and efficient solution techniques for such equations can also be applied. Along with additional equations for water and sediment concentration, a set of continuous food chain equations forms a framework for a simplified analysis of toxic substances in lakes.

To do this, Thomann had to choose a metric to mark location along the kinetic dimension. Although a number of parameters could be used for the purpose (organism mass, surface area, lipid content for certain lipophilic compounds, etc.), he chose length because of the ease with which organisms can be fractionated with filters and nets. He then defined a contaminant density function, Ψ, with units of contaminant concentration per organism length. This quantity represents contaminant concentration along the food chain continuum. Using the same approach as for the river model in Section 12.2.2, a balance can be taken around an element, ΔL, over a time period, Δt, as in

$$\Delta L \Delta \Psi = v_1 \Psi \Delta t - v_1 \left(\Psi + \frac{\partial \Psi}{\partial L} \Delta L \right) \Delta t \qquad (15.90)$$

where L = organism length [L]
           Ψ = contaminant density function $[ML^{-3}L^{-1}]$
           v_L = transfer velocity up the food chain $[LT^{-1}]$

Dividing by ΔL and Δt and taking the limit yields

$$\frac{\partial \Psi}{\partial t} = -v_L \frac{\partial \Psi}{\partial L} \qquad (15.91)$$

This advection equation indicates that if a molecule of contaminant were introduced at the lower end of the food chain, it would move along the kinetic dimension at a rate of v_L.

Of course, in a lake the situation is more complicated than in Equation 15.91. For one thing, this simple representation does not include interactions between the food chain and the water, i.e., it has no sources and sinks. In fact, for most substances, matter is exchanged through a number of uptake and release mechanisms as in

$$V\left(\frac{\partial \Psi}{\partial t} + v_L \frac{\partial \Psi}{\partial L} \right) = -Q(L)\Psi = K(L)V\Psi + k_u(L)m(L)Vc \qquad (15.92)$$

where $K(L)$ = excretion rate $(T^{-1}]$
$k_u(L)$ = uptake rate $(L^3 M^{-1} T^{-1}]$
$m(L)$ = mass density function $[M L^{-3} L^{-1}]$

(L) means that the parameter is a function of organism length. For example, $Q(L)$ represents the fact that some organisms (i.e., motile forms like fish) are not subject to flushing.

An accompanying equation for the water is

$$V\frac{dc}{dt} = W - Qc - \lambda Vc + V \int_{L_o}^{L_f} K(L)\Psi \, dL$$

$$\qquad (15.93)$$

$$- Vc \int_{L_i}^{L_f} K_u(L)m(L) \, dL$$

where λ = miscellaneous mechanisms, such as vaporization and photolysis, that break down contaminants in the water $[T^{-1}]$
L_o, L_f = the minimum and maximum lengths of the organisms [L]

Equations 15.91 and 15.92 represent a framework for relating input-output fluxes to contaminant levels along the food chain. Since the parameters may be complex functions of organism length, some simplifications are required to obtain analytical solutions. One method is to divide the food chain into regions of constant parameters. This is analogous to the exact solutions obtained previously by dividing a river-run lake into segments (Section 12.2.2). At steady state, a region of constant parameters is defined by

$$v_L \frac{d\Psi}{dL} + \alpha\Psi = k_u m\bar{c} \qquad (15.94)$$

and

$$\bar{c} = \frac{\overline{W} + V \int_{L_i}^{L_f} K\Psi\, dL}{Q + \lambda V + V \int_{L_0}^{L_f} k_u m\, dL} \qquad (15.95)$$

where

$$\alpha = \frac{Q}{V} + K \qquad (15.96)$$

Notice that Equation 15.95 is similar to the completely mixed model with first-order decay (Equation 11.16) with the exception that the loading term (the numerator) is supplemented by the integrated effect of food chain release. In addition, the assimilation factor (the denominator) is enhanced by the integrated effect of food chain uptake.

In order to solve these equations, a value for the biomass density function, m, must be developed. Thomann suggests the following formulation

$$m = m_0 \exp[-(b/v_L)L] \qquad (15.97)$$

where m_0 = biomass density function of the organisms at the lower end of the food chain region [M-organism $L^{-3} L^{-1}$]
   b = effective biomass respiration along the food chain [T^{-1}]

Equation 15.97 can be substituted into Equation 15.94, which can be solved for (recall Equation 11.41)

$$\Psi = \frac{k_u \bar{c} m_0}{\alpha - b} \{\exp[-(b/v_L)L] - \exp[-(\alpha/v_L)L]\} + \Psi_0 \exp[-(\alpha/v_L)L] \qquad (15.98)$$

where Ψ_0 is the contaminant density at the lower end of the food chain region.

Although Equation 15.98 provides a relationship to compute contaminant density, the mass-specific body burden for the organisms is more meaningful. This quantity, ν, refers to the mass of contaminant per mass of organism and can be derived by dividing Equation 15.98 by Equation 15.97 to yield

$$\nu = \frac{k_u \bar{c}}{\alpha - b}(1 - \exp\{-[(\alpha - b)/v_L]L\}) + \nu_0 \exp\{-[(\alpha - b)/v_L]L\} \qquad (15.99)$$

where

$$\nu_o = \frac{\Psi_o}{m_o} \qquad\qquad (15.100)$$

§ § §

Example 15.9. Assuming the concentration of PCB in Lake Ontario is 5 μg m^{-3}, use the data in Table 15.14 to compute the mass-specific body burden for the food chain. Lake Ontario's volume is 1634 km^3 and its outflow is 212 km^3 yr^{-1}. Assume that ν_o at L $= 10^2$ is zero. Equation 15.99 can be used to compute ν for each of the three regions. The results are given in Figure 15.10; specific values are listed in Table 15.15.

§ § §

While the continuous approach is elegant and provides theoretical insight into toxicant-food chain dynamics, the version in the preceding section has several limitations. The physical interpretation of the transfer velocity is unclear since it is a composite of feeding rates and efficiencies. In addition, the model computes food chain toxicant levels independently of the input-output fluxes for the contaminant. For example, a fixed contaminant concentration in the water is used to drive the food chain. Also, the computation deals solely with biota greater than 100 μm and does not consider smaller organisms and particles that are nonmotile and subject to flushing and sedimentation. Although these factors can be included in Thomann's framework, solutions become somewhat difficult as further detail is incorporated. In particular, time variable solutions become unwieldy. As in other parts of this volume, an approximate or compartmentalized approach offers increased flexibility.

Table 15.14 Coefficients Used in Analysis of PCB Data with Steady-State Size-Dependent Model

	Trophic Region		
	1	2	3
Coefficient	10^2–10^4 μm	10^4–2.5×10^5 μm	2.5×10^5–10^6 μm
Water Uptake, k_u (g l^{-1} day^{-1})$^{-1}$	0.5	0.38	0.23
Excretion, K (day^{-1})	0.05	0.0072	0.0025
Transfer Velocity, v_L (μm day^{-1})	12	190	728
Biomass Respiration, b(day^{-1})	0.01	0.0024	0.001
(K$'$ − b)/v_L (μm)$^{-1}$	3.0×10^{-3}	2.5×10^{-5}	2.0×10^{-6}
k_u/(K$'$ − b)(g l^{-1})$^{-1}$	13.4	79	158

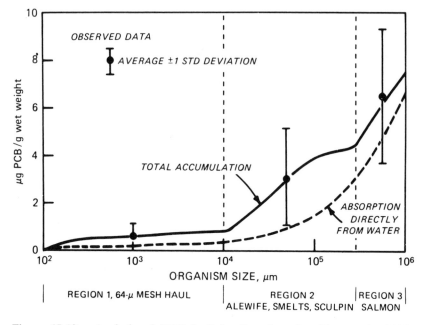

Figure 15.10 Analysis of PCB in Lake Ontario using Thomann's (1979) continuous food chain approach.

Table 15.15   Mass-Specific Body Burden of PCB for Lake Ontario as Computed with a Continuous Food Chain Model

L (μm)	ν [(μg PCB) g wet wt^{-1}]
10^2	0
3.16×10^2	0.446
10^3	0.657
3.16×10^3	0.681
10^4	0.681
3.16×10^4	2.600
10^5	3.991
2.5×10^5	4.346
10^6	7.499

The Compartmentalized Food Chain

A number of possible mathematical formulations characterize interactions among the elements of the food chain. As described in Chapter 14, fairly elaborate nonlinear models are typically used to simulate seasonal dynamics. However, for long-term computations, these seasonal models are costly to implement. One alternative is to integrate a seasonal model over the annual cycle in order to estimate transfer rates for a long-term food chain model. Hydroscience (1973) used such an approach to calibrate a linear, donor-dependent model for cadmium in western Lake Erie. A second alternative is to directly develop a long-term model based on seasonal predator-prey mathematics but using constant average annual rates. Thomann (1981) developed such a model to characterize mass and contaminant cycling for individual organisms in the food chain.

Thomann (1981) divides the motile food chain into three compartments (Figure 15.11). A mass balance equation for the wet weight of the average individual in the i-th compartment, w_i [g(w)], can be written as

$$\frac{dw_i}{dt} = (a_{i,i-1}C_{i,i-1} - r_i)w_i \qquad (15.101)$$

where $a_{i,i-1}$ = biomass assimilation efficiency, i.e., the amount of biomass of organism i that is generated by consuming a unit amount of biomass of organism $i-1$ [g(w) predator (g(w) prey)$^{-1}$]

$C_{i,i-1}$ = weight-specific consumption of organism i on $i-1$ [g(w) prey (g(w) predator)$^{-1}$ d^{-1}]

r_i = weight loss due to routine metabolism, swimming and other activities [d^{-1}]

Equation 15.101 is a homogeneous, linear, ordinary differential equation. If the coefficients are assumed to be constant for the average individual of a particular compartment, it is of the same form as Equation 11.17 and the following solution results

$$w_i = w_{oi} \exp(G_i t) \qquad (15.102)$$

where w_{oi} = initial weight [g(w)]

G_i = net growth rate of the organism [d^{-1}], representing the combined effect of growth due to grazing and weight loss due to activity where

$$G_i = \frac{dw_i/dt}{w_i} = a_{i,i-1}C_{i,i-1} - r_i \qquad (15.103)$$

Since we are dealing with growing organisms, G_i is positive and, as in Figure 15.12a, the organism's body weight increases exponentially.

Aside from the weight change of the organism, the major processes governing its contaminant concentration are: (1) direct uptake from the water, (2) excretion, and (3) consumption of contaminated food. These processes are incorporated in a general mass balance of the contaminant for the i-th compartment as in,

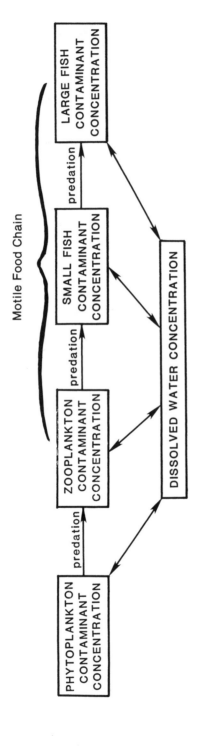

Figure 15.11   Schematic of Thomann's (1981) compartmentalized food chain.

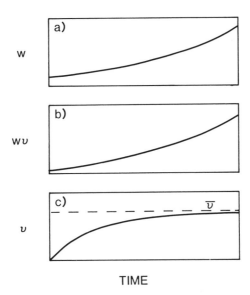

TIME

Figure 15.12   Illustration of dynamics of model equations for a) mass of organism (Equation 15.102), b) mass of contaminant per organism (Equation 15.106) and c) mass of contaminant per mass of organism (Equation 15.112). Redrawn from Thomann (1981).

$$\frac{d(w\nu)_i}{dt} = k_{ui}w_i c_{d,w} - K_i(w\nu)_i + \alpha_{i,i-1}C_{i,i-1}w_i\nu_{i-1} \qquad (15.104)$$

where ν_i = mass-specific contaminant concentration of the i-th compartment $[\mu g\ g(w)^{-1}]$

k_{ui} = uptake rate for the i-th compartment $[m^3\ d^{-1}\ g(w)^{-1}]$

K_i = excretion rate $[d^{-1}]$

$\alpha_{i,i-1}$ = chemical assimilation efficiency, i.e., the portion of the grazed contaminant that is incorporated into the body tissue of organism i $[\mu g$ contaminant absorbed $(\mu g$ contaminant ingested$)^{-1}]$

Equations 15.102 and 15.104 can be combined and rearranged to yield

$$\frac{d(w\nu)_i}{dt} + K_i(w\nu)_i = (k_{ui}c_{d,w} + \alpha_{i,i-1}C_{i,i-1}\nu_{i-1})w_{oi}\exp(G_i t)$$

$$(15.105)$$

For constant coefficients and constant contaminant sources (i.e., $\bar{c}_{d,w}$ and $\bar{\nu}_{i-1}$), Equation 15.105 is identical to the well mixed lake with exponentially increasing loading as discussed on pp. 35 and 36. The solution to Equation 15.105 is, therefore,

$$(w\nu)_i = \frac{k_{ui}\bar{c}_{d,w} + \alpha_{i,i-1}C_{i,i-1}\bar{\nu}_{i-1}}{K_i + G_i}[\exp(G_it) - \exp(-K_it)] + (w\nu)_{oi}\exp(-K_it)$$

$$(15.106)$$

where $(w\nu)_{oi}$ is the initial mass of contaminant in i $[\mu g]$. This solution, plotted in Figure 15.12b, indicates that the mass of contaminant per organism (called the average chemical whole body burden) increases exponentially with time.

Although these equations and solutions can be developed, we are more interested in predicting the mass-specific concentration of the organism. This can be done by returning to Equation 15.104. Note that since both ν_i and w_i change in time (Figure 15.12a and b), the accumulation term must be represented as

$$\frac{d(w\nu)_i}{dt} = w_i\frac{d\nu_i}{dt} + \nu_i\frac{dw_i}{dt}$$

$$(15.107)$$

This differs from previous cases in this book, where one of the variables being differentiated could be assumed constant and, therefore, treated as a parameter. Such was the case for the mass balance around the well mixed lake in Chapter 11 where we implicitly assumed that lake volume was approximately constant over the simulation period and accumulation could be represented as

$$\frac{d(Vc)}{dt} = V\frac{dc}{dt} + c\cancel{\frac{dV}{dt}}^{0} = V\frac{dc}{dt}$$

$$(15.108)$$

since if V is constant, $dV/dt = 0$.

When modeling a growing organism, this simplification cannot be made and both differentials must be maintained. However, Equation 15.101 provides a means to express the differential for weight in terms of variables and parameters. Therefore, Equations 15.101, 15.104, and 15.108 are combined to give

$$w_i\frac{d\nu_i}{dt} + \nu_i(a_{i,i-1}C_{i,i-1} - r_i)w_i = k_{ui}w_ic_{d,w} - K_iw_i\nu_i$$

$$(15.109)$$

$$+ \alpha_{i,i-1}C_{i,i-1}w_i\nu_{i-1}$$

which can be rearranged to yield a differential equation for mass-specific contaminant concentration

$$\frac{d\nu_i}{dt} + K_i'\nu_i = k_{ui}c_{d,w} + \alpha_{i,i-1}C_{i,i-1}\nu_{i-1}$$

$$(15.110)$$

where K_i' can be thought of as a bulk rate that accounts for decrease in mass-specific concentration due to both excretion and the weight gain of the organism as it grows [d^{-1}] where

$$K_i' = K_i + G_i = K_i + a_{i,i-1}C_{i,i-1} - r_i \qquad (15.111)$$

Equation 15.110 is an ordinary differential equation that is directly analogous to the completely mixed lake model with step input described on p. 32. The solution is

$$\nu_i = \frac{k_{ui}\bar{c}_{d,w} + \alpha_{i,i-1}C_{i,i-1}\bar{\nu}_{i-1}}{K_i'}[1 - \exp(-K_i't)] + \nu_{oi}\exp(-K_i't) \qquad (15.112)$$

In contrast to Equations 15.102 and 15.106, Equation 15.112 does not increase exponentially but levels off to a constant value as in Figure 15.12c. A 90% response time (p. 43) can be used to estimate the time required to reach this constant level,

$$t_{90} = \frac{2.3}{K_i'} \qquad (15.113)$$

Using Thomann's data, the response times for the contaminants in his study can be calculated and listed in Table 15.16. If the age-class represented by the compartment is greater than t_{90}, then Equation 15.112 can be approximated by the steady state value

$$\bar{\nu}_i = \frac{k_{ui}\bar{c}_{d,w} + \alpha_{i,i-1}C_{i,i-1}\bar{\nu}_{i-1}}{K_i'} \qquad (15.114)$$

Notice that the mass-specific concentration is composed of the summation of two components due to direct uptake and to grazing gains as in

$$\bar{\nu}_i = \frac{k_{ui}}{K_i'}\bar{c}_{d,w} + \frac{\alpha_{i,i-1}C_{i,i-1}}{K_i'}\bar{\nu}_{i-1} \qquad (15.115)$$

Application of this equation to the zooplankton compartment (i = 2) yields

$$\bar{\nu}_2 = \frac{k_{u2}}{K_2'}\bar{c}_{d,w} + \frac{\alpha_{2,1}C_{2,1}}{K_2'}\bar{\nu}_1 \qquad (15.116)$$

Thus, the zooplankton mass-specific concentration is a linear function of the dissolved concentration, $\bar{c}_{d,w}$ and the phytoplankton concentration, $\bar{\nu}_1$.

Table 15.16   90% Response for Steady State of Mass-
Specific Contaminant Concentration for Contaminants and
Compartments Modeled by Thomann (1981)

Food Chain Compartment	^{239}Pu	^{137}Cs	PCB	
			K = 0	K ≠ 0
Zooplankton	0.11	0.16	0.70	0.33
Small Fish	0.25	0.80	1.29	0.71
Large Fish	0.54	1.80	3.71	2.33

Equation 15.116 can be divided by $\bar{c}_{d,w}$ and rewritten as

$$N_2 = N_{2w} + \frac{\alpha_{2,1}C_{2,1}}{K_2'}N_{1w} \tag{15.117}$$

where N_2 is called a concentration factor representing the mass-specific concentration normalized to dissolved concentration as in

$$N_2 = \bar{\nu}_2/\bar{c}_{d,w} \tag{15.118}$$

and N_{iw} is the concentration factor due solely to direct uptake. Notice that for phytoplankton

$$N_1 = N_{1w} = k_{ul}/K_1 \tag{15.119}$$

since these organisms do not receive contaminant by grazing, whereas for the zooplankton

$$N_2 \neq N_{2w} = k_{u2}/K_2' \tag{15.120}$$

Similar equations can be developed for the other compartments of the food chain. For example, the small fish can be represented as

$$\bar{\nu}_3 = N_{3w} + \frac{\alpha_{3,2}C_{3,2}}{K_3'}N_{2w} + \frac{\alpha_{3,2}C_{3,2}}{K_3'}\frac{\alpha_{2,1}C_{2,1}}{K_2'}N_{1w} \tag{15.121}$$

An equation could also be written for the large fish that would have four terms. A generalized relationship can be expressed as

$$N_n = N_{nw} + \sum_{j=1}^{n-1}\left(\prod_{i=j+1}^{n}f_{i,i-1}\right)N_{jw} \tag{15.122}$$

where $f_{i,i-1}$ is called a food chain transfer number which represents the potential relative increase or decrease in the concentration factor due to feeding on contaminated prey where

$$f_{i,i-1} = \frac{\alpha_{i,i-1} C_{i,i-1}}{K_i'} \qquad (15.123)$$

The quantity $\Pi f_{i,i-1}$ is called the food chain multiplier. It is designated by the symbol Γ and represents the accumulated effect of transfer through the prior levels of the food chain. As a further simplification, Thomann assumes that for a given contaminant $f_{i,i-1}$ is constant across the food chain and Equation 15.122 can be reexpressed as

$$N_n = N_{nw} + \sum_{j=1}^{n-1} f^{n-j} N_{jw} \qquad (15.124)$$

and the food chain multiplier is

$$\Gamma = f^{n-j} \qquad (15.125)$$

where $n - j$ is the number of levels in the food chain below the level under consideration.

It can be shown that a food chain transfer number greater than one coupled with several passes through lower levels of the food chain will result in magnification of the contaminant concentration in the large fish. Conversely, for transfer numbers less than one, the concentration of the top predators becomes independent of that of the lower levels and is solely a function of direct uptake from the water.

§ § §

Example 15.10. Thomann (1981) applied his model to calculate concentration factors for three contaminants: PCB, ^{137}Cs and ^{239}Pu. Using the data in Table 15.17, compute concentration factors for PCB.

For the zooplankton, Equation 15.111 yields

$$K_2' = 0 + 0.8(0.105) - 0.075 = 0.009 \, \text{d}^{-1}$$

Direct concentration from the water is computed using Equation 15.120

$$N_{2w} = \frac{753 \times 10^{-6}}{0.009} = 0.0837 = 10^{-1.077} \frac{\mu\text{g g(w)}^{-1}}{\mu\text{g m}^{-3}}$$

Table 15.17   Parameters Used by Thomann (1981) to Model
Bioconcentration of PCB for the Case Where Clearance of
PCB is Zero (i.e., K = 0)

Parameter	Phytoplankton	Zooplankton	Small Fish	Large Fish
Weight Loss Rate, r (d^{-1})		0.075	0.0087	0.0055
Food Conversion Efficiency, a (g(w) pred [g(w) prey]$^{-1}$)		0.8	0.8	0.8
Food Consumption, c (g(w) prey [g(w) pred d]$^{-1}$)		0.105	0.017	0.009
Ratio of Wet to Dry Weight, β (g(w) [g(d)]$^{-1}$)	10	5	4	4
Uptake Rate, k_u (10^{-6} m^3 [g(w) d]$^{-1}$)		753	86	55
Excretion Rate, K (d^{-1})		0	0	0
Assimilation Efficiency, α (μg $(\mu$g$)^{-1}$)		0.9	0.9	0.9
Bioconcentration from Water Only, N_{iw} (μg g(w)$^{-1}$ [μg m^{-3}]$^{-1}$)[a]	$10^{-1.5}$	$10^{-1.08}$	$10^{-1.76}$	$10^{-1.49}$
Bulk Loss Rate, K' (d^{-1})		0.009	0.0049	0.0017
Food Chain Transfer Number, f		10.5	3.12	4.65

[a]Multiply by 10^6 to obtain dimensionless form.

The food chain transfer number for the zooplankton (Equation 15.123) is

$$f_{21} = \frac{0.9(0.105)}{0.009} = 10.5$$

Consequently, since $f > 1$, we would expect some biomagnification. This can be verified by using Equation 15.117 and 15.123 to compute

$$N_2 = 10^{-1.077} + 10.5(10^{-1.5})$$

$$N_2 = 10^{-1.077} + 10^{-0.479} = 10^{-0.381}$$

or in dimensionless form $N_2 = 10^{5.62}$. Therefore, there is approximately an order-of-magnitude increase from the phytoplankton to the zooplankton.

The computation can be continued for the small and large fish with resulting dimensionless concentration factors of $10^{6.12}$ and $10^{6.80}$, respectively. These increases would be anticipated on the basis of computed f values of 3.12 and 4.76 for these organisms (see Table 15.16).

The results along with computations for other contaminants are presented in Figure 15.13. Whereas PCB indicates biomagnification, ^{137}Cs is relatively constant and ^{239}Pu decreases. Thomann (1981) includes data

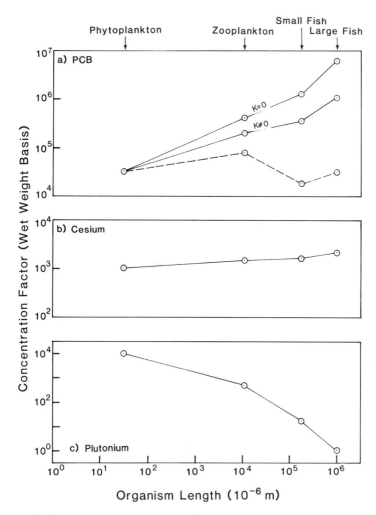

Figure 15.13   Dimensionless wet weight concentration factors for a) PCB, b) cesium (fresh water) and c) plutonium as calculated using Thomann's (1981) compartmentalized food chain/contaminant model. The PCB plot shows calculations for cases with and without excretion (K) as well as the concentration factor in the absence of food chain transfer (the dashed line). The difference between the dashed and the solid lines suggests the importance of food chain transfer as a mechanism for biomagnification of PCB in the environment.

verifying that these trends are approximately correct. The PCB plot also includes the computation for the case where food chain transfer is assumed to be nonexistent. This case does not fit existing data. On the basis of this result, Thomann suggests that laboratory-derived concentration factors based solely on water uptake could be inadequate for environmental prediction. For substances such as PCB, food chain magnification must be included for an adequate representation.

§ § §

Thomann's model is particularly important in that it represents a framework for incorporating laboratory and field data into predictions of contaminant behavior in the environment. In the next section, it will be combined with an input-output model in order to relate large fish contamination to toxic substance loadings.

15.2.3 Incorporating Food Chain/Contaminant Interactions into Input-Output Models

There are a variety of options for combining food chain interactions with contaminant input-output models. First, the nutrient/food chain models described in Chapter 14 can be expanded to include higher organisms and contaminants. Although this is possible, it would not be a viable option for most engineering work because, among other things, the seasonal resolution of the nutrient/food chain models is not consistent with the long-term time frame of the toxic substance issue.

A second option is to use a contaminant budget model to predict the mean annual dissolved concentration of the toxic substance. Then, if an estimate of the environmental concentration factor is available, it can be used to compute contaminant levels in the higher organisms. Values of N can either be obtained by measurements or from models and experimental results as explained in the previous section.

The contaminant budget model could include sediment-water interactions as in Equation 15.74 or could be of the simplified form of Equation 15.53. For the latter case, the steady state solution for total contaminant concentration in the water would be

$$c_{t,w} = \frac{W_c}{Q + k_{t,w}V_{t,w} + v_pF_{pw}A_w} \tag{15.126}$$

which can be used to compute dissolved concentration by

$$c_{d,w} = F_{dw}c_{t,w} \tag{15.127}$$

which in turn can be used to compute

$$\nu_4 = N_4 c_{d,w} \tag{15.128}$$

or combining the above

$$\nu_4 = \frac{W_c}{\P_4} \tag{15.129}$$

where $\P_4$ is an assimilation factor (recall p. 11) for large fish body burden $\mu g\,yr^{-1}\,[\mu g\,g(w)^{-1}]^{-1}$ where

$$\P_4 = \frac{Q + k_{t,w}V_{t,w} + v_p F_{pw}A_w}{N_4 F_{dw}} \tag{15.130}$$

Equation 15.129 provides a framework for predicting contaminant body burden in large fish as a function of external loadings. Conversely, it can be rearranged to compute the loading required to meet a prescribed standard as in

$$W_c = \P_4 \nu_4 \tag{15.131}$$

In addition to the above steady state estimates, time variable solutions for large fish body burden can be computed by merely integrating Equation 15.53 or 15.56 (or the comparable equations with sediment-water interactions from Chapter 13) and multiplying the result by $F_{dw}N_4$.

§ § §

Example 15.11. (a) Use the results of Example 15.7 along with estimates of F_{dw} and N_4 to compute trends of PCB in large fish for Lake Michigan, and (b) determine the loading rate required to maintain a standard of 2 $\mu g\,g(w)^{-1}$ for large fish.
   (a) Values of N_4 and F_{dw} for Lake Michigan PCB (K = 0) are

$$N_4 = 10^{0.779}\,\mu g\,g(w)^{-1}\,(\mu g\,m^{-3})^{-1}$$

$$F_{dw} = 1/[1 + 1(0.1)] = 0.9091$$

Therefore, to determine ν_4, the results in Table 15.6 for $c_{t,w}$ can be multiplied by $0.9091\,(10^{0.779}) = 5.46$. For example, the peak value in 1970 would be

$$\nu_4(1970) = 5.46(9.93) = 54.3\,\mu g\,g(w)^{-1}$$

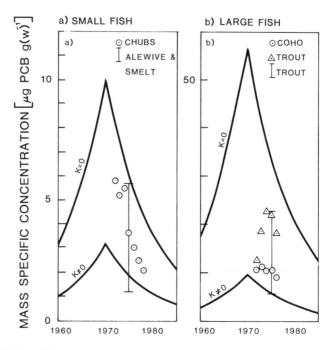

Figure 15.14   Simulated and measured values for PCB in small and large fish in Lake Michigan.

The computation can be performed for the other years and the results plotted in Figure 15.14b. In addition, computations were also performed for the case where $K \neq 0$ and plotted on Figure 15.14b along with data. The results indicate that the model provides a valid order of magnitude estimate for ν_4.

The computation was also repeated for small fish. The results (Figure 15.14a) also indicate consistency with available data.

(b) The large fish assimilation factor for PCB ($K = 0$) in Lake Michigan is (Equation 15.130 and Tables 15.3–15.5)

$$\P_4 = \frac{7.12 \times 10^{10} + 0 + 84(0.0909)5.78 \times 10^{10}}{5.46} = 9.39 \times 10^{10} \frac{\mu g \ yr^{-1}}{\mu g \ g(w)^{-1}}$$

Therefore, to maintain a level of $2 \ \mu g \ g(w)^{-1}$ the appropriate loading can be computed as

$$W_c = 9.39 \times 10^{10}(2) = 1.9 \times 10^{11} \ \mu g \ yr^{-1}$$

For the case where $K \neq 0$, $N_4 = 10^{0.027}$ and the computation can be repeated to yield

$$\P_4 = 5.30 \times 10^{11} \frac{\mu g \ yr^{-1}}{\mu g \ g(w)^{-1}}$$

and

$$W_c = 1.1 \times 10^{12} \ \mu g \ yr^{-1}$$

Therefore, the loadings vary by a factor of 6.

§ § §

15.2.4 General Comments

The material in this section is certainly not intended as a comprehensive review of the burgeoning literature related to toxic substance modeling of natural waters. We have deliberately limited ourselves to those contributions that we feel are consistent with our defined engineering approach and which could have immediate utility for lake water quality management. In so doing we have neglected excellent work that will likely affect the development of a toxicant loading concept. Noteworthy among these are the models of Mackay (1977, 1982) and the EPA Environmental Research Laboratory, Athens, Georgia (e.g., Baughman and Lassiter 1978).

With regard to the material in this section, the most serious methodological omission is the lack of an error analysis of the toxic substance computations. Techniques such as first-order error analysis and Monte Carlo simulation are available and could be applied for this purpose. In any event, it should be obvious that toxic substance predictions will typically exhibit significant uncertainty. Methods for incorporating this uncertainty in a management context are explored in the next section.

15.3 RISK ANALYSIS

The models developed in this book have been expressly designed as decision-making aids. In the first chapter of this volume we introduced the notion of assimilative capacity as a conceptual framework for the integration of models into the policy arena. Implicit to the validity of the assimilative capacity concept is the assumption that (1) we have at our command "very good" models relating pollutant loadings to water quality response and (2) we have a "very good" idea (as expressed in terms of a water quality standard or objective) of what constitutes acceptable water quality. By "very good" we mean that the models and standards are accurate and precise.

Although classical water quality problems, such as dissolved oxygen depletion and eutrophication, may manifest the certainty required for an adequate assimilative capacity computation, toxic substance contamination of natural waters typically exhibits much greater uncertainty. As depicted in Figure 15.15, this is reflected in both model predictions and water quality standards (Wicke 1983).

The effective use of models under such conditions of uncertainty requires a broadening of the assimilative capacity concept. One vehicle for this broadening is risk analysis. The following material represents a preliminary attempt to show how risk analysis might be applied to lake water quality management (from Reckhow et al. 1983).

15.3.1 The Concept of Risk

Risk has been defined and used in many different ways in the literature. Often, it is used to refer to a hazard. This is frequently the manner in which it is employed in assessing the effects of toxic substances. In contrast, ecosystem modelers use risk to designate the variance or uncertainty of outcomes related to an action. In traditional decision theory, decision under risk (when the underlying probability model was assumed to be known) was distinguished from decision under uncertainty (when the underlying probability model was unknown). This distinction has tended to disappear, probably because one rarely knows the true probability model that is generating the state of nature in a decision problem.

Current literature on decision theory defines risk as the expected loss or the expected utility. The decision problem typically combines a model, expressing the probability of occurrence of alternative states of nature along with a loss (or utility) function representing a decision-maker's value judgment concerning the states of nature (Raiffa and Schlaifer 1968). Risk analysis, therefore, is defined here as both the process and the study of this type of decision problem, leading to the estimation of expected loss or utility.

Given that definition, a risk analysis conducted for the management of PCBs in the Great Lakes, for example, must have the following components. First, a mathematical model is required that describes the physical system from sources to effects. In specific terms, this means that the

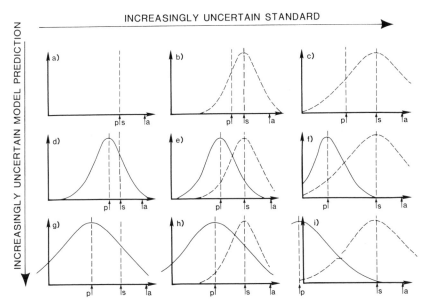

Figure 15.15   Graphical depiction of the load required, p, to meet a water quality standard, s, under a specified level of uncertainty (adapted from Wicke 1983). The abscissa of each plot represents pollutant concentration in a lake. The letter "p" is used to represent a load because a model prediction must be used to relate the load to an in-lake concentration. The ambient level, a, of the pollutant is also shown. The cases range from plot (a) where there is no uncertainty associated with either the prediction or the standard (as might be the case for a pollutant such as chloride) to plot (i) where both are highly uncertain (as is the case for many toxic substances). Note that more stringent loading requirements (as manifested by lower values of p) are required as either the prediction, the standard or both become more uncertain.

model must relate human and ecosystem effects of PCB contamination to the sources of PCB in the Great Lakes. This is essential, since it is human and ecosystem effects that impart utility (or disutility) to various PCB management strategies, and it is the scientist, or modeler, who is best able to express this relationship between sources and effects. In addition, uncertainty analysis must accompany the solution of the model so that the effects are expressed probabilistically. This will result in one component of the risk analysis: the probability model predicting the states of nature (which, for this problem, are the ecosystem effects and the human health effects). The models described in the present chapter could serve as a part of this component.

The second component of the risk analysis involves quantification of the decision-maker's loss or utility function. This function expresses the decision-maker's preferences or values associated with different states of nature.

15.3.2 The Concept of Utility

The utility function is invariably multiattribute, involving issues of consequence in more than one sector, for example, decisions involving water quality may affect human health, recreation, esthetics and the economy. In order to understand and properly address these complex issues, all meaningful attributes must first be identified. It makes little sense (and may result in unpopular, inefficient decisions) to evaluate a multi-attribute water quality issue strictly on the basis of recreational enjoyment (unless all other attributes are assigned a zero weight, which reduces the issue to a single attribute problem).

Identification of meaningful attributes may be expeditiously undertaken by the preparation of an objectives hierarchy as illustrated in Ellis and Keeney (1972). For the management of PCBs in the Great Lakes, an objectives hierarchy has been constructed and is presented in Figure 15.16. This begins with an all-encompassing objective at the top; issue-specific objectives are then derived that are consistent with the overall objective. Finally, attributes that are measurable (and can be modeled) are defined from each specific objective.

At this point, it would be important to present the objectives hierarchy in Figure 15.16 to affected individuals (decision-makers, interest groups, etc.) for critique and refinement. This may lead to the identification of additional objectives or the elimination of objectives. In this regard, Ellis and Keeney (1972) and Zeleny (1982) present methods for assessing attribute importance. Attributes may be excluded, if, for example, the decision-maker believes that an assessment of policy that affects that attribute will have no bearing on the decision (the "test of importance" from Ellis and Keeney). Occasionally it may be difficult to assign a measurable attribute to an important objective, so proxy attributes may have to be found at this time (see Keeney and Raiffa 1976). The overall task of objectives and attributes characterization is extremely important, as it determines the measures of success or effectiveness of a particular management strategy. Therefore, the analyst is wise to devote full attention to this endeavor.

Once the attributes are identified, the analyst must derive the multi-attribute utility function. Under certain, often quite reasonable, conditions the multiattribute utility function may be decomposed for ease of analysis. Keeney and Raiffa identify these conditions as preference

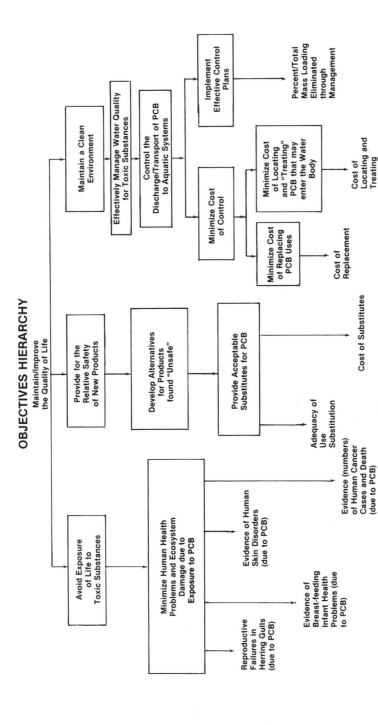

Figure 15.16 An objectives hierarchy for PCB in the Great Lakes. The hierarchy begins with an all-encompassing objective at the top; issue-specific objectives are then derived that are consistent with the overall objective. Finally, attributes that are measurable (and can be modeled) are defined for each specific objective. (From Reckhow et al. 1983.)

independence and utility independence*; they involve simple tests of the sensitivity of the decision-maker's preferences for attributes to changes in other attributes. These conditions generally hold in most decision problems, permitting decomposition of the utility function. Therefore, it is a reasonable approximation to break the multiattribute function into single attribute utility functions. After the individual utility functions are estimated in the manner briefly described below, they are combined in a multiplicative or additive manner, according to the values of estimated scaling coefficients. The entire procedure is presented in detail in Keeney and Raiffa.

For each attribute, a utility function is estimated. This is accomplished through a set of questions posed to the decision-maker concerning attitude toward risk. The questions are expressed in terms of simple hypothetical lotteries, and the responses are checked for consistency. An equation (the utility function) can then be fitted to the responses relating utility to the value of an attribute. Once all of the individual utility functions are estimated they are combined as stated above.

As a brief example, Figure 15.16 identifies objectives and measurable/meaningful attributes for PCB management in the Great Lakes. The analyst must first establish that the attributes are pairwise preferentially independent and utility independent through a series of questions posed to the decision-maker. Assuming that independence is established, the analyst must define the individual utility functions. For example, assume that the specific proxy attribute for reproductive failure in herring gulls is "estimated percent reduction in annual hatching of healthy young birds." The following dialog might lead to the development of the needed utility function:

- Analyst: What are the best and worst possible values for the proxy attribute [These are assigned utilities (U) of one and zero, respectively]?
- Decision-Maker: I would say that 0 and 40% are reasonable values.
- Analyst: Okay, now at what value of this proxy attribute would you be indifferent to a 50–50 lottery involving the extreme values or achieving the chosen value with certainty?
- Decision-Maker: Probably 10%.
- Analyst: That is the value assigned a utility of 0.5.

Preferential independence: The pair (w,x) is preferentially independent of (y,z) if one's preference order for w,x combinations in (w,x,y,z), given that y and z are held fixed, does not depend on the levels where they are fixed. *Utility independence*: Attribute w is utility independent of (x,y,z) if one's preference order for lotteries on w with x,y,z held fixed does not depend on the levels where they are fixed (definitions taken from Buehring et al. 1976)

A question similar to the second question posed by the analyst is asked to determine the "certainty equivalent" to a 50–50 lottery for the utility at $U = 0.75$ and for $U = 0.25$. These five points (at $U = 0$, 0.25, 0.5, 0.75 and 1.0) begin to describe the utility function. After checks for consistency, the analyst could express the utility function mathematically, perhaps using regression analysis. The utility functions are then combined into a single multiattribute function.

The management of toxic substances in aquatic systems is clearly a multiattribute problem. Any decision analytic study of this issue must consider the multiple objectives. Accordingly, multiattribute utility theory can be employed to assess the value side of the decision "equation." When this is combined with the uncertainty analysis of system state, the complete risk analysis should aid in the consideration of policy alternatives.

15.3.3 The Decision Resolution

In mathematical terms, the decision problem is expressed in the following way. The decision-maker has a set of actions (or strategies) that are identified by an action space $[A = (a_i)]$. Correspondingly, there exists a state space $[\Omega = (\Theta_j)]$ consisting of all possible states of nature that could occur in that situation. A probability model $[p(\Theta)]$ is identified and calibrated for prediction of the state of nature, and a loss function $[L(a_i, \Theta_j)]$ is identified that represents the utility of the action-state pair. The expected loss or risk is:

$$E[L(a_i)] = \int_{\Theta} L(a_i, \Theta) p(\Theta) d\Theta \qquad (15.132)$$

An action that minimizes risk is one that results in a minimum loss in the above equation.

Finally, it is often helpful to express the decision problem using a decision tree. This useful graphical device may be employed to display and perhaps simplify the issues involved. For the example of PCB management in the Great Lakes, two decision trees are presented in Figures 15.17 and 15.18. The decision moves from left to right, beginning from the square node at the far left. Two kinds of nodes are used; the square node represents a decision to be made and the circular node represents an outcome governed by chance. The analyst estimates the probability of these outcomes (often using expert judgment), determines the utility of each result (system state), and identifies the best (minimum risk) decision tree path.

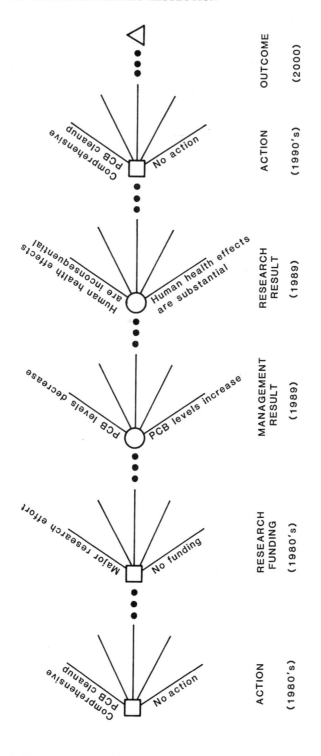

Figure 15.17   A decision tree for PCB management in the Great Lakes presented in abbreviated form. The decision moves from left to right, beginning with the square node on the left. Square nodes represent an outcome resulting from a decision, circular nodes represent outcomes governed by chance and a triangular node represents a terminus. Each node has a number of outcomes representing extreme and intermediate cases. The three dots between each node are meant to signify that every branch leads to an individual node which in turn branches out. The result is a spreading tree, as in Figure 15.18.

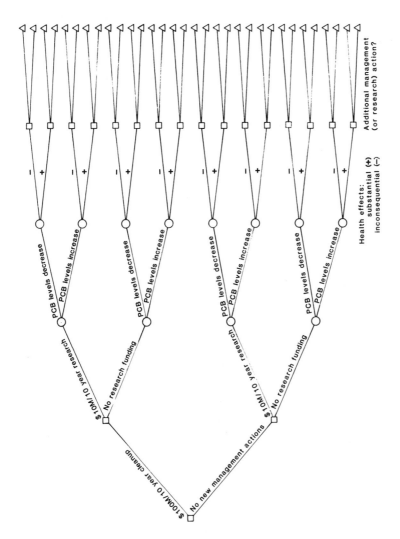

Figure 15.18 A decision tree example for Great Lakes PCB using extreme outcomes and actions.

In Figure 15.17, PCB management is presented as a sequence of decisions and "chances" concerning management actions and research funding. This illustrates the multitude of options and outcomes. It is presented on the assumption that decisions will soon be made on management strategies and research support; the decision-maker(s) will then observe the outcome at the end of the decade and perhaps then modify the strategy. Other scenarios could of course be analyzed in the same way.

The decision is simplified in Figure 15.18 by considering only the extremes. This permits the development of a completely connected tree. The analyst must then assess the probabilities at the chance nodes and the utilities for the health effects outcomes. This would allow the calculation of the minimum risk path. Once the options have been outlined, a display of the major features of the decision using a decision tree can help to convey information concerning the choices and the outcomes.

The foregoing is an attempt to suggest how models might be integrated into the decision-making process under conditions of uncertainty. Although it was stimulated in response to the toxic substance problem, it could also be relevant to other areas, such as oxygen depletion and eutrophication, that also exhibit uncertainty.

REFERENCES

Alexander, M. 1979. "Biodegradation of Toxic Chemicals in Water and Soil," in *Dynamics, Exposure and Hazard Assessment of Toxic Chemicals,* R. Haque, Ed. (Ann Arbor, MI: Ann Arbor Science Publishers, Inc.), pp. 179–191.

Alexander, M. 1981. "Biodegradation of Chemicals of Environmental Concern," *Science* 211:132–211.

Baughman, G. L., and R. R. Lassiter. 1978. "Prediction of Environmental Pollutant Concentration," in *Estimating the Hazard of Chemical Substances to Aquatic Life,* J. Cairns, Jr., K. L. Dickson and A. W. Maki, Eds., ASTM Special Technical Publication 657, American Society for Testing and Materials, Philadelphia, PA, pp. 55–70.

Baughman, G. L., D. F. Paris and W. C. Steen. 1980. "Quantitative Expression of Biotransformation," pp. 105–111.

Bierman, V. J., Jr. 1980. "A Comparison of Models Developed for Phosphorus Management in the Great Lakes," in *Phosphorus Management Strategies for Lakes,* R. C. Loehr, C. S. Martin and W. Rast, Eds. (Ann Arbor, MI: Ann Arbor Science Publishers, Inc.), pp. 235–255.

Bierman, V. J., Jr., and W. R. Swain. 1982. "Mass Balance Modeling of DDT

Dynamics in Lakes Michigan and Superior," *Environ. Sci. Technol.* 16:572–579.

Buehring, W. A., W. K. Foell and R. L. Keeney. 1976. "Energy/Environment Management: Application of Decision Analysis," International Institute for Applied Systems Analysis.

Chapra, S. C. 1975. "Comment on 'An Empirical Method of Estimating the Retention of Phosphorus in Lakes', by W. B. Kirchner and P. J. Dillon," *Water Resources Res.* 11:1033–1034.

Chapra, S. C. 1977. "Total Phosphorus Model for the Great Lakes," *J. Environ. Eng. Div. ASCE* 103(EE2):147–161.

Chapra, S. C. 1982. "Long-Term Models of Interactions Between Solids and Contaminants in Lakes," PhD Dissertation, The University of Michigan, Ann Arbor.

Chapra, S. C., and S. J. Tarapchak. 1976. "A Chlorophyll Model and Its Relationship to Phosphorus Loading Plots for Lakes," *Water Resources Res.* 12:1260–1264.

Cohen, Y., W. Cocchio and D. Mackay. 1978. "Laboratory Study of Liquid-Phase Controlled Volatilization Rates in Presence of Wind Waves," *Environ. Sci. Technol.* 12(5):553–558.

Council on Environmental Quality. 1978. "Environmental Quality, The Ninth Annual Report of the Council on Environmental Quality, U.S. Government Printing Office, Washington, DC, 599 pp.

Dankwertz, P. V. 1970. *Gas-Liquid Reactions* (New York: McGraw-Hill Book Company).

Deacon, E. L. 1977. "Gas Transfer to and across an Air-Water Interface," *Tellus* 29:363–374.

Dillon, P. J., and F. H. Rigler. 1974. "A Test of a Simple Nutrient Budget Model Predicting the Phosphorus Concentration in Lake Water," *J. Fish. Res. Bd. Can.* 31(11):1771–1778.

Doskey, P. V., and A. W. Andren. 1981. "Modeling the Flux of Atmospheric Polychlorinated Biphenyls Across the Air/Water Interface," *Environ. Sci. Technol.* 15(6):705–711.

Ellis, H. M., and R. L. Keeney. 1972. "A Rational Approach for Government Decisions Concerning Air Pollution," in *Analysis of Public Systems,* A. W. Drake, Ed. (Cambridge, MA: The MIT Press).

Emerson, S. 1975. "Gas Exchange in Small Canadian Shield Lakes," *Limnol. Oceanogr.* 20:754.

Froment, G. F., and K. B. Bischoff. 1979. *Chemical Reactor Analysis and Design* (New York: John Wiley & Sons, Inc.), 765 pp.

Hydroscience, Inc. 1973. "Limnological Systems Analysis of the Great Lakes: Phase I—Preliminary Model Design," Hydroscience, Inc., Westwood, NJ.

Keeney, R. L., and H. Raiffa. 1976. *Decisions with Multiple Objectives: Preferences and Value Tradeoffs* (New York: John Wiley & Sons, Inc.).

Larsen, D. P., and H. T. Mercier. 1976. "Phosphorus Retention Capacity of Lakes," *J. Fish. Res. Bd. Can.* 33(8):1742–1750.

Lewis, W. K., and W. G. Whitman. 1924. "Principles of Gas Absorption," *Ind. Eng. Chem.* 16(12):1215:1220.

Liss, P. S. 1975. "Chemistry of the Sea Surface Microlayer," *Chem. Oceanogr.,* 2, J. P. Riley and G. Skirrow, Eds., 193, Academic Press, London.

Liss, P. S., and P. G. Slater. 1974. "Flux of Gases Across the Air-Sea Interface," *Nature* 247:181–184.

Mackay, D. 1977. "Volatilization of Pollutants from Water," in *Aquatic Pollutants: Transformations and Biological Effects,* O. Hutzinger et al., Eds. (Amsterdam: Pergamon Press), p. 175.

Mackay, D. 1979. "Finding Fugacity Feasible," *Environ. Sci. Technol.* 13(10): 1218–1223.

Mackay, D. 1980. "Solubility, Partition Coefficients, Volatility, and Evaporation Rates," in *Vol. 2 Part A: Reactions and Processes Handbook* (New York: Springer-Verlag).

Mackay, D. 1982. "Fugacity Revisited," *Environ. Sci. Technol.* 16(12): 654A–660A.

Mackay D., A. Bobra, D. W. Chan and W. Y. Shiu. 1982. "Vapor Pressure Correlations for Low-Volatility Environmental Chemicals," *Environ. Sci. Technol.* 16:645–649.

Mackay, D., A. Bobra and W. Y. Shiu. 1980. "Relationship Between Aqueous Solubility and Octanol-Water Partition Coefficients," *Chemosphere* 9:701–711.

Mackay, D., and P. J. Leinonen. 1975. "Rate of Evaporation of Low-Solubility Contaminants from Water Bodies to Atmosphere," *Environ. Sci. Technol.* 9(13):1178–1180.

Mackay, D., and W. Y. Shiu. 1977. "Aqueous Solubility of Polynuclear Aromatic Hydrocarbons," *J. Chem. Eng. Data* 22(4):399–402.

Mackay, D., W. Y. Shiu and R. J. Sutherland. 1979. "Estimating Volatilization and Water Column Diffusion Rates of Hydrophobic Contaminants," in *Dynamics, Exposure and Hazard Assessment of Toxic Chemicals,* R. Haque, Ed. (Ann Arbor, MI: Ann Arbor Science Publishers, Inc.), pp. 127–142.

Mackay, D., and A. W. Wolkoff. 1973. "Rate of Evaporation of Low-Solubility Contaminants from Water Bodies to Atmosphere," *Environ. Sci. Technol.* 7(7):611–614.

Murphy, T. J., and C. P. Rzeszutko. 1978. "Polychlorobiphenyls in Precipitation in the Lake Michigan Basin," EPA-600/3-18-071, U.S. Environmental Protection Agency, Duluth, MN, 33 pp.

PLUARG. 1978. "Environmental Management Strategy for the Great Lakes System," International Joint Commission, Windsor, Ontario, 115 pp.

Raiffa, H., and R. Schlaifer. 1968. *Applied Statistical Decision Theory* (Cambridge, MA: The MIT Press).

Reckhow, K. H., and S. C. Chapra. 1983. *Engineering Approaches for Lake Management: Vol. 1. Data Analysis and Empirical Modeling* (Ann Arbor, MI: Ann Arbor Science Publishers).

Reckhow, K. H., R. Cupery and J. E. Ramig. 1983. "Risk Analysis for Water Quality Management," National Oceanic and Atmospheric Administration, Ann Arbor, MI.

Schnoor, J. L. 1981. "Fate and Transport of Dieldrin in Coralville Reservoir: Residues in Fish and Water Following a Pesticide Ban," *Science* 211:840–842.

Smith, J. H., W. R. Mabery, N. Bohonos, B. R. Holt, S. S. Lee, T.-W. Chou, D. C. Bomberger and T. Mill. 1977. "Environmental Pathways of Selected Chemicals in Freshwater Systems," EPA-600/7-77-113, U.S. Environmental Protection Agency, Athens, GA, 91 pp.

Strachan, W. M. J., and H. Huneault. 1979. "Polychlorinated Biphenyls and Organochlorine Pesticides in Great Lakes Precipitation, *J. Great Lakes Res.* 5:61–68.

Stumm, W., and J. J. Morgan. 1981. *Aquatic Chemistry* (New York: Wiley-Interscience), 780 pp.

Thomann, R. V. 1978. "Size Dependent Model of Hazardous Substances in Aquatic Food Chain," EPA-600/3-78-036, U.S. Environmental Protection Agency, Washington, DC, 40 pp.

Thomann, R. V. 1979. "An Analysis of PCB in Lake Ontario Using a Size-Dependent Food Chain Model," in *Perspectives on Lake Ecosystem Modeling,* D. Scavia and A. Robertson, Eds. (Ann Arbor, MI: Ann Arbor Science Publishers, Inc.), pp. 293–320.

Thomann, R. V. 1981. "Equilibrium Model of Fate of Microcontaminants in Diverse Aquatic Food Chains," *Can. J. Fish. Aquat. Sci.* 38:280–296.

Thomann, R. V., R. P. Winfield, and D. M. Di Toro. 1974. "Modeling of Phytoplankton in Lake Ontario (IFYGL)," Proc. 17th Conf. Great Lakes Res. Internat. Assoc. Great Lakes Res., pp. 135–149.

Vollenweider, R. A. 1968. "The Scientific Basis of Lake and Stream Eutrophication with Particular Reference to Phosphorus and Nitrogen as Eutrophication Factors," Technical Report DAS/DSI/68.27, Organization for Economic Cooperation and Development, Paris, France.

Vollenweider, R. A. 1969. "Möglichkeiten und Grenzen Elementarer Modelle der Stoffbilanz von Seen," *Arch. Hydrobiol.* 66:1–36.

Vollenweider, R. A. 1975. "Input-Output Models with Special Reference to the Phosphorus Loading Concept in Limnology," *Schweiz. Z. Hydrol.* 37:53–84.

Vollenweider, R. A. 1976. "Advances in Defining Critical Loading Level for Phosphorus in Lake Eutrophication," *Mem. Ist. Ital. Idrobiol.* 33:53–83.

Whitman, W. G. 1923. "The Two-Film Theory of Gas Absorption," *Chem. Metallurg. Eng.* 29(4):146–148.

Whitmore, F. C. 1977. "First Order Mass Balance Model for the Sources, Distribution and Fate of PCB's in the Environment," EPA–560/6–77–006, U.S. Environmental Protection Agency, Washington, DC, 180 pp.

Wicke, H. D. 1983. "Risk Assessment for Water Quality Management," PhD Dissertation, The University of Michigan, Ann Arbor.

Wolfe, N. L. 1979. "Determining the Role of Hydrolysis in the Fate of Organics in Natural Waters," in *Dynamics, Exposure and Hazard Assessment,* R. Haque, Ed. (Ann Arbor, MI: Ann Arbor Science Publishers, Inc.), pp. 163–178.

Wolfe, N. L., R. G. Zepp, G. N. Baughman, R. C. Fincher and J. A. Gordon. 1976. "Chemical and Photochemical Transformation of Selected Pesticides in Aquatic Systems, EPA–600/3–76–067, U.S. Environmental Protection Agency, Athens, GA, 151 pp.

Zeleny, M. 1982. *Multiple Criteria Decision Making.* (New York: McGraw-Hill Book Company).

Zepp, R. G. 1980. "Assessing the Photochemistry of Organic Pollutants in Aquatic Environments," in *Dynamics, Exposure and Hazard Assessment,* R. Haque, Ed. (Ann Arbor, MI: Ann Arbor Science Publishers, Inc.), pp. 69–110.

Zepp, R. G., and D. M. Cline. 1977. "Rates of Direct Photolysis in Aquatic Environment," *Environ. Sci. Technol.* 11(4):359–366.

SECTION 7

MODEL IMPLEMENTATION

CHAPTER 16

CONFIRMATION OF MECHANISTIC
WATER QUALITY MODELS

Mathematical model development begins with the conceptualization of the functions and relationships of the characteristics of the issue or system under study and proceeds with specification of the mathematical relationships, estimation of the model parameters, and validation of the model as a reliable representation (see Chapter 1). The process may be iterative. All steps are important; the validation step, however, may be most important because it provides confirmation (or lack thereof) that the conduct of the other steps resulted in a reliable model. Ironically, validation is also the step that most often is conducted inadequately in water resource model development.

In fact, validation, or the ascertainment of truth, is inconsistent with the logic of scientific research. As Anscombe (1967) notes, "The word valid would be better dropped from the statistical vocabulary. The only real validation of a statistical analysis, or of any scientific enquiry, is confirmation by independent observations." The testing of scientific models may be considered an inductive process, which means that, even with true premises, we can at best assign high probability to the correctness of the model. Philosophers of science have long debated the appropriate criteria for the effectiveness of arguments of this nature, considering characteristics such as the severity of tests and the goodness-of-fit.

How can this be translated into statistical terms for practical applications? Generalization of verifying criteria is possible only to a limited extent; beyond that, issue-specific criteria must be determined. Still, guidelines may be proposed for the composition of tests that are rigorous and for the selection of goodness-of-fit tests and acceptance levels. Both model developers and model users should benefit from careful consideration and application of criteria for model confirmation.

These issues are not strictly of academic interest. In the past 15 years, a number of water quality simulation models have been developed and then promoted as predictive methods to aid in the management of environmental quality. In most cases, however, these models have not been subjected to a rigorous validation or confirmation. Therefore, the model user often has no assurance that the model will yield reliable and informative predictions. This has potentially serious consequences since an inadequately confirmed planning model may lead to the implementation of economically inefficient or socially unacceptable water quality management plans. It is the purpose of this chapter to outline some philosophical and statistical issues relevant to the problem of confirmation, and then to recommend appropriate applications of statistical confirmatory criteria.

16.1 PHILOSOPHY AND SCIENTIFIC CONFIRMATION

Until the 1950s, virtually all scientists and philosophers of science viewed the advancement of science and the scientific method as endeavors dominated by empiricism and logic. The empiricism of Hume and the deductive logic of Russell and Whitehead formed the basis for the approaches of the logical positivists and, later, the logical empiricists. In particular, the logical empiricists have enjoyed widespread support during the twentieth century.

Logical empiricism (see Hempel 1965) is based on the presupposition that observations and logic advance scientific knowledge. For example, when a scientific hypothesis (model) is proposed under logical empiricism, observations of relevant phenomena are acquired, and inductive or deductive logic is used to determine the degree of confirmational support. Inductive arguments, we may recall, cannot strictly be proven as true, but at best can be assigned a high likelihood of being correct. In statistical inference, inductive arguments often are associated with reasoning from the specific to the general. Deductive logic (reasoning from the general to the specific), on the other hand, must yield true conclusions if the premises are true and the arguments are valid.

Logical empiricists are divided on the importance and appropriate applications of deduction and induction in science. For example, under the hypothetico-deductive approach (Kyburg 1970), a scientific hypothesis is proposed and criteria that can be tested are deduced logically. The scientist then must be concerned with constructing rigorous tests which, depending on rigor and the results of testing, confer a degree of confirmation upon the hypothesis. When competing hypotheses are offered, philosophers have recommended acceptance of the simplest one that is consistent with the empirical evidence, possibly because it is most probable.

Inductive logic, on the other hand, is important in a class of problems concerned with statistical explanation (Salmon 1971). Scientists and philosophers who subscribe to this approach argue that there are many scientific analyses in which the information content of the conclusion exceeds that of the premises. In those circumstances, inductive logic is appropriate, and we, at best, can assign high probability to the conclusion based on the premises. Alternatively, using reasoning similar to Bayes' Theorem, we may state that the degree of confirmation, or the probability of a hypothesis [P(H)], is conditional on the available empirical evidence (E):

$$P(H \mid E) = \frac{P(H,E)}{P(E)} \qquad (16.1)$$

In contrast, Edwards (1972) advocates a likelihood interpretation (without Bayes' Theorem) for the support provided to a hypothesis from a set of data; Rosenkrantz (1977), however, takes a strictly Bayesian view and conditionalizes this likelihood with an often informationless prior.

Popper (1968) has proposed a variation on the hypothetico-deductive approach that has undergone a variety of interpretations since its introduction (Brown 1977). Popper rejects the notion that induction should be called logic, since the nature of induction is to support a conclusion that contains more information than the premises. Therefore, if we accept the logical empiricist view that science is based on logic, then deductive logic is necessary. Consistent with the hypothetico-deductivists, Popper requires the deduction of observational consequences of a scientific hypothesis; but in a break from previous thought, he bases scientific knowledge on a criterion of falsification rather than confirmation. This means, according to Popper, that scientific statements are distinguished not by the fact that they can be confirmed by observation, but rather by the fact that they can be falsified by observation. Popper believes that candidate hypotheses should be subjected to severe tests, and from among the successful hypotheses, the one that is deemed most falsifiable is the one that tentatively should be accepted. Although this at first may seem counterintuitive, it is reasonable since, following the application of severe tests, the hypothesis that was most likely to be falsified yet survived is the hypothesis receiving the greatest empirical support. Popper then would say that this highly falsifiable hypothesis had been corroborated through the application of rigorous tests. Like confirmation, corroboration has a vague quantitative meaning associated with the severity of the applied tests and the degree of test success.

Finally, to complete this discussion of the philosophy and methods of science, we must consider the thinking of some philosophers during the past 30 years (see Kuhn 1970 or Brown 1977). Specifically, it has been suggested that the logical empiricist notion of observation and logic, as fundamental to scientific research, biases our view of science. When these presuppositions are eliminated, other criteria may become important, such as the consensus of opinion of the scientific community (Brown 1977). Under one view of this new philosophy, most scientific research is "normal science" (Kuhn 1970), in which the existing theoretical framework determines the research and the nature of the scientific inferences drawn from the observations. In contrast to normal science, scientific "revolutions" change the basic theoretical framework. These ideas represent an important new philosophical view of the conduct of science. Without rejecting this view, however, we justifiably may consider logical empiricism as the dominant theoretical framework at present. This means that methods proposed for the testing of mathematical models must draw their support from the philosophy and methods of the logical empiricists.

Independent of the preference we may have for a particular logical empiricist approach for evaluating scientific hypotheses, there are consistencies among the approaches that the scientist should note well. Without doubt, tests must be rigorous. This means that the hypothesis should be subjected to conditions that are most likely to identify its weaknesses or falsity. Mathematical simulation models must be tested with data that reflect conditions noticeably different from the calibration conditions; without this, there is no assurance that the model is anything more than a descriptor of a unique set of conditions (i.e., those representing the calibration state). To assess the degree of confirmation or corroboration that a hypothesis or model should enjoy, a statistical goodness-of-fit criterion is necessary. Finally, the modeler should prepare a set of candidate model formulations and then base the model choice in part on the relative performance of the models on statistical tests and on consistency with theoretical system behavior. Comparison of rival models/hypotheses is an important step in the testing of scientific hypotheses.

The severity of the tests employed often is dependent on the intended use of the hypothesis or model. For example, the user normally faces a risk associated with the application of an incorrect model and a cost associated with testing candidate models. A cost/risk trade-off determines the appropriate level of test severity. Likewise, the statistical criterion is use-dependent. Specifically, it is noted below that the needs of a particular application generally determine the best criteria for assessing statistical goodness-of-fit.

16.2 SOME PRACTICAL ISSUES

The selection of a statistical test for the confirmation of a mathematical model may be facilitated through consideration of the following issues:

1. What characteristics of the prediction are of interest to the modeler? The answer may be one or more of: mean values, variability, extreme values, all predicted values, and so forth. If one of the limited, specific responses is given, then the test statistical criterion should focus on that specific feature.

2. Is it intended that the model be primarily descriptive (identifying hypothesized cause-effect relationships) or primarily predictive? Different statistical tests are appropriate in each case.

3. What is the criterion for successful confirmation? In statistical inference, mean square error often is adopted, although many statistical tests (e.g., nonparametric methods) do employ other error criteria. In some situations, a decision theoretic approach such as regret minimization is warranted (see Chernoff and Moses 1959).

4. Are there any peculiar features to the model application of concern? This is a "catch-all" question intended to alert the model user to the fact that each application is unique, and therefore the confirmation process must be designed on that basis. For example:

   a. When prediction and observation uncertainty are considered, are all error terms quantified? It should be noted that model specification error rarely is estimated for water quality simulation models. This means that the corresponding prediction error is underestimated. Omission or mis-specification of any prediction/observation error terms will influence model confirmation.

   b. Are the assumptions behind any of the statistical tests violated? In particular, since time series or spatial series of data are often examined in model confirmation, autocorrelation may be a problem. When the validity of the statistical procedures is sensitive to a violated assumption (as is generally true for the assumption of independence), then some modifications or alternatives must be considered.

16.3 CONFIRMATION OF SIMULATION MODELS: LITERATURE REVIEW

Although there have been few, if any, rigorous attempts at confirmation of a water quality simulation model, this is not because of a complete lack of attention to this issue in the recent literature. General discussions on the importance of model confirmation or on confirmation as a step in simulation model development are noteworthy in this regard (Van Horn 1969, Naylor and Finger 1971, Mihram 1973, Davis et al. 1976, Caswell 1977). In addition, the Environmental Protection Agency recently sponsored a workshop on this topic (Hydroscience 1980). Unfortunately, the discussion groups convened as part of this workshop generally offered mixed or mild endorsement of rigorous statistical confirmatory criteria. While some of the papers presented at this workshop contained strongly worded statements on the importance of confirmation (e.g., Velz) or presented statistical criteria for confirmation (e.g., Thomann, or Chi and Thomas), the workshop missed an opportunity to produce and to promulgate a set of confirmatory guidelines necessary for proper model development.

Despite the claims by some that statistical confirmatory criteria generally should not be recommended because of the unique demands of each model application, there are in fact statistical tests that may be adapted to virtually any situation. A number of researchers (Mihram 1973, Shaeffer 1980, Thomann 1980, Thomann and Segna 1980, Thomann and Winfield 1976) have suggested various statistics useful for model confirmation. Thomann's work in particular stands out as one of the few statistical statements on confirmation specific to water quality simulation models. In the field of simulation modeling in hydrology, James and Burges (1981) have prepared a useful practical guide to model selection and calibration. Many of the statistical tests that they propose and apply to calibration are equally applicable for confirmation.

In further support of the argument against those reluctant to adopt statistical confirmatory criteria, consider the alternative. The extremes are those cases where simulations are performed in the absence of data. Although these can have some academic significance, their relevance to decision-making is minimal. However, even where an effort at validation has been made, the comparisons undertaken are often cursory. Figures 16.1 through 16.3 were selected from the water quality simulation literature as examples of current practice in prediction/observation comparison or model "validation." Commenting on Figure 16.1, the authors described the prediction/observation match as "good." Ignoring this debatable judgment on the fit, we still may question any conclusion on model fit in the absence of statistical tests (which are clearly possible with these quantitative measures). Figures 16.2 and 16.3 specifically are labeled as "verification" plots, yet again there is no statistical goodness-of-fit criterion. In Figure 16.3, the authors take the commendable step of displaying a shaded region for the observations. Regrettably, this region is so large that it may detract from meaningful confirmation by preventing model discrimination. A shaded observation region in conjunction with a time series for central tendency would be a more useful representation of the observations.*

Several investigators (Meyer 1971, Miller 1974, Miller et al. 1976, Hornberger and Spear 1980, 1981, Spear and Hornberger 1980, Majkowski et al. 1981) have advocated the use of sensitivity analysis for the confirmation and evaluation of simulation models. It is clear that a measure of the importance and error levels of model terms can be helpful during model development and also can provide some insight into the confirmation process. Gardner et al. (1981) caution that the standard form of sensitivity analysis (partial derivative with respect to the parameter of concern) may result in a misleading approximation of effect when nonlinearity and parameter covariance are large (see Chapter 2 on first-order error analysis). In contrast, Hornberger and Spear (1980, 1981) avoid this problem by using Monte Carlo simulation in their sensitivity analyses. Factorial methods from experimental design also can be useful in simulation model studies of single variable and interaction effects. Sensitivity analysis, then, does not yield a measure of model confirmation, but it can provide information that is extremely useful in model testing and development.

Several studies (Beck 1980, Fedra 1980, 1981, Fedra et al. 1980) at the International Institute for Applied Systems Analysis have examined issues in the development, calibration, confirmation, and prediction of water quality simulation models. Sensitivity analysis and Monte Carlo simulation have been used to examine the impact of error terms on the prediction error. Among the strong conclusions apparent from this work (and from examination of Figure 16.1) is that data often are inadequate for effective calibration and confirmation of mathematical models. This situation clearly limits the degree to which we may apply statistical confirmatory criteria and ultimately affects the reliability of planning models and methods.

16.4 STATISTICAL METHODS FOR CONFIRMATION

Several statistical methods may be found useful for assessing the degree of confirmation of a mathematical model. Some of the more common techniques are listed in Table 16.1. Before selecting a technique

---

*It should be noted that the authors of Figures 16.2 and 16.3 are cognizant of the issues under discussion and have moved to address them in more recent work. However, the examples are still representative of current practice by most other investigators.

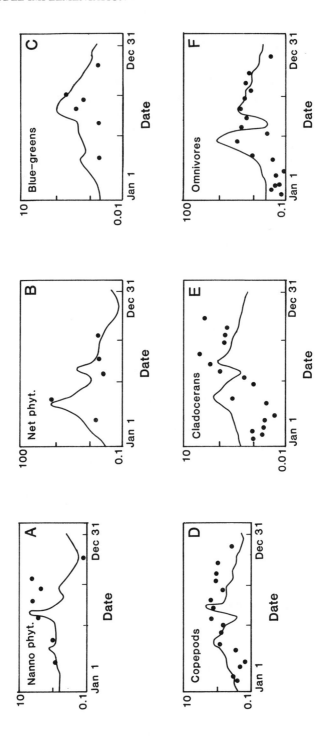

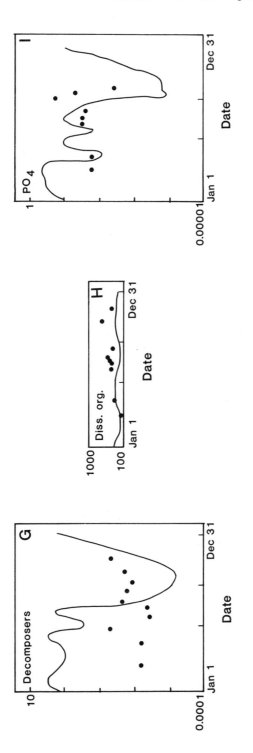

Figure 16.1 An example of a comparison of observations with predictions for a water quality simulation model (Park et al. 1975).

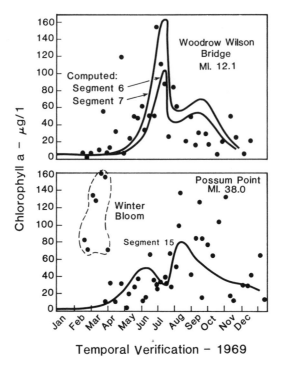

Figure 16.2   An example of a model verification plot (Thomann et al. 1974).

(or, for that matter, before acquiring data for model development), the investigator should consider the issues presented in previous sections of this chapter. For example, it is likely that model applications primarily are concerned with only certain features of the model. It is appropriate, then, for confirmation to focus on those features of concern. In addition, statistical assumptions must be considered. Common assumptions include normality, homogeneity of variance, and independence. Many procedures are robust to mild violations of the first two assumptions, but not to lack of independence. Transformations often may be applied to achieve approximate normality or to stabilize variance, while some robust and nonparametric procedures mentioned below may be useful under nonnormality.

Violation of the independence assumption poses more difficult problems. Predictions and observations in water quality simulation often are time series, and autocorrelation may be present in one or both of these series. In a dependent (autocorrelated) series, the information content is less than in an equivalent-length, independent series because each data point, to some degree, is redundant with respect to the preceding point.

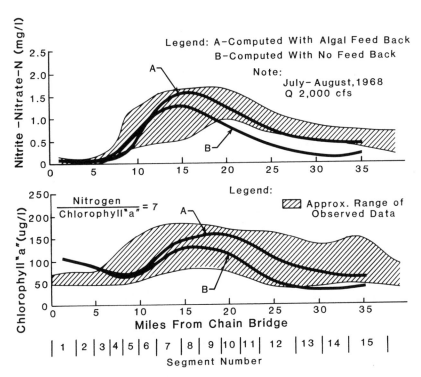

Figure 16.3   An example of a model verification plot with observation error shown (O'Connor et al. 1976).

This means that confidence intervals and significance tests that falsely assume independence will be overly optimistic—that is, the intervals will be too small.

For a single data series x_i, the autocorrelation coefficient for lag k is defined as:

$$r_k = \frac{\text{covar}[x_i, x_{i+k}]}{s(x_i)s(x_{i+k})} \qquad (16.2)$$

where   covar = covariance
         s = standard deviation

When predictions and observations are compared, the Durbin-Watson test may be used to examine the residuals for autocorrelation (see Wonnacott and Wonnacott 1981). However, as Wonnacott and Wonnacott note (page 232) the estimate of autocorrelation from residuals tends to be low. In fact, Lenton et al. (1973) observe that the small sample sizes

Table 16.1   Statistical Methods for Confirmation

1. Deterministic Modeling
   a. Measures of error
   b. t-test
   c. Mann-Whitney-Wilcoxon test
   d. Regression
   e. Cross-correlation
   f. Graphical comparison—box plots
2. Stochastic Modeling
   a. Deterministic methods for particular percentile
   b. Probability density function "slices"
      i.   chi-square test
      ii. Kolmogorov-Smirnov test
      iii. Comparison of moments
      iv. Graphical comparisons—box plots

usually found in water resources can cause large estimation errors for the autocorrelation coefficient.

Fortunately, when autocorrelation is found and quantified, there are some steps that can then be taken to permit application of many of the standard statistical tests. Yevjevich (1972) presents several relationships for calculating the effective sample size, which is the size of an independent series that contains the same amount of information as contained in the autocorrelated series. For example, in the common situation when the lag one autocorrelation coefficient is positive and the first-order Markov model is appropriate, the effective sample size $N(e)$ is:

$$N(e) = N \left[\frac{1 - r_1}{1 + r_1} \right] \qquad (16.3)$$

where N is the actual sample size.

A less efficient but computationally easy alternative to $N(e)$ is to use or to aggregate data covering intervals greater than the period of autocorrelation influence. For example, weekly data may exhibit autocorrelation but monthly data may not; therefore, confine the analysis to monthly data.

A particularly useful method for time series confirmation is cross-correlation of the prediction and observation series. Here, too, auto-correlation is important, but methods have been developed to address the problem. Yevjevich (1972) presents an equation from Bartlett (1935) for the effective sample size in two autocorrelated series:

$$N(e) = \frac{N}{1 + 2r_i(x)r_i(y) + \cdots + 2r_k(x)r_k(y)} \qquad (16.4)$$

where $r_i(x)$ = lag i autocorrelation for series 1
            $r_i(y)$ = lag i autocorrelation for series 2

N(e) then may be used in the significance test for the cross-correlation coefficient. Note that N(e) equals N if one of the two series contains no autocorrelation.

An alternative solution to autocorrelation in cross-correlation analysis is prewhitening (Box and Jenkins 1976, McCleary and Hay 1980). Under this procedure, the Box-Jenkins methods are used to transform each series into a white noise process. Cross-correlation analysis then is performed on the two white noise series.

To summarize this discussion on autocorrelation, considerable attention has been devoted to this topic because of the impact of lack of independence on statistical tests of significance. Further, even those water quality simulation model studies that have employed statistical confirmatory criteria—for example, Thomann and Segna (1980)—have neglected autocorrelation in situations where it probably is present. Since "data generated by dynamic simulation (models) usually are highly correlated" (Naylor 1971) and since time series of natural phenomena also may be correlated, the attention paid to autocorrelation seems appropriate.

Following consideration of these application-specific and statistical issues that help to determine the model terms and statistical methods to be involved in confirmation, the investigator likely will employ one or more of the techniques listed in Table 16.1. Graphical examination of data sets or series usually is a necessary part of any statistical analysis, and it certainly can be helpful in model confirmation. However, it is not listed in Table 16.1 because of concern that confirmation will begin and end with a graphical study and thus not advance beyond Figures 16.1 to 16.3.

One view of model output and, hence, confirmation approaches leads to the separate groupings of deterministic and stochastic modeling. Most water quality simulation models are deterministic, and this limits the set of available statistical methods. The trend toward error analysis in modeling is important for model confirmation, although difficulties in the estimation of model error may restrict the confirmation study. Some of the methods listed in Table 16.1 under deterministic modeling use aggregated data (prediction and observation samples), and some of the methods are appropriate for data series. Under "measures of error," we may include various weighting functions for the difference between the predictions and the observations (see Chapter 3). For example, the relative error is:

$$\text{relative error} = \frac{|x_{obs} - x_{pred}|}{x_{obs}} \qquad (16.5)$$

Another alternative, the squared error, is:

$$\text{squared error} = (x_{obs} - x_{pred})^2 \tag{16.6}$$

In each case, the average value (e.g., mean square error) is the appropriate form for expressing these error terms.

However, to assess the degree of confirmation (beyond a relative comparison of models), we need to use a test of statistical significance such as the t-test (parametric) or the Mann-Whitney-Wilcoxon test (nonparametric). Both tests require assumptions of independent identically distributed (i.i.d.) observations, but the t-test adds a normality assumption. While the t-test is fairly robust to violations of the normality assumptions (Box et al. 1978), neither test is robust to violation of independence. (See Chapters 3 and 4 for discussions of these issues.)

The t-test is conducted from Student's t distribution which, for a null hypothesis of no difference between the mean of the observations ($\bar{x}_{obs}$) and the mean of the predictions ($\bar{x}_{pred}$), is expressed as:

$$t = \frac{\bar{x}_{obs} - \bar{x}_{pred}}{s_{dif}/\sqrt{n}} \tag{16.7}$$

where s_{dif} = standard deviation of the paired differences ($x_{obs} - x_{pred}$)
n = number of ($x_{obs} - x_{pred}$) pairs

The nonparametric alternative to the t-test is the Mann-Whitney or Wilcoxon test. This procedure, which may be preferred under certain conditions of nonnormality, although perhaps not strongly so (see Box et al. (1978), is based on the relative ranks achieved when the data are ordered. Both the t-test and the Mann-Whitney test are described clearly in Chapters 3 and 4 and in Snedecor and Cochran (1967).

A second set of related statistical methods useful for model confirmation is regression and correlation (see Chapter 6). Here the method chosen would be used to relate one data series to another, and thus autocorrelation again is a problem. Following analysis and adjustment (if necessary) for autocorrelation, the investigator may regress the predictions on the observations. The fit may be assessed through the standard error statistic, or perhaps using the reliability index proposed by Leggett and Williams (1981). This index reflects on a plot of predictions vs observations, the angle between the 1:1 line (line of best fit), and a line through each data point from the origin. Cross-correlation (see Davis 1973) is calculated in a manner similar to that for the Pearson product moment correlation. Davis (1973) provides a test statistic for assessing the significance of the cross-correlation coefficient between two series. Remember that it is important to adhere to the assumptions behind the statistical methods; failure to do this under certain conditions can lead to faulty inferences concerning confirmation.

The final method presented here for deterministic model confirmation (from by no means an exhaustive list of options in Table 16.1) is the box plot (McGill et al. 1978, Reckhow 1980). The box plot is an extremely informative method for graphing one or more sets of data for the purpose of comparing order statistics. For each data set, the plot displays the median, the relative statistical significance of the median, the interquartile range, and the minimum and maximum points (see Figure 16.4). With aggregated (nonseries) data, the box plot yields perhaps the best visual comparison of two or more data sets. A detailed example illustrating box plot construction and several applications is presented in Chapter 4. McGill et al. (1978) and Reckhow (1980) also describe the construction and interpretation of box plots.

Before examining some statistical options for confirming stochastic models, consider one of the important practical issues that the model developer must face with a multivariate deterministic model. Specifically, the model developer may have calculated a confirmation statistic (e.g., a cross-correlation coefficient) for each variable in the model and/or for certain features of the model such as for extreme values. How might these confirmatory statistics be aggregated into a single confirmation measure?

First, the modeler must realize that to aggregate statistics and to make the confirmation decision on the basis of a single measure means the loss of potentially valuable model evaluation information. If this loss is acceptable, then the modeler must decide on an aggregation scheme for the individual confirmation statistics, for example, for the cross-correlation coefficients. This decision should be based on the relative importance of the model characteristics (e.g., model variables) for which confirmation statistics are available. The confirmation statistics then are aggregated using weights reflecting this importance. For example, if chlorophyll and dissolved oxygen are deemed most important in an aquatic ecosystem model, then the confirmatory statistics for these two variables should receive the highest weights. The final confirmation measure is a weighted sum of, for example, cross-correlation coefficients:

$$\text{confirmation measure} = \sum w(x)r(x) \tag{16.8}$$

where x = model characteristic (variable)
  w = weight reflecting the importance of x
  r = cross-correlation confirmation statistic for x

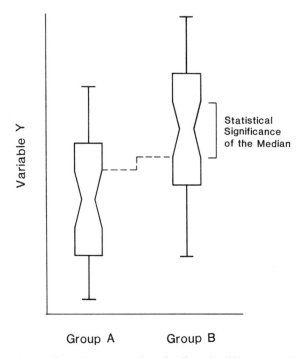

Figure 16.4   Box plots possessing signficantly different medians.

The particular scheme presented above merely is meant to suggest one option for aggregating statistics; others certainly are possible.

Less common at present than the deterministic simulation model, the stochastic model nonetheless is important and quite amenable to a number of statistical confirmatory approaches. In fact, all of the methods discussed above for the deterministic model are appropriate for a number of features (e.g., the time stream of mean values) of the three-dimensional prediction and observation surfaces. In addition, we can take a two-dimensional slice of these three-dimensional distributions. Several statistical goodness-of-fit tests listed in Table 16.1 then can be employed.

The chi-square test (Figure 16.5) and the Kolmogorov-Smirnov test (Figure 16.6) yield test statistics based on the comparison of two distributions. The chi-square statistic, χ^2, is calculated as the sum:

$$\chi^2 = \sum \frac{(n_{i,\,obs} - n_{i,\,pred})^2}{n_{i,\,obs}} \qquad (16.9)$$

where $n_{i,\,obs}$ = number of observations in cell i
        $n_{i,\,pred}$ = number of predictions in cell i

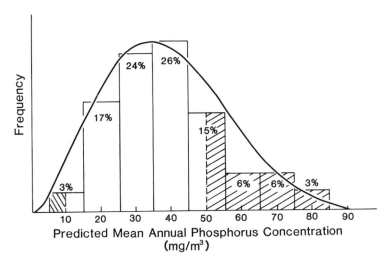

Figure 16.5   A comparison of a histogram with a probability density function for the chi-square test.

The chi-square test is conducted from the probability density function (pdf); each pdf is divided into a number of cells from which the chi-square counts are made. The somewhat arbitrary nature of the pdf division unfortunately can affect the results of the test. Benjamin and Cornell (1970) provide an excellent discussion of the merits of the chi-square test, as well as a table of chi-square statistics for the significance of the test.

The Kolmogorov-Smirnov test perhaps is preferred to the chi-square test because it is based on the cumulative distribution function (cdf). This removes the arbitrariness and investigator influence because cells are not required; rather, the data are ordered and the deviations of the order statistics are examined. In Figure 16.6, the fit of a model is examined and the goodness-of-fit is portrayed graphically with the Kolmogorov-Smirnov statistic.

Either of these methods may be used when the data are arranged in histogram or cumulative distribution form. Test statistics are available to assess the degree of confirmation. Benjamin and Cornell (1970) present a superb discussion on these goodness-of-fit methods for probability models.

Other statistics or procedures certainly may be considered to support model confirmation. The comparison of moments, particularly higher moments, can be useful in some situations (see Benjamin and Cornell 1970). In addition, the box plot is quite effective for examining and displaying differences between distributions.

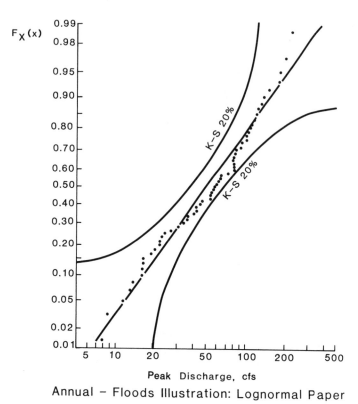

Figure 16.6   A lognormal probability plot illustrating the Kolmogorov-Smirnov test (Benjamin and Cornell 1970).

From a practical standpoint, the stochastic water quality simulation modeler probably does not have two three-dimensional distributions representing predictions and observations, respectively. Rather, he may have a continuous prediction "cloud" representing one standard error around the central points and either continuous point observations (Figure 16.7) or discrete observations with error bars (Figure 16.8). If the prediction error cloud does not include all error (is model error included?), then the error region is too small and "rejection" is more likely. Otherwise, the modeler for Figure 16.7 could cross-correlate the two central time series or test the overlap of the error region with the observation line. For Figure 16.8, the modeler could compare the points and regions statistically during the discrete observation times. Remember that the preferred approach involves comparison of a number of candidate models.

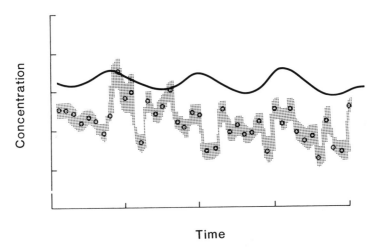

Figure 16.7   Prediction-observation comparison for model confirmation: continuous point observations.

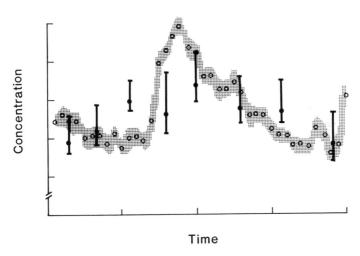

Figure 16.8   Prediction-observation comparison for model confirmation: error bars on observations.

In closing this discussion of statistical methods for confirmation, two additional model types deserve mention: cross-sectional regression models and descriptive (causal) models. Confirmation of cross-sectional regression models often does not pose the problem experienced with simulation models. This is particularly true if the cases studied are truly representative (e.g., a random sample) of the population of concern. Nonetheless, "shrinkage of the coefficient of multiple correlation" (Stone 1974) between model development and application data sets is to be expected. The methods of cross-validation* and the jackknife are useful for both regression model confirmation and estimation of a non-shrinking standard error or correlation. Mosteller and Tukey (1977) and Stone (1974) discuss these methods in detail.

To this point, the statistical confirmatory methods proposed largely are intended for predictive applications of models. Another important use of mathematical models is as descriptors of hypothesized causal relations. The methods presented above also may be found useful for confirming descriptive (causal) models. In addition, though, a causal confirmation process may be proposed.

The causal model confirmation procedure is based on a comparison of synthetic data generated from the model with actual observations. The statistical methods employed are path analysis (Kenny 1979) and the confirmatory approaches of Joreskog for linear structural equations (Kenny 1979, Joreskog and Sorbom 1980). The following procedure is recommended:

1. Experimental design and/or Monte Carlo simulation are used to generate "data" from each model. It is important that a number of plausible candidate models be evaluated.

2. The statistical tests presented in Table 16.1 may be used to compare real and simulated output data.

3. Using path analysis and LISREL (Joreskog and Sorbom 1980), construct linear structural equation models for both the real and synthetic data. These models are intended to represent causal behavior, from the point of view of the real data and from the point of view of each candidate simulation model.

4. Use the statistical tests presented in Table 16.1 to compare the real and synthetic structural equation models. The degree of confirmation of the causal model is then a measure of confirmation of the descriptive nature of the original simulation model. Several evaluative criteria may be posed:

   a. What "parts" of the model are most consistent (inconsistent) with observation? To what extent?

   b. What changes might be appropriate? This suggests an iterative approach alternating model development with causal confirmation analysis.

---

*Calibrate on half of the data and confirm on the other half; if no significant difference occurs, recalibrate using all the data.

    c. How do the models (and model subroutines) compare in performance?

It appears likely that there are many applications of path analysis and confirmatory methods for structural equations in the areas of simulation model development and testing.

16.5   CONCLUDING COMMENTS

To end this discussion of the philosophy and statistics of simulation model confirmation, a few points deserve restating.

1. Inadequate model confirmation increases the risks associated with the application of the model. Admittedly, there is a data cost and an analysis cost associated with model confirmation. This cost is to be compared with the risk resulting from the use of an unconfirmed model.
2. If confirmation is to be meaningful:
   a. rigorous statistical tests must be applied; and
   b. calibration-independent data are needed.
3. A number of plausible candidate models (or model subroutines) should undergo confirmation. Comparison of the performance of the candidates aids the modeler in the determination of the degree of confirmation.

Finally, it must be recognized that the proposed confirmation criteria rarely can be applied in practice to the extent outlined in this chapter. This realization does not reduce the importance of these criteria. Rather, a confirmation goal has been proposed, and the modeler may assess the extent of achievement of this goal. This degree of confirmation, estimated in terms of test rigor, test success, and data set independence, represents a measure of confidence to be assigned to the model as a predictive tool.

REFERENCES

Anscombe, P. J. 1967. "Topics in the Investigation of Linear Relations Fitted by the Method of Least Squares," *J. R. Statist. Soc. B* 29:1–52.

Bartlett, M. S. 1935. "Some Aspects of the Time Correlation Problem in Regard to Tests of Significance," *J. R. Statist. Soc.* 98:536–543.

Beck, M. B. 1980. "Hard or Soft Environmental Systems?" International Institute for Applied Systems Analysis Working Paper 80-25.

Benjamin, J. R., and C. A. Cornell. 1970. *Probability, Statistics and Decision for Civil Engineers* (New York: McGraw Hill Book Co.), 684 pp.

Box, G. E. P., W. G. Hunter and J. S. Hunter. 1978. *Statistics for Experimenters: An Introduction to Design, Data Analysis, and Model Building* (New York: John Wiley & Sons, Inc.)

Box, G. E. P., and G. M. Jenkins. 1976. *Time Series Analysis, Forecasting and Control* (San Francisco: Holden-Day, Inc.), 553 pp.

Brown, H. I. 1977. *Perception, Theory, and Commitment* (Chicago: The University of Chicago Press), 202 pp.

Caswell, H. 1977. "The Validation Problem," in *Systems Analysis and Simulation in Ecology, Vol. IV,* B. C. Patten, Ed. (New York: Academic Press), pp. 313–325.

Chernoff, H., and L. E. Moses. 1959. *Elementary Decision Theory* (New York: John Wiley & Sons, Inc.), 364 pp.

Davis, J. C., 1973. *Statistics and Data Analysis in Geology* (New York: John Wiley & Sons, Inc.), 550 pp.

Davis, D. R., L. Duckstein and C. C. Kisiel. 1976. "Model Choice and Evaluation from the Decision Viewpoint," in *Theories of Decision in Practice* (New York: Crane, Russak & Co., Inc.), pp. 341–351.

Edwards, A. W. F., 1972. *Likelihood* (Cambridge, U.K.: Cambridge University Press), 235 pp.

Fedra, K., 1980. "Estimating Model Prediction Accuracy: A Stochastic Approach to Ecosystem Modeling," International Institute for Applied System Analysis Working Paper 80-168.

Fedra, K., 1981. "Hypothesis Testing by Simulation: An Environmental Example," International Institute for Applied System Analysis Working Paper 81-74.

Fedra, K., G. van Straten and M. B. Beck, 1980. "Uncertainty and Arbitrariness in Ecosystem Modeling: A Lake Modeling Example," International Institute for Applied Systems Analysis Working Paper 80-87.

Gardner, R. H., R. V. O'Neill, J. B. Mankin and J. H. Carney. 1981. "A Comparison of Sensitivity Analysis Based on a Stream Ecosystem Model," *Ecol. Modelling* 12:173–190.

Hempel, C. G. 1965. *Aspects of Scientific Explanation* (New York: The Free Press), 504 pp.

Hornberger, G. M., and R. C. Spear. 1980. "Eutrophication in Peel Inlet— I. The Problem-Defining Behavior and a Mathematical Model for the Phosphorus Scenario," *Water Res.* 14:29–42.

Hornberger, G. M., and R. C. Spear. 1981. "An Approach to the Preliminary Analysis of Environmental Systems," *J. Environ. Management* 12:7–18.

Hydroscience, Inc. 1980. "Workshop on Verification of Water Quality Models," U.S. Environmental Protection Agency. EPA-600/9-80-016.

James, L. D., and S. J. Burges, 1981. "Selection, Calibration, and Testing of Hydrologic Models," Am. Soc. Agr. Engrs. Monograph.

Joreskog, K. G., and D. Sorbom. 1978. *LISREL: Analysis of Linear Structural Relationships by the Method of Maximum Likelihood. User's Guide, Version IV* (Chicago: National Educational Resources, Inc.), 165 pp.

Kenny, D. A. 1979. *Correlation and Causality* (New York: John Wiley & Sons, Inc.), 277 pp.

Kuhn, T. S. 1970. *The Structure of Scientific Revolutions,* 2nd ed. (Chicago: University of Chicago Press).

Kyburg, Jr., H. E. 1970. *Probability and Inductive Logic* (London: The Macmillian Co.), 272 pp.

Leggett, R. W., and L. R. Williams. 1981. "A Reliability Index for Models," *Ecol. Modelling* 13:303–312.

Lenton, R. L., I. Rodriquez-Iturbe and J. C. Schaake, Jr. 1973. "A Bayesian Approach to Autocorrelation Estimation in Hydrologic Autoregressive Models," MIT Water Res. Rpt. 163, Cambridge, MA. 121 pp.

Majkowski, J., J. M. Ridgeway and D. R. Miller. 1981. "Multiplicative Sensitivity Analysis and its Role in Development of Simulation Models," *Ecol. Modelling* 12:191–208.

McCleary, R., and R. A. Hay, Jr. 1980. *Applied Time Series Analysis for the Social Sciences* (Beverly Hills: Sage Publications), 331 pp.

McGill, R., J. W. Tukey and W. A. Larsen. 1978. "Variations of Box Plots," *Am. Stat.* 32:12–16.

Meyer, C. F. 1971. "Using Experimental Models to Guide Data Gathering," *J. Hydro. Div., ASCE* HYIO:1681–1697.

Mihram, G. A. 1973. "Some Practical Aspects of the Verification and Validation of Simulation Models," *Op. Res. Q.* 23:17–29.

Miller, D. R. 1974. "Sensitivity Analysis and Validation of Simulation Models," *J. Theor. Biol.* 48:345–360.

Miller, D. R., G. Butler and L. Bramall. 1976. "Validation of Ecological System Models," *J. Environ. Management* 4:383–401.

Mosteller, F., and J. W. Tukey. 1977. *Data Analysis and Regression: A Second Course in Statistics* (Reading, MA: Addison-Wesley), 588 pp.

Naylor, T. H. 1971. *Computer Simulation Experiments with Models of Economic Systems* (New York: John Wiley & Sons, Inc.), 502 pp.

Naylor, T. H., and J. M. Finger. 1971. "Validation," in *Computer Stimulation Experiments with Models of Economic Systems,* T. H. Naylor, Ed. (New York: John Wiley & Sons, Inc.), pp. 153–164.

O'Connor, D. J., R. V. Thomann and D. M. Di Toro. 1976. "Ecologic Models," in *Systems Approach to Water Management,* A. K. Biswas, Ed. (New York: McGraw-Hill Book Company), pp. 294–334.

Park, R. A., D. Scavia and N. L. Clesceri. 1975. "Cleaner: The Lake George Model," in *Ecological Modelling,* C. S. Russell, Ed. (Washington, DC: Resources for the Future), pp. 49-81.

Popper, K. R. 1968. *The Logic of Scientific Discovery* (New York: Harper & Row Publishers, Inc.), 480 pp.

Reckhow, K. H. 1980. "Techniques for Exploring and Presenting Data Applied to Lake Phosphorus Concentration," *Can. J. Fish. Sci.* 37:290-294.

Rosenkrantz, R. D. 1977. *Inference, Method and Decision: Toward a Bayesian Philosophy of Science* (Dordrecht, The Netherlands: D. Reidel Publishing Co.), 262 pp.

Salmon W. C. 1971. *Statistical Explanation and Statistical Relevance* (Pittsburgh: University of Pittsburgh Press), 117 pp.

Schaeffer, D. L. 1980. "A Model Evaluation Methodology Applicable to Environmental Assessment Models," *Ecol. Modelling* 8:275-295.

Snedecor, G. W., and W. G. Cochran. 1967. *Statistical Methods.* (Ames, IA: The Iowa State University Press), 593 pp.

Spear, R. C., and G. M. Hornberger. 1980. "Eutrophication in Peel Inlet—II. Identification of Critical Uncertainties via Generalized Sensitivity Analysis," *Water Res.* 14:43-49.

Stone, M. 1974. "Cross-Validatory Choice and Assessment of Statistical Predictions," *J. R. Statis. Soc. B* 36:111-147.

Thomann, R. V. 1980. "Measures of Verification," in *Workshop on Verification of Water Quality Models.* Hydroscience, Inc. U.S. Environmental Protection Agency. EPA-600/9-80-016, Athens, GA 258 pp.

Thomann, R. V., D. M. Di Toro and D. J. O'Connor. 1974. "Preliminary Model of Potomac Estuary Phytoplankton," *J. Environ. Eng. Div., ASCE* 100:699-715.

Thomann, R. V., and J. S. Segna. 1980. "Dynamic Phytoplankton – Model of Lake Ontario: Ten Year Verification and Simulations," in *Phosphorus Management Strategies for Lakes,* R. C. Loehr, C. S. Martin and W. Rast, Eds. (Ann Arbor, MI: Ann Arbor Science Publishers, Inc.), pp. 153-190.

Thomann, R. V., and R. P. Winfield. 1976. "On the Verification of a Three-Dimensional Phytoplankton Model of Lake Ontario," in *Environmental Modelling and Simulation,* W. R. Ott, Ed., U.S. Environmental Protection Agency, EPA-600/9-76-016, Washington, DC, pp. 568-572.

Van Horn, R. 1969. "Validation," in *The Design of Computer Simulation Experiments,* T. H. Naylor, Ed. (Durham, NC: Duke University Press), pp. 232-251.

Wonnacott, T. H., and R. J. Wonnacott. 1981. *Regression: A Second Course in Statistics* (New York: John Wiley & Sons, Inc.), 556 pp.

Yevjevich, V., 1972. *Probability and Statistics in Hydrology* (Fort Collins, CO: Water Resources Publications), 302 pp.

CHAPTER 17

ASSIMILATIVE CAPACITY MODELS AND WATER QUALITY MANAGEMENT*

17.1 TWO PLUS TWO, REVISITED

This book's preface begins with a joke concerning the differing problem-solving perspectives of a scientist, an engineer and a laywer. It articulates our perception of the roles of these professionals in the water quality management process. Whereas the scientist and engineer proffer ostensibly objective answers to the question: "What is two plus two?", the lawyer subjectively asks: "What would you like it to be?"

Although this dialogue is an obvious oversimplification, it is relevant to the roles of these professionals in establishing the past and future direction of water quality management in the United States. The water quality management process involves the integration of scientific and technical information to define management alternatives to achieve environmental objectives within a legally enforceable regulatory framework. The development and implementation of national water quality policy is due, in large measure, to the productive interactions among scientists, engineers, lawyers and the American public.

Scientists have been relied on to provide an understanding of the physical, chemical and biological aspects of the aquatic environment. Their research efforts have been applied to determining cause-and-effect relationships, that is, the identification of a measurable connection between the presence of a substance in the water and its eventual effect on the aquatic ecosystem and/or human health.

Lawyers have developed procedures for implementing the management options, defined by scientists and engineers, into a regulatory

---

*This chapter was written by S. C. Chapra, H. D. Wicke and K. H. Reckhow.

system codified into law. This regulatory framework evolves in the political arena and is, therefore, shaped by lawmakers' perceptions of societal goals.

Engineers have participated in various activities in support of water quality management. They have been called on to devise management mechanisms and strategies based on scientific, technical and economic information. These efforts range from developing design specifications for sewage treatment works to formulating a multisource load reduction plan for the Great Lakes. In these efforts, environmental engineers have derived the models surveyed in this book as methods for systematic analysis of diverse types of information. The following section reviews these models, which have been and will continue to be vital tools of the engineering approach to lake water quality management.

17.2 ASSIMILATIVE CAPACITY MODELS

In the first chapter of this volume, we introduced the notion of assimilative capacity as the amount of external loading that a water body can absorb and still maintain an acceptable level of quality. In classical environmental engineering, this "acceptable level" was usually expressed quantitatively as a water quality standard. The traditional concept of assimilative capacity can, therefore, be given simple mathematical expression as (recall Equation 10.16)

$$\begin{pmatrix} \text{external} \\ \text{loading} \end{pmatrix} = \P \begin{pmatrix} \text{water quality} \\ \text{standard} \end{pmatrix} \tag{17.1}$$

where $\P$ = assimilation factor [M T^{-1} (M L^{-3})$^{-1}$] that reflects the net effect of the transport and kinetic mechanisms acting to purge the pollutant from the system

For a given quality standard, Equation 17.1 indicates that a water body with strong purging mechanisms will assimilate a larger external loading than one with a small value of $\P$.

This book describes a variety of techniques to predict $\P$ for lakes. Volume 1 employs primarily empirical techniques, whereas the present volume uses a more mechanistic approach. For example, in Chapter 11, we developed a simple model to predict the assimilation factor for well mixed lakes. Equation 11.16, which is applicable to a pollutant that decays with first order kinetics, can be used to determine

$$\P = Q + kV \tag{17.2}$$

where Q = water flow through the lake's outlet $[L^3\ T^{-1}]$
          kV = the product of the pollutant's first-order decay rate and the lake's volume $[L^3 T^{-1}]$

Consequently, the assimilation factor in this case reflects both the flushing and decay mechanisms acting to purge the pollutant.

In Chapter 12, we derived a multi-dimensional expression of ¶ based on Thomann's (1972) control volume approach. Thomann's approach is required when, because of spatial heterogeneity, the system under study cannot be modeled as a single well mixed volume. For such cases, the water body is divided into a series of interconnected, well mixed volumes and the assimilative capacity computation is reexpressed as

$$(\text{loadings}) = [A]^{-1}\ (\text{standards}) \qquad\qquad (17.3)$$

where   **(loadings)** = vector containing the external loading for each of the interconnected, well mixed volumes
      (standards) = vector containing the water quality standard for each volume
         $[A]^{-1}$ = spatial system response matrix that, in essence, represents the multidimensional expression of ¶

The response matrix has the same units—$[M\ T^{-1}(M\ L^{-3})^{-1}]$—and performs the same function as the assimilation factor. That is, its elements represent the response concentration of each of the volumes due to a unit external loading to any of the other volumes. Thus, Equation 17.3 can be used for assimilative capacity computations for systems that cannot be adequately described as single, well mixed entities.

The material in Chapter 13 on the transport and fate of contaminants in lake sediments represented somewhat of a digression from the assimilative capacity theme. However, as described in the latter parts of that chapter and in Chapter 15, such approaches can be combined with a water column model to compute assimilative capacity for substances that associate strongly with solid matter.

In Chapter 14, we explored model frameworks to simulate seasonal dynamics of nutrients and the food chain. Although these models are time-variable, they reach a long-term dynamic equilibrium under constant loading conditions that is suited for assimilative capacity computations. In addition, as in Table 14.1 and Section 14.7, the differential equations for such models can be combined to yield an input-output version that can be used to express

$$\P = Q + \left(\frac{v_1}{z}F_1 + \frac{v_4}{z}F_4\right)V_{t,w} \qquad\qquad (17.4)$$

where v_1, v_4 = settling velocities of phytoplankton and detritus, respectively
  F_1, F_4 = fractions of the total phosphorus in phytoplankton and detrital forms, respectively

Finally, in Chapter 15, we returned to the assimilative capacity theme in our discussion of toxic substance models. Two types of models were used for this purpose:

1. For cases where the standard is expressed in terms of total contaminant concentration in the water we developed screening models to, among other things, compute assimilative capacity. In the absence of sediment water interaction (recall Equation 15.53),

$$\P = Q + k_{t,w}V_{t,w} + v_wF_{pw}A_w \qquad (17.5)$$

   If sediment-water interactions were important, a more elaborate relationship for settling velocity (Equation 15.88) could be used.
2. For the more common case where the standard would be expressed in terms of contaminant concentration in large fish, simple proportionality factors can be used to reformulate the assimilative capacity computation as in Equation 15.130.

Thus, this book describes a variety of techniques for determining the loading required to meet a water quality objective or standard. This cause-and-effect approach can be implemented in a number of ways to support water quality management and planning:

Straight Assimilative Capacity Computations. For cases where there is either a single waste discharge or there are multiple discharges but a uniform treatment program (i.e., all sources must treat their effluents to the same level), the assimilative capacity computation is implemented as in Equations 17.1 or 17.3. For the multidimensional case, the uniform treatment level would typically be dictated by the water quality standard of one of the segments. This limiting segment represents the last part of the system to meet its standard as treatment levels are made more stringent. Consequently, such a strategy would be economically suboptimal, as all the other segments would be brought to quality levels in excess of their standards (see Chapra et al. 1983).

Optimal Assimilative Capacity Computations. If information on treatment cost is available, assimilative capacity models can be used to determine economically optimal treatment levels to meet water quality standards. Linear programming techniques are available to compute the least costly treatment program to meet the standards of a multidimensional system. In essence, the approach determines the different treatment levels for each source (or group of sources) that are needed to meet water quality standards in every segment. Thus, the approach allows more stringent treatment requirements for those segments where they will do the most good. Such techniques were first developed for estuaries (see Thomann 1972) but can also be used for lakes (Chapra et al. 1983) and streams. Aside from economic optimization, these approaches can also be used for cost-effectiveness studies, i.e., to rank treatment options as to how much water quality improvement will be reaped per dollar spent.

Risk Analysis. As discussed in Section 15.3, assimilative capacity models can provide information for a risk analysis of a particular water quality problem. The risk analysis combines information on utility, uncertainty, environmental modifications and cause-and-effect relationships in nature to quantify which of a group of alternative actions poses the least risk to society and the ecosystem.

§ § §

Example 17.1. Great Lakes eutrophication provides an excellent case study demonstrating the constructive application of engineering models for lake water quality management. In the 1960s, both scientific evidence (e.g., Beeton 1965) and public perception indicated that accelerated eutrophication was developing into a major problem. On the basis of a number of studies (notably Vollenweider 1968), phosphorus was identified as the limiting nutrient that could be practically controlled to reverse the process.

As the result of the mounting evidence and public concern, the United States and Canada signed the 1972 Great Lakes Water Quality Agreement. This initial attempt to reverse the eutrophication of the system required that the phosphorus concentration of major point source effluents be limited to 1 mg l^{-1}. The assumption was that the strategy would be less costly than diffuse source controls and that it would hopefully result in compliance with water quality objectives. In addition, the uniform treatment of point sources to 1 mg l^{-1} was an excellent example of a technology-based approach in that (1) it represented the treatment level that was practicably attainable using conventional phosphorus removal technology; and (2) it was considered politically and legally advantageous because it seemed equitable.

Although there was hope that the 1-mg l^{-1} effluent would result in compliance with objectives, there was no assurance that such would be the case. Consequently, the United States and Canada agreed to reconvene in five years to reassess the impact of the 1-mg l^{-1} strategy and decide on possible future actions and alternatives. In the meantime, a number of investigators began developing phosphorus assimilative capacity models. These ranged from simple empirical and input-output models (e.g., Vollenweider 1975, 1976; Chapra 1977) to more complex seasonal models (e.g., Thomann et al. 1975, Snodgrass and O'Melia 1975; Bierman and Dolan 1976; Di Toro and Connolly 1980). Although the models spanned a broad range of complexity, they were all capable of predicting in-lake response as a function of external loadings. Consequently, they could be used to evaluate the effectiveness of the 1-mg l^{-1} strategy as well as any other control programs that the managers might devise.

For example, one such model evaluation is shown in Figure 17.1 (Chapra and Robertson 1977). The height of each bar represents the total phosphorus concentration in the early 1970s for each lake with contributions indicated for several anthropogenic and natural loads and with the improvement due to the 1-mg l^{-1} effluent represented by the dashed line. To assist in interpretation of the results, total phosphorus concentration is related to trophic state by assuming that mesotrophy is bounded by concentrations of 10 and 20 μg of phosphorus per liter.

The immediately obvious observation is that the 1-mg l^{-1} effluent restriction would significantly improve the water quality over much of the Great Lakes. For example, the concentration of total phosphorus in the central and eastern basins of Lake Erie and in Lake Ontario would fall from levels of 20 μg l^{-1} or above to values approaching 10 μg l^{-1}.

However, in the western basin of Lake Erie and in Saginaw Bay and lower Green Bay the model predicted that the 1-mg l^{-1} limitation would not bring the total phosphorus concentration below 20 μg l^{-1}. Thus, to restore the trophic conditions in lower Green Bay, Saginaw Bay and western Lake Erie to levels that more nearly approach their natural state and that would be considered generally satisfactory, further management actions would be required. An examination of Figure 17.1 showed that these drainage basins have large inputs from land runoff and suggested that, in addition to the point source limitation, steps to reduce diffuse sources might be necessary to bring about a return to acceptable trophic conditions.

Such results demonstrate the utility of engineering models in defining the bounds of a management problem. For instance, Figure 17.1 indicates that parts of the system, (Green Bay, Saginaw Bay and western

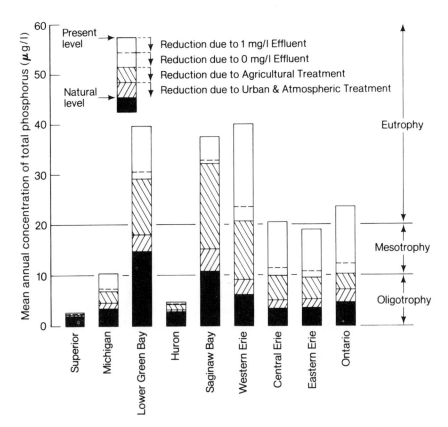

Figure 17.1 Total phosphorus concentrations (micrograms per liter) resulting from various treatment schemes for the Great Lakes (from Chapra and Robertson 1977).

Lake Erie) had naturally higher phosphorus concentrations than other areas of the Great Lakes. The very name—Green Bay—bears witness to the fact that some parts of the Great Lakes were not originally crystal clear and oligotrophic. From a management perspective, however, the result suggested a very real limit to water quality improvement in the basin. The calculation implies that total removal of cultural wastes would never bring Green Bay, Saginaw Bay and western Erie to the levels possible in the other lakes.

Although Figure 17.1 provides insight into control of Great Lakes eutrophication, such work was not formally integrated into the decision-making process. However, in 1977 as part of the renegotiation of the Great Lakes Water Quality Agreement, models played a direct role in the process (see Bierman 1980 for a complete description). A Task Group under the aegis of the U.S. Department of State and the Canadian Department of External Affairs was convened to recommend phosphorus loading objectives for each of the Great Lakes. In order to estimate lake response to changes in phosphorus load, the Task Group used five mathematical models. The results of these assimilative capacity computations were summarized in graphical form. These plots (e.g., Figure 17.2) were then used by the Task Group to set phosphorus treatment requirements for the system. Thus, the models represented a critical link in the process of managing Great Lakes eutrophication. All too often this is not the case and decision makers must develop remedial programs on the basis of intuition, politics and legal concerns. In the Great Lakes case, the model results provided an objective estimate of cause-and-effect that could be combined with other factors in making the ultimate control decision.

The result of the process was that the 1-mg l^{-1} policy was modified. The Task Group recommended that point source effluents for Lakes Erie and Ontario be reduced further to 0.5 mg l^{-1}. In addition, a 30% reduction in diffuse sources was also recommended for Erie and Ontario. These new treatment guidelines were based on the combination of the model results with other information of an economic, social and political nature. However, no comprehensive estimates were made of the cost-effectiveness of these measures. In addition, the choice of the 0.5-mg l^{-1} effluent and the 30% diffuse source reduction for Erie and Ontario were arrived at in a somewhat nonsystematic fashion.

Engineering approaches can be used to systematically incorporate economic information into the process in order to:

1. determine the most economical mix of point and nonpoint source controls to meet water quality objectives in all segments; and
2. rank the various control options according to their cost-effectiveness.

A recent study used optimization techniques to address both of these questions (Chapra et al 1983). This analysis demonstrated two key points about the nature and costs of an optimal phosphorus management program. First, the least-cost strategy for phosphorus management relies on a mix of both point and diffuse source controls and zoned, rather than uniform treatment. Second, the rate of treatment costs accelerates rapidly as water quality objectives become more stringent. The analysis indicates that the attainment of the highest levels (for example, the last 17% of the water quality objectives) will require a large portion (77%) of the total expenditure for the optimal treatment program (see Figure 17.3).

The shape of Figure 17.3 is extremely significant. It indicates that as treatment levels are made more stringent, costs increase exponentially.

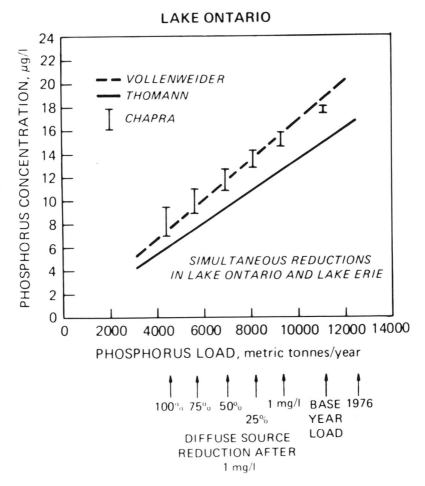

Figure 17.2   Assimilative capacity plot for Lake Ontario based on three water quality models (from Bierman 1980).

Of course, this result depends on the assumption that treatment is implemented in a cost-effective manner, i.e., installing the cheapest measures first. These escalating costs represent a strong pressure to develop optimal, cost effective strategies for pollution control. The Great Lakes phosphorus case study is a fine example of how this pressure influences policy-making. At first, a suboptimal, uniform treatment program (the 1-mg l^{-1} effluent) was the best choice because of its legal advantages. However, as the easy options are exhausted, economic arguments figure more prominently in determining the configuration of the treatment program. The focus on problem areas such as Lakes Erie and Ontario in the

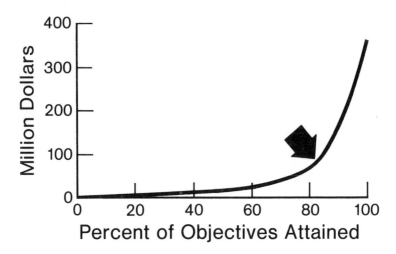

Figure 17.3   Plot of treatment cost (million dollars) vs % of objectives obtained for an optimal phosphorus control program for the Great Lakes (from Chapra et al. 1983).

1977–1978 recommendations of the Phosphorus Task Group are manifestations of this shift.

As should be clear from this chapter, engineering and economic analyses should never be the sole basis for water quality management. However, as in Figure 17.3, they often focus debate, raise questions and provide options that might otherwise be omitted from the decision-making process.

§ § §

17.3 ENGINEERS AND WATER QUALITY MANAGEMENT

This book can be regarded as a manual of methodologies that an environmental engineer can use to provide vital information to water quality managers and decision-makers. The type of information we are asked to supply depends on a variety of factors and regulatory programs. Therefore, the instruction offered here to students would not be complete without a brief description of the current state of water quality management in the United States. This is the context within which you and we practice our craft.

A basis for water quality management actions in this country is provided by the Federal Water Pollution Control Act (FWPCA) of 1972 (also known as the Clean Water Act). This statute represents one of the most comprehensive and complex pieces of legislation ever passed by Congress. It embodies the philosophical stance that no individual has the right to pollute the nation's waters. This view is supported by the declaration of a "zero discharge" goal by 1985, with the interim 1983 goal of attaining fishable, swimmable waters throughout the country. Administrative and enforcement timetables and procedures are established for the control of pollutant discharges consistent with these goals.

FWPCA was formulated in response to public outcry over the visible deterioration of the Nation's water. The existing state-controlled water quality management programs had been ineffective in reducing pollutant loads adversely affecting aquatic environments in significant parts of the country. There was a perceived need to make dramatic changes in the Federal and State responsibilities, in the amount of public funds committed to water quality maintenance and improvement, and in the fundamental approach to water quality regulation.

Prior to 1972 the states had the authority to establish water quality management programs for intrastate waters. Water quality standards served as the basis for pollutant load regulation. The concept of assimilative capacity provided the technical foundation for development of water quality standards. This approach proved to be ineffective because of a number of factors: the scarcity of available data on which these judgments were based, the developing state of engineering models, the increasing discharges of toxic substances, and the lack of funds for construction of treatment works.

FWPCA displaced the state water quality based management approach for a uniform technology approach controlled by federal authority. Required reductions of pollutant loads were to be determined not by estimated water quality effects but by the technology available to do the job. Technology standards formulated by the U.S. Environmental Protection Agency (EPA) were based strictly on the technical considerations of "best practicable technology" and "best available technology" economically achievable. Engineers and lawyers have worked together to identify uniform standards for wastewater treatment plants and industrial processes that are legally defensible from a technical viewpoint. All discharges of conventional (biochemical oxygen demand, suspended solids) and toxic pollutants were to be issued discharge permits based on technological standards.

The concept of assimilative capacity was not completely eliminated from management activities. States are required to develop water quality standards, consisting of a designated use of the water body (drinking, body contact, fishing, agricultural, industrial, navigation) and water quality criteria to support these uses, for all intrastate waters. These water quality standards are to be used as the basis for renegotiating discharge permits where technological limitations are not sufficient to avoid degradation.

The effectiveness of the technology-based approach cannot yet be thoroughly assessed. All standards have not been issued and all dischargers are not planned to come into compliance until 1988. However, visible and measurable results have been achieved with mandated actions to this point. The existing program has been particularly effective in reducing the discharge of conventional pollutants. However, toxic discharges continue to be a severe and threatening problem.

Renewed discussion of the roles of technology-based and water quality-based management approaches has been generated in anticipation of national compliance with required technology standards. Water quality problems will persist in some locations due particularly to concentrated toxic loadings and nonpoint source pollution. Water quality standards may then provide the basis for subsequent control actions. In addition, as in Example 17.1, once conventional technology is in place, economic considerations make optimization and cost-effectiveness more important in determining appropriate actions. In these cases, the concept of assimilative capacity will come to the fore as guidance for required loading reductions. Therefore, the techniques surveyed in this book will be used to inform future water quality management decision-making. Uncertainty analyses of these models will be necessary to use them as effective aids for control of toxics.

The future concerns of national water quality management will focus on solving those quality problems that persist after the required phases of technology are implemented. The shift of emphasis to water quality oriented activities will modify specific information and program needs thereby altering the necessary tasks of the professionals involved. Scientists will be expected to raise the level of objective knowledge about interactions of obscure toxic substances within aquatic environments. Lawyers will be relied on to continue to define procedures to ensure compliance with subjective program aims.

As engineers, we will be encouraged to apply our skills of systematic data analysis and modeling to provide objective judgments of achievable water quality standards and associated costs. In addition, we must facilitate assimilative capacity approaches wherever possible. Although there are cases where such approaches may not be legally advantageous, we must, in part as a consequence of our training, strive for the optimal economic solution to a problem. The present dilemma of water quality management makes this stance more important than ever.

On one hand, we know that a water-quality approach failed to produce adequate results prior to 1970. On the other, the alternative is to embark on a costly, suboptimal control program during hard economic times. In George Orwell's novel it is suggested that in 1984 two plus two would be five. While we are far from the society envisioned by Orwell, the zero discharge of pollutants by 1985 seems almost as implausible. Although we should always consider the perspectives and constraints of our legal and scientific colleagues, engineers must persist in their efforts to promulgate cost-effective solutions to water quality problems as our positive contribution to the collective decision process. Only in this way can we do our part to nudge a very approximate world in the direction of a cleaner environment.

REFERENCES

Bierman, V. J., Jr. 1980. "A Comparison of Models Developed for Phosphorus Management in the Great Lakes," in *Phosphorus Management Strategies for Lakes,* R. C. Loehr et al., Eds. (Ann Arbor, MI: Ann Arbor Science Publishers, Inc.), pp. 235–255.

Bierman, V. J., Jr., and D. M. Dolan. 1976. "Mathematical Modeling of Phytoplankton Dynamics in Saginaw Bay, Lake Huron," in *Environmental Modeling and Simulation* (Cincinnati, OH: U.S. Environmental Protection Agency), pp. 773–779.

Beeton, A. M. 1965. "Eutrophication of the St. Lawrence Great Lakes," *Limnol. Oceanog.* 10(2):240–254.

Chapra, S. C. 1977. "Total Phosphorus Model for the Great Lakes," *J. Environ. Eng. Div., ASCE* 103(EE2):147–161.

Chapra, S. C., and A. Robertson. 1977. "Great Lakes Eutrophication: The Effect of Point Source Control of Total Phosphorus," *Science* 196(4297): 1448–1450.

Chapra, S. C., H. D. Wicke and T. M. Heidtke. 1983. "Effectiveness of Treatment to Meet Phosphorus Objectives in the Great Lakes," *J. Water Poll. Control Fed.* 55(1):81–91.

Di Toro, D. M., and J. P. Connolly. 1980. "Mathematical Models of Water Quality in Large Lakes; Part 2: Lake Erie," EPA-600/3-80-065, U.S. Environmental Protection Agency, Washington, DC.

Snodgrass, W. J., and C. R. O'Melia. 1975. "Predictive Model for Phosphorus in Lakes," *Environ. Sci. Technol.* 9:937–944.

Thomann, R. V. 1972. *Systems Analysis and Water Quality Management* (New York: McGraw-Hill Book Company).

Thomann, R. V., D. M. Di Toro, R. P. Winfield, and D. J. O'Connor. 1975. "Mathematical Modeling of Phytoplankton in Lake Ontario. 1. Model Development and Verification," EPA-660/3-75-005, U.S. Environmental Protection Agency Ecological Research Series.

Vollenweider, R. A. 1968. "Scientific Fundamentals of the Eutrophication of Lakes and Flowing Waters, with Particular Reference to Nitrogen and Phosphorus as Factors in Eutrophication," Technical Report DAS/CSI/68.27, OECD, Paris, France.

Vollenweider, R. A. 1975. "Input-Output Models (with Special Reference to the Phosphorus Loading Model in Limnology)," *Schweiz. Z. Hydrol.* 37(1):53–84.

Vollenweider, R. A. 1976. "Advances in Defining Critical Loading Levels for Phosphorus in Lake Eutrophication," *Mem. Ist. Ital. Idrobiol.* 33:53–83.

APPENDIX

Table A.1   Index of Commonly Used Symbols

Symbol	Definition Given on Page:	Symbol	Definition Given on Page:
a	376	$c_{d,w}$	199
$[A]^{-1}$	128	c_{dt}	182
A_c	76	c_g	25
$[A_c]$	309	C_{gc}	275
$a_{i,i-1}$	407	c_i	359
A_m	203	$C_{i,i-1}$	407
a_p	272	$c_{i,w}$	225
a_{pc}	168	C_m	273
$a_{pd,o}$	219	c_o	97
a_{po}	170	$c_{o,w}$	225
A_s	22	c_p	25
A_t	146	c_{pt}	180
A_w	168	c_s	365
α	25	C_T	305
α_i	281	c_{tt}	180
$\alpha_{i,i-1}$	407	D	77
α_{ij}	125	D_m	185
b	404	D_n	200
β	182	D_s	185
β_e	35	$D_s{'}$	207
β_{ij}	125	D_v	167
β_ℓ	34	DO_e	169
c	6	DO_h	169
$\bar{c}$	25	DO_s	177
C	145	δ	30
c_a	6	e	166
c_d	182	E	82
c_{di}	188	$E{'}$	86

Symbol	Definition Given on Page:	Symbol	Definition Given on Page:
E_a	9	I_o	109,271
$E_{B,p}$	188	I_s	271
E_I	189	j	371
E_t	146	J	76
ϵ_i	281	J_B	397
ϵ_λ	370	$J_{B,d}$	188
f	271	$J_{B,p}$	188
F	185	J_s	188
f_b	211	J_{sr}	52
F_D	107	J_{wm}	203
F_{dm}	226	K	9,403
F_{dp}	198	k'	381
F_{ds}	227	k_a	370
F_{dw}	226	k_A	374
f_i	273	k_{ad}	189
$f_{i,i-1}$	413	k_{ad}'	191
F_{iw}	225	$k_{a,\lambda}$	370
F_{ow}	225	k_b	377
F_{ow}'	220	k_B	374
F_{pw}	391	k_d	370
f_s	46	K_d	191
g	142	K_d'	191
G_i	407	k_{de}	190
G_m	269	$K_{di,m}$	226
$G_{m,20}$	269	$K_{di,w}$	225
h	166	$k_{d,\lambda}$	370
H	145,360	$K_{d,m}$	392
H'	360	$K_{do,m}$	227
η	185	$K_{do,w}$	225
$\eta_{d,\lambda}$	372	$K_{d,s}$	392
η_λ	371	$k_{d,w}$	381
$\eta_{p,\lambda}$	372	$K_{d,w}$	392
$\eta_{w,\lambda}$	372	k_e	271
θ	10,36	k_f	8
θ^{10}	10	k_g	359
$\theta_{i,g}$	269	K_g	362
$\theta_{i,r}$	273	k_h	374
$\theta_{2,g}$	273	K_h	361
$\theta_{2,r}$	275	k_l	359
$\theta_{3,g}$	275	K_l	362
$\theta_{3,r}$	275	k_m	203,259,398
$\theta_{4,r}$	276	k_N	374
I	271	K_o	109
I'	370	k_{pr}	370
I_a	271	$k_{p,w}$	381
I_λ	370	$k_{r,e}$	166

Symbol	Definition Given on Page:	Symbol	Definition Given on Page:
k_{re}	219	p_{CO_2}	301
$k_{r,h}$	166	$p_{d,w}$	219
k_s	203,259,370	P_e	97
k_{sc}	275	p_g	359
k_{sh}	273	p_i	359
k_{sp}	272	$p_{i,w}$	219
k_{su}	286	p_k	266
$k_{t,w}$	377	p_m	211
k_u	403	$p_{n,e}$	165
$k_{u,e}$	166	$p_{n,h}$	166
k_{up}	219	$p_{o,w}$	219
$K_{u,2}$	275	Pr	167
$K_{u,3}$	275	Pr_s	167
k_w	228	Pr_w	167
K_w	298	$p_{s,e}$	165
L	97,402	$p_{s,h}$	166
L_a	209	p_t	278
L_d	210	$p_{t,w}$	220
L_p	388	p_w	211
ℓ	125	π	220
λ	403	q	286
m	19,211,403	Q	6
M	369	Q_a	6
M_d	182	q_o	286
$m_{i,w}$	224	q_s	388
m_ℓ	81	Q_{10}	10
m_o	404	r	108
$m_{o,w}$	224	R	9,97,282,359
m_p	75,181	R_a	388
M_p	181	$R_a{}'$	388
M_t	180	R_{ad}	189
μ	286	R_{de}	189
μ_m	286	R_{df}	394
n	22,166	R_{fw}	394
N_i	412	R_h	358
N_{iw}	412	r_i	407
ν	404	$R_{i,o}$	141
$\nu_{i,w}$	224	R_k	266
ν_o	405	R_p	358,394
$\nu_{o,w}$	224	R_v	358
ν_p	181	ρ	145
$\nu_{p,m}$	203	ρ_i	223
$\nu_{p,max}$	189	ρ_o	223
$\nu_{p,s}$	203	ρ_p	181
$\nu_{p,w}$	203	ρ_w	183
P	368	s	89,166,203

Symbol	Definition Given on Page:	Symbol	Definition Given on Page:
S	146,368,376	v_s	211
S_i	100	v_t	146
$s_{i,w}$	218	V_t	180
$s_{o,w}$	219	$V_{t,m}$	203
$s_{t,w}$	223	$V_{t,w}$	211
s_w	199	v_w	199
t	143	ϕ	180,370
T	10	ϕ'	182
T_a	9	ϕ_d	370
t_m	36	ϕ_i	223
T_p	36	ϕ_o	223
t_s	148	w	211
t_ϕ	43	W	369
t_{50}	43	$\overline{W}$	25
t_{90}	43	W_c	380
τ_c	42	W_e	35
τ_E	41	w_i	407
τ_m	179	W_i	218
τ_w	41	W_i'	128
u	142	$W_{n,e}$	167
U	83	$W_{n,h}$	167
v	22,285	W_o	36
V	19	W_p	388
v_a	394	W_s	389
v_b	183	$W_{s,e}$	167
v_d	183	$W_{s,h}$	167
V_d	180	$W(t)$	20
v_e	166	Ψ	402
V_e	167	ψ	45
v_f	211	z	23
v_h	166	z_b	199
V_h	167	z_e	167
v_i	223	z_f	368
V_i	100	z_h	167
v_L	402	z_m	203
v_m	203,286	z_w	381
v_o	223	ω	36
v_p	183	¶	11
V_p	180	¶$_c$	394
$v_{p,s}$	203	¶$_p$	388
v_r	389	¶$_4$	417

AUTHOR INDEX

SUBJECT INDEX

phosphorus models
  autochthonous matter   219-221
  Great Lakes budget   132-135
  nutrient/food chain   265-283
  rapid losses   46
  sediment-water model   210-216
  Simplest Seasonal Approach
    161-178
  total phosphorus   62-65,132-135,
    221,278,387-389
  transport across thermocline
    148-150
photolysis   369-373
  attenuation   371-372
  direct   370
  sensitized or indirect   371
  variation   372-373
photosynthesis/respiration
  see production/decomposition
phytoplankton
  functional groups   254-256,
    333-334
    physiological consideration   256
    size   255-256
  kinetics   269-273
    light   270-272
    nutrient limitation   272,283-287
    self-shading   247,272
  predator-prey   260-265
  seasonal dynamics   282,335-337
  space/time scales   288-289
  toxic substances   378-379,401-416
plane source   75n
plug flow
  see advection; river-run lake
    models
polychlorinated biphenyls,
    PCB   354,365-367,383-385,
    398-401,405-406,413-419
  risk analysis   420-428
porosity   179-185
  compaction   182-183
  diffusion   185
production/decomposition
  dissolved oxygen   176
  inorganic carbon   300-302
  long-term approach   219-221
  nutrient/food chain   245-247
  Simplest Seasonal Approach
    161-163

Q_{10} 10

radionuclides   227-230,396-401
  estimating vertical transport   160
  food chain transfer   413-416
  units   204n
  ^{137}Cs 227-230,398-400
  ^{90}Sr 52-56,227-230,398-400
  ^{210}Pb 204-206,208,398-400
  $^{239,240}Pu$ 227-230,398-400
random walk   72-76
reactions   8-11,22-23
  coupled   46-49
  equilibrium constant   9
  first-order   25-45
  heterogeneous   23
  homogeneous   23
  inorganic carbon   296-310
  law of mass action   9-10
  order   22
  predator-prey   260-263
  saturating   258-260
  sedimentation   23
  temperature dependence   9-10
  toxic substances
    biodegradation   376-377
    hydrolysis   374-376
    photolysis   369-373
    van't Hoff-Arrhenius equation   9
    vaporization   359-369
    zero-order reaction   45-46
reaction rates
  temperature effect   10,269
reservoirs
  see river-run lakes
residence time   41-42
  pollutant   41-42
  sediment   179
  water   41
response time   27,42-45
  contaminants   385
  Lake Ontario   230-234
  simplifying assumptions   395-396
  lakes in series   52-56
  sediment-water phosphorus
    model   214
  Simplest Seasonal Approach
    171-173
retention coefficient (R_p)   389,
    394-400
Richardson number   141-142